TENTS

THE
MICHE
GUID
HONG
MAC
20
RES
& H

CON

目錄

DEAR READER

This year, the Michelin Guide Hong Kong and Macau celebrates its 11th anniversary.

Both Hong Kong and Macau are world-class gourmet destinations. There are so many food choices that visitors always have a hard time making up their mind. Among the fastest-paced metropolises in the world, both cities constantly undergo transformations in all areas, including the food and beverage industry. The cityscape can change beyond recognition within a few years, let alone the shops and eateries, so keeping this guide up-to-date and relevant has never been more challenging.

As always, our full-time inspectors have searched every nook and cranny of the cities to compile a list of recommended food options, ranging from simple congee and noodle shops and traditional Chinese teahouses, to the most exclusive haute cuisine establishments. They visit all of the restaurants and shops anonymously to ensure their experiences are the same as any other paying customer and to keep their reviews objective.

Alongside our world-famous Michelin Stars ✿, good value Bib Gourmands ☺ and terrific street food stalls ⛟, we have a newer category – The Michelin Plate 🍽. This identifies restaurants using fresh ingredients to create simple yet delicious meals.

As well as the restaurants, our inspectors have chosen a selection of quality hotels, from the cosy to the hip, the elegant to palatial.

We care about what you think and would love to hear from you. If you have any comments about our guide, please write to:
michelinguide.hongkong-macau@michelin.com

We wish you many wonderful culinary and hotel experiences in Hong Kong and Macau.

Bon appétit!

親愛的讀者

不經不覺，香港澳門米芝蓮指南已出版至第十一版了！

香港和澳門均是世界知名的美食天堂，遊客到訪，不愁餓着，就怕選擇太多。而兩城急促的生活節奏也聞名於世，餐飲業的變化也像城市發展一樣瞬息萬變，幾年光景，有些街道可能就變了模樣，這也為指南的評選帶來巨大挑戰。

一如既往，我們的全職專業評審員在過去一年走遍大街小巷，為讀者挑選了一系列餐館，種類範圍涵蓋甚廣，從簡單粥麵店到傳統中菜館，至奢華的食府一應俱全。為確保體驗到與一般顧客同等的待遇，讓評審結果更客觀公正，評審員會以匿名身份到訪各大食肆。

獲得本指南推薦的，其食材質素與烹調水準全屬優質之列。除了聞名遐邇的米芝蓮星級餐廳、車胎人美食推介和充滿本地風味的街頭小吃外，還有去年增設的米芝蓮餐盤，推介的是材料新鮮、烹調用心，評審員萬裏挑一的餐館。

此外，評審員亦在芸芸酒店中挑選了一系列優質酒店，從時尚型格以至豪華典雅，各個級別和風格的酒店，只要服務水準高、房間舒適及設備完善均會獲得推薦。

讀者的回饋一直是我們重要的資訊來源，如閣下對本指南有任何意見或提議，歡迎電郵至下列電子郵箱：

michelinguide.hongkong-macau@michelin.com

祝願閣下在香港和澳門擁有愉快的美食和住宿體驗！

Bon appétit !

THE MICHELIN GUIDE'S COMMITMENTS

"This volume was created at the turn of the century and will last at least as long".

This foreword to the very first edition of the MICHELIN Guide, written in 1900, has become famous over the years and the guide has lived up to the prediction. It is read across the world and the key to its popularity is the consistency of its commitment to its readers, which is based on the following promises:

Anonymous inspections:

Our inspectors make regular and anonymous visits to restaurants and hotels to gauge the quality of the products and services offered to an ordinary customer. They settle their own bill and may then introduce themselves and ask for more information about the establishment. Our readers' comments are also a valuable source of information, which we can then follow up with another visit of our own.

Independence:

Our choice of establishments is a completely independent one, made for the benefit of our readers alone. The decisions to be taken are discussed around the table by the inspectors and the editor. Inclusion in the guide is completely free of charge.

Selection and choice:

Our guide offers a selection of the best restaurants and hotels. This is only possible because all the inspectors rigorously apply the same methods.

Annual updates:

All the practical information, the classifications and awards are revised and updated every single year to give the most reliable information possible.

Consistency:

The criteria for the classifications are the same in every country covered by the MICHELIN Guide.

...And our aim:

To do everything possible to make travel, holidays and eating out a pleasure, as part of Michelin's ongoing commitment to improving travel and mobility.

承諾

「這冊書於世紀交替時創辦，亦將繼續傳承下去。」

這是1900年首冊米芝蓮指南的前言，多年來享負盛名，並一直傳承下去。指南在世界各地均大受歡迎，關鍵在其秉承一貫宗旨，履行對讀者的承諾。

匿名評審

我們的評審員以匿名方式定期到訪餐廳和酒店，以一般顧客的身份對餐廳和酒店的食品和服務質素作出評估。評審員自行結賬後，在需要時會介紹自己，並會詳細詢問有關餐廳或酒店的資料。讀者的評語和推薦也是寶貴的資訊來源，我們會根據讀者的推薦到訪該餐廳。

獨立性

餐廳的評選完全是我們獨立的決定，純以讀者利益為依歸。經評審員和編輯一同討論後才作出決定，亦不會向收錄在指南內的餐廳和酒店收取任何費用。

選擇

全賴一眾評審員使用一致且嚴謹的評選方法，本指南才能向讀者推介一系列優質餐廳和酒店。

每年更新

每年都會修訂和更新所有實用資訊、分類及評級，務求為讀者提供最可靠的資料。

一致性

每個國家地區的米芝蓮指南均採用相同的評審和分類準則。

我們的目標

盡全力令旅遊、度假及在外用膳成為一大樂事，實踐米芝蓮一貫優化旅遊和生活的承諾。

ONCE UPON A TIME, IN THE HEART OF FRANCE...

It all started way back in 1889, in Clermont-Ferrand, when the Michelin brothers founded the Manufacture Française des Pneumatiques Michelin tyre company – this was at a time when driving was considered quite an adventure!

In 1900, fewer than 3,000 cars existed in France. The Michelin brothers hit upon the idea of creating a small guide packed with useful information for the new pioneers of the road, such as where to fill up with petrol or change a tyre, as well as where to eat and sleep. The MICHELIN Guide was born!

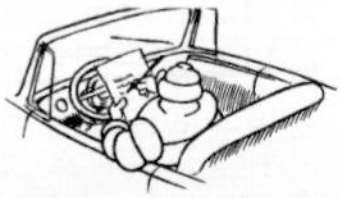

The purpose of the guide was obvious: to track down the best hotels and restaurants across the country. To do this, Michelin employed a veritable armada of anonymous professional inspectors to scour every region – something that had never before been attempted!

Over the years, bumpy roads were replaced by smoother highways and the company continued to develop, as indeed did the country's cuisine: cooks became chefs, artisans developed into artists, and traditional dishes were transformed into works of art. All the while, the MICHELIN Guide, by now a faithful travel companion, kept pace with – and encouraged – these changes. The most famous distinction awarded by the guide was created in 1926: the "étoile de bonne table" – the famous star which quickly established itself as the reference in the world of gastronomy!

Bibendum – the famous tyre-clad Michelin Man – continued to widen his reach and by 1911, the guide covered the whole of Europe.

In 2006, the collection crossed the Atlantic, awarding stars to 39 restaurants in New York. In 2007 and 2008, the guide moved on to San Francisco, Los Angeles and Las Vegas, and in 2011 it was the turn of Chicago to have its own Michelin guide – The Michelin Man had become truly American!

In November 2007, The Michelin Man took his first steps in Asia: in recognition of the excellence of Japanese cuisine, stars rained down on Tokyo, which was gripped by culinary fever! A guide to Kyoto, Kobe, Osaka and Nara followed, with Yokohama and Shonan then joining Tokyo. Thereafter the Michelin Man set his feet down in Southern China, with the publication in 2009 of a guide to Hong Kong and Macau.

The Red Guide was now firmly on the map in the Far East. The Michelin Man then explored Southeast Asia and China. In 2016 the first editions of the MICHELIN Guide Singapore and the MICHELIN Guide Shanghai were published. The MICHELIN guides collection now covers 32 titles in 30 countries, with over 30 million copies sold in a century. Quite a record!

Meanwhile, the search continues... Looking for a delicious pot-au-feu in a typical Parisian bistro, or a soothing bowl of congee in Hong Kong? The Michelin Man continues to span the globe making new discoveries and selecting the very best the culinary world has to offer!

從前，在法國中部……

這一切始於1889年，米芝蓮兄弟在法國克萊蒙費朗(Clermont-Ferrand)創辦Manufacture Française des Pneumatiques Michelin 輪胎公司──當年駕駛汽車仍被視為一大冒險。

在1900年，法國的汽車總數量少於3,000輛。米芝蓮兄弟靈機一觸，想到為道路駕駛的先驅提供含實用資訊的小指南，如補充汽油或更換輪胎，以至用餐和睡覺的好去處。米芝蓮指南就這樣誕生了！

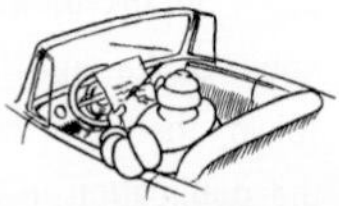

指南的宗旨非常清晰：搜羅全國各地最好的酒店和餐廳。為達目的，米芝蓮招攬了一整隊神秘專業評審員，走遍全國每一個角落尋找值得推介的酒店和餐廳，這在當時是前所未有的創舉。

多年來，崎嶇不平的道路早已被平順的高速公路取代，米芝蓮公司持續茁壯成長。同時間，全國各地餐飲業的發展亦一日千里：廚子成為大廚、傳統手藝成為藝術，傳統菜餚亦轉化成為藝術傑作。現今米芝蓮指南已成為廣受信賴的旅遊夥伴，不僅與時並進，更致力推動這些轉變。指南中最著名的是早在1926年面世，並迅即成為美食界權威指標的「星級推介」。

由米芝蓮車胎人必比登為代言人的米芝蓮指南，不斷拓展其版圖，到1911年已覆蓋全歐洲。

2006年，米芝蓮指南系列成功跨越大西洋，授予紐約39家餐廳星級推介。在2007及2008年，米芝蓮指南在三藩市、洛杉磯和拉斯維加斯出版，2011年已拓展至芝加哥，米芝蓮車胎人必比登也正式落戶美國。

2007年11月，米芝蓮車胎人首次踏足亞洲，在東京廣發星級推介，以表揚日本料理的卓越成就，同時亦掀起美食熱潮。其後，旋即推出京都、神戶、大阪及奈良指南，並繼東京之後推出橫濱和湘南指南。香港和澳門指南亦於2009年推出。

2016年，米芝蓮車胎人更涉足新加坡和中國，推出首本米其林新加坡指南及米其林上海指南，令這本以紅色為標誌的指南，在遠東地區的覆蓋範圍更見廣泛。

時至今日，米芝蓮指南系列共計32本，涵蓋30個國家，一個世紀以來，總銷量超過三千萬。這是個令人鼓舞的紀錄！

此時此刻，我們仍然繼續對美食的追尋……是巴黎餐廳的美味雜菜鍋，還是香港令人窩心的粥品？米芝蓮車胎人將會努力不懈，發掘全球美食，為你們挑選最出色的佳餚美饌！

HOW TO USE
THIS RESTAURANT GUIDE
如何使用餐廳指南

Map number / coordinates
地圖號碼 / 座標

New entry in the guide
新增推介

Cuisine type
菜式種類

Name of restaurant
餐廳名稱

Stars for good food
美食星級
✿ to ✿✿✿

**Bib Gourmand
(Inspectors' favourite
for good value)**
車胎人美食推介

Plate
米芝蓮餐盤
⽤

**Restaurant classification
according to comfort**
餐廳── 以舒適程度分類
Particularly pleasant if in red
紅色代表上佳

	Simple shop 簡單的食店
✗	Quite comfortable 頗舒適
✗✗	Comfortable 舒適
✗✗✗	Very comfortable 十分舒適
✗✗✗✗	Top class comfort 高級舒適
✗✗✗✗✗	Luxury 豪華

TAIWANESE 台灣菜

MAP 地圖 26/A-2

What To Eat 🅝
吃什麼

The two Taiwanese mums have revived the old name of their first bento shop. The menu is now bigger, but the food is just as good and the service just as warm and homely. The egg crepe roll is made with ingredients imported from Taiwan and the beef shin in the noodle soup is braised for more than five hours in a spiced broth. Taiwanese veggies such as citron daylily and vegetable fern are hard to find elsewhere.

兩位台灣媽媽的食店之路雖經一番波折，但初心依然；希望客人能安然坐下好好享用一頓簡單的餐點，感受當中濃濃的人情味。原班人馬帶來種類更多的食品，猶幸食材和手法不變；燜煮逾五小時的牛肉美味依然；招牌蛋餅的蛋皮始終由台灣進口；麵條經特別調配，在本地現做。多款小吃及時令台灣土產均值得一試。

TEL. 2810 9278
Shop A, GF, Carfield Commercial
Building, 75-77 Wyndham Street,
Central
中環雲咸街 75-77號
嘉兆商業大廈地下 A號地鋪

■ PRICE 價錢
Lunch 午膳
à la carte 點菜 $65-250
Dinner 晚膳
à la carte 點菜 $65-250

■ OPENING HOURS 營業時間
Lunch 午膳　12:00-15:00 (L.O.)
Dinner 晚膳　18:00-21:00 (L.O.)

■ ANNUAL AND WEEKLY CLOSING 休息日期
Closed 4 days Lunar New Year and
Sunday 農曆新年 4 天及週日休息

Restaurant promoted to a Bib Gourmand or Star
評級有所晉升的餐廳

FRENCH CONTEMPORARY 時尚法國菜 MAP 地圖 24/B-2

Belon

18

Frenchman Daniel Calvert cut his teeth cooking in some of the best restaurants in London, New York and Paris. His appealing little bistro has a subtle French look and a relaxed feel made even more enjoyable by his personable team who deliver excellent service. He is a chef who understands sophisticated simplicity perfectly and his pared-back, delicious classic French dishes are delivered with consummate skill and accuracy.

這間法式餐館與蘇豪區的風格如出一轍，環境優雅舒適，團隊親切殷勤的服務更讓食客賓至如歸。法籍廚師曾先後於倫敦、紐約及巴黎的頂級餐廳效力，擅於烹調傳統法國菜，所作的菜式精緻簡約，盡顯其熟練而精湛的烹調技巧，每道菜都令人垂涎欲滴。

TEL. 2152 2872
41 Elgin Street, Central
中環伊利近街41號
www.belonsoho.com

■ PRICE 價錢
Sunday lunch 週日午膳
set 套餐 $ 458
Dinner 晚膳
set 套餐 $ 1,088-1,488
à la carte 點菜 $ 700-1,100

■ OPENING HOURS 營業時間
Sunday lunch 週日午膳
12:00-14:30 (L.O.)
Dinner 晚膳 18:00-22:30 (L.O.)

■ ANNUAL AND WEEKLY CLOSING 休息日期
Closed Monday 週一休息

69

Restaurant symbols
餐廳標誌

- Cash only 只接受現金
- Wheelchair access 輪椅通道
- Terrace dining 陽台用餐
- Interesting view 上佳景觀
- Valet parking 代客泊車
- Car park 停車場
- Private room with maximum capacity 私人廂房及座位數目
- Counter 櫃枱式
- Reservations required 需訂座
- Reservations not accepted 不設訂座
- Interesting wine list 供應優質餐酒

HOW TO USE THIS HOTEL GUIDE
如何使用酒店指南

Map number / coordinates
地圖號碼 / 座標

New entry in the guide
新增推介

Name of hotel
酒店名稱

Hotel classification according to comfort
酒店——以舒適程度分類

Particularly pleasant if in red
紅色代表上佳

- Quite comfortable 頗舒適
- Comfortable 舒適
- Very comfortable 十分舒適
- Top class comfort 高級舒適
- Luxury 豪華

Restaurants recommended in MICHELIN Guide
米芝蓮指南內的推薦餐廳

DESIGN 型格 MAP 地圖 43/C-2

Morpheus Ⓝ
摩珀斯

This hotel, part of the City of Dreams, is set to become a landmark in Cotai. It's architecturally stunning exterior was designed by the late Dame Zaha Hadid. Its interior is no less striking with a rooftop pool, a spa and numerous eateries, including two restaurants from Alain Ducasse. Bedrooms are luxurious, beautifully styled and equipped with the latest technology.

摩珀斯由已故建築師札哈・哈蒂女爵士設計，其縱橫交錯的外觀別樹一格，目光難以從中移離，勢將成為區內新的地標建築。客房同樣時尚奢華，先進科技設施應有盡有。酒店餐飲選擇良多，包括兩家法國大廚Alain Ducasse名下的餐廳，以及各式環球美食。欲肆意享受怎能錯過天台泳池及水療設施？

TEL. 8868 8888
City of Dreams, Estrada do Istmo, Cotai
路氹連貫公路新濠天地
www.cityofdreamsmacau.com/en/stay/morpheus/index.html

= MOP 2,998-5,298
Suites 套房 = MOP 10,998-16,998
= MOP 288

Rooms 客房 604
Suites 套房 168

RECOMMENDED RESTAURANTS 餐廳推薦
Alain Ducasse at Morpheus 杜卡斯 XxxX
Voyages by Alain Ducasse 風雅廚 XX
Yi 天頤 XxX

410

CONTEMPORARY 時尚 MAP 地圖 25/C-1

Four Seasons
四季

Four Seasons hotel not only offers some of the most spacious accommodation in Hong Kong but the bedrooms, which have wall-to-wall windows, also feature an impressive array of extras. Choose between a Western style room and one with a more Asian feel; all have large and luxurious bathrooms. The hotel also boasts two bars, two swimming pools and three world class restaurants.

四季酒店與維港毗鄰，景色壯麗，提供香港最寬敞時尚的客房。客房佈置分為現代風格和東方情調兩種，且設有大型豪華浴室。Blue Bar專為享受雞尾酒和現場音樂演奏而設。水療設施令人印象難忘，更設有兩個溫度不同的泳池。舒適的環境與高質素服務兩者俱備。

TEL. 3196 8888
8 Finance Street, Central
中環金融街 8號
www.fourseasons.com/hongkong

RECOMMENDED RESTAURANTS 餐廳推薦
Caprice ✿✿✿ XXXXX
Lung King Heen 龍景軒 ✿✿✿ XXXX
Sushi Saito 鮨·齋藤 ✿✿ XX

= $ 4,100-5,500
= $ 4,300-5,600
Suites 套房 = $ 11,800-13,500
= $ 340

Rooms 客房 345
Suites 套房 54

283

Hotel symbols
酒店標誌

Wheelchair access
輪椅通道

Interesting view
上佳景觀

Valet parking
代客泊車

Car park
室外停車場

Garage
室內停車場

Non smoking rooms
非吸煙房

Conference rooms
會議室

Outdoor / Indoor swimming pool
室外 / 室內游泳池

Spa
水療服務

Exercise room
健身室

Casino
娛樂場所

360°
DINING EXPERIENCE

MICHELIN ARE EXPERTS AT FINDING THE BEST RESTAURANTS AND INVITE YOU TO EXPLORE THE DIVERSITY OF THE GASTRONOMIC UNIVERSE. AS WELL AS EVALUATING A RESTAURANT'S COOKING, WE ALSO CONSIDER ITS DÉCOR, THE SERVICE AND THE AMBIENCE – IN OTHER WORDS, THE ALL-ROUND CULINARY EXPERIENCE.

360°
用餐體驗

米芝蓮是追尋最佳餐廳的專家，邀請您共同發掘豐富多元的餐飲世界。在品評餐廳烹調質素同時，我們亦將其裝潢、服務和整體氛圍加入考慮，換言之，是包含味覺、感官和整體用餐經驗的全方位評估。

FRENCH CONTEMPORARY 時尚法國菜
ITALIAN 意大利菜
INDONESIAN 印尼菜
CHIU CHOW 潮州菜
HAKKANESE 客家菜
CANTONESE ROAST MEATS 燒味
RAMEN 拉麵
NOODLES 麵食
JAPANESE 日本菜
CANTONESE 粵菜
Comfortable
舒適
Top class comfort
高級舒適
Luxury
豪華
Quite comfortable
頗舒適
Very comfortable
十分舒適
Simple shop
簡單的食店

Hong Kong, a gourmet paradise, has much to offer when it comes to dining. Here, foodies can find cuisine from across the globe – but what are the authentic tastes of Hong Kong?

With its meticulously prepared, top quality ingredients and no-frills preparation, every flavourful bite of Hong Kong's classic dishes embody the chefs' skills and attention to detail. The collective memory that Hongkongers can't part with and the true culinary gems that visitors applaud, these include piping hot dim sum steamed to order in traditional teahouses; succulent Cantonese roast meats with crispy skin; home-style dishes and stir-fries from neighbourhood eateries; and velvety congee or wonton soup noodles from 'holes-in-the-wall'.

BIB GOURMAND, A GOOD VALUE!

價廉物美的味道

香港餐廳數目多如繁星，中、西、日、韓各地佳餚應有盡有，而當說起香港味道，你會想到什麼？

香港味道，存在於早上的茶市中，午後的粥麵檔裏，晚上的爐火間——不論是即叫即蒸的點心、皮脆肉嫩的燒味、街坊小店內的鑊氣小炒或家常小菜，還是一碗綿滑粥品或雲吞麵，皆是香港名物。這些食物，賣相樸實無華，但卻真材實料，滋味無窮，每一口都顯示出廚師的心思和功架，叫香港人念念不忘，也令旅客舉手稱頌。

DO YOU KNOW THE BIB GOURMAND?

The MICHELIN Guide has been in existence for over 100 years and today it covers many countries, from Brazil to Japan. Its best known awards are its Michelin Stars, which are awarded to the top restaurants in the world.

...but how well do you know the Bib Gourmand?

Originally, a red 'R ' or 'M' (and later changed to 'Repas' or 'Meals'), it identifies restaurants offering 'good quality, good value cooking'. In 1997, an astute artist gave life to this award by using the face of Bibendum, the Michelin Man, for which the Michelin Tyre Company was already known: the Bib Gourmand was born!
An indefatigable globe-trotter and an ambassador of well-crafted, inexpensive cuisine, he invites you to follow him throughout the world on his gourmet journeys.

你知道車胎人美食推介嗎？

米芝蓮指南面世已超過一世紀，時至今日，米芝蓮指南系列介紹的國家持續增長，從巴西至日本皆可找到米芝蓮評審員的足跡。星級食店推介是指南最著名的評級，標示的是獲評為食物質素卓越出色的餐廳，而關於「車胎人美食推介」你又所知多少？

最初，指南將經濟實惠而食物具質素的餐廳標注紅色的「R」或「M」字（其後改為「Repas」和「Meals」）。至1997年，一位觸覺敏銳的設計師決定將栩栩如生的必比登先生形象用在這推介上，從此，米芝蓮輪胎公司的代表人物——必比登先生——就成為了車胎人美食推介的象徵！

這從不歇息、行動勤快、象徵經濟實惠美食的親善大使，將帶領您走遍全球，體驗各種味覺旅程。

HONG KONG
香港

RESTAURANTS
餐廳

STARRED RESTAURANTS
星級餐廳

Within this selection, we have highlighted a number of restaurants for their particularly good cooking. When awarding one, two or three Michelin Stars there are a number of factors we consider: the quality and compatibility of the ingredients, the technical skill and flair that goes into their preparation, the clarity and combination of flavours, the value for money and above all, the taste. Equally important is the ability to produce excellent cooking not once but time and time again. Our inspectors make as many visits as necessary, so that you can be sure of the quality and consistency.
A two or three star restaurant has to offer something very special that separates it from the rest. Three stars – our highest award – are given to the very best.
Cuisines in any style of restaurant and of any nationality are eligible for a star. The decoration, service and comfort levels have no bearing on the award.

在這系列的選擇裏，推薦的是食物質素特別出色的餐廳。給予一、二或三粒米芝蓮星時，我們考慮到以下因素：材料的質素和配搭、烹調技巧和特色、氣味濃度和組合、價錢是否相宜及味道層次。同樣重要的是該餐館的食物能恆常保持高水平。閣下對我們的推薦絕對可以放心！我們的評審員會因應需要多次到訪同一家餐館，以確認其食物品質恆常保持高水準。

二或三星餐廳必有獨特之處，比同類型其他餐廳更出眾。最高評級——三星——只會給予最出色的餐廳。

星級評定不會受到餐廳風格、菜式、裝潢陳設、服務及舒適程度影響。只要烹調技巧出色，食物品質特別優秀，都有機會獲得米芝蓮星星。

Exceptional cuisine, worth a special journey.
卓越的烹調，值得專程造訪。

Our highest award is given for the superlative cooking of chefs at the peak of their profession. The ingredients are exemplary, the cooking is elevated to an art form and their dishes are often destined to become classics.

獲得最高級別的餐館，其廚師的烹調技巧卓絕，選材用料堪稱典範，並將烹飪提升至藝術層次，菜式大多會成為經典。

Bo Innovation		XXX	Innovative 創新菜	71
Caprice		XXXXX	French contemporary 時尚法國菜	77
L'Atelier de Joël Robuchon		XX	French contemporary 時尚法國菜	142
Lung King Heen 龍景軒		XXXX	Cantonese 粵菜	159
8 1/2 Otto e Mezzo - Bombana		XXXX	Italian 意大利菜	173
Sushi Shikon 志魂		X	Sushi 壽司	211
T'ang Court 唐閣		XXXX	Cantonese 粵菜	220

Excellent cooking, worth a detour.
烹調出色，不容錯過！

The personality and talent of the chef and their team is evident in the refined, expertly crafted dishes.

主廚的個人風格與烹飪天賦及其團隊的優秀手藝完全反映在精巧味美的菜式上。

Amber		XXXX	French contemporary 時尚法國菜	62
Écriture	N	XX	French contemporary 時尚法國菜	99
Forum 富臨飯店		XX	Cantonese 粵菜	106
Kashiwaya 柏屋		XX	Japanese 日本菜	134
Pierre		XXXX	French contemporary 時尚法國菜	178
Sun Tung Lok 新同樂		XXX	Cantonese 粵菜	206
Sushi Saito 鮨・齋藤	N	XX	Sushi 壽司	210
Ta Vie 旅		XX	Innovative 創新菜	214

High quality cooking, worth a stop!
優質烹調，不妨一試！

Within their category, these establishments use quality ingredients and serve carefully prepared dishes with distinct flavours.

此名單上的餐館，在同類型餐館中，其食材較具質素，烹調細緻用心、味道出色。

N : New entry in the guide 新增推介

: Restaurant promoted to a Bib Gourmand or Star 評級有所晉升的餐廳

BIB GOURMAND RESTAURANTS
車胎人美食推介餐廳

This symbol indicates our inspectors' favourites for good value. These restaurants offer quality cooking for $400 or less (price of a 3-course meal excluding drinks).

車胎人標誌表示該餐廳提供具質素且經濟實惠的美食：費用在400元或以下（三道菜但不包括飲品）。

N : New entry in the guide 新增推介

: Restaurant promoted to a Bib Gourmand or Star 評級有所晉升的餐廳

RESTAURANTS BY AREA
餐廳 — 以地區分類

Hong Kong Island 香港島

Admiralty 金鐘

Café Gray Deluxe	IO	XX	European contemporary 時尚歐陸菜	75
Petrus 珀翠	IO	XXXXX	French 法國菜	177
Summer Palace 夏宮	✿	XXX	Cantonese 粵菜	204

Causeway Bay 銅鑼灣

Din Tai Fung (Causeway Bay) 鼎泰豐 (銅鑼灣)	☺	X	Shanghainese 滬菜	94
Farm House 農圃	IO	XX	Cantonese 粵菜	102
Forum 富臨飯店	✿✿	XX	Cantonese 粵菜	106
Fu Sing (Causeway Bay) 富聲 (銅鑼灣)	☺	XXX	Cantonese 粵菜	109
Ho Hung Kee 何洪記	✿	X	Noodles and Congee 粥麵	119
Involtini	IO	X	Italian 意大利菜	127
Kung Tak Lam (Causeway Bay) 功德林 (銅鑼灣)	IO	XX	Vegetarian 素食	137
La Bombance	IO	XX	Japanese 日本菜	140
Pak Loh Chiu Chow (Hysan Avenue) 百樂潮州 (希慎道)	IO	XX	Chiu Chow 潮州菜	174
Putien (Causeway Bay) 莆田 (銅鑼灣)	☺	XX	Fujian 福建菜	180
Ramen Jo (Causeway Bay) 拉麵Jo (銅鑼灣)	☺	🍜	Ramen 拉麵	183
Shanghai Yu Yuan 豫園 (N)	IO	XXX	Shanghainese 滬菜	191
She Wong Yee 蛇王二	☺	🍜	Cantonese 粵菜	192
Snow Garden 雪園	☺	XX	Shanghainese 滬菜	201
Tai Woo (Causeway Bay) 太湖海鮮城 (銅鑼灣)	☺	XX	Cantonese 粵菜	216
Town	IO	XX	Innovative 創新菜	237
Wu Kong (Causeway Bay) 滬江 (銅鑼灣)	IO	XX	Shanghainese 滬菜	250
Yee Tung Heen 怡東軒	✿	XXX	Cantonese 粵菜	257

(N) : New entry in the guide 新增推介

☺ : Restaurant promoted to a Bib Gourmand or Star 評級有所晉升的餐廳

Central 中環

Restaurant	New	Award	Comfort	Cuisine	Page
Sing Kee (Central) 星記 (中環)		Bib	X	Cantonese 粵菜	198
Steak on Elgin	N	Plate	XX	Steakhouse 扒房	203
Sushi Saito 鮨・齋藤	N	★★	XX	Sushi 壽司	210
Ta Vie 旅		★★	XX	Innovative 創新菜	214
Tasty (Central) 正斗粥麵專家 (中環)		Bib	X	Noodles and Congee 粥麵	221
The Chairman 大班樓		Plate	XX	Cantonese 粵菜	225
Toritama 酉玉		Plate	X	Japanese 日本菜	235
Tsim Chai Kee (Wellington Street) 沾仔記 (威靈頓街)		Bib	Street food	Noodles 麵食	241
VEA		★	XX	Innovative 創新菜	245
Wang Fu (Central) 王府 (中環)		Bib	Street food	Dumplings 餃子	246
What To Eat 吃什麼	N	Bib	Street food	Taiwanese 台灣菜	247
Yat Lok 一樂燒鵝		★	Street food	Cantonese Roast Meats 燒味	253
Ying Jee Club 營致會館		★★	XXX	Cantonese 粵菜	258

Happy Valley 跑馬地

Restaurant	New	Award	Comfort	Cuisine	Page
Locanda dell' Angelo	N	Plate	XX	Italian 意大利菜	156
Pang's Kitchen 彭慶記		★	X	Cantonese 粵菜	175

North Point 北角

Restaurant	New	Award	Comfort	Cuisine	Page
Ancient Moon 古月		Bib	Street food	Singaporean and Malaysian 星馬菜	63
Chiuchow Delicacies 潮樂園		Bib	Street food	Chiu Chow 潮州菜	88
Lei Garden (North Point) 利苑酒家 (北角)		Plate	XX	Cantonese 粵菜	150
Sun Fook Kee 新福記		Plate	XX	Fujian 福建菜	205
Tim Ho Wan (North Point) 添好運 (北角)		Bib	Street food	Dim Sum 點心	229
Yuè (North Point) 粵 (北角)		Plate	XX	Cantonese 粵菜	261

Quarry Bay 鰂魚涌

Restaurant	New	Award	Comfort	Cuisine	Page
Congee and Noodle Shop 粥麵館		Bib	Street food	Noodles and Congee 粥麵	92
Shugetsu Ramen (Quarry Bay) 麵鮮醬油房周月 (鰂魚涌)		Bib	Street food	Ramen 拉麵	197

Repulse Bay 淺水灣

Restaurant	New	Award	Comfort	Cuisine	Page
The Ocean		★	XXX	French 法國菜	226
TRi		Plate	XXX	Balinese 峇里菜	238

Sheung Wan 上環

Bibo	Plate	XX	French contemporary 時尚法國菜	70
Chan Kan Kee Chiu Chow (Sheung Wan) 陳勤記鹵鵝飯店 (上環)	Bib Gourmand	X	Chiu Chow 潮州菜	81
Frantzén's Kitchen	Plate	XX	Scandinavian 北歐菜	107
Lin Heung Kui 蓮香居	Bib Gourmand	Street food	Cantonese 粵菜	153
Sun Yuen Hing Kee 新園興記	Bib Gourmand	Street food	Cantonese Roast Meats 燒味	207
Sushi Shikon 志魂	✪✪✪	X	Sushi 壽司	211
Sushi Wadatsumi	✪	X	Sushi 壽司	213
Tate	✪	XX	Innovative 創新菜	222
Tim's Kitchen (Sheung Wan) 桃花源小廚 (上環)	Plate	XXX	Cantonese 粵菜	232
Upper Modern Bistro	Plate	XX	French 法國菜	243

Tai Hang 大坑

IM Teppanyaki & Wine	✪	XX	Teppanyaki 鐵板燒	125

Tai Koo Shing 太古城

CIAK - All Day Italian	Bib Gourmand	X	Italian 意大利菜	91

Tin Hau 天后

Shek Kee Kitchen 石記廚房	Bib Gourmand	Street food	Cantonese 粵菜	193
Sister Wah (Tin Hau) 華姐清湯腩 (天后)	Bib Gourmand	Street food	Noodles 麵食	199
Sushi Mori Tomoaki	Plate	X	Sushi 壽司	209

Wan Chai 灣仔

Akrame	Plate	XX	French contemporary 時尚法國菜	61
Bo Innovation	✪✪✪	XXX	Innovative 創新菜	71
Brass Spoon (Wan Chai)	Bib Gourmand	Street food	Vietnamese 越南菜	74
Che's 車氏粵菜軒	Plate	XX	Cantonese 粵菜	82
Fook Lam Moon (Wan Chai) 福臨門 (灣仔)	Plate	XXX	Cantonese 粵菜	105
Fu Sing (Wan Chai) 富聲 (灣仔)	Bib Gourmand	XX	Cantonese 粵菜	110
Giando N	Plate	XXX	Italian 意大利菜	113
Grand Hyatt Steakhouse	Plate	XX	Steakhouse 扒房	116
Jardin de Jade (Wan Chai) 蘇浙滙(灣仔)	✪	XXX	Shanghainese 滬菜	129
Kaiseki Den by Saotome	✪	XX	Japanese 日本菜	131

Kam's Roast Goose 甘牌燒鵝	✿	🍜	Cantonese Roast Meats 燒味	133
Le Garçon Saigon (N)	ıO	X	Vietnamese 越南菜	144
Lei Garden (Wan Chai) 利苑酒家 (灣仔)	ıO	XX	Cantonese 粵菜	152
Liu Yuan Pavilion 留園雅敘	☺	XX	Shanghainese 滬菜	154
Megan's Kitchen 美味廚	☺	XX	Cantonese 粵菜	163
New Shanghai 新滬坊	☺	XXX	Shanghainese 滬菜	167
One Harbour Road 港灣壹號	ıO	XXX	Cantonese 粵菜	172
Qi (Wan Chai) 呇 (灣仔)	✿	XX	Sichuan 川菜	182
Sabah (Wan Chai) 莎巴 (灣仔)	☺	X	Malaysian 馬拉菜	185
Samsen 泰麵	☺	X	Thai 泰國菜	187
Sang Kee 生記	☺	X	Cantonese 粵菜	188
Seventh Son 家全七福	ıO	XX	Cantonese 粵菜	189
Sushi Masataka	ıO	X	Sushi 壽司	208
Takumi by Daisuke Mori	✿	XX	Innovative 創新菜	219
Trusty Congee King (Wan Chai) 靠得住 (灣仔)	☺	🍜	Noodles and Congee 粥麵	239
Trusty Gourmet 信得過	☺	🍜	Cantonese 粵菜	240
Xin Rong Ji 新榮記 (N)	✿	XXX	Taizhou 台州菜	251
Yixin 益新	☺	XX	Cantonese 粵菜	259
Zhejiang Heen 浙江軒	✿	XX	Zhejiang 浙江菜	265

Western District 西環

Ba Yi 巴依	☺	X	Xinjiang 新疆菜	66
Café Hunan (Western District) 書湘門第 (西環)	☺	X	Hunanese 湖南菜	76
Eng Kee Noodle Shop 英記麵家	☺	🍜	Noodles 麵食	100
Fish School	ıO	X	Seafood 海鮮	103
Kaum	ıO	XX	Indonesian 印尼菜	136
Kwan Kee Clay Pot Rice (Queen's Road West) 坤記煲仔小菜 (皇后大道西)	☺	🍜	Cantonese 粵菜	139
Po Kee 波記	☺	🍜	Cantonese Roast Meats 燒味	179
Sheung Hei Claypot Rice 嚐囍煲仔小菜	☺	🍜	Cantonese 粵菜	194
Sheung Hei Dim Sum 嚐囍點心皇	☺	🍜	Dim Sum 點心	195
Tak Kee 德記	☺	🍜	Chiu Chow 潮州菜	217

Kowloon 九龍

Cheung Sha Wan 長沙灣

Kwan Kee Bamboo Noodles (Cheung Sha Wan) 坤記竹昇麵 (長沙灣)	Noodles 麵食	138

Hung Hom 紅磡

Takeya 竹家	Japanese 日本菜	218
Wing Lai Yuen 詠藜園	Chinese 中國菜	249

Jordan 佐敦

Mak Man Kee 麥文記	Noodles 麵食	160
Yat Tung Heen (Jordan) 逸東軒 (佐敦)	Cantonese 粵菜	254
Yau Yuen Siu Tsui (Jordan) 有緣小敍 (佐敦)	Shaanxi 陝西菜	255

Kowloon Bay 九龍灣

Lei Garden (Kowloon Bay) 利苑酒家 (九龍灣)	Cantonese 粵菜	147
Siu Shun Village Cuisine (Kowloon Bay) 肇順名匯河鮮專門店 (九龍灣)	Shun Tak 順德菜	200

Kwun Tong 觀塘

Lei Garden (Kwun Tong) 利苑酒家 (觀塘)	Cantonese 粵菜	148
Lucky Indonesia 好運印尼餐廳	Indonesian 印尼菜	157

Lei Yue Mun 鯉魚門

Hyde Park Garden 海德花園	Seafood 海鮮	123
Kam Fai 金輝	Seafood 海鮮	132

Mong Kok 旺角

Chuen Cheung Kui (Mong Kok) 泉章居 (旺角)	Hakkanese 客家菜	89
Fung Shing (Mong Kok) 鳳城 (旺角)	Shun Tak 順德菜	111
Good Hope Noodle (Fa Yuen Street) 好旺角麵家 (花園街)	Noodles and Congee 粥麵	115

Lei Garden (Mong Kok) 利苑酒家（旺角）	Cantonese 粵菜	149
Ming Court 明閣	Cantonese 粵菜	165
Yuet Lai Shun 粵來順	Cantonese 粵菜	263

Prince Edward 太子

Ah Chun Shandong Dumpling 阿純山東餃子	Dumplings 餃子	59
Ju Xing Home 聚興家	Cantonese 粵菜	130
Lan Yuen Chee Koon 蘭苑饍館	Cantonese 粵菜	141

Sham Shui Po 深水埗

Glorious Cuisine 增輝藝廚	Cantonese 粵菜	114
Lau Sum Kee (Fuk Wing Street) 劉森記麵家（福榮街）	Noodles 麵食	143
Thai Chiu (Sham Shui Po) 泰潮（深水埗）	Thai 泰國菜	224
Tim Ho Wan (Sham Shui Po) 添好運（深水埗）	Dim Sum 點心	230

Tai Kwok Tsui 大角咀

Tim Ho Wan (Tai Kwok Tsui) 添好運（大角咀）	Dim Sum 點心	231

Tsim Sha Tsui 尖沙咀

Above & Beyond 天外天	Cantonese 粵菜	58
Ah Yat Harbour View (Tsim Sha Tsui) 阿一海景飯店（尖沙咀）	Cantonese 粵菜	60
Bostonian Seafood & Grill	Steakhouse 扒房	73
Celestial Court 天寶閣	Cantonese 粵菜	80
Chesa 瑞樵閣	Swiss 瑞士菜	83
China Tang (Tsim Sha Tsui) 唐人館（尖沙咀）	Cantonese 粵菜	86
Cuisine Cuisine at The Mira 國金軒（尖沙咀）	Cantonese 粵菜	93
Din Tai Fung (Silvercord) 鼎泰豐（新港中心）	Shanghainese 滬菜	95
Dong Lai Shun 東來順	Chinese 中國菜	96
Épure	French contemporary 時尚法國菜	101

New Territories 新界

Sai Kung 西貢

Sha Tin 沙田

Sham Tseng 深井

Yue Kee 裕記	Cantonese 粵菜	262

Tuen Mun 屯門

Chinese Legend (Tuen Mun) 廣東名門 (屯門)	Cantonese 粵菜	87
Dragon Inn 容龍	Seafood 海鮮	97
Hoi Tin Garden 海天花園	Cantonese 粵菜	121
Yuè (Gold Coast) 粵 (黃金海岸)	Cantonese 粵菜	260

Yuen Long 元朗

Ho To Tai (Yuen Long) 好到底 (元朗)	Noodles 麵食	120
Tai Wing Wah 大榮華	Cantonese 粵菜	215
Tin Hung 天鴻燒鵝	Cantonese Roast Meats 燒味	233

RESTAURANTS BY CUISINE TYPE
餐廳 — 以菜式分類

Cantonese 粵菜

Above & Beyond 天外天	🍽	XXX	Tsim Sha Tsui 尖沙咀	58
Ah Yat Harbour View (Tsim Sha Tsui) 阿一海景飯店（尖沙咀）	✿	XXX	Tsim Sha Tsui 尖沙咀	60
Celebrity Cuisine 名人坊	✿	XX	Central 中環	79
Celestial Court 天寶閣	🍽	XXX	Tsim Sha Tsui 尖沙咀	80
Che's 車氏粵菜軒	🍽	XX	Wan Chai 灣仔	82
China Tang (Tsim Sha Tsui) 唐人館 (尖沙咀)	🍽	XX	Tsim Sha Tsui 尖沙咀	86
Chinese Legend (Tuen Mun) 廣東名門 (屯門)	🍽	X	Tuen Mun 屯門	87
Cuisine Cuisine at The Mira 國金軒 (尖沙咀)	🍽	XXX	Tsim Sha Tsui 尖沙咀	93
Duddell's 都爹利會館	✿	XXX	Central 中環	98
Farm House 農圃	🍽	XX	Causeway Bay 銅鑼灣	102
Fook Lam Moon (Wan Chai) 福臨門 (灣仔)	🍽	XXX	Wan Chai 灣仔	105
Forum 富臨飯店	✿✿	XX	Causeway Bay 銅鑼灣	106
Fu Ho (Tsim Sha Tsui) 富豪 (尖沙咀)	✿	XXX	Tsim Sha Tsui 尖沙咀	108
Fu Sing (Causeway Bay) 富聲 (銅鑼灣)	☺	XXX	Causeway Bay 銅鑼灣	109
Fu Sing (Wan Chai) 富聲 (灣仔)	☺	XX	Wan Chai 灣仔	110
Glorious Cuisine 增輝藝廚	☺	X	Sham Shui Po 深水埗	114
Guo Fu Lou 國福樓 Ⓝ	✿	XXX	Central 中環	117
Hoi Tin Garden 海天花園	🍽	X	Tuen Mun 屯門	121
Imperial Treasure Fine Chinese Cuisine 御寶軒	✿	XXX	Tsim Sha Tsui 尖沙咀	126
Ju Xing Home 聚興家	☺	🍜	Prince Edward 太子	130
Kwan Kee Clay Pot Rice (Queen's Road West) 坤記煲仔小菜（皇后大道西）	☺	🍜	Western District 西環	139
Lan Yuen Chee Koon 蘭苑饎館	☺	🍜	Prince Edward 太子	141
Lei Garden (Central) 利苑酒家 (中環)	🍽	XX	Central 中環	146

Ⓝ : New entry in the guide 新增推介

☺ : Restaurant promoted to a Bib Gourmand or Star 評級有所晉升的餐廳

Trusty Gourmet 信得過	☺	♨	Wan Chai 灣仔	240
Tsui Hang Village (Tsim Sha Tsui) 翠亨邨 (尖沙咀)	ıO	XX	Tsim Sha Tsui 尖沙咀	242
Yan Toh Heen 欣圖軒	✿✿	XXXX	Tsim Sha Tsui 尖沙咀	252
Yat Tung Heen (Jordan) 逸東軒 (佐敦)	✿	XX	Jordan 佐敦	254
Yee Tung Heen 怡東軒	✿	XXX	Causeway Bay 銅鑼灣	257
Ying Jee Club 營致會館 🍷	✿✿	XXX	Central 中環	258
Yixin 益新	☺	XX	Wan Chai 灣仔	259
Yuè (Gold Coast) 粵 (黃金海岸)	ıO	XX	Tuen Mun 屯門	260
Yuè (North Point) 粵 (北角)	ıO	XX	North Point 北角	261
Yue Kee 裕記	☺	X	Sham Tseng 深井	262
Yuet Lai Shun 粵來順	☺	♨	Mong Kok 旺角	263

American-Italian 美國意大利菜

Carbone	ıO	XX	Central 中環	78

Balinese 峇里菜

TRi	ıO	XXX	Repulse Bay 淺水灣	238

Cantonese Roast Meats 燒味

Kam's Roast Goose 甘牌燒鵝	✿	♨	Wan Chai 灣仔	133
Po Kee 波記	☺	♨	Western District 西環	179
Sun Yuen Hing Kee 新園興記	☺	♨	Sheung Wan 上環	207
Tin Hung 天鴻燒鵝 Ⓝ	ıO	♨	Yuen Long 元朗	233
Yat Lok 一樂燒鵝	✿	♨	Central 中環	253

Chinese 中國菜

China Tang (Central) 唐人館 (中環)	ıO	XXX	Central 中環	85
Dong Lai Shun 東來順	ıO	XXX	Tsim Sha Tsui 尖沙咀	96
Wing Lai Yuen 詠藜園	☺	X	Hung Hom 紅磡	249

Chiu Chow 潮州菜

Chan Kan Kee Chiu Chow (Sheung Wan) 陳勤記鹵鵝飯店 (上環)	☺	X	Sheung Wan 上環	81
Chiuchow Delicacies 潮樂園	☺	♨	North Point 北角	88
Pak Loh Chiu Chow (Hysan Avenue) 百樂潮州 (希慎道)	ıO	XX	Causeway Bay 銅鑼灣	174

Tak Kee 德記		☺	𝌆	Western District 西環	217

Dim Sum 點心

Sheung Hei Dim Sum 嚐囍點心皇		☺	𝌆	Western District 西環	195
Tim Ho Wan (North Point) 添好運 (北角)		☺	𝌆	North Point 北角	229
Tim Ho Wan (Sham Shui Po) 添好運 (深水埗)		✿	𝌆	Sham Shui Po 深水埗	230
Tim Ho Wan (Tai Kwok Tsui) 添好運 (大角咀)		☺	𝌆	Tai Kwok Tsui 大角咀	231

Dumplings 餃子

Ah Chun Shandong Dumpling 阿純山東餃子		☺	𝌆	Prince Edward 太子	59
Wang Fu (Central) 王府 (中環)		☺	𝌆	Central 中環	246

European 歐陸菜

Hugo's 希戈		℩O	XXX	Tsim Sha Tsui 尖沙咀	122

European contemporary 時尚歐陸菜

Arcane		✿	XX	Central 中環	65
Beet	N	℩O	X	Central 中環	68
Café Gray Deluxe		℩O	XX	Admiralty 金鐘	75
Mandarin Grill + Bar 文華扒房+酒吧		✿	XXXX	Central 中環	162
Mic Kitchen	N	℩O	X	Central 中環	164
Whisk		℩O	XX	Tsim Sha Tsui 尖沙咀	248

French 法國菜

Gaddi's 吉地士		℩O	XXXX	Tsim Sha Tsui 尖沙咀	112
ON		℩O	XX	Central 中環	171
Petrus 珀翠		℩O	XXXXX	Admiralty 金鐘	177
The Ocean		✿	XXX	Repulse Bay 淺水灣	226
Upper Modern Bistro		℩O	XX	Sheung Wan 上環	243

French contemporary 時尚法國菜

Akrame		℩O	XX	Wan Chai 灣仔	61
Amber		✿✿	XXXX	Central 中環	62

Italian 意大利菜

CIAK - All Day Italian		☺	X	Tai Koo Shing 太古城	91
Giando	N	🍽	XXX	Wan Chai 灣仔	113
Involtini		🍽	X	Causeway Bay 銅鑼灣	127
Locanda dell' Angelo	N	🍽	XX	Happy Valley 跑馬地	156
Octavium	N	✿	XXX	Central 中環	170
8 1/2 Otto e Mezzo - Bombana		✿✿✿	XXXX	Central 中環	173
Tosca		✿	XXXX	Tsim Sha Tsui 尖沙咀	236

Japanese 日本菜

Kaiseki Den by Saotome		✿	XX	Wan Chai 灣仔	131
Kashiwaya 柏屋		✿✿	XX	Central 中環	134
La Bombance		🍽	XX	Causeway Bay 銅鑼灣	140
Nishiki 錦		☺	X	Tsim Sha Tsui 尖沙咀	169
Takeya 竹家		☺	🍜	Hung Hom 紅磡	218
Tenku RyuGin 天空龍吟		✿✿	XX	Tsim Sha Tsui 尖沙咀	223
Toritama 酉玉		🍽	X	Central 中環	235

Malaysian 馬拉菜

Sabah (Wan Chai) 莎巴 (灣仔)		☺	X	Wan Chai 灣仔	185

Middle Eastern 中東菜

Le Souk	☺	☺	X	Central 中環	145

Noodles 麵食

Eng Kee Noodle Shop 英記麵家		☺	🍜	Western District 西環	100
Ho To Tai (Yuen Long) 好到底 (元朗)		☺	🍜	Yuen Long 元朗	120
Kau Kee 九記		☺	🍜	Central 中環	135
Kwan Kee Bamboo Noodles (Cheung Sha Wan) 坤記竹昇麵 (長沙灣)		☺	🍜	Cheung Sha Wan 長沙灣	138
Lau Sum Kee (Fuk Wing Street) 劉森記麵家 (福榮街)	☺	☺	🍜	Sham Shui Po 深水埗	143
Mak Man Kee 麥文記		☺	🍜	Jordan 佐敦	160
Sister Wah (Tin Hau) 華姐清湯腩 (天后)		☺	🍜	Tin Hau 天后	199
Tsim Chai Kee (Wellington Street) 沾仔記 (威靈頓街)		☺	🍜	Central 中環	241

Noodles and Congee 粥麵

Congee and Noodle Shop 粥麵館	㊝	🍜	Quarry Bay 鰂魚涌	92
Good Hope Noodle (Fa Yuen Street) 好旺角麵家 (花園街)	㊝	🍜	Mong Kok 旺角	115
Ho Hung Kee 何洪記	✿	X	Causeway Bay 銅鑼灣	119
Tasty (Central) 正斗粥麵專家 (中環)	㊝	X	Central 中環	221
Trusty Congee King (Wan Chai) 靠得住 (灣仔)	㊝	🍜	Wan Chai 灣仔	239

Pekingese 京菜

Peking Garden (Central) 北京樓 (中環)	IO	XXX	Central 中環	176

Peru 秘魯菜

ICHU Ⓝ	IO	XX	Central 中環	124

Ramen 拉麵

Ramen Jo (Causeway Bay) 拉麵Jo (銅鑼灣)	㊝	🍜	Causeway Bay 銅鑼灣	183
Shugetsu Ramen (Central) 麵鮮醬油房周月 (中環)	㊝	🍜	Central 中環	196
Shugetsu Ramen (Quarry Bay) 麵鮮醬油房周月 (鰂魚涌)	㊝	🍜	Quarry Bay 鰂魚涌	197

Scandinavian 北歐菜

Frantzén's Kitchen	IO	XX	Sheung Wan 上環	107

Seafood 海鮮

Chuen Kee Seafood 全記海鮮	IO	X	Sai Kung 西貢	90
Dragon Inn 容龍	㊝	XX	Tuen Mun 屯門	97
Fish School	IO	X	Western District 西環	103
Hing Kee 避風塘興記	IO	X	Tsim Sha Tsui 尖沙咀	118
Hyde Park Garden 海德花園	IO	X	Lei Yue Mun 鯉魚門	123
Kam Fai 金輝	IO	X	Lei Yue Mun 鯉魚門	132
Rech	✿	XXX	Tsim Sha Tsui 尖沙咀	184
Sai Kung Sing Kee 勝記	IO	X	Sai Kung 西貢	186

Shaanxi 陝西菜

Yau Yuen Siu Tsui (Jordan) 有緣小敘 (佐敦)		☺	🍜	Jordan 佐敦	255

Shanghainese 滬菜

Din Tai Fung (Causeway Bay) 鼎泰豐 (銅鑼灣)		☺	X	Causeway Bay 銅鑼灣	94
Din Tai Fung (Silvercord) 鼎泰豐 (新港中心)		☺	X	Tsim Sha Tsui 尖沙咀	95
Jardin de Jade (Wan Chai) 蘇浙滙 (灣仔)		✿	XXX	Wan Chai 灣仔	129
Liu Yuan Pavilion 留園雅敘		☺	XX	Wan Chai 灣仔	154
New Shanghai 新滬坊		☺	XXX	Wan Chai 灣仔	167
Shanghai Yu Yuan 豫園	Ⓝ	ıO	XXX	Causeway Bay 銅鑼灣	191
Snow Garden 雪園		☺	XX	Causeway Bay 銅鑼灣	201
Wu Kong (Causeway Bay) 滬江 (銅鑼灣)		ıO	XX	Causeway Bay 銅鑼灣	250
Yè Shanghai (Tsim Sha Tsui) 夜上海 (尖沙咀)		✿	XXX	Tsim Sha Tsui 尖沙咀	256

Shun Tak 順德菜

Fung Shing (Mong Kok) 鳳城 (旺角)	☺	X	Mong Kok 旺角	111
Siu Shun Village Cuisine (Kowloon Bay) 肇順名匯河鮮專門店 (九龍灣)	☺	X	Kowloon Bay 九龍灣	200

Sichuan 川菜

Chilli Fagara 麻辣燙	ıO	X	Central 中環	84
Qi (Tsim Sha Tsui) 呇 (尖沙咀)	ıO	XX	Tsim Sha Tsui 尖沙咀	181
Qi (Wan Chai) 呇 (灣仔)	✿	XX	Wan Chai 灣仔	182

Singaporean and Malaysian 星馬菜

Ancient Moon 古月	☺	🍜	North Point 北角	63

Spanish 西班牙菜

FoFo by el Willy	ıO	X	Central 中環	104

Steakhouse 扒房

Beefbar	✿	XXX	Central 中環	67

Bostonian Seafood & Grill		🍽	XX	Tsim Sha Tsui 尖沙咀	73
Grand Hyatt Steakhouse		🍽	XX	Wan Chai 灣仔	116
Steak on Elgin	Ⓝ	🍽	XX	Central 中環	203
The Steak House winebar + grill		🍽	XXX	Tsim Sha Tsui 尖沙咀	227

Sushi 壽司

Sushi Masataka		🍽	X	Wan Chai 灣仔	208
Sushi Mori Tomoaki		🍽	X	Tin Hau 天后	209
Sushi Saito 鮨・齋藤	Ⓝ	✿✿	XX	Central 中環	210
Sushi Shikon 志魂		✿✿✿	X	Sheung Wan 上環	211
Sushi Tokami		✿	X	Tsim Sha Tsui 尖沙咀	212
Sushi Wadatsumi		✿	X	Sheung Wan 上環	213

Swiss 瑞士菜

Chesa 瑞樵閣		🍽	XX	Tsim Sha Tsui 尖沙咀	83
The Swiss Chalet 瑞士餐廳		🍽	X	Tsim Sha Tsui 尖沙咀	228

Taiwanese 台灣菜

What To Eat 吃什麼	Ⓝ	☺	🍜	Central 中環	247

Taizhou 台州菜

Xin Rong Ji 新榮記	Ⓝ	✿	XXX	Wan Chai 灣仔	251

Tempura 天婦羅

Ippoh 一宝		🍽	X	Central 中環	128

Teppanyaki 鐵板燒

IM Teppanyaki & Wine		✿	XX	Tai Hang 大坑	125

Thai 泰國菜

Samsen 泰麵		☺	X	Wan Chai 灣仔	187
Thai Chiu (Sham Shui Po) 泰潮 (深水埗)		☺	🍜	Sham Shui Po 深水埗	224

Vegetarian 素食

Kung Tak Lam (Causeway Bay) 功德林 (銅鑼灣)		🍽	XX	Causeway Bay 銅鑼灣	137

Vietnamese 越南菜

Brass Spoon (Wan Chai)	Wan Chai 灣仔	74
Le Garçon Saigon	Wan Chai 灣仔	144

Xinjiang 新疆菜

Ba Yi 巴依	Western District 西環	66

Zhejiang 浙江菜

Zhejiang Heen 浙江軒	Wan Chai 灣仔	265

RESTAURANTS WITH INTERESTING WINE LISTS
供應優質餐酒的餐廳

ⓝ : New entry in the guide 新增推介

↗ : Restaurant promoted to a Bib Gourmand or Star 評級有所晉升的餐廳

RESTAURANTS WITH VIEWS
有景觀的餐廳

(N) : New entry in the guide 新增推介
☺ : Restaurant promoted to a Bib Gourmand or Star 評級有所晉升的餐廳

quel cadre!

Looking for a taste of local life? Check out our top street food picks.
到哪兒尋找本土特色小食？請翻閱本年度的街頭小吃推介。

Read 'How to use this guide' for an explanation of our symbols, classifications and abbreviations.
請細閱「如何使用餐廳／酒店指南」，當中的標誌、分類等簡介助你掌握使用本指南的訣竅，作出智慧選擇。

STREET FOOD
街頭小吃

Above & Beyond
天外天

Its stylish and vibrant décor comes as no surprise given its location in the Hotel Icon. The vast array of menus offers everything from lunchtime dim sum to a dedicated Peking duck tasting menu. They also have healthier options and at the weekends serve Cantonese-style afternoon tea. Signature dishes include crispy chicken, and wok-fried lobster with egg white and black truffles.

位處風格鮮明的唯港薈之內，由泰倫斯・康藍 (Sir Terence Conran) 設計的天外天時尚典雅，加上坐擁醉人維港景致，叫人讚歎不已，臨窗的座位無疑是最佳選擇。叫人花多眼亂的餐單包羅萬有，從午市點心、健怡套餐至港式片皮鴨皆能找到。招牌菜包括脆皮炸子雞和黑松露蛋白炒龍蝦球。週末設粵式下午茶。

TEL. 3400 1318
28F, Hotel Icon, 17 Science Museum Road, East Tsim Sha Tsui
尖東科學館道 17號唯港薈 28樓
www.hotel-icon.com/dining/above-beyond

■ PRICE 價錢
Lunch 午膳
set 套餐 $ 198-298
à la carte 點菜 $ 250-2,100
Dinner 晚膳
set 套餐 $ 568-918
à la carte 點菜 $ 250-2,100

■ OPENING HOURS 營業時間
Lunch 午膳 11:00-14:30 (L.O.)
Dinner 晚膳 18:00-22:30 (L.O.)

Ah Chun Shandong Dumpling
阿純山東餃子

The shop has a traditional feel to it after renovation. Green wooden window frames on the wall are reminiscent of old-time Hong Kong. Dumplings are handmade daily and only the freshest ingredients are used in the fillings. Try their most-ordered item lamb and Peking scallion dumplings. Or surprise yourself with the specialty, such as mackerel dumplings and cuttlefish dumplings. Shandong roast lamb and meat pie are also recommended.

翻新後的店子帶點傳統味道，牆上的綠色木窗框很有老香港感覺。多款不同味道的傳統餃子以新鮮食材作餡料，每天在店內以人手包製，其中以京蔥羊肉餃最受歡迎。此外，特色推介如馬鮫魚餃和墨魚餃，常給顧客帶來驚喜！其他推介菜式還有山東紅燒羊肉和餡餅。最新推出的薺菜餃也值得一試。

TEL. 2789 9611
60 Lai Chi Kok Road, Prince Edward
太子荔枝角道 60號

■ PRICE 價錢
à la carte 點菜 $ 30-100

■ OPENING HOURS 營業時間
11:00-22:30 (L.O.)

■ ANNUAL AND WEEKLY CLOSING 休息日期
Closed 6 days Lunar New Year and Wednesday
農曆新年 6 天及週三休息

Ah Yat Harbour View (Tsim Sha Tsui)
阿一海景飯店 (尖沙咀)

60

A large photo of owner-chef Yeung Koon Yat greets you as you come out of the lift – and he's enjoying his most famous dish: abalone. Ah Yat signature fried rice and stewed oxtail with homemade sauce and red wine casserole is also worth a try. The good value set lunch menu is a great way of experiencing many more of their Cantonese specialities. The contemporary dining room takes full advantage of the wonderful views; Table 11 is the best.

身處位於iSquare 29樓的阿一海景，當然要一嘗名廚老闆楊貫一的名菜：阿一鮑魚。此外，不妨試試其他馳名菜如一哥招牌砂鍋炒飯及紅酒醬燜牛尾。飯店供應來自波爾多、加州、新西蘭和澳洲的高級紅酒。店內設有四間私人廂房，大部分座位都能欣賞宜人的維港兩岸美景，11號餐桌景觀最佳。

TEL. 2328 0983
29F, iSquare, 63 Nathan Road, Tsim Sha Tsui
尖沙咀彌敦道63號 iSquare 29樓

SPECIALITIES TO PRE-ORDER 預訂食物
Poached sliced fresh sea whelk 白灼響螺盞 / Baked chicken filled with abalone matsutake mushroom and morchella mushroom 松茸羊肚菌吉濱鮮鮑魚焗雞 / Baked salty chicken 一哥鹽焗雞

■ PRICE 價錢
Lunch 午膳
set 套餐 $ 300-500
à la carte 點菜 $ 400-2,200
Dinner 晚膳
set 套餐 $ 800-1,500
à la carte 點菜 $ 400-2,200

■ OPENING HOURS 營業時間
Lunch 午膳 11:30-15:00 (L.O.)
Dinner 晚膳 18:00-22:30 (L.O.)

Akrame

XX

12

The restaurant takes its name from Akrame Benallal who also owns restaurants in Paris and Shanghai. His team here offers their own interpretation of his style, which is highly creative and uses imaginative combinations of flavours and textures, with each dish relying on just a few ingredients to deliver impact. Choose the 8-course 'Surprise' menu at dinner which features dishes like avocado/snail and pineapple/charcoal.

以在巴黎和上海均有開設餐廳的大廚Akrame Benallal命名，團隊專業演繹Akrame的風格，以無限創意組合不同味道和質感，每道菜僅以數款食材便帶出不同效果。晚餐建議點選八道菜的菜單。以黑白色作主調的餐室，線條簡潔且具時尚魅力。

TEL. 2528 5068
9B Ship Street, Wan Chai
灣仔船街 9號 B
www.akrame.com.hk

■ PRICE 價錢
Lunch 午膳
set 套餐 $ 280-680
à la carte 點菜 $ 650-750
Dinner 晚膳
set 套餐 $ 1,280
à la carte 點菜 $ 650-750

■ OPENING HOURS 營業時間
Lunch 午膳 12:00-14:00 (L.O.)
Dinner 晚膳 18:00-21:30 (L.O.)

■ ANNUAL AND WEEKLY CLOSING 休息日期
Closed Lunar New Year and Monday
農曆新年及週一休息

FRENCH CONTEMPORARY 時尚法國菜 MAP 地圖 25/D-2

Amber

Closed for a radical revamp from December 2018 to May 2019, this restaurant helmed by the Dutch-born chef Richard Ekkebus is famous for its bold and adventurous haute cuisine, which is deeply rooted in classical French techniques and uses top-notch ingredients, mostly from Japan. Check their official website to make sure the re-opening is on schedule.

由荷蘭廚師Richard Ekkebus帶領的團隊將以法國菜烹調技巧，配合日本進口的高質食材，為客人帶來全新的餐飲體驗。Amber將於2018年12月開始進行大型裝修，並計劃於翌年5月重新營業，相關資訊敬請留意官方公佈。

TEL. 2132 0066
7F, The Landmark Mandarin Oriental Hotel, 15 Queen's Road Central, Central
中環皇后大道中 15號置地文華東方酒店 7樓
www.amberhongkong.com

■ PRICE 價錢
Lunch 午膳
set 套餐 $ 618-2,138
Weekend set 週末套餐 $ 1,028
à la carte 點菜 $ 1,600-2,500
Dinner 晚膳
set 套餐 $ 1,598-2,138
à la carte 點菜 $ 1,600-2,500

■ OPENING HOURS 營業時間
Lunch 午膳 12:00-14:30 (L.O.)
Public Holiday lunch 公眾假期午膳 12:00-14:00 (L.O.)
Dinner 晚膳 18:30-22:30 (L.O.)

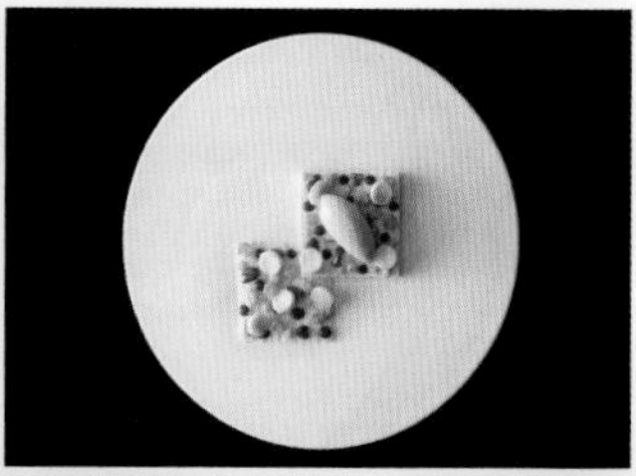

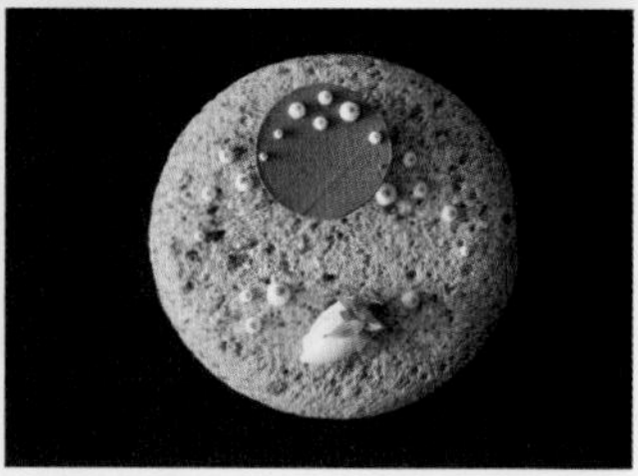

Ancient Moon
古月

It was Singaporean and Malaysian street food enjoyed whilst travelling that inspired owners Fanni and Lico to open their fun little place. The small menu lists about 12 items and avoids serving the more standard dishes. Instead, it's one of the few places to offer Malaysian chilli pan mee (a flavoursome white noodle dish with dried fish and homemade chilli sauce) and Singaporean bak kut teh, made with pork ribs and garlic.

藏身於鬧市中，古月的位置確是有點隱蔽，你須從書局街進入方能找到。看着牆上帶有地方特色的卡通繪畫，不難猜中這裏提供的是星、馬兩地美食。餐單貴精不貴多，當中多是在香港較少見，甚或是首家供應的菜式，包括以胡椒和生蒜作湯底的新加坡肉骨茶及配自製辣椒乾進食非常惹味的馬來西亞板麵等。

TEL. 3568 4530
29A, Kam Ping Street, North Point
北角錦屏街29號A舖

■ PRICE 價錢
Lunch 午膳
set 套餐 $ 50-90
à la carte 點菜 $ 50-100
Dinner 晚膳
à la carte 點菜 $ 50-100

■ OPENING HOURS 營業時間
12:00-21:30 (L.O.)

■ ANNUAL AND WEEKLY CLOSING 休息日期
Closed 5 days Lunar New Year and Sunday 農曆新年5天及週日休息

Arbor N

Its calming Mediterranean colours make this something of an oasis from the bustle of Central. The experienced chef hails from Finland; he uses mostly French techniques in his cooking and sources quality ingredients, mainly from Japan. His sophisticated dishes exhibit typical Nordic precision and deliver intense natural flavours. The service style is quite formal and there's an impressive wine list.

室內設計採用悠閒的地中海風格，讓人暫時遠離中環區的繁囂。祖籍芬蘭、經驗老到的大廚對食材瞭解透徹，秉持對食材的尊重，堅持採用新鮮且大部分皆源自日本的材料。嫻熟的法式烹調技術加上北歐精準細緻的態度，食材的自然滋味得以充分顯露。酒單使人眼前一亮，服務專業周到。

TEL. 3185 8388
25F, H Queen's, 80 Queen's Road Central, Central
中環皇后大道中 80號 H Queen's 25樓
www.arbor-hk.com

■ PRICE 價錢
Lunch 午膳
set 套餐 $ 488-568
Dinner 晚膳
set 套餐 $ 1,488-1,888

■ OPENING HOURS 營業時間
Lunch 午膳 12:00-14:00 (L.O.)
Dinner 晚膳 18:30-22:00 (L.O.)

■ ANNUAL AND WEEKLY CLOSING 休息日期
Closed Sunday 週日休息

Arcane

Aussie chef Shane Osborn lets diners witness how quality ingredients turn into artistic culinary creations in the open kitchen. Simple recipes are done with a refined edge which allows authentic flavours to shine through. The affable manager and sommelier is more than happy to pair your food with wine from their extensive cellar covering Europe, Oceania, The Americas and which includes a lavish Burgundy selection.

開放式廚房讓食客能注視主廚Shane Osborn烹調時的專注、體會他的熱情，以簡易方式烹調日本海鮮、澳洲牛肉、意大利小牛肉和法國有機雞肉等食材，也反映了他對食材的尊重。經理兼侍酒師的熱情招待，完滿了客人的用餐經驗，其挑選的餐酒涵蓋布根地、大洋洲和美國等地產物。

TEL. 2728 0178
3F, 18 On Lan Street, Central
中環安蘭街 18號 3樓
www.arcane.hk

■ PRICE 價錢
Lunch 午膳
set 套餐 $ 350
à la carte 點菜 $ 700-1,000
Dinner 晚膳
à la carte 點菜 $ 700-1,000

■ OPENING HOURS 營業時間
Lunch 午膳 12:00-14:30 (L.O.)
Dinner 晚膳 18:30-22:30 (L.O.)

■ ANNUAL AND WEEKLY CLOSING 休息日期
Closed Saturday lunch and Sunday
週六午膳及週日休息

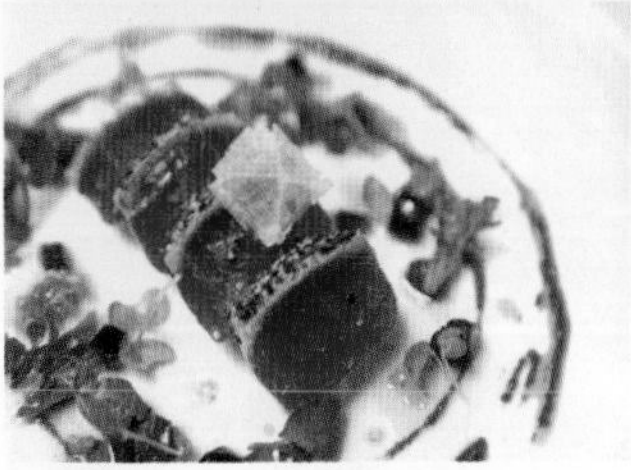

Ba Yi
巴依

Despite being somewhat out of the way, lamb-lovers gather here in numbers for items such as stewed lamb, roast leg and mutton skewers, prepared by the Xinjiangese kitchen team. Besides lamb, it's also worth trying the chicken stew with potato and chilli, the Ketik yoghurt drink, and the goat's milk curd dessert with almonds. The updated dining room still features the map of the Silk Road on a stretched canvas.

開業多年，標誌性的巨型絲路圖始終佔據着店中央的顯著位置。同是新疆人的廚師團隊與店主合作無間，一直堅守着同一使命：為客人提供地道而優質、價錢相宜的新疆菜。羊肉特色菜如手抓肉、烤羊腿和羊肉串燒等固然是主角，此外，大盤雞、酸奶和杏仁羊奶凍也值得一試，店主還會不時加入新菜式。

TEL. 2484 9981
43 Water Street, Sai Ying Pun
西營盤水街 43號

■ PRICE 價錢
Lunch 午膳
set 套餐 $ 40-80
à la carte 點菜 $ 50-150
Dinner 晚膳
à la carte 點菜 $ 150-250

■ OPENING HOURS 營業時間
Lunch 午膳 12:00-14:30 (L.O.)
Dinner 晚膳 18:00-22:30 (L.O.)

■ ANNUAL AND WEEKLY CLOSING 休息日期
Closed 2 weeks Lunar New Year and Monday
農曆新年兩星期及週一休息

Beefbar

XXX ♿ 18

With branches all over the world now, this Monte Carlo based group has created a rather stylish restaurant whose décor blends marble and leather. Naturally, meat is the real focus, with the prime cuts broiled then chargrilled to keep in all the flavour. To start, consider beef tartare prepared tableside or one of the lighter ceviches and tacos. They offer some interesting Kobe beef street food snacks too which show refinement as well as flavour.

源自摩納哥的扒房在雪廠街的店子別具型格，時尚氣息來自白色雲石和黑色皮革裝潢。主打頂級牛扒：美國安格斯牛、澳洲安格斯牛、澳洲和牛及神戶牛，多種不同部位的牛肉給烤至恰到好處。前菜不妨考慮柑橘汁醃魚生、墨西哥卷餅或席前炮製的牛肉他他。以神戶牛製作的小食也不錯。

TEL. 2110 8853
2F, Club Lusitano, 16 Ice House Street, Central
中環雪廠街 16號西洋會所 2樓
www.beefbar.hk

■ PRICE 價錢
Lunch 午膳
set 套餐 $ 320-600
à la carte 點菜 $ 450-1,500
Dinner 晚膳
set 套餐 $ 1,180
à la carte 點菜 $ 450-1,500

■ OPENING HOURS 營業時間
Lunch 午膳 12:00-14:30 (L.O.)
Dinner 晚膳 18:30-22:30 (L.O.)

■ ANNUAL AND WEEKLY CLOSING 休息日期
Closed 3 days Lunar New Year and Sunday 農曆新年 3 天及週日休息

Beet

As humble as the vegetable after which it's named, this casual, tucked away little eatery makes everything from scratch in-house and that includes smoking and curing their bacon and churning their own butter. Try the signature New Territories pork, seasonal seafood and the creamy chicken liver parfait bursting with flavour. The ingredients are organic and there are plenty of vegetarian and vegan options too.

餐廳格調簡單樸素，為食客提供了輕鬆舒適的用餐環境。只採用有機食材，當中九成為本地生產，確保用料新鮮。主廚尤愛從零開始自家製作食物，不論是牛油和麵包，以至煙肉的煙燻過程均親自操刀。招牌菜包括New Territories Pork及時令海鮮菜式，並有素食可供選擇。綿滑而味道濃郁的雞肝醬亦是必試之選。

TEL. 2824 3898
Shop C, 6-10 Kau U Fong, Central
中環九如坊 6-10號 C舖
www.beetrestaurant.com

■ PRICE 價錢
Lunch 午膳
set 套餐 $ 195-245
à la carte 點菜 $ 375-655
Dinner 晚膳
set 套餐 $ 630-810
à la carte 點菜 $ 375-655

■ OPENING HOURS 營業時間
Wednesday to Friday lunch
週三至週五午膳 12:00-14:00 (L.O.)
Dinner 晚膳 18:30-22:00 (L.O.)

■ ANNUAL AND WEEKLY CLOSING 休息日期
Closed 3 days Lunar New Year and Sunday 農曆新年 3 天及週日休息

Belon

18

Frenchman Daniel Calvert cut his teeth cooking in some of the best restaurants in London, New York and Paris. His appealing little bistro has a subtle French look and a relaxed feel made even more enjoyable by his personable team who deliver excellent service. He is a chef who understands sophisticated simplicity perfectly and his pared-back, delicious classic French dishes are delivered with consummate skill and accuracy.

這間法式餐館與蘇豪區的風格如出一轍，環境優雅舒適，團隊親切殷勤的服務更讓食客賓至如歸。法籍廚師曾先後於倫敦、紐約及巴黎的頂級餐廳效力，擅於烹調傳統法國菜，所作的菜式精緻簡約，盡顯其熟練而精湛的烹調技巧，每道菜都令人垂涎欲滴。

TEL. 2152 2872
41 Elgin Street, Central
中環伊利近街 41號
www.belonsoho.com

■ PRICE 價錢
Lunch 午膳
set 套餐 $ 458
Dinner 晚膳
set 套餐 $ 1,088-1,488
à la carte 點菜 $ 700-1,100

■ OPENING HOURS 營業時間
Sunday lunch 週日午膳
12:00-14:30 (L.O.)
Dinner 晚膳 18:00-22:30 (L.O.)

■ ANNUAL AND WEEKLY CLOSING 休息日期
Closed Monday 週一休息

HONG KONG 香港

Bibo

Once you've found the door button that lets you in you'll be confronted by a remarkable collection of original art. Banksy, Basquiat, Murakami and Kaws are just a few artists whose works make this restaurant so unique. Creative French cuisine is served in this rather sparse, dimly lit but intimate restaurant; choose the 'Chef's Imagination' menu to see the creativity of the kitchen. A remarkable selection of wines by the glass includes Château Palmer.

要進入餐廳，你先要找到隱藏在金色滑門上的神秘開關。金屬門趟開後，迎接你的會是一件件別出心裁、出自當代藝術家的作品，街頭壁畫及雕塑遍佈四周，恍若置身藝廊一樣。餐室燈光昏黃而寬敞。「大廚想像菜單」可讓你體驗廚師的無窮創意，杯裝酒更是選擇眾多。

TEL. 2956 3188
163 Hollywood Road, Sheung Wan
上環荷李活道 163號
www.bibo.hk

■ PRICE 價錢
Dinner 晚膳
set 套餐 $ 858
à la carte 點菜 $ 620-900

■ OPENING HOURS 營業時間
Dinner 晚膳 18:00-22:30 (L.O.)

Bo Innovation

10

Alvin Leung celebrates Hong Kong's culture, traditions and people here, from the kitchen façade inspired by the typhoon shelters of Aberdeen Harbour to the graffiti walls which illustrate the journey of this chef. Each vibrant, imaginative and at times 'X-treme' dish comes with its own story and blends strong Chinese techniques with subtle French influences. Ingredients are superb and the flavours are clearly defined and memorable.

靈感來自香港仔避風塘的廚房佈置，記述着主廚研製菜式旅程的牆上塗鴉，甚或是餐廳內各式本地特製食具和古董，通通都是主廚梁經倫獻給香港文化的讚歌。他以上乘的用料創作，天馬行空地以食物訴說故事，菜式透出穩紮的中式烹調技巧和法式手法，味道教人難以忘懷。

TEL. 2850 8371
Shop 8, Podium 1F, J Senses,
60 Johnston Road, Wan Chai
灣仔莊士敦道 60號
J Senses一樓平台 8號舖
www.boinnovation.com

■ PRICE 價錢
Lunch 午膳
set 套餐 $ 750-900
Dinner 晚膳
set 套餐 $ 2,280-2,680

■ OPENING HOURS 營業時間
Lunch 午膳 12:00-14:00 (L.O.)
Dinner 晚膳 19:00-22:00 (L.O.)

■ ANNUAL AND WEEKLY CLOSING 休息日期
Closed 3 days Lunar New Year, Saturday lunch and Sunday 農曆新年 3 天，週六午膳及週日休息

Bombay Dreams

Tucked away on the 4th floor of an unremarkable building is something of an institution – this Indian restaurant has been operating here since 2002. The jars of spices that line the shelves tell you this is a kitchen which takes spicing seriously. There's a great value lunch buffet but go for the à la carte for original, well-crafted dishes with an emphasis on northern India – specialities from the tandoor are a highlight.

這印度餐廳自2002年開始營業，雖然其位置不甚顯眼，卻一直不乏捧場客。一列列香料瓶置滿架上，說明了廚師對香料的重視。午市供應豐富的自助餐，經濟實惠，深得上班族喜愛。如欲品嘗餐廳最出色、正宗的菜式，自選餐單是更佳選擇，以北印度泥爐炭火(Tandoor)烹調的菜式非試不可，新增的六道菜套餐亦不妨一試。

TEL. 2971 0001
4F, 75-77 Wyndham Street, Central
中環雲咸街 75-77號 4樓
www.diningconcepts.com

■ PRICE 價錢
Lunch 午膳
set 套餐 $ 158-498
à la carte 點菜 $ 200-400
Dinner 晚膳
set 套餐 $ 498
à la carte 點菜 $ 200-400

■ OPENING HOURS 營業時間
Lunch 午膳 12:00-15:00 (L.O.)
Dinner 晚膳 18:00-23:00 (L.O.)

Bostonian Seafood & Grill

16

The self-assured Bostonian is a handsome and sophisticated restaurant offering all the things you'd expect from an American restaurant: plenty of hearty salads, lots of lobster, oysters, assorted seafood and, of course, a huge choice of prime beef from the grill. The set lunch with the seafood buffet is particularly popular, as is brunch on a Sunday. It's unlikely anyone has ever left here still feeling hungry.

深色系和木製傢具為餐廳添上型格感覺，牆上的藝術畫令環境生色不少，生蠔吧變成了小型酒吧，供客人餐前或飯後淺酌。任職多年的大廚繼續提供具水準的美食，波士頓龍蝦等各類海鮮仍然是餐牌的焦點所在，當然亦少不了種類多樣而且處理得恰到好處的特級烤牛扒，完全符合你對美式餐廳的期望。

TEL. 2132 7898
Lower Lobby Level, The Langham Hotel,
8 Peking Road, Tsim Sha Tsui
尖沙咀北京道 8號朗廷酒店低層大堂
www.langhamhotels.com/hongkong

■ PRICE 價錢
Lunch 午膳
set 套餐 $ 378
à la carte 點菜 $ 510-1,600
Dinner 晚膳
à la carte 點菜 $ 510-1,600

■ OPENING HOURS 營業時間
Lunch 午膳 12:00-14:30 (L.O.)
Sunday lunch 週日午膳
11:00-14:30 (L.O.)
Dinner 晚膳 18:00-22:30 (L.O.)

Brass Spoon (Wan Chai)

The chef has barely had time to draw breath since he opened his small shop selling pho, Vietnam's national dish. He learnt to cook in France, where his family had a Vietnamese restaurant, and chose this small street to recreate the feeling you get when you come across a little ramen shop in Tokyo. He uses US Angus beef and Danish pork and, for the noodles' soup base, slow-cooks beef shank bone for more than 16 hours.

這小小的越式河粉店選址於一條寧靜小街上，源於店東對日本街頭小巷拉麵店的嚮往。於法國習廚的主廚兼店東注重細節，堅決不用味精，湯底以牛小腿骨熬煮逾十六小時而成，味道濃郁；客人可揀選不同級別的美國牛肉，也可自選配料。餐單也提供各種越式小食，如春卷和蒸粉卷等。不設訂座，建議提早前往輪候。

TEL. 2877 0898
Shop B, GF, 1-3 Moon Street, Wan Chai
灣仔月街 1-3號地下 B舖
www.thebrassspoon.com

■ PRICE 價錢
à la carte 點菜 $ 90-220

■ OPENING HOURS 營業時間
12:00-18:45 (L.O.)

■ ANNUAL AND WEEKLY CLOSING 休息日期
Closed Public Holidays and Sunday
公眾假期及週日休息

Café Gray Deluxe

12

The fashionable Upper House hotel hosts this stylish bistro deluxe on its 49th floor and its great views, relaxed atmosphere and fluent, efficient service make it a very popular spot, especially at lunch. The kitchen uses plenty of modern techniques and adds its own twists to what are mostly European and American dishes. The speciality from consulting chef Gray Kunz is steak tartare ketjap. The restaurant also serves afternoon tea.

型格餐廳Café Gray Deluxe位處奕居49樓，用餐的同時能欣賞維港的超凡美景，服務亦極為周到。年輕主廚烹調技巧高超，在歐陸佳餚中混入獨特的材料變化，香草汁鮮茄車輪意粉、芥末汁牛小排等均值得一試。菜單中有不少輕盈選擇，而下午茶頗受歡迎。

TEL. 3968 1106
49F, The Upper House Hotel,
Pacific Place, 88 Queensway,
Admiralty
金鐘道88號太古廣場奕居49樓
www.cafegrayhk.com

■ PRICE 價錢
Lunch 午膳
set 套餐 $395-445
à la carte 點菜 $600-1,300
Dinner 晚膳
set 套餐 $725
à la carte 點菜 $600-1,300

■ OPENING HOURS 營業時間
Lunch 午膳 12:00-14:30 (L.O.)
Dinner 晚膳 18:00-22:30 (L.O.)

Café Hunan (Western District)
書湘門第 (西環)

He honed his skills at his mother's restaurant, so the young Hunanese chef is passionate about his home-town cooking. Ingredients such as chillies and smoked pork are sourced directly from farmers in Hunan. The speciality braised pork elbow entails four complicated cooking steps spanning over 10 hours to develop layered flavours and the right texture. Stir-fried pork with Youxian beancurd and spicy organic cauliflower are also worth trying.

來自湖南的廚師從小已在母親的菜館幫忙，奠定了扎實的廚藝基礎。他熱衷烹調風味正宗的湖南菜，店內使用食材大部分來自湖南，例如從農戶採購而來的煙燻臘肉和各種辣椒。推介菜式包括經四個工序以十小時製作的霸王肘子，還有攸縣香乾炒肉和乾鍋有機花菜。部分菜式設不同辣度供選擇。

TEL. 2803 7177
420-424 Queen's Road West,
Western District
西環皇后大道西 420-424號

SPECIALITIES TO PRE-ORDER 預訂食物
Steamed fish head with diced red and yellow pepper 鴛鴦魚頭王 / Braised pork elbow Hunan style 霸王肘子 / Sauteed crab in spicy sauce 湘辣蟹 / Braised wild Chinese softshell turtle in spicy sauce 野生甲魚煲 / Farmer's steamed chicken 乾蒸雞

■ PRICE 價錢
Lunch 午膳
set 套餐 $ 48
à la carte 點菜 $ 100-200
Dinner 晚膳
à la carte 點菜 $ 100-200

■ OPENING HOURS 營業時間
Lunch 午膳 11:00-14:30 (L.O.)
Dinner 晚膳 18:00-21:30 (L.O.)

■ ANNUAL AND WEEKLY CLOSING 休息日期
Closed 4 days Lunar New Year
農曆新年休息 4 天

Caprice

12

Not only is this one of the most glamourous and elegant restaurants in Hong Kong but it also boasts impressive views of the harbour. French cuisine of the highest order features luxurious ingredients, superb techniques and a mastery of flavours and harmony. A stunning wine list accompanies specialities like crab royale, and turbot with sea urchin sauce. The wonderful array of cheeses is another highlight. Dining here is always an amazing experience.

餐室裝潢古典優雅而不失格調，更有迷人海景及貼心專業的服務，在這裏用餐實是非凡享受。先到酒吧呷杯雞尾酒，再享用各式以高級食材輔以精湛烹調技巧所作的法國菜式，每一道都將味道發揮到極致。招牌菜包括多寶魚伴海膽汁和蟹肉拌生蠔及海鮮啫喱；芝士和餐酒的選擇叫人驚歎。

TEL. 3196 8860
6F, Four Seasons Hotel,
8 Finance Street, Central
中環金融街8號四季酒店6樓
www.fourseasons.com/hongkong

■ PRICE 價錢
Lunch 午膳
set 套餐 $ 550-895
à la carte 點菜 $ 1,200-2,600
Dinner 晚膳
set 套餐 $ 1,720-2,080
à la carte 點菜 $ 1,200-2,600

■ OPENING HOURS 營業時間
Lunch 午膳 12:00-14:30 (L.O.)
Dinner 晚膳 18:30-22:00 (L.O.)

Carbone

24

As with the original Carbone in Greenwich Village, this colourful restaurant pays homage to the American-Italian eateries of the 1950s. Tiles, wood panelling, red armchairs and a counter bar all help to create that typical Manhattan feel. The menu features classics like Caesar salad, spicy rigatoni vodka and veal parmesan – and the regulars would never allow the meatballs to be removed. From the dessert trolley, choose the lemon cheesecake.

色彩明艷式樣懷舊的地磚、牆上的木窗框裝飾、懷舊天花、紅色扶手靠背椅和入口處的小吧枱，將你帶進五十年代的紐約。餐單以美國意大利菜為主，凱撒沙律、辣伏特加酒汁通心粉和肉丸等是招牌菜。餐後侍應會推着載有意大利芝士蛋糕、檸檬芝士蛋糕等甜品的餐車服務顧客。酒單上羅列的均是意國佳釀。

TEL. 2593 2593
9F, LKF Tower, 33 Wyndham Street, Central
中環雲咸街 33號蘭桂芳大廈 9樓
www.carbone.com.hk

■ PRICE 價錢
Lunch 午膳
set 套餐 $ 398
à la carte 點菜 $ 480-1,200
Dinner 晚膳
à la carte 點菜 $ 480-1,200

■ OPENING HOURS 營業時間
Lunch 午膳 12:00-14:30 (L.O.)
Dinner 晚膳 18:00-23:30 (L.O.)
Friday and Saturday dinner
週五及週六晚膳 18:00-00:00 (L.O.)

■ ANNUAL AND WEEKLY CLOSING 休息日期
Closed Sunday lunch 週日午膳休息

Celebrity Cuisine
名人坊

⊕13

Having just six tables and a host of regulars makes booking ahead vital at this very discreet and colourful restaurant concealed within the Lan Kwai Fong hotel. The Cantonese menu may be quite short but there are usually plenty of specials; highlights of the delicate, sophisticated cuisine include whole superior abalone in oyster sauce; baked chicken with Shaoxing wine and, one of the chef's own creations, 'bird's nest in chicken wing'.

這家隱藏於蘭桂坊酒店內的餐廳，看似不甚出眾但別具魅力，地方雖小卻常客眾多，故此必須提早預約。這裏的廣東菜餐牌頗為精簡，但全是大廚富哥的特選菜式，精美菜餚推介包括富哥頂級鮑魚、花雕焗飛天雞及自創菜式燕窩釀鳳翼。

TEL. 3650 0066
1F, Lan Kwai Fong Hotel, 3 Kau U Fong, Central
中環九如坊 3號蘭桂坊酒店 1樓

SPECIALITIES TO PRE-ORDER 預訂食物
Baked chicken with Shaoxing wine 花雕焗飛天雞 / Whole duck stuffed with eight goodies 八子全鴨 / Steamed crab pincers in egg white 蛋白蒸蟹拑

■ PRICE 價錢
Lunch 午膳
à la carte 點菜 $ 200-400
Dinner 晚膳
à la carte 點菜 $ 350-1,000

■ OPENING HOURS 營業時間
Lunch 午膳 12:00-14:30 (L.O.)
Dinner 晚膳 18:00-22:15 (L.O.)

■ ANNUAL AND WEEKLY CLOSING 休息日期
Closed 4 days Lunar New Year
農曆新年休息 4 天

Celestial Court
天寶閣

XXX

♿ 🅿 96

The room may be windowless but that at least puts the emphasis on the decoration – which features plenty of wood veneer – and, of course, onto the food. The chef has over 40 years of Cantonese culinary experience and also spent time in Japan – and his cooking is informed by his travels. Specialities include roasted whole suckling pig with pearl barley and black truffles; and deep-fried prawns with spicy termite mushrooms and crispy rice toast.

天寶閣位於喜來登酒店內，雖然餐室欠窗戶，但典雅堂皇的裝潢和具水準的菜餚足以彌補。主廚於不同粵菜餐廳和日本打拼超過四十年，遊歷於不同城市也豐富了他的創作，黑松露薏米燒釀乳豬和飯焦雞瑽菌鳳尾蝦是其得意之作。

TEL. 2732 6991
2F, Sheraton Hotel, 20 Nathan Road, Tsim Sha Tsui
尖沙咀彌敦道 20號喜來登酒店 2樓
www.sheratonhongkonghotel.com

SPECIALITIES TO PRE-ORDER 預訂食物
Roasted whole suckling pig, pearl barley, black truffles, glutinous rice, Yunnan ham
黑松露薏米燒釀乳豬

■ PRICE 價錢
Lunch 午膳
set 套餐 $ 350-2,150
à la carte 點菜 $ 200-3,300
Dinner 晚膳
set 套餐 $ 650-5,850
à la carte 點菜 $ 200-3,300

■ OPENING HOURS 營業時間
Lunch 午膳 11:30-15:00 (L.O.)
Dinner 晚膳 18:00-23:00 (L.O.)

Chan Kan Kee Chiu Chow (Sheung Wan)
陳勤記鹵鵝飯店 (上環)

Ms Chan's grandfather set up this family business in 1948 in Sheung Wan; it moved to its current location in 1997 and was completely refurbished in 2010, when the kitchen was also expanded. Chiu Chow goose, cooked in a secret family recipe, remains the main event here, but there are other Chiu Chow specialities on offer such as pan fried baby oyster with egg, steamed goby fish with salted lemon, and double-boiled pig's lung with almond soup.

陳勤記於1948年在上環開始營業，1997年遷至現址，並於2010年進行大規模翻新。樓高兩層的餐廳裝潢佈置充滿中國特色。店子現由第三代經營，以家傳秘方炮製的潮州滷鵝仍然是招牌菜，另外還提供其他潮州特色美食，如潮州蠔仔粥、檸檬蒸烏魚和杏汁燉白肺湯等。

TEL. 2858 0033
11 Queen's Road West, Sheung Wan
上環皇后大道西 11號

SPECIALITIES TO PRE-ORDER 預訂食物
Chiu Chow crab 潮州凍花蟹

■ PRICE 價錢
Lunch 午膳
set 套餐 $ 50-80
à la carte 點菜 $ 100-400
Dinner 晚膳
à la carte 點菜 $ 100-400

■ OPENING HOURS 營業時間
11:00-22:15 (L.O.)

■ ANNUAL AND WEEKLY CLOSING 休息日期
Closed 3 days Lunar New Year
農曆新年休息 3 天

Che's
車氏粵菜軒

35

This unremarkable-looking little restaurant is popular with the local businessmen who come here in their droves for speedy service of the house speciality – crispy pork buns. But there are other reasons to visit: the dim sum at lunch; the extensive menu of classic dishes like crispy chicken or crab and dry scallop soup with bitter melon; and for simpler offerings such as congee or braised claypot dishes. The menu has been reworked by the chef and you may find some Sichuan dishes too.

這家小餐館看似不起眼，但在本地商界人士間卻享負盛名，選擇豐富的經典粵菜如脆皮炸子雞，簡單卻美味的粥品和煲仔菜，還有午市點心，都使一眾食客趨之若鶩。在經驗老到的廚師加盟後更令菜單改良不少，例如新增了四川菜式；服務快速且有效率，午餐時分往往座無虛席。

TEL. 2528 1123
4F, The Broadway,
54-62 Lockhart Road, Wan Chai
灣仔駱克道 54-62號博匯大廈 4樓

SPECIALITIES TO PRE-ORDER 預訂食物
Braised duck stuffed with eight types of delicacies 蓮子八寶鴨 / Baked chicken in rock salt 古法鹽焗雞

■ PRICE 價錢
Lunch 午膳
à la carte 點菜 $ 120-350
Dinner 晚膳
à la carte 點菜 $ 200-750

■ OPENING HOURS 營業時間
Lunch 午膳 11:00-14:30 (L.O.)
Dinner 晚膳 18:00-22:30 (L.O.)

Chesa
瑞樵閣

The room may be windowless but the authentic chalet-style decor is unmistakably Alpine. It has been welcoming devotees of all things Swiss since 1965, having originally opened as a 'pop-up' by the Swiss-born manager at the time. It offers everything from fondue and raclette to the famous Chemin de Fer wines. Authenticity is assured as the current executive chef of the hotel is also Swiss and keeps a close eye on everything they do here.

只要推開餐廳的木門，彷彿瞬間踏進了瑞士農舍，四處的木製裝飾更顯親切。自1965年開始瑞士美食的魅力在此得以展現，店內的傳統瑞士菜式與特選芝士系列，包括瑞士芝士火鍋或瓦萊州烤芝士(熱熔的芝士配馬鈴薯、醃洋蔥及青瓜)均惹人垂涎。現任主廚生於瑞士，保證所有出品均是正宗風味。

TEL. 2696 6769
1F, The Peninsula Hotel,
Salisbury Road, Tsim Sha Tsui
尖沙咀梳士巴利道半島酒店 1樓
http://hongkong.peninsula.com

■ PRICE 價錢
Lunch 午膳
set 套餐 $ 300-500
à la carte 點菜 $ 500-1,000
Dinner 晚膳
set 套餐 $ 1,000-1,800
à la carte 點菜 $ 500-1,000

■ OPENING HOURS 營業時間
Lunch 午膳 12:00-14:30 (L.O.)
Dinner 晚膳 18:30-22:30 (L.O.)

Chilli Fagara
麻辣燙

The name will be known to all fans of Sichuan cooking as this is their second site and replaces the original one in Graham Street which closed in 2016. It's quite a large space and is moodily dark at night. Dishes are classified 'Ma', 'La' and 'Tang' according to their level of spiciness – it's best to end with a 'La' dish. Chilli crab always delivers, but you won't regret ordering the glazed beef with caramelised garlic and ginger-infused sauce.

店如其名，裝潢離不開火辣辣的紅色，昏暗的燈光，並沒影響食客在此品嘗美食的興致，為免白行一趟，請預訂座位。以麻、辣、燙作為分類的主餐單，供應的是辣度不同的四川小菜，建議從辣度較低的燙菜單開始，嗜辣者不妨挑戰一下辣菜單。麻菜單的霸王登格斯辣蟹和辣菜單的薑煸蒜片牛肉均不能錯過。

TEL. 2796 6866
GF, 7 Old Bailey Street, Central
中環奧卑利街 7號地下
www.chillifagara.com

■ PRICE 價錢
Lunch 午膳
set 套餐 $ 108-168
à la carte 點菜 $ 200-400
Dinner 晚膳
à la carte 點菜 $ 300-500

■ OPENING HOURS 營業時間
Lunch 午膳 11:30-14:30 (L.O.)
Dinner 晚膳 17:00-22:30 (L.O.)

■ ANNUAL AND WEEKLY CLOSING 休息日期
Closed 4 days Lunar New Year
農曆新年休息 4 天

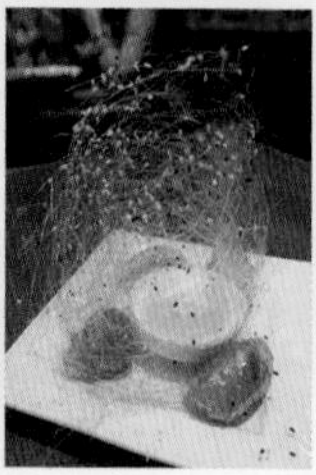

China Tang (Central)
唐人館 (中環)

Decorated with a mix of traditional Chinese art and contemporary Western design, this handsome restaurant was conceived and designed by the late Sir David Tang as a sister to the London branch. Tables are set closely together and there are several private rooms. Dishes from Beijing, Sichuan and Canton feature and dim sum is popular. The chef has introduced a more modern element to the menu.

由已故鄧永鏘爵士構思及設計，是其繼倫敦唐人館後又一傑作。人手刺繡的牆紙、獨特的鏡飾、古董燈飾及線裝中式排版菜譜，中式傳統藝術與西方美學結合得天衣無縫，流露出典雅貴氣。菜單涵蓋粵、京、川等地美食及精製南北點心：老北京傳統掛爐烤鴨、唐人館叉燒和琉璃蝦球等，滋味無窮。

TEL. 2522 2148
Shop 411-413, 4F, Landmark Atrium,
15 Queen's Road Central, Central
中環皇后大道中 15號
置地廣場中庭 4樓 411-413號舖
www.chinatang.hk

SPECIALITIES TO PRE-ORDER 預訂食物
Traditional Beijing roasted duck 老北京傳統掛爐烤鴨 / Hangzhou Vagabond chicken 火焰杭州富貴雞

■ PRICE 價錢
Lunch 午膳
à la carte 點菜 $300-1,000
Dinner 晚膳
à la carte 點菜 $800-1,200

■ OPENING HOURS 營業時間
Lunch 午膳 12:00-14:30 (L.O.)
Dinner 晚膳 18:00-22:30 (L.O.)

■ ANNUAL AND WEEKLY CLOSING 休息日期
Closed 3 days Lunar New Year
農曆新年休息 3 天

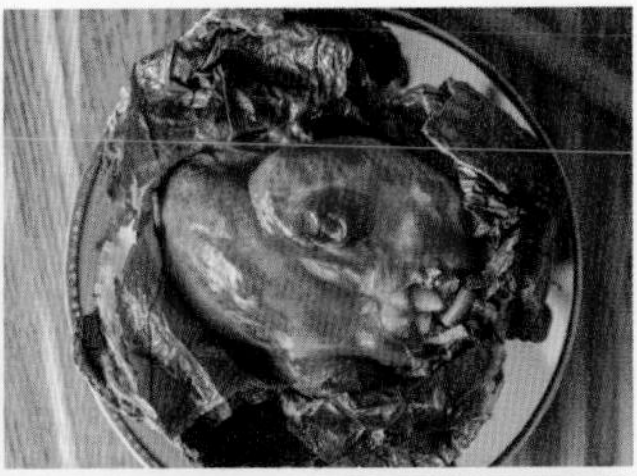

China Tang (Tsim Sha Tsui)
唐人館 (尖沙咀)

40

The second China Tang to open in Hong Kong was another ingenious work by the late Sir David Tang. Traditional Chinese embroidery is set against bold-coloured chinoiserie fabrics for a dynamic yet graceful look. The menu is dominated by Cantonese cuisine, but chefs are hired from their respective provinces to take care of other regional dishes. Recommendations include marinated shrimps in plum-scented Huadiao wine, and crystal prawns in lobster bisque.

唐人館在香港的第二家店子設計同樣出自已故鄧永鏘爵士手筆，他巧妙地將歐陸式裝潢和中式元素融合，色彩繽紛的布料配搭優雅的花卉圖案，雅致舒適。粵菜是餐單的主角，也不乏南北點心、佐酒小食和大笪地爐端燒菜式；廚師團隊來自中國不同地區，各負責不同菜系。陳年花雕話梅蝦和琥珀水晶大蝦球值得一試。

TEL. 2157 3148
Shop 4101, 4F, Gateway Arcade,
Harbour City, 17 Canton Road,
Tsim Sha Tsui
尖沙咀廣東道 17號
海港城港威商場 4樓 4101號舖
www.chinatang.hk

SPECIALITIES TO PRE-ORDER 預訂食物
Hangzhou Vagabond chicken 杭州富貴雞

■ PRICE 價錢
Lunch 午膳
set 套餐 $ 988
à la carte 點菜 $ 300-800
Dinner 晚膳
set 套餐 $ 988
à la carte 點菜 $ 400-1,000

■ OPENING HOURS 營業時間
Lunch 午膳 12:00-15:00 (L.O.)
Weekend & Public Holiday lunch
週末及公眾假期午膳 11:30-15:00 (L.O.)
Dinner 晚膳 18:00-22:30 (L.O.)

Chinese Legend (Tuen Mun)
廣東名門 (屯門)

15

Located right opposite the seafood market, this popular glass-walled restaurant not only cooks the critters you get from the market, but also serves their own famous Cantonese roast meat, such as lychee wood-roasted goose, available in limited daily quantity. Despite its plain interior, antique pieces add some interest and there is even a stone grinder hidden underneath each round table.

門上刻有「廣東名門」的牌匾是店主從廣東運來，是菜館名字的由來。位處海鮮市場，客人會先購買海鮮，再拿到菜館前台的籃子量重並作記號。每晚都人頭湧湧輪候入座，不僅是為了烹調出色的海鮮，還為了以荔枝柴燻烤的各款燒味，如限量供應的荔枝柴燒鵝。店內有許多古董傢具，連圓形桌子底部都藏了一個石磨，煞是有趣。

TEL. 2955 1313
Shop 1, GF, Sam Shing Market,
Sam Shing Estate, Tuen Mun
屯門三聖村三聖市場1號地下
www.kingmen.com.hk

SPECIALITIES TO PRE-ORDER 預訂食物
Roasted duck with lychee wood (dinner only) 荔枝柴燒鵝（晚市供應）

■ PRICE 價錢
Lunch 午膳
à la carte 點菜 $ 200-300
Dinner 晚膳
à la carte 點菜 $ 300-400

■ OPENING HOURS 營業時間
11:00-22:00 (L.O.)

■ ANNUAL AND WEEKLY CLOSING 休息日期
Closed 1 day Lunar New Year
農曆新年休息1天

Chiuchow Delicacies
潮樂園

Walls covered in photos the chef took with celebrities speak volumes about the popularity of this no-frills shop. Velvety goose meat steeped in its signature spiced marinade, baby oyster porridge, oyster omelette, and pork blood curd with chives keep the regulars coming. Sourced from a local fish farm, the fatty grey mullet is juicy but without a muddy taste. It also serves rare traditional Chiu Chow gems, such as raw marinated red ark clams.

簡樸的店子，牆上滿是東主與廚師和名人的合照，其受歡迎程度不言而喻。滷水汁的香料成分有特定比例，因此，每天供應的滷水食物味道絕無差異。不含味精的滷汁令鵝肉更嫩滑。採用的烏頭是元朗楊氏烏頭，帶黃油且沒泥味。還供應時下較罕見的潮式生醃蛳蚶。蠔仔粥、蠔餅及韭菜豬紅很受常客歡迎。

TEL. 3568 5643
GF, Ngan Fai Building,
84-94 Wharf Road, North Point
北角和富道 84-94號銀輝大廈地下

SPECIALITIES TO PRE-ORDER 預訂食物
Cold crab in Chiu Chow style 潮州凍花蟹 / Double-boiled duck soup with salted lemon 鹹檸檬燉鴨湯 / Double-boiled eel soup 荷包燉白鱔湯 / Chicken with Puning bean sauce 普寧豆醬雞

■ PRICE 價錢
Lunch 午膳
à la carte 點菜 $ 40-150
Dinner 晚膳
à la carte 點菜 $ 100-250

■ OPENING HOURS 營業時間
11:00-22:30 (L.O.)

■ ANNUAL AND WEEKLY CLOSING 休息日期
Closed 3 days Lunar New Year
農曆新年休息 3 天

Chuen Cheung Kui (Mong Kok)
泉章居 (旺角)

This two-storey restaurant has been owned by the same family since the 1960s. It moved to this location in 2004 and has been jam-packed at night ever since. Diners line up to enjoy its traditional Hakkanese fare, including the unmissable salt-baked chicken and braised pork belly with dried mustard greens. The ground floor is smaller in size and rice plates that are less complicated to prepare are served there during lunch hours.

菜館自六十年代起一直由同一家族經營，直至2004年才遷至現址。雖然餐廳樓高兩層，但晚上經常座無虛席，門外排隊等候的客人，為的都是這裏的傳統客家菜，不能錯過的有鹽焗雞和梅菜扣肉。下層地舖面積較小，中午時分主要供應烹調工序較簡單的碟頭飯。

TEL. 2396 0672
Lisa House, 33 Nelson Street, Mong Kok
旺角奶路臣街 33號依利大廈

■ PRICE 價錢
à la carte 點菜 $ 100-300

■ OPENING HOURS 營業時間
11:00-23:15 (L.O.)

■ ANNUAL AND WEEKLY CLOSING 休息日期
Closed 4 days Lunar New Year
農曆新年休息 4 天

Chuen Kee Seafood
全記海鮮

50

Two family-run restaurants overlook a pleasant harbour to distant islands; choose the one with the rooftop terrace and the quayside plastic seats. An extraordinary range of seafood is available from adjacent fishmongers: cuttlefish, bivalve, crab and lobster, mollusc, shrimps, prawns… Go to the tank, select your meal, and minutes later it appears in front of you: steamed, poached, or wok-fried. Try the abalone or mantis shrimp in peppered salt.

兩家相連的餐廳是家族生意，可選擇有陽台的那一家，坐在碼頭邊的膠座椅上觀賞宜人海灣及離島景致。魚缸內的海鮮種類繁多，墨魚、貝類、蟹、龍蝦、瀨尿蝦等任你隨意挑選，蒸、灼、炒也好，不一會就奉到餐桌上，然後你便可輕鬆地邊品嘗海鮮邊細覽海上景色。推介菜式有古法椒鹽鮑魚和椒鹽瀨尿蝦。

TEL. 2791 1195
53 Hoi Pong Street, Sai Kung
西貢海傍街53號

SPECIALITIES TO PRE-ORDER 預訂食物
Double-boiled soups 燉湯

■ PRICE 價錢
à la carte 點菜 $ 250-500

■ OPENING HOURS 營業時間
11:00-22:30 (L.O.)

CIAK - All Day Italian

The name helpfully explains what to expect – fresh and revitalising Italian food, at any time of the day. Most ingredients are imported from Italy and the pasta and sausages really stand out, as does the bread which is made with Italian flour, mineral water and home-grown wild yeast. All pizzas come in two sizes and there is a takeaway counter at the door. From time to time it also hosts wine pairing dinners that oenophiles should not miss.

取名All Day Italian，食客可在此嘗到各款意式美食，其中麵包和麵條均自家製作，廚師選材嚴謹，除特地由意大利進口麵粉和礦泉水，更自行培養發酵用的酵母。各款薄餅設有兩種尺寸，點餐更具彈性，其中豬肉腸仔拼蘑菇芝士薄餅值得一試。餐廳不定期舉行葡萄酒晚宴，嗜酒的你不容錯過。

TEL. 2116 5128
Shop 265, 2F, Cityplaza,
18 Taikoo Shing Road, Tai Koo Shing
太古太古城道 18號
太古城中心 2樓 265號舖
www.ciakconcept.com

■ PRICE 價錢
Lunch 午膳
set 套餐 $ 168-198
Weekend set 套餐 $ 230-260
à la carte 點菜 $ 150-300
Dinner 晚膳
set 套餐 $ 298
à la carte 點菜 $ 250-500

■ OPENING HOURS 營業時間
11:30-21:30 (L.O.)

Congee and Noodle Shop
粥麵館

Hidden in a glass office tower, this simple shop may have no ambiance or character to speak of, but guests come for the creamy congee made by a chef with over 30 years of experience. Bestsellers include fresh crab congee and salted pork ribs congee with bitter melon. Regulars also customize with their favourite ingredients such as fish belly and beef. Expect to sit on plastic chairs and share a table with strangers.

隱藏在充滿藝術氣息的嘉里中心內，店內裝潢卻不講究，食客全是慕粥品之名而來。為了品嘗逾三十年經驗老師傅精心炮製的傳統靚粥，客人都不介意坐塑膠椅及跟陌生人拼桌。暢銷粥品有原味蟹皇粥及涼瓜鹹排骨粥，但食客通常會自選配粥材料，如魚腩及牛肉等，魚片頭撈麵或新增的福丸湯米等麵食也是不錯的選擇。

TEL. 2750 0208
Shop 2A, 2F, Kerry Centre,
683 King's Road, Quarry Bay
鰂魚涌英皇道 683號
嘉里中心 2樓 2A號舖

■ PRICE 價錢
set 套餐 $ 35
à la carte 點菜 $ 50-150

■ OPENING HOURS 營業時間
10:30-20:15 (L.O.)

■ ANNUAL AND WEEKLY CLOSING 休息日期
Closed 4 days Lunar New Year
農曆新年休息 4 天

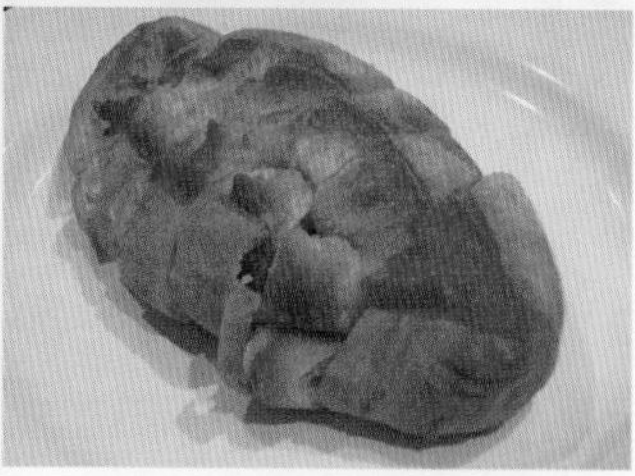

Cuisine Cuisine at The Mira
國金軒 (尖沙咀)

44

You'll be greeted by a striking feature of crystal glass spheres hanging from the ceiling and calming blue and green colours, which help bring the feel of the outside gardens into the room at the Mira hotel. They like to add the odd modern slant to the Cantonese cooking too and regularly create special dim sum, such as crispy frogs' legs with spicy salt. The wine pairings are thoughtfully matched.

這家型格餐廳充滿現代感，圓球狀的水晶吊燈引人注目，在此享受融入精巧現代元素的廣東美食，可謂相得益彰。午市供應多達三十款精美點心，目不暇給。欲體驗廚房的功力則可自選菜式。侍酒師能為你提供餐酒配搭的建議。宜先作預訂，以免撲空。

TEL. 2315 5222
3F, The Mira Hotel, 118 Nathan Road, Tsim Sha Tsui
尖沙咀彌敦道 118號 The Mira 3樓
www.themirahotel.com

SPECIALITIES TO PRE-ORDER 預訂食物
Roasted Peking duck served two ways
北京烤鴨（一鴨兩吃）

■ PRICE 價錢
Lunch 午膳
set 套餐 $ 250-300
à la carte 點菜 $ 400-2,500
Dinner 晚膳
set 套餐 $ 500-700
à la carte 點菜 $ 400-2,500

■ OPENING HOURS 營業時間
Lunch 午膳 11:30-14:30 (L.O.)
Sunday lunch 週日午膳 10:30-15:00 (L.O.)
Dinner 晚膳 18:00-22:30 (L.O.)

Din Tai Fung (Causeway Bay)
鼎泰豐 (銅鑼灣)

14

Worry not – the Xiao Long Bao are good enough to justify the long queueing time. The group's executive chef visits here frequently to ensure quality. Ingredients are still sourced from the same suppliers and the same team has been running the kitchen all these years. Other standouts are double-boiled chicken soup and braised beef brisket noodle soup. This efficiently run branch is bigger than the one in Tsim Sha Tsui.

鼎泰豐在銅鑼灣的分店多年來備受追捧，歸功於餐廳始終如一的水準，供應商合作良久，而行政總廚蔡師傅每月專程從台灣到店巡查，監察出品及服務，難怪很多時都需要輪候入座。小籠包固然是重點所在，原盅雞湯和紅燒牛肉湯麵也鬱受歡迎。飯店還為初次光顧的客人提供進食小籠包的說明，非常周到。

TEL. 3160 8998
Shop G3-G11, GF, 68 Yee Woo Street, Causeway Bay
銅鑼灣怡和街 68號地下 G3-G11號舖
www.dintaifung.com.hk

■ PRICE 價錢
à la carte 點菜 $ 150-280

■ OPENING HOURS 營業時間
11:30-22:00 (L.O.)

■ ANNUAL AND WEEKLY CLOSING 休息日期
Closed 4 days Lunar New Year
農曆新年休息 4 天

Din Tai Fung (Silvercord)
鼎泰豐 (新港中心)

12

From Mr Yang's first shop in Taiwan in 1958 grew a multinational chain with branches in all major Asian cities. It's famous for good service, competitive prices and listening to its customer's feedback, but mostly for its Xiao Long Bao made on the spot. Taiwanese chefs visit regularly to ensure the quality is maintained. Even the vinegar, free of artificial colours and preservatives, is shipped from Taiwan. Expect long queues at peak hours.

楊先生在1958年於台灣開辦首家小籠包店，至今分店遍佈各個主要亞洲城市。主打的上海小籠包以人手製作，材料新鮮，餡料充足，並選用無色素及防腐劑的台灣米醋佐吃，令人食指大動。創辦人特別注重品質、服務及價格，除了定期監控品質，也重視客人反饋，台灣師傅亦會定期來港交流，確保食物水準。

TEL. 2730 6928
Shop 306, 3F, Silvercord,
30 Canton Road, Tsim Sha Tsui
尖沙咀廣東道 30號新港中心 3樓 306號舖
www.dintaifung.com.hk

■ PRICE 價錢
à la carte 點菜 $ 150-280

■ OPENING HOURS 營業時間
11:30-22:00 (L.O.)

■ ANNUAL AND WEEKLY CLOSING 休息日期
Closed 4 days Lunar New Year
農曆新年休息 4 天

HONG KONG 香港

Dong Lai Shun
東來順

XXX ♿ 🅿 60

The original may have opened in Beijing in 1903 but the room here shows more of a contemporary style of décor and also includes a relaxing water feature and a bridge. The cooking blends recipes from Beijing and Huaiyang. Paper thin slices of Mongolian black-headed mutton remains a speciality, along with the drunken chicken.

東來順將北京與淮陽菜共冶一爐，火鍋、北京填鴨及涮羊肉等菜式自然齊備；當中涮羊肉採用蒙古黑頭白羊的上乘部分，肉質極為細軟；而醉雞也值得一試。餐室裝潢混搭現代和傳統格調，牆板和壁畫展現出鮮明的亞洲特色；坐在人工噴泉旁用餐，更是別有一番閒情逸致。

TEL. 2733 2020
B2F, The Royal Garden Hotel,
69 Mody Road, East Tsim Sha Tsui
尖東麼地道69號帝苑酒店地庫2樓
www.rghk.com.hk

SPECIALITIES TO PRE-ORDER 預訂食物
Roasted Beijing duck 烤北京填鴨 / Roasted chicken fillet with wild mushrooms and black truffles 黑松露野生菌烤雞柳 / Baked beggar's chicken 叫化雞

■ PRICE 價錢
Lunch 午膳
set 套餐 $ 120-300
à la carte 點菜 $ 200-700
Dinner 晚膳
set 套餐 $ 300-600
à la carte 點菜 $ 200-700

■ OPENING HOURS 營業時間
Lunch 午膳 11:30-14:30 (L.O.)
Sunday lunch 週日午膳 11:00-14:30 (L.O.)
Dinner 晚膳 18:00-22:30 (L.O.)

Dragon Inn
容龍

XX ♿ P 18

This restaurant is known by almost everyone in the neighbourhood and was revamped in 2017 to include more private rooms alongside the main dining hall. Most guests pick their seafood from the nearby wet market for the chefs here to cook up; others choose the catch of the day without looking at the menu. Baked baby lobster with cheese and baked oysters with port are not to be missed. It also serves dim sum during the day.

容龍在本區可謂赫赫有名，裝修後換上更時尚的佈置，新增更多私人廂房，滿足注重私人空間的食客，其中兩間更坐擁海畔美景。為數不少的客人會自來海鮮加工，個別更不看主菜牌，直接從海鮮單上挑選食物。招牌菜包括芝士焗龍蝦與砵酒焗生蠔；日間則有點心供應。

TEL. 2450 6366
Miles 19, Castle Peak Road, Tuen Mun
屯門青山公路19咪
www.dragoninn1939.com

■ PRICE 價錢
à la carte 點菜 $ 300-500

■ OPENING HOURS 營業時間
10:00-22:30 (L.O.)

■ ANNUAL AND WEEKLY CLOSING 休息日期
Closed 2 days Lunar New Year
農曆新年休息 2 天

Duddell's
都爹利會館

24

Not many restaurants come with their own 'Art Manager' but then Duddell's has always been about more than just serving food and hosts regular art exhibitions and screenings. The upstairs bar is a cool spot for a pre-dinner drink, while the restaurant itself is a stylish and contemporary space. In contrast to the surroundings, the Cantonese menu keeps things fairly traditional, with ingredients very much from the luxury end of the scale.

都爹利會館是少數設有藝術項目經理的餐館，除了專營傳統粵菜，餐館會定期舉行藝術展覽、電影欣賞和藝術沙龍等活動。閣樓酒吧宜於餐前歇息淺酌。主餐室布置時尚且風格獨特，廚師團隊的更替為菜單添上不少新菜式，但仍然以時尚粵菜為主，選用的是高級矜貴食材。團隊服務周到。

TEL. 2525 9191
3F, Shanghai Tang Mansion,
1 Duddell Street, Central
中環都爹利街 1號上海灘 3樓
www.duddells.co

■ PRICE 價錢
Lunch 午膳
set 套餐 $ 680
à la carte 點菜 $ 450-1,000
Dinner 晚膳
set 套餐 $ 1,480
à la carte 點菜 $ 450-1,000

■ OPENING HOURS 營業時間
Lunch 午膳 12:00-14:30 (L.O.)
Dinner 晚膳 18:00-22:30 (L.O.)

■ ANNUAL AND WEEKLY CLOSING 休息日期
Closed New Year's Day
元旦休息 1 天

Écriture

Plenty of creativity went into the design of this intimate, understated restaurant from chef Maxime Gilbert, formerly of Amber – and the views are pretty good too. Japan provides many of the ingredients and some of the inspiration, but French techniques bring it all together. To best experience the creative, original and occasionally theatrical cooking, go for the 8-course 'Library of Flavours' menu. Piqniq is their rooftop bar on the floor above.

位於H Queen's頂層的Écriture裝潢簡約而別具特色，窗外有迷人景觀。餐廳採用日本食材以法式手法烹調，包括八道菜的品嘗菜單「Library of Flavours」盡展食材的原汁原味，菜式充滿創意，部分甚至在席前烹調，各種味道配搭使人眼前一亮且難以忘懷。天台酒吧Piqniq是時尚潮流好去處。

TEL. 5365 5701
26F, H Queen's,
80 Queen's Road Central, Central
中環皇后大道中 80號 H Queen's 26樓
www.lecomptoir.hk/ecriture

■ PRICE 價錢
Lunch 午膳
set 套餐 $ 488-688
Dinner 晚膳
set 套餐 $ 1,488
à la carte 點菜 $ 1,400-2,400

■ OPENING HOURS 營業時間
Lunch 午膳 12:00-14:30 (L.O.)
Dinner 晚膳 18:30-22:30 (L.O.)

■ ANNUAL AND WEEKLY CLOSING 休息日期
Closed Sunday 週日休息

Eng Kee Noodle Shop
英記麵家

This family-run shop has been feeding hungry locals with Cantonese noodle soup since 1994. It prides itself on its signature beef brisket – braised one night ahead and steeped in a spiced marinade overnight for silky tenderness and deep flavours. Their oven-grilled char siu is made with pork shoulder and pork neck and has a juicy, springy texture thanks to the fine marbling. The deep-fried wontons also earn unanimous praise.

於1994年開業的英記一直以帶住家風味的潮式和廣東麵食服務食客。以牛坑腩製作的招牌牛腩每天晚上就開始燜煮，以滷水浸泡過夜後，開店前再燜煮，是以軟腍入味。用焗爐烹調的自家製叉燒除了選用脢頭肉，也以豬頸肉製作，因其肥瘦分佈比例使油分均勻滲透，吃起來肉爽且多汁。淨牛腩、叉燒湯麵和炸雲吞深受食客歡迎。

TEL. 2540 7950
GF, 32 High Street, Sai Ying Pun
西營盤高街 32號地下

■ PRICE 價錢
à la carte 點菜 $ 40-110

■ OPENING HOURS 營業時間
09:00-19:00 (L.O.)

■ ANNUAL AND WEEKLY CLOSING 休息日期
Closed 7 days Lunar New Year
農曆新年休息 7 天

Épure

Have a drink on the terrace of this professionally run Harbour City restaurant before enjoying French dishes that are classically based in their makeup but enhanced by clever modern touches. You can expect perfectly matched combinations of flavours of textures – and their vol-au-vents are renowned! Alongside the carte are three tasting menus with carefully considered wine pairings. There's also a café which is a great spot for afternoon tea.

由法國廚師及侍酒師帶領，菜式毋庸置疑是正宗法國口味，餐酒亦是一絲不苟地奉上。菜式選材經典，卻是以現代手法演繹，配合得恰到好處。除了單點菜單外，還有數款精選套餐，佐以經過精心配搭的餐酒。馳名酥皮餡餅不容錯過。位處購物熱點，逛累了不妨到附設的咖啡廳享用下午茶。

TEL. 3185 8338
Shop 403, 4F, Ocean Centre,
Harbour City, Canton Road,
Tsim Sha Tsui
尖沙咀廣東道海港城海洋中心 4樓 403號舖
www.epure.hk

■ PRICE 價錢
Lunch 午膳
set 套餐 $ 388-588
Dinner 晚膳
set 套餐 $ 1,488-1,888
à la carte 點菜 $ 880-1,650

■ OPENING HOURS 營業時間
Lunch 午膳 12:00-14:00 (L.O.)
Dinner 晚膳 18:30-21:30 (L.O.)

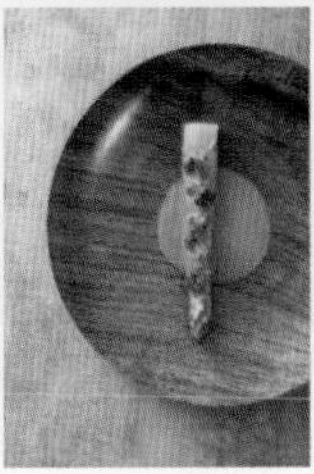

Farm House
農圃

XX 24

The aquarium running the entire length of one wall of this modern dining room certainly catches the eye. But it's the quality food made with fresh, top-notch ingredients that wins the hearts of the regulars. The famous fried chicken wing stuffed with sticky rice is the must-try item. Baked sea whelk stuffed with foie gras, and steamed rice with chicken, abalone and dried scallops are also well-executed. Service is friendly and thoughtful.

飯店裝潢時尚，巨型水族箱延伸整道牆，非常引人注目。年中無休的農圃一直堅持以新鮮、優質的特級食材烹調粵菜，著名菜式有古法糯米雞翼、鵝肝焗釀響螺和瑤柱鮑魚雞粒飯等。配合細心周到的服務團隊，令用餐經驗更稱心滿意。飯店更出售鮑魚及海參等處理步驟繁複的食品。

TEL. 2881 1331
1F, China Taiping Tower,
8 Sunning Road, Causeway Bay
銅鑼灣新寧道 8號中國太平大廈 1樓
www.farmhouse.com.hk

■ PRICE 價錢
Lunch 午膳
set 套餐 $ 448-888
à la carte 點菜 $ 200-900
Dinner 晚膳
set 套餐 $ 448-888
à la carte 點菜 $ 200-900

■ OPENING HOURS 營業時間
Lunch 午膳 11:00-14:45 (L.O.)
Dinner 晚膳 18:00- 22:30 (L.O.)

Fish School

♿ 28

You'll first need to find its discreet entrance before you get to taste this restaurants' fresh seafood, meticulously prepared by an experienced team. Their insistence of buying local doesn't stop there – they also ask local farmers to grow certain produce specifically for them. The 10-course tasting menu showcases modern aesthetics and precise techniques while the ebullient servers add to the atmosphere. Ask for counter seats to feel part of the action.

富有經驗的廚師除了盼以合理價格提供高質素的海鮮，也着意以經營方法支持本地漁農業，除了每天新鮮購入各類海鮮，更會定期到訪本地農場以作採購。餐廳至少七成食材為本地生產，包括特別訂購的本地農產品。餐單不定期更新，心猿意馬的食客不妨點選有十道菜的品嘗餐單。欲坐於吧台觀看烹調過程，建議於訂座時説明。

TEL. 2361 2966
GF, 100 Third Street, Sai Ying Pun, Western District
西環西營盤第三街 100號地舖
www.fishschool.hk

■ PRICE 價錢
Lunch 午膳
set 套餐 $ 850
à la carte 點菜 $ 600-800
Dinner 晚膳
set 套餐 $ 850
à la carte 點菜 $ 600-800

■ OPENING HOURS 營業時間
Sunday Lunch 週日午膳
12:00-14:30 (L.O.)
Dinner 晚膳 18:00-22:30 (L.O.)

■ ANNUAL AND WEEKLY CLOSING 休息日期
Closed 3 days Lunar New Year and Monday 農曆新年 3 天及週一休息

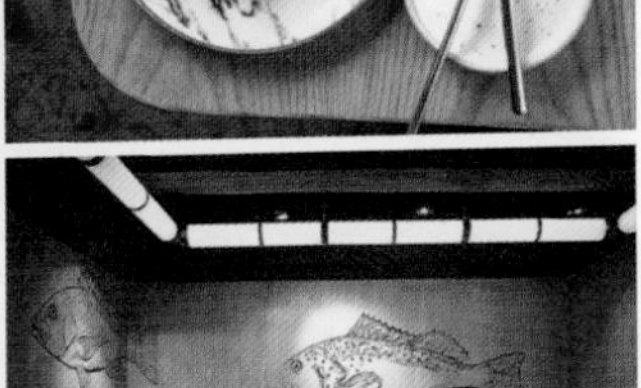

FoFo by el Willy

FoFo means 'chubby' and, judging by the look on the faces of the plump pig and penguin figures dotted around the room, therein lies contentment. For those eating here, three of the authentic Spanish dishes for each person, plus a little rice, should bring equal joy. The appealing tapas range from the popular suckling pig, which is slow-roasted, to fried croquettes of Iberian ham and fried gambas with garlic and chilli. Try the roof terrace for even better views.

FoFo是圓胖之意。小豬與企鵝裝飾臉上滿足的表情，與店名非常相配。在這兒，每位食客能享用三道傳統西班牙菜和少許飯，那份滿足非筆墨能形容。從以慢火烤製的脆皮乳豬，到脆炸伊比利亞火腿丸子和蒜椒炸蝦等，全是令人垂涎的西班牙小菜。在屋頂露台用餐景觀更佳。

TEL. 2900 2009
20F, M88, 2-8 Wellington Street, Central
中環威靈頓街 2-8號 M88 20樓
www.fofo.hk

■ PRICE 價錢
Lunch 午膳
set 套餐 $ 288-350
à la carte 點菜 $ 350-600
Dinner 晚膳
à la carte 點菜 $ 350-600

■ OPENING HOURS 營業時間
Lunch 午膳 12:00-14:30 (L.O.)
Dinner 晚膳 18:00-22:30 (L.O.)

■ ANNUAL AND WEEKLY CLOSING 休息日期
Closed 4 days Lunar New Year and Sunday 農曆新年 4 天及週日休息

Fook Lam Moon (Wan Chai)
福臨門 (灣仔)

150

Thanks to 70 years of glorious history, Fook Lam Moon is held dear by its faithful regulars as an institution in classic Cantonese cuisine. Thanks to a stable kitchen team, the food has always been consistently good. Seasonal ingredients – including live seafood that is shipped daily – are cooked in traditional ways. Standouts such as deep-fried crispy chicken, baked stuffed crab shell, and gourmet soup in whole winter melon, are true delights.

由1948年開業至今，福臨門一直是城中具標誌性的酒家之一。多年來水準保持一致，全賴默契十足、服務多年的團隊。家族第三代秉承父輩持守烹調粵菜的宗旨，以傳統烹調手法，配合優質食材奉客。時令菜單全年供應，海鮮則每天進貨，確保嘗到真鮮味。招牌菜包括釀焗鮮蟹蓋及炸子雞等。

TEL. 2866 0663
35-45 Johnston Road, Wan Chai
灣仔莊士敦道 35-45號
www.fooklammoon-grp.com

SPECIALITIES TO PRE-ORDER 預訂食物
Barbequed suckling pig (whole) 大紅片皮乳豬全體 / Double-boiled whole chicken stuffed with bird's nest 上湯鳳吞燕

■ PRICE 價錢
Lunch 午膳
à la carte 點菜 $ 300-1,000
Dinner 晚膳
à la carte 點菜 $ 800-2,000

■ OPENING HOURS 營業時間
Lunch 午膳 11:30-14:30 (L.O.)
Dinner 晚膳 18:00-22:00 (L.O.)

■ ANNUAL AND WEEKLY CLOSING 休息日期
Closed 2 days Lunar New Year
農曆新年休息 2 天

Forum
富臨飯店

48

The iconic dish here, Ah Yat braised abalone, has become as famous as Forum's owner-chef after whom it is named. Indeed, its international fame is such that some even travel from abroad just to taste it – tender and flavoursome abalone slow-cooked in a gourmet broth for days. Try also the braised oxtail, crispy fried chicken and stuffed crab shell with dried scallops. The dining room is spacious and comfortable.

餐廳老闆楊貫一的招牌菜阿一鮑魚赫赫有名，不論是本地食客或世界知名人士皆慕名而至。幕後團隊對此菜式絕不馬虎，採用日本乾鮑燜煮數天而成，且由專人主理。鮑魚以外，燒汁焗牛尾、脆皮雞和瑤柱焗釀蟹蓋也是一絕。室內裝潢豪華且富時代感，視覺味覺同時得到滿足。

TEL. 2869 8282
1F, Sino Plaza,
255-257 Gloucester Road,
Causeway Bay
銅鑼灣告士打道 255-257號信和廣場 1樓

■ PRICE 價錢
Lunch 午膳
set 套餐 $ 500
à la carte 點菜 $ 200-600
Dinner 晚膳
à la carte 點菜 $ 500-2,000

■ OPENING HOURS 營業時間
Lunch 午膳 11:30-14:30 (L.O.)
Dinner 晚膳 18:00-22:30 (L.O.)

Frantzén's Kitchen

Bjorn Frantzén's first restaurant outside Sweden aims to bring Nordic cooking with an Asian influence to Hong Kong. He gave the head chef full autonomy on its concept, from the menu to the interior. A sleek but cosy warmth characterises the interior. Every course has a story to tell and matches perfectly with their exciting wine list and Scandinavian craft beers. Food comes in moderate portions so that diners can try more variety.

東主在瑞典以外首家海外分店，主打斯堪的納維亞菜，亦是本地暫時唯一一家供應該菜式的餐廳。每道菜式都是一個故事。廚師帶着對食材的尊重，以簡單的方式炮製美食，務使食客品嘗到食材的原汁原味，分量亦較少，讓食客可嘗試更多菜式。店內還供應斯堪的納維亞雞尾酒和手工啤酒。

TEL. 2559 8508
11 Upper Station Street, Sheung Wan
上環差館上街 11號
www.frantzenskitchen.com

■ PRICE 價錢
Lunch 午膳
set 套餐 $ 595
à la carte 點菜 $ 600-1,000
Dinner 晚膳
à la carte 點菜 $ 600-1,000

■ OPENING HOURS 營業時間
Saturday lunch 週六午膳
12:00-14:00 (L.O.)
Dinner 晚膳 17:30-23:00 (L.O.)

■ ANNUAL AND WEEKLY CLOSING 休息日期
Closed Sunday and Monday
週日及週一休息

Fu Ho (Tsim Sha Tsui)
富豪 (尖沙咀)

P ⊡36

Thanks to his considerable experience, the head chef has been enticing diners back here for over a decade with his skilfully executed dishes, such as pan-fried Longgang chicken with ginger and scallion, and fried Chinese kale with dried plaice. Named after the owner, the signature Ah Yung abalone is slow-braised in a secret sauce for up to 20 hours. The dining room now has a contemporary, elegant and relaxing feel.

位於商場內不甚起眼的位置，這家酒家十多年來依然屹立不倒，足證正宗而不花巧的粵菜自有引人入勝之處。掌勺二十多年的廚師一直堅持用心烹煮傳統菜式，招牌菜阿翁鮑魚採用自家調製的鮑汁燜煮近二十小時，製作需時且考功夫；以龍崗雞製作的薑葱煎鹽香雞和方魚炒芥蘭亦值得一試。

TEL. 2736 2228
Shop 402, 4F, FoodLoft, Mira Place One,
132 Nathan Road, Tsim Sha Tsui
尖沙咀彌敦道 132號美麗華廣場一期
食四方 4樓 402號舖

■ PRICE 價錢
Lunch 午膳
à la carte 點菜 $ 250-1,500
Dinner 晚膳
à la carte 點菜 $ 600-1,500

■ OPENING HOURS 營業時間
Lunch 午膳 11:00-15:00 (L.O.)
Dinner 晚膳 18:00-22:00 (L.O.)

Fu Sing (Causeway Bay)
富聲 (銅鑼灣)

32

The regulars keep coming back for a number of reasons: the convenient location, reasonable prices, attentive service, and of course the delectable food, such as dim sum, steamed crab in Shaoxing wine and soy sauce chicken. Pork lung soup with fish maw and almond milk is available in individual servings. Seasonal specialities include double-boiled whole winter melon soup in summer and fried glutinous rice with preserved meat in winter.

富現代感的裝潢，細心的服務，加上地點便利，難怪這家富聲的常客眾多！點心選擇多且價錢合理，除了招牌菜富聲花雕蒸蟹和鮑汁豉油雞外，順德無骨魚雲羹和杏汁花膠筒豬肺湯同樣值得一試。品嘗粵菜當然少不了時令菜式，夏季不妨試試原個燉煮四小時的冬瓜盅，冬天自然不能錯過臘味糯米飯。

TEL. 2504 4228
1F, 68 Yee Wo Street, Causeway Bay
銅鑼灣怡和街68號1樓
www.fusinggroup.hk

■ PRICE 價錢
Lunch 午膳
à la carte 點菜 $ 150-450
Dinner 晚膳
à la carte 點菜 $ 200-450

■ OPENING HOURS 營業時間
Lunch 午膳 11:00-14:30 (L.O.)
Weekend lunch 週末午膳 11:00-15:30 (L.O.)
Dinner 晚膳 18:00-22:30 (L.O.)

■ ANNUAL AND WEEKLY CLOSING 休息日期
Closed 2 days Lunar New Year
農曆新年休息 2 天

Fu Sing (Wan Chai)
富聲 (灣仔)

40

Since 2004 food-lovers have been gathering at this contemporary dining room. The kitchen brigade may have changed slightly, but the current team boast plenty of experience. The menu features an array of Cantonese fare and is updated with seasonable items from time to time. Dim sum is recommended, as is fish head soup in Shun Tak style, soy sauce chicken, and steamed crab in Huadiao wine.

2004年開業的富聲位處時尚大樓之中，升降機可帶你直達這佔地寬廣、設計富現代感的粵菜酒家。十多年來廚師團隊雖略有變動，但皆為資歷深厚的老師傅，難怪食客紛至沓來。餐單選擇多樣，且不時跟隨季節推出時令菜式。推介包括順德無骨魚雲羹、鮑汁豉油雞、花雕蒸蟹及乾燒粉絲煲，當然更少不了精美點心。

TEL. 2893 2228
3F, Sunshine Plaza, 353 Lockhart Road, Wan Chai
灣仔駱克道 353號三湘大廈 3樓
www.fusinggroup.hk

■ PRICE 價錢
Lunch 午膳
set 套餐 $ 498-698
à la carte 點菜 $ 130-600
Dinner 晚膳
set 套餐 $ 498-698
à la carte 點菜 $ 200-600

■ OPENING HOURS 營業時間
Lunch 午膳 11:00-14:45 (L.O.)
Dinner 晚膳 18:00-22:15 (L.O.)

■ ANNUAL AND WEEKLY CLOSING 休息日期
Closed 2 days Lunar New Year
農曆新年休息 2 天

Fung Shing (Mong Kok)
鳳城 (旺角)

This family business has been going since 1954; and their story has been published along with assorted recipes. Owner-chef Mr Tam looks to the region of Shun Tak for inspiration for his tasty Cantonese cooking – must try dishes are stir-fried milk with egg whites and roasted suckling pig. The two-storey restaurant is always busy, so it's well worth booking in advance.

由家族經營的鳳城創於1954年，這家旺角總店共佔兩層，仍然經常人頭湧湧，除了因為其傳統順德菜甚具水準，親民的價格亦是受歡迎原因，不少客人更選擇於此設宴。主廚兼老闆譚國景從順德菜中尋找烹調美味廣東菜的靈感，大良炒鮮奶及馳名燒乳豬絕對值得一試。三五知己聚會建議訂座。

TEL. 2381 5261
1-2F, 749 Nathan Road, Mong Kok
旺角彌敦道749號1-2樓

■ PRICE 價錢
Lunch 午膳
à la carte 點菜 $ 100-350
Dinner 晚膳
à la carte 點菜 $ 150-350

■ OPENING HOURS 營業時間
Lunch 午膳 09:00-15:00 (L.O.)
Dinner 晚膳 18:00-22:30 (L.O.)

■ ANNUAL AND WEEKLY CLOSING 休息日期
Closed 4 days Lunar New Year
農曆新年休息 4 天

Gaddi's
吉地士

16

This grand restaurant opened in 1953 and now occupies what was once The Peninsula's ballroom – it even has its own dedicated entrance on Nathan Road. The well-versed team looks after the guests so well here you may find yourself loathed to leave. The chef uses the finest ingredients but brings a certain lightness to the classic French cuisine. For those wanting something a little different book the Chef's Table in the kitchen.

穿過專用入口到達這家於1953年開業的傳奇食店。這裏原是酒店宴會廳，原來的典雅格調依舊保存，餐室內盡是酒店的珍藏品。主廚擅於把上乘材料烹調成融入現代元素的法國佳餚。想要一趟與眾不同的體驗，可預訂位於餐廳廚房內的「廚師之桌」，在享受美食的同時欣賞大廚風采。

TEL. 2696 6763
1F, The Peninsula Hotel,
Salisbury Road, Tsim Sha Tsui
尖沙咀梳士巴利道半島酒店 1樓
http://hongkong.peninsula.com

■ PRICE 價錢
Lunch 午膳
set 套餐 $ 500-900
à la carte 點菜 $ 1,000-3,500
Dinner 晚膳
set 套餐 $ 1,000-3,000
à la carte 點菜 $ 1,000-3,500

■ OPENING HOURS 營業時間
Lunch 午膳 12:00-14:30 (L.O.)
Dinner 晚膳 18:30-22:30 (L.O.)

Giando

Italian chef Gianni Caprioli owns several restaurants in Hong Kong but this one, minutes from Wan Chai but tucked away in a quiet corner, is his jewel. The look inside is smart and sophisticated, with the booths along one side being the prized seats. Expect to see dishes from all over Italy, with strozzapreti – hand-twisted pasta – and Milanese-style veal chop being two specialities. They have a real passion for wine too – Italian, naturally.

意籍廚師Gianni Caprioli名下餐廳眾多，此店可視為其珍寶，自有其因由。位處鬧市中的寧謐一隅，別有洞天，室內設計精巧富心思；餐單中意大利各地區口味俱備，配上招牌的自製捲意粉及米蘭式小牛扒，視、味覺均感受到濃厚的意式風情。酒單由身兼侍酒師的釀酒師設計，包羅意國佳釀，不妨細酌一番。

TEL. 2511 8912
Shop 1, GF, Tower 1, Starcrest,
9 Star Street, Wan Chai
灣仔星街 9號星域軒 1座地下 1號舖
www.giandorestaurant.com

■ PRICE 價錢
Lunch 午膳
set 套餐 $ 278-348
à la carte 點菜 $ 450-1,000
Dinner 晚膳
à la carte 點菜 $ 450-1,000

■ OPENING HOURS 營業時間
Lunch 午膳 12:00-14:30 (L.O.)
Dinner 晚膳 18:00-22:00 (L.O.)

Glorious Cuisine
增輝藝廚

14

The owner shops for seafood daily to ensure freshness and quality. Picking out your favourite live critters from the tank is part of the fun – Hokkaido scallops, Thai marble goby, and even Hanasaki crab if you're lucky. Apart from the signature braised chicken stuffed with abalone and sea cucumber, try also their salt-baked sea whelks or virgin crabs. Double-boiled chicken soup with conpoy and Yunnan ham is available in limited quantities every night.

北海道帶子、泰國筍殼魚……門外的魚缸內是來自各地的海鮮，幸運的話，或能吃到日本花咲蟹。曾經營雞隻生意的老闆乘貨源之便，每天親自選購當造的新鮮食材。自創的金瑤雲腿落湯雞，選用清遠雞加上瑤柱及雲腿等，清燉約一小時而成，每晚限量供應；同樣大受歡迎的頭抽雞需提前預訂。

TEL. 2778 8103
31-33 Shek Kip Mei Street,
Sham Shui Po
深水埗石硤尾街 31-33號

SPECIALITIES TO PRE-ORDER 預訂食物
Chicken stuffed with fresh abalone and braised sea cucumber 鮑魚海參雞 / Double-boiled chicken soup with conpoy and Yunnan ham 金瑤雲腿落湯雞 / Soy sauce chicken 頭抽雞

■ PRICE 價錢
à la carte 點菜 $ 200-300

■ OPENING HOURS 營業時間
17:30-01:30 (L.O.)

■ ANNUAL AND WEEKLY CLOSING 休息日期
Closed 3 days Lunar New Year
農曆新年休息 3 天

Good Hope Noodle (Fa Yuen Street)
好旺角麵家 (花園街)

Mong Kok residents will know the name, as Good Hope Noodle has been around for over 40 years, but now they have a more comfortable spot in which to enjoy their favourite dishes. The brightly lit dining room is neatly furnished with booths and tiles. Food is prepared in the open kitchen, with noodles, congee and snacks served all day. Try the distinctive flavour of Zha Jiang Mian (fried noodles).

好旺角麵家在旺角區開業至今逾四十載，街坊對這名字一定不會陌生。店內以卡座為主，開放式廚房、光潔的牆身、地磚和明亮的燈光，為顧客提供了一個整潔的環境。店家全日供應粥品、粉麵和各式小吃。這兒的炸醬麵別具風格，不容錯過。

TEL. 2384 6898
18 Fa Yuen Street, Mong Kok
旺角花園街 18號

■ PRICE 價錢
Lunch 午膳
set 套餐 $ 55-66
à la carte 點菜 $ 40-80
Dinner 晚膳
à la carte 點菜 $ 40-80

■ OPENING HOURS 營業時間
11:00-00:45 (L.O.)

■ ANNUAL AND WEEKLY CLOSING 休息日期
Closed 3 days Lunar New Year
農曆新年休息 3 天

Grand Hyatt Steakhouse

XX

32

As this was once the hotel's JJ's nightclub it should come as no surprise that there's a moody, sultry feel to the place. The chef is Argentinian and whilst they don't yet feature meat from his country the vast array includes Wagyu, Galician from Spain and American bison. The chips cooked in duck fat are a must and the sherry berry trifle is big enough for two to share. The best seats are at the counter or by the window.

專屬升降機帶你到達這帶剛陽味的扒房，不論是富情調的吧枱座位或臨窗的二人桌皆為客人所喜愛。新任的阿根廷廚師深諳烹調肉類的法門，食客可在和牛、美國Bison野牛，甚至西班牙加利西亞牛肉中作挑選；配菜別錯過以鴨油炮製的厚切薯條，和足夠二人共享的雪梨酒漿果蛋糕。葡萄酒和香檳選擇目不暇給。

TEL. 2584 7722
MF, Grand Hyatt Hotel,
1 Harbour Road, Wan Chai
灣仔港灣道1號君悅酒店閣樓
www.hongkong.grand.hyatt.com

■ PRICE 價錢
Dinner 晚膳
à la carte 點菜 $ 480-2,200

■ OPENING HOURS 營業時間
Dinner 晚膳 18:00-22:30 (L.O.)

Guo Fu Lou
國福樓

24

It may have moved from Wan Chai to Central, but the kitchen team stayed the same, so all your favourites are still on the menu. Classics such as stewed garoupa belly with Chinese lettuce and garlic cloves, and jasmine tea smoked chicken are exquisitely made. Ask about the seasonal items and their signature deep-fried sesame balls. The interior befits the smart hotel in which it's located, with glass and frosted gold creating a modern, lavish feel.

國福樓移師至新開業的美利酒店，原班人馬繼續以頂級食材精心炮製各式手工粵菜。菜單上包括了多款精緻傳統菜品，例如以黃皮老虎斑烹調的蒜子唐生菜燜斑翅，以及選用新鮮清遠雞的茉莉花茶燻雞；不妨考慮時令推介，夏天獨有的冬瓜盅需提前預訂。充滿芝麻香、只在晚市供應的燈影煎堆香脆煙韌，萬勿錯過。

TEL. 3468 8188
The Pavilion at The Murray Hotel,
22 Cotton Tree Drive, Central
中環紅棉路22號美利酒店平台亭樓
http://fooklammoon-grp.com

■ PRICE 價錢
Lunch 午膳
à la carte 點菜 $ 400-1,000
Dinner 晚膳
à la carte 點菜 $ 800-2,000

■ OPENING HOURS 營業時間
Lunch 午膳 12:00-14:30 (L.O.)
Dinner 晚膳 18:00-22:00 (L.O.)

■ ANNUAL AND WEEKLY CLOSING 休息日期
Closed 2 days Lunar New Year
農曆新年休息 2 天

Hing Kee
避風塘興記

It started two generations ago in Causeway Bay but the family's reputation for Boat People style cuisine was made in Tsim Sha Tsui; further testimony comes from the celebrity signatures lining the walls. Elder sister heads the serving team; younger brother runs the kitchen. They are famous for their stir-fried crabs with black beans and chilli, roast duck and rice noodles in soup and congee. Guests aren't seated until everyone in the party has arrived.

歷經三代，原址在銅鑼灣，其後才遷到尖沙咀現址，這家由祖父輩創辦的餐廳主打仍是避風塘特色小菜。廚房由弟弟掌舵，大家姐則負責領導服務團隊。海鮮每天新鮮進貨，供應有限，不妨於訂座時預留，招牌菜包括避風塘炒蟹、燒鴨湯河及艇仔粥。座位不多，食客須人齊方能入座。

TEL. 2722 0022
1F, Bowa House, 180 Nathan Road, Tsim Sha Tsui
尖沙咀彌敦道 180號寶華商業大廈 1樓

■ PRICE 價錢
Dinner 晚膳
à la carte 點菜 $ 300-700

■ OPENING HOURS 營業時間
Dinner 晚膳 18:00-02:30 (L.O.)

■ ANNUAL AND WEEKLY CLOSING 休息日期
Closed 2 days Lunar New Year
農曆新年休息 2 天

Ho Hung Kee
何洪記

No discussion about Hong Kong's historic noodle shops would be complete without mentioning Ho Hung Kee, which originally opened in Wan Chai in the 1940s and is famed for its springy wonton noodles and fresh, sweet soup. More elements have been added here at its new address – dim sum and some Cantonese dishes are now served too. For the interior, they've adopted a more contemporary, Western style aesthetic.

何洪記是香港歷史悠久的麵家之一，自四十年代起在灣仔區營業，多年來其招牌雲吞麵憑着麵條彈牙、湯底鮮甜而口碑載道；其粥品也很出色。遷至商場後，設計變得西化，但重視食品質素的經營方針始終不變，更增加了食物種類，除粥麵外，還供應點心和廣式小菜，難怪吸引到新舊客人到此用膳。

TEL. 2577 6028
Shop 1204-1205, 12F, Hysan Place,
500 Hennessy Road, Causeway Bay
銅鑼灣軒尼詩道 500號希慎廣場 12樓
1204-1205號舖

■ PRICE 價錢
à la carte 點菜 $ 100-200

■ OPENING HOURS 營業時間
11:30-22:45 (L.O.)
Weekends & Public Holidays
週末及公眾假期 11:00-22:45 (L.O.)

■ ANNUAL AND WEEKLY CLOSING 休息日期
Closed 2 days Lunar New Year
農曆新年休息 2 天

Ho To Tai (Yuen Long)
好到底 (元朗)

Traditional shops that make their own noodles from scratch are hard to come by. Founded in 1946, this household name is among the remaining few. The nostalgic two-storey shop has quintessential Cantonese dumplings on the menu, the must-try wonton soup and fish skin dumplings. Those craving more carbs can order the hugely popular tossed noodles with shrimp roe. The owner also runs a dried noodle factory with retail outlets all over town.

自家製麵的傳統店鋪愈來愈少，這家於1946年開業、位處元朗的老字號麵家是其中之一。樓高兩層的店鋪內是濃濃的懷舊氣氛。蝦籽撈麵和特製魚皮水餃向來是最受歡迎的食物，而雲吞更是非試不可！麵店附近設有製麵工場，店主同時在市區設立多個麵食銷售店，出售自製乾麵及蝦籽。

TEL. 2476 2495
67 Fau Tsoi Street, Yuen Long
元朗阜財街 67號

■ PRICE 價錢
à la carte 點菜 $ 30-70

■ OPENING HOURS 營業時間
10:00-20:00 (L.O.)

■ ANNUAL AND WEEKLY CLOSING 休息日期
Closed 10 days Lunar New Year
農曆新年休息 10 天

WHAT IS NATURAL MINERAL WATER?

Natural mineral water originates from an underground aquifer, is protected from all risks of pollution, and emerges from a unique source. It is characterized by a **constant level of minerals and purity at the source.**

This makes the water UNIQUE

PLAIN WATERS	EVIAN NATURAL MINERAL WATER	NATURAL MINERAL WATER	DRINKING WATER	FILTERED WATER
UNIQUE SOURCE	●	●	Variable	Variable
STABLE NATURAL MINERAL COMPOSITION	●	●	●	○
NATURAL FILTRATION PROCESS	●	●	○	○
CHEMICAL OR PHYSICAL TREATMENT	○	○	●	●

March 2018 Danone internal source

SPARKLING WATERS	BADOIT SPARKLING NATURAL MINERAL WATER	FILTERED SPARKLING WATER
UNIQUE SOURCE	●	Variable
NATURAL GAS FROM SOURCE	●*	○
BICARBONATED (Meaning > 600 mg/L according to law)	●	○

Hoi Tin Garden
海天花園

One of the biggest and best known restaurants on the seafood street in Sam Shing, this three-storey establishment, complete with its own parking lot, has been in business for over 30 years. Seafood lovers travel from around town to shop for their favourite catch at the wet market nearby and ask their chefs to cook it up. Dim sum is served in the morning. A private room on the third floor caters to bigger parties.

位於三聖村海鮮街入口，稱得上是該處規模最大的酒家，樓高三層且設有停車場，街坊對海天這個名字一定不會感到陌生，概因她已在區內開業逾三十年。與海鮮街毗鄰的便利，食客都會在市場購買海鮮後帶到酒家，由廚師烹調處理。上午有早茶點心供應。三五知己聚餐，可選擇三樓的廂房。

TEL. 2450 6331
5 Sam Shing Street, Castle Peak Bay, Tuen Mun
屯門青山灣三聖街 5號

■ PRICE 價錢
à la carte 點菜 $ 400-500

■ OPENING HOURS 營業時間
11:00-22:00 (L.O.)

Hugo's
希戈

12

There aren't many restaurants in Hong Kong with a medieval theme, complete with swords and suits of armour, but then Hugo's is all about the charms of yesteryear. The European menu includes plenty of French classics like Dover sole meunière and escargot à la bourguignonne; there are also plenty of dishes finished at the table, like steak tartare and steak au poivre. At lunch, desserts and a large hors d'oeuvre selection are served from a trolley.

完整的銀鎧甲、大型金屬燭台加上兵器裝飾，令這餐廳瀰漫着不一樣的中世紀懷舊風情。餐單上的是具濃厚法國特色的傳統歐洲菜，如法式洋葱湯、布根地式焗田螺等，部分菜式如生牛肉他他或法式黑胡椒牛柳，更是席前調製，帶來多一重享受。午市的套餐提供大量餐前開胃菜和甜品選擇。

TEL. 3721 7733
Lobby, Hyatt Regency Tsim Sha Tsui,
18 Hanoi Road, Tsim Sha Tsui
尖沙咀河內道 18號凱悅酒店大堂
www.hongkongtsimshatsui.regency.hyatt.com

SPECIALITIES TO PRE-ORDER 預訂食物
Roasted US rib of beef 燒美國牛肋骨肉

■ PRICE 價錢
Lunch 午膳
set 套餐 $ 500-800
à la carte 點菜 $ 800-1,800
Dinner 晚膳
set 套餐 $ 1,000-1,500
à la carte 點菜 $ 800-1,800

■ OPENING HOURS 營業時間
Lunch 午膳 12:00-14:30 (L.O.)
Sunday lunch 週日午膳 11:30-14:30 (L.O.)
Dinner 晚膳 18:30-22:30 (L.O.)

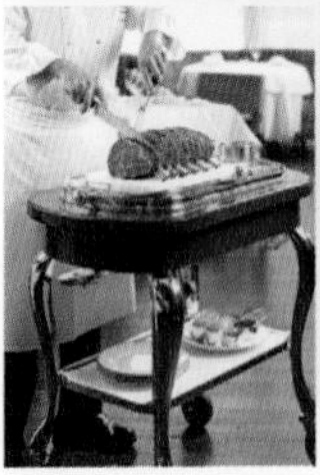

Hyde Park Garden
海德花園

20

The owner also sells seafood from a nearby stall so diners can pick from the selection that is flown in daily and have it cooked in the restaurant for a fee. Also try their razor clams in chilli black bean sauce, or the signature fish soup which is simmered for hours with freshwater fish and tofu. Other recommendations include ginger and scallion abalone in a clay pot, and tofu skin sweet soup with pearl barley.

店東同時經營對面的明月海鮮檔，客人可先到此挑選空運到港的生猛海鮮，再交給廚房處理。師傅烹調海鮮的時間拿捏精準，如鮮甜爽脆豉椒炒蟶子就火候十足；推介淡水鮮魚湯，以大量淡水魚加入豆腐熬煮至少兩小時，每天新鮮製作。此外，腐竹洋薏米糖水、炸茄子皇和無添加人造色素的咕嚕肉也是招牌菜。

TEL. 2717 6381
44 Hoi Pong Road Central,
Lei Yue Mun
鯉魚門海傍道中 44號
www.hydeparkdeli.com

■ PRICE 價錢
Lunch 午膳
à la carte 點菜 $ 500-1,000
Dinner 晚膳
à la carte 點菜 $ 500-1,000

■ OPENING HOURS 營業時間
Lunch 午膳 11:30-14:30 (L.O.)
Dinner 晚膳 16:30-22:00 (L.O.)

■ ANNUAL AND WEEKLY CLOSING 休息日期
Closed 4 days Lunar New Year
農曆新年休息 4 天

ICHU Ⓝ

This is the first Asian venture of chef Martínez, who helms the famed restaurant 'Central' in Peru; in fact, three key members from there were relocated to Hong Kong to ensure his vision is replicated here. The interior is inspired by Peru's landscape and the chef's cooking. Signatures include pargo al rocoto (sliced snapper with celeriac, avocado and aji rocoto) and tacu tacu chupe (tiger prawns with beans and aji panca). Don't miss the aperitivos.

秘魯廚師Virgilio Martínez於亞洲的首家餐廳，廚房、酒吧和服務團隊的領軍人物均曾於秘魯店效力多年，韓籍主廚將當地多樣化的特產融入菜式，確保風味不變。酒單側重南美風味，雞尾酒Aperitivos與生醃前菜是不錯的配搭。以秘魯為題的大型抽象畫作高懸於餐室，中央懸浮的樹木及電梯旁的雕像更使人眼前一亮。

TEL. 2477 7717
3F, H Queen's, 80 Queen's Road Central, Central
中環皇后大道中 80號 H Queen's 3樓
www.ichu.com.hk

■ PRICE 價錢
Lunch 午膳
à la carte 點菜 $ 300-700
Dinner 晚膳
à la carte 點菜 $ 300-700

■ OPENING HOURS 營業時間
Lunch 午膳 12:00-14:30 (L.O.)
Dinner 晚膳 18:00-22:30 (L.O.)
Friday and Saturday dinner
週五及週六晚膳 18:00-23:30 (L.O.)

IM Teppanyaki & Wine

XX 8

Less a meal, more a full multi-sensory experience. Sit at the teppanyaki bar, admire the cooking show and enjoy contemporary Japanese flavours that make great use of prime ingredients like lobster and premium quality Wagyu. You also get to hear all about owner-chef Lawrence Mok's extraordinary triathlon experiences straight from his own mouth while he prepares your food. There is a private room available for small groups.

這間僅設二十個座位的鐵板燒餐廳，由經驗豐富的創辦人兼總廚莫師傅主理。客人可嘗到鮑魚、龍蝦、黑毛和牛等高級食材，不能錯過的有甘鯛魚配海膽忌廉汁，酥脆的魚鱗和幼嫩多汁的魚肉配合得天衣無縫。坐在鐵板燒桌前，食客會看到廚師預備食材的嚴謹態度及對細節的執著。如要親嘗莫師傅手藝，務必提前預訂並註明。

TEL. 2570 7088
134 Tung Lo Wan Road, Tai Hang
大坑銅鑼灣道 134號
www.imteppanyaki.com

■ PRICE 價錢
Lunch 午膳
set 套餐 $ 320-880
à la carte 點菜 $ 1,000-2,000
Dinner 晚膳
set 套餐 $ 1,480-1,800
à la carte 點菜 $ 1,000-2,000

■ OPENING HOURS 營業時間
Lunch 午膳 12:00-14:30 (L.O.)
Dinner 晚膳 18:00-22:30 (L.O.)

Imperial Treasure Fine Chinese Cuisine
御寶軒

XXX 20

Finding success in Singapore and Shanghai, Imperial Treasure opened its first Hong Kong branch in the sky-scraping landmark, with panoramic views of the harbour. The stylish dining room is embellished with subtle Chinese touches, such as the ceramic Koi carps and calligraphy. A fish tank in the kitchen ensures live seafood is available every day. Poached garoupa in fish soup with crispy rice and stuffed crab shell are worth a try.

御寶軒在香港的首家分店選址在九龍半島地標北京道1號，坐擁無敵維港兩岸景色，加上時尚中帶點中國風的設計——水泥牆上的立體陶瓷鯉魚和樑柱上的書法——令人悠然神往！廚房內附設魚缸，每天都有鮮活的海鮮供應。脆米海鮮浸東星、糯米釀脆皮乳豬及法式蟹蓋是招牌菜。

TEL. 2613 9800
10F, One Peking, 1 Peking Road,
Tsim Sha Tsui
尖沙咀北京道1號10樓
www.imperialtreasure.com

■ PRICE 價錢
Lunch 午膳
à la carte 點菜 $ 200-300
Dinner 晚膳
à la carte 點菜 $ 500-1,000

■ OPENING HOURS 營業時間
Lunch 午膳 11:30-14:30 (L.O.)
Dinner 晚膳 18:00-22:30 (L.O.)

Involtini

The young chef of this fairly diminutive Italian restaurant is an alumnus of both Otto e Mezzo and CIAK. The speciality of the house is homemade pasta, freshly made every day and served with a variety of good quality, imported seasonal ingredients ranging from seafood to truffles. Recommendations include orecchiette in tomato sauce with homemade sausage, and black truffle tagliolini. The open kitchen adds plenty of animation to the simply furnished, monochrome room.

餐廳面積不大，以白色為主調配上簡樸的裝飾。揀選開放式廚房邊上的座位，能盡情注視廚師為你炮製美食的過程。每天鮮製的手造意粉是這裏的主打食品，配以時令進口食材如新鮮海產和松露等，黑松露幼麵和配上自家製香腸的貓耳意粉值得一試。午市供應的意粉套餐，味美且價錢實惠，適合上班族。

TEL. 2658 2128
11F, The L. Square,
459-461 Lockhart Road, Causeway Bay
銅鑼灣駱克道 459-461號
The L. Square 11樓
www.involticoncept.com

■ PRICE 價錢
Lunch 午膳
set 套餐 $ 68-248
à la carte 點菜 $ 250-500
Dinner 晚膳
set 套餐 $ 568
à la carte 點菜 $ 290-600

■ OPENING HOURS 營業時間
Lunch 午膳 12:00-15:00 (L.O.)
Dinner 晚膳 18:00-22:00 (L.O.)

■ ANNUAL AND WEEKLY CLOSING 休息日期
Closed 3 days Lunar New Year
農曆新年休息 3 天

Ippoh
一宝

Now run by the fifth generation, this family business rooted in Osaka still strictly follows the traditional rules of making tempura. The owner-chef insists on battering and frying every morsel himself without delegating his duty. Seafood is flown in daily from Osaka and Toyosu fish market and they use flavourless safflower oil, so as not to overpower the ingredients' natural tastes. The sauce is made to a secret recipe. Omakase is the best way to go.

大廚兼東主是這家餐館的第五代傳人，時令的日本海產從大阪和東京豐洲市場空運抵達，放入輕純的紅花油中以明火烹調，並配上每天鮮製的醬汁佐吃。餐館水準多年來始終如一，除因為規模不大有助保持穩定，亦因為大廚堅持親自烹調每件天婦羅，從不假手於人。建議點選廚師套餐，可盡嘗最時令的食材。

TEL. 2468 0641
39 Aberdeen Street, Central
中環鴨巴甸街39號
www.ippoh.com.hk

■ PRICE 價錢
Lunch 午膳
set 套餐 $ 480-1,100
Dinner 晚膳
set 套餐 $ 1,200-1,500

■ OPENING HOURS 營業時間
Lunch 午膳 12:00-14:00 (L.O.)
Dinner 晚膳 18:00-21:30 (L.O.)

■ ANNUAL AND WEEKLY CLOSING 休息日期
Closed New Year's Day, 4 days Lunar New Year and Wednesday
元旦、農曆新年4天及週三休息

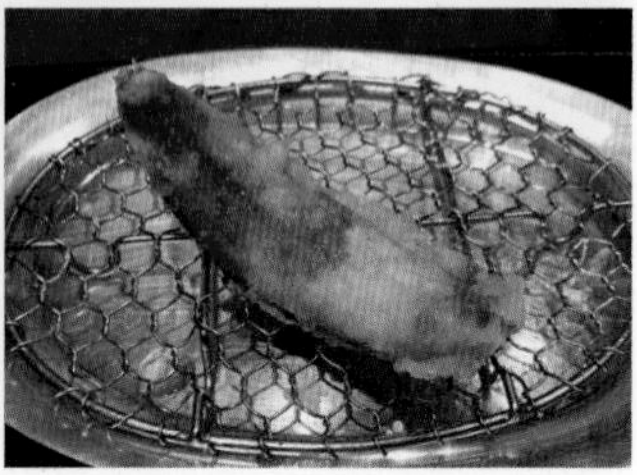

Jardin de Jade (Wan Chai)
蘇浙滙 (灣仔)

16

The first Hong Kong venture from this renowned Shanghai restaurant group is certainly not lacking in grandeur, thanks to its double-height ceiling and striking chandelier. The kitchen naturally focuses on Shanghainese cooking and makes good use of traditional recipes but presents the dishes in a more modern style. High quality ingredients are sourced from the mainland. A seasonal menu is offered to reflect the produce available. Try steamed reeves shad or smoked duck.

作為上海著名餐飲集團的首家香港分店，餐廳的裝潢雅致，特高樓底配上引人注目的吊燈，別具氣派。餐館以時尚包裝演繹傳統上海菜式，味美且外形精緻。集團注重選料，從內地搜羅優質食材，更每季推出時令菜單。推介菜式包括清蒸鰣魚、樟茶鴨和清炒河蝦仁等。

TEL. 3528 0228
GF, Sun Hung Kai Centre,
30 Harbour Road, Wan Chai
灣仔港灣道 30號新鴻基中心地下
www.jade388.com

SPECIALITIES TO PRE-ORDER 預訂食物
Eight-treasure duck with spicy salt 椒鹽八寶鴨 / Deboned fish head with mung bean vermicelli 拆骨魚頭粉皮

■ PRICE 價錢
Lunch 午膳
à la carte 點菜 $ 200-500
Dinner 晚膳
à la carte 點菜 $ 200-500

■ OPENING HOURS 營業時間
Lunch 午膳 11:30-14:30 (L.O.)
Dinner 晚膳 17:30-22:00 (L.O.)

Ju Xing Home
聚興家

This hole-in-the-wall that occupies two units is always jam-packed – because of its food, not because of its décor or service. Regulars range from hotel chefs to local stars. Chef-owner Ng gets hands on in the kitchen and tries out new recipes with other cooks. The menu was mostly Cantonese at first, but now comes with a few Sichuan options. His succulent salt-baked chicken and lobster with pan-fried rice vermicelli are must-tries. Reservations are highly recommended.

沒有豪華裝修及五星級服務，即使已擴充至隔鄰鋪位，仍然經常滿座，且是許多酒店大廚和明星的飯堂，因此想在此用餐，請務必訂座。店東兼主廚吳師傅喜歡親自下廚，亦愛與各大廚師交流並學習新菜式，由最初主攻粵菜到現在店內添加了少量川菜。用鮮雞炮製的鹽焗雞及上湯澳洲龍蝦煎米粉底是招牌菜。

TEL. 2392 9283
GF, 416 & 418 Portland Street, Prince Edward
太子砵蘭街 416及 418號地下

SPECIALITIES TO PRE-ORDER 預訂食物
Long-boiled soups 老火湯

■ PRICE 價錢
à la carte 點菜 $ 250-350

■ OPENING HOURS 營業時間
17:00-01:00 (L.O.)

■ ANNUAL AND WEEKLY CLOSING 休息日期
Closed 4 days Lunar New Year
農曆新年休息 4 天

Kaiseki Den by Saotome

14

Formerly occupying a glitzy space in Sheung Wan, this Japanese haute cuisine restaurant embraces a zen-inspired aesthetic with bamboo, grass green and birch panels at this new location, opened in 2017. Only the freshest food in season prepared flawlessly makes it to the table. Seats at the counter let you observe chef Saotome and his team's artistic touch. Try their signature dishes of sea urchin truffle rice and chargrilled wagyu beef.

從上環舊店遷至現址，以深淺啡色配搭木材的裝潢，帶着強烈的時尚日式風格。店內仍設有開放式廚房，令你可以觀賞廚師埋首製作食物的過程。由大廚決定的廚師發辦懷石料理，一如既往，食材會隨着季節而轉換，炭烤和牛及黑松露海膽飯是招牌菜。

TEL. 2851 2820
Shop 3-4, The Oakhill, 28 Wood Road, Wan Chai
灣仔活道 28號萃峯3-4號舖

■ PRICE 價錢
Dinner 晚膳
set 套餐 $ 2,480-3,580

■ OPENING HOURS 營業時間
Dinner 晚膳 18:30-21:30 (L.O.)

■ ANNUAL AND WEEKLY CLOSING 休息日期
Closed 3 days Lunar New Year and Sunday
農曆新年 3 天及週日休息

Kam Fai
金輝

20

It has over 50 years of history and is managed by a head chef with over 40 years of kitchen experience. Cooking is customised so you can specify how you want your seafood prepared – oysters can be lightly floured, tempura-battered, or breadcrumbed before being deep-fried. Try their salt-baked virgin crabs, and deep-fried mantis shrimps in peppered salt. Pre-order the braised abalone in peppercorn soup to avoid missing out.

開業逾五十年，歷史悠久之餘更向以信譽和品質見稱。有四十年入廚經驗的羅先生既是店舖掌舵，亦是廚房主帥，其烹調海鮮的技術毋庸置疑。靈活的經營模式，服務以客為本，如酥炸生蠔可應客人要求以不同作法烹調。招牌菜包括油鹽焗奄仔蟹、火候十足的椒鹽瀨尿蝦，及建議預訂的胡椒扣鮑魚。

TEL. 2347 7434
10 Hoi Pong Road Central, Lei Yue Mun
鯉魚門海傍道中 10號

■ PRICE 價錢
à la carte 點菜 $ 600-1,100

■ OPENING HOURS 營業時間
12:00-22:30 (L.O.)

■ ANNUAL AND WEEKLY CLOSING 休息日期
Closed 4 days Lunar New Year
農曆新年休息 4 天

Kam's Roast Goose
甘牌燒鵝

The Kam family name is synonymous with their famous roast goose restaurant. This little place is owned by the third generation of the family and he wisely hired his father's former chef to ensure the goose is as crisp and succulent as ever. There's also suckling pig, goose neck and head, and goose blood pudding available. With only 30 seats, don't be surprised to see a queue.

從祖父輩創業至今歷七十多年，甘氏出品的燒鵝早已遠近馳名，現由第三代傳人在灣仔開設全新餐館，承傳父輩廚藝。與父輩共事多年的老師傅以甘氏家傳秘方炮製的燒鵝，掛在窗前令人垂涎欲滴。燒乳豬、鵝頭和鵝紅也非常美味。小店僅有三十個座位，故常見輪位或買外賣的人龍。

TEL. 2520 1110
226 Hennessy Road, Wan Chai
灣仔軒尼詩道 226號
www.krg.com.hk

■ PRICE 價錢
Lunch 午膳
set 套餐 $ 60-80
à la carte 點菜 $ 50-150
Dinner 晚膳
à la carte 點菜 $ 50-150

■ OPENING HOURS 營業時間
11:30-21:15 (L.O.)

Kashiwaya
柏屋

The head chef worked for twenty years at the much celebrated, original Kashiwaya restaurant in Osaka before being charged with opening their Hong Kong branch here in Central. It's a predictably discreet, impeccably run operation with around 80% of the menu the same as the original. For the kaiseki cuisine, all the fiercely seasonal ingredients are flown in from Japan, including the soft water for the cooking of the rice.

柏屋在大阪的總店享負盛名，這家首間海外分店於2015年開業，食客可在這兒嘗到正宗的懷石料理。主廚曾於總店效力長達二十年，秉承懷石料理食物精緻、製作嚴謹的宗旨侍客，除了選用最頂尖的時令食材，連用於製作煮物、飯和上湯的軟水亦來自日本。每一道菜式均值得細味品嘗。

TEL. 2520 5218
8F, 18 On Lan Street, Central
中環安蘭街 18號 8樓
jp-kashiwaya.com/hongkong/

■ PRICE 價錢
Lunch 午膳
set 套餐 $ 680-4,000
Dinner 晚膳
set 套餐 $ 1,800-4,000

■ OPENING HOURS 營業時間
Lunch 午膳 12:00-13:30 (L.O.)
Dinner 晚膳 18:30-21:00 (L.O.)

■ ANNUAL AND WEEKLY CLOSING 休息日期
Closed Sunday 週日休息

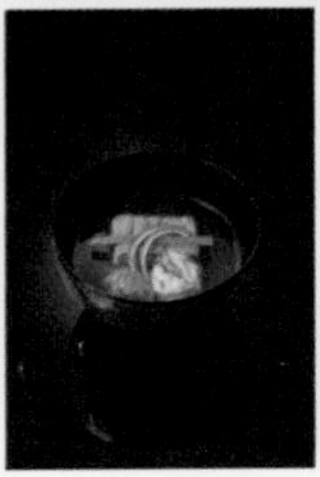

Kau Kee
九記

Kau Kee has been trading since the 1930s and has consequently built up such a huge following that you'll probably have to line up in the street first to eat here. It's all very basic and you'll have to share your table but the food is delicious. Beef noodles are the speciality; different cuts of meat with a variety of noodles in a tasty broth or spicy sauce. Try the milk tea too.

開業於三十年代的九記深得食客支持，每天自十二時起，即使店舖還未正式營業，來自世界各地的食客都已整裝待發在門外輪候，午膳時間尤其擠擁。店內陳設簡單，進餐時要和其他人共用餐桌。歷久不衰的食物當然要數清湯牛腩，而咖喱牛腩亦不乏老饕捧場，配上更能掛湯的伊府麵，滋味無窮。

TEL. N/A
21 Gough Street, Central
中環歌賦街 21號

■ PRICE 價錢
à la carte 點菜 $40-90

■ OPENING HOURS 營業時間
12:30-22:30 (L.O.)

■ ANNUAL AND WEEKLY CLOSING 休息日期
Closed 10 days Lunar New Year, Public Holidays and Sunday
農曆新年 10 天、公眾假期及週日休息

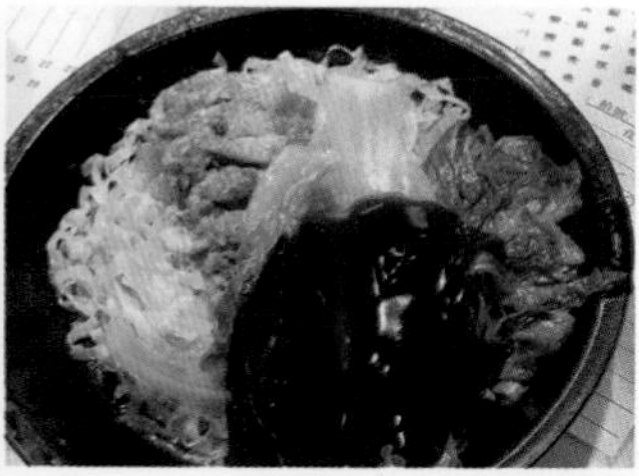

Kaum

An all-in-one boutique, bar-lounge and restaurant that celebrates all things Indonesian. The latter is furnished with beautiful Toraja tiles and upholstery, which lend a nostalgic feel. The menu covers different styles of the vibrant indigenous cuisine. All dishes are appealingly priced and come in portion sizes big enough for a few to share. Parties of six or more can order the special menu to sample a variety of culinary highlights.

衣物手工藝店、酒吧和兩個風格截然不同的主餐室，組合成這家供應印尼菜的餐廳。位處店子最深處的餐室以五、六十年代風格傢具布置，綴以由印尼少數民族製造的天花鑲板、布藝品和裝飾，別具特色。餐單羅列印尼各地佳餚，菜式分量頗大，且設不少可供分享的選擇，例如原隻甜辣烤雞和烤乳豬等。

TEL. 2858 6066
GF, 100 Third Street, Sai Ying Pun
西營盤第三街100號地下
www.kaum.com

■ PRICE 價錢
Lunch 午膳
set 套餐 $ 95-160
à la carte 點菜 $ 200-400
Weekend and Public Holiday set
週末及公眾假期套餐 $ 398
Dinner 晚膳
à la carte 點菜 $ 200-400

■ OPENING HOURS 營業時間
12:00-22:30 (L.O.)
Monday dinner 週一晚膳
18:00-22:30 (L.O.)

■ ANNUAL AND WEEKLY CLOSING 休息日期
Closed Monday lunch 週一午膳休息

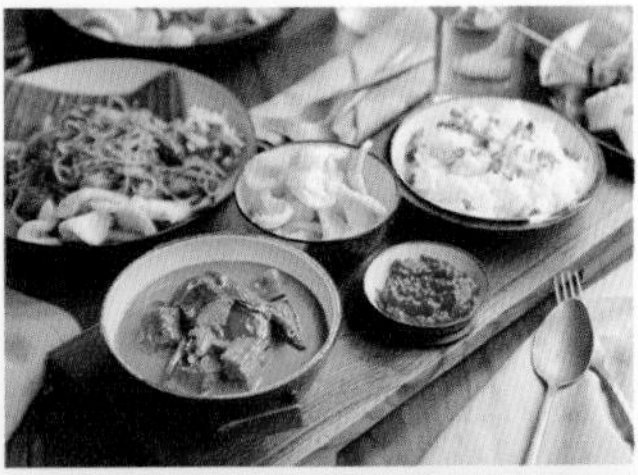

Kung Tak Lam (Causeway Bay)
功德林 (銅鑼灣)

24

Don't be alarmed to find 'chicken', 'pork' and 'seafood' on the menu of this vegan restaurant – they are all made with soy. The food is based on Shanghainese cooking, minus the fattening sauces, and is easy on the salt and oil; the creations have punchy flavours and are exquisitely presented. Items such as dim sum and traditional stir-fries have been added to the menu recently. A set lunch is available in individual portions.

菜單上出現豬、雞、海鮮等菜式，乍看與一般餐廳無異，但其實全是以大豆製品烹調的素菜。店家以傳統上海菜作藍本，配合少鹽少油的烹調方法，製作出的素食菜式健康與風味兼備，且外型賣相精緻。菜單種類愈來愈多樣化，近年加入多款點心和懷舊小菜，午市更設一人套餐。裝潢以翠綠配米白色系，予人清新自然之感。

TEL. 2881 9966
10F, World Trade Centre,
280 Gloucester Road, Causeway Bay
銅鑼灣告士打道 280號世貿中心 10樓

■ PRICE 價錢
Lunch 午膳
set 套餐 $ 88
à la carte 點菜 $ 150-250
Dinner 晚膳
à la carte 點菜 $ 250-500

■ OPENING HOURS 營業時間
11:00-22:30 (L.O.)

Kwan Kee Bamboo Noodles (Cheung Sha Wan)
坤記竹昇麵 (長沙灣)

It's inside a local market but easy to spot, thanks to the big yellow sign. Watch the kitchen at work through the glass wall as egg noodles are made the traditional way – with the chef seesawing on a bamboo pole to painstakingly knead the dough for that stringy texture. Don't miss the signature noodles tossed in shrimp roe and oyster sauce. Try replicating it all at home by buying their pre-packaged noodles, dried shrimp roe and ground dried plaice.

秉承店東在廣州的家族麵店做法，麵條全在工房經人手以傳統竹竿壓法每日新鮮打製，配方含大量雞蛋和少量鹼水，製成的麵條彈牙爽口，啖啖蛋香卻無鹼水味，配以自製的大地魚湯和蝦籽更是滋味；萬勿錯過招牌蝦籽蠔油撈麵。店家另有出售樽裝蝦籽、大地魚粉、秘製XO醬及盒裝竹昇蛋麵。

TEL. 3484 9126
Shop E, 1 Wing Lung Street,
Cheung Sha Wan
長沙灣永隆街 1號 E鋪
www.kknoodles.com

■ PRICE 價錢
à la carte 點菜 $ 50-70

■ OPENING HOURS 營業時間
10:00-22:45 (L.O.)

CANTONESE 粵菜 MAP 地圖 23/C-1

Kwan Kee Clay Pot Rice (Queen's Road West)
坤記煲仔小菜 (皇后大道西)

Its gigantic red sign, typical greasy spoon style interior and traditional stir-fries all point to an authentic Hong Kong culinary experience. Clay pot rice is only served at night and features a three-rice blend enrobed in the oil brushed on the bottom of the pot. The rice is chewy and fragrant, with a crispy crust at the bottom perfectly scorched from the right amount of heat and time. Their signature white eel clay pot rice is the top choice.

親切而熟悉的飯店大門帶着滿滿的地道香港風味，飯店供應的是傳統港式小炒，晚上亦可點選煲仔小菜及煲仔飯。其馳名煲仔飯用上了三種米混合而成，均勻地塗在瓦煲底的油滲透於飯內，米飯吃起來特別香滑軟糯；控制得宜的時間與火候令飯焦變得十分香脆。不妨一試其招牌白鱔飯。

TEL. 2803 7209
Shop 1, GF, Wo Yick Mansion,
263 Queen's Road West, Sai Ying Pun
西營盤皇后大道西 263號和益大廈地下
1號舖

■ PRICE 價錢
Lunch 午膳
à la carte 點菜 $ 40-80
Dinner 晚膳
à la carte 點菜 $ 80-120

■ OPENING HOURS 營業時間
Lunch 午膳 11:00-14:30 (L.O.)
Dinner 晚膳 18:00-23:00 (L.O.)

■ ANNUAL AND WEEKLY CLOSING 休息日期
Closed 7 days Lunar New Year and Sunday lunch 農曆新年 7 天及週日午膳休息

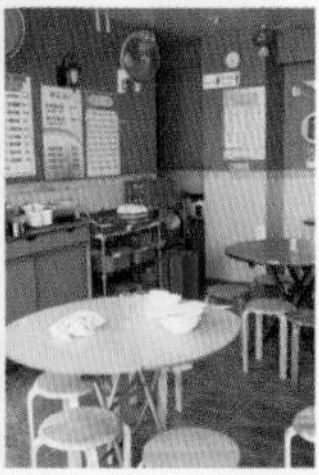

La Bombance

12

La Bombance is celebrated in Tokyo for its creative 'new Japanese cuisine' and opened its first overseas branch here at V Point in 2016. Dinner sees two monthly-changing, 6- or 8-course kaiseki menus – although there are more menu options at lunch. Nearly all the produce is flown in from Japan but don't be surprised to see certain ingredients more associated with French cuisine, like foie gras, as well as some French cooking techniques.

東京La Bombance首家海外分店。以和風裝潢的餐室內最顯眼的是中央的長木餐桌，座位皆面向窗外動人的維港景色。餐廳以日本直送的時令食材奉客，菜式走日法融和路線，晚膳只供應六或八道菜的套餐；午膳除了壽司、魚生及和牛套餐，也可預訂迷你懷石料理套餐。餐單每月更新，供應多款清酒和葡萄酒。

TEL. 3188 3326
30F, V Point, 18 Tang Lung Street, Causeway Bay
銅鑼灣登龍街18號V Point 30樓
www.labombance.com.hk

SPECIALITIES TO PRE-ORDER 預訂食物
Lunch mini kaiseki 午膳迷你懷石料理套餐

■ PRICE 價錢
Lunch 午膳
set 套餐 $ 260-680
Dinner 晚膳
set 套餐 $ 880-1,280

■ OPENING HOURS 營業時間
Lunch 午膳 12:00-14:00 (L.O.)
Dinner 晚膳 18:00-21:30 (L.O.)

■ ANNUAL AND WEEKLY CLOSING 休息日期
Closed 1 day Lunar New Year
農曆新年休息1天

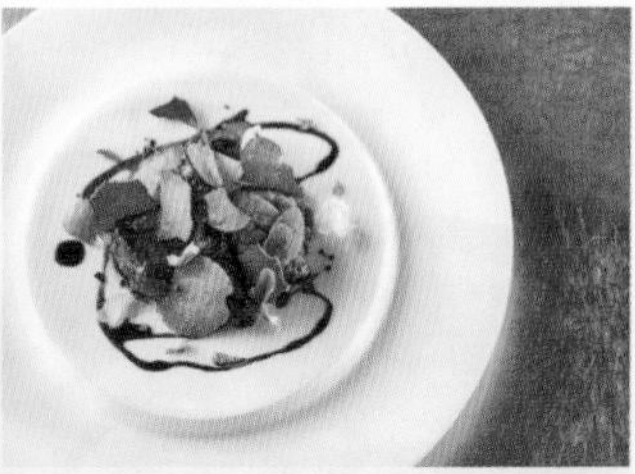

Lan Yuen Chee Koon
蘭苑饎館

The Chan's first place opened back in '84; they moved here in '98 to premises with a proper kitchen and now offer Cantonese claypots, healthy home-style steamed dishes, noodles and deliciously sweet puddings. Fine Chinese furniture is a feature of the small dining room, where Mrs Chan does the cooking and her husband the serving. The set menus at dinner prove particularly popular so be prepared to queue outside. It only serves dessert on Mondays.

陳氏夫婦於1984年創辦這家食館，並於1998年遷到有正規廚房的現址；廚房由陳太掌舵，陳先生則負責招呼客人。菜單上有各種粵式煲仔菜、健康家常蒸煮菜式、麵食、糕點和糖水；晚飯時間的套餐特別受歡迎，亦有不少客人到來一嘗具保健功效的龜苓膠。週一則只供應甜品。

TEL. 2381 1369
318 Sai Yeung Choi Street North,
Prince Edward
太子西洋菜北街 318號

■ PRICE 價錢
set 套餐 $ 90-108
à la carte 點菜 $ 100-150

■ OPENING HOURS 營業時間
12:00-22:00 (L.O.)
Monday 週一 12:00-20:30 (L.O.)
Sunday 週日 12:00-21:30 (L.O.)

■ ANNUAL AND WEEKLY CLOSING 休息日期
Closed 9 days Lunar New Year and Chinese festivals 農曆新年 9 天及中國節日休息

FRENCH CONTEMPORARY 時尚法國菜 MAP 地圖 25/D-3

L'Atelier de Joël Robuchon

8

If you want to feel part of the action sit at the counter; if you prefer a more intimate setting then ask for a table in Le Jardin. The signature red and black décor, along with the living garden wall, have become as much a signature in a Joël Robuchon restaurant as the cooking. The contemporary French cuisine is executed to the highest level, using ingredients which are the best available. Expect professional service to match.

乘搭專屬電梯或升降機皆可到達這餐廳。如欲充分感受餐室的氣氛與節奏，開放式廚房前的櫃枱座位無疑是最佳位置；屬意較親密的環境則不妨要求能看到露台的座位。標誌性的紅黑裝潢代表着處理精細的時尚法國菜餚將輪流登場，不論用料或烹調技巧皆無懈可擊，專業的服務令用餐經驗更稱心滿意。

TEL. 2166 9000
Shop 401, 4F, The Landmark,
15 Queen's Road Central, Central
中環皇后大道中 15號置地廣場 4樓
401號舖
www.robuchon.hk

■ PRICE 價錢
Lunch 午膳
set 套餐 $ 598-2,080
à la carte 點菜 $ 1,150-1,770
Dinner 晚膳
set 套餐 $ 2,080
à la carte 點菜 $ 1,150-1,770

■ OPENING HOURS 營業時間
Lunch 午膳 12:00-14:30 (L.O.)
Dinner 晚膳 18:30-22:30 (L.O.)

Lau Sum Kee (Fuk Wing Street)

劉森記麵家 (福榮街)

Since 1956, this branch (and the original shop around the corner) has been packed with customers buzzing in and out. The third-generation family business still kneads noodle dough with a bamboo pole like it used to be done. Wontons are made on the spot with whole prawns and pork and even the crunchy radish pickles on the table are homemade. Recommendations include wonton noodles, and tossed noodles with dry shrimp roe or pork knuckle.

始創於1956年，此家族經營的麵店已傳至第三代。這分店與轉角位的總店位於麵店林立的街道上，店內依然人頭湧湧，質素自是不言而喻。店家所有竹昇麵及雲吞均在店內新鮮人手製造，雲吞包入原隻鮮蝦及豬肉，飽滿爽口。推薦雲吞麵、蝦籽撈麵及豬手撈麵。餐桌上的自製醃蘿蔔爽脆美味，亦不可不試。

TEL. 2386 3583
82 Fuk Wing Street, Sham Shui Po
深水埗福榮街 82號

■ PRICE 價錢
à la carte 點菜 $ 30-50

■ OPENING HOURS 營業時間
12:00-22:00 (L.O.)

■ ANNUAL AND WEEKLY CLOSING 休息日期
Closed 3 days Lunar New Year
農曆新年休息 3 天

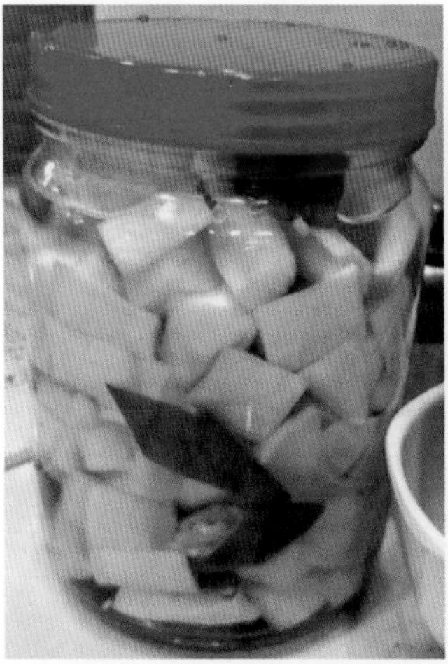

Le Garçon Saigon N

The head chef used to be a sous chef at Ho Lee Fook, where chefs also take turns to cook for the staff, and his Vietnamese cuisine was especially popular. Later on, the owner opened this brasserie-style Vietnamese grill house and asked him to run the kitchen. On the menu, DIY rice paper rolls stand out, where guests have to wrap their own rolls. You'll also find a selection of French wines, Vietnamese beers and coffee.

主廚因製作員工膳食廣受好評而得到老闆賞識，獲邀主理此越南餐廳。可別以為會吃到越式湯粉，糅合了奧地利元素的越南燒烤才是主角。特色菜有DIY米紙卷，食客需動手將材料用米紙捲好享用；佐餐飲料包括越南咖啡、法國餐酒及兩地的啤酒。設計兼具法國及越南風格，牆身模仿越南街頭寫上食物名稱及價錢，饒有特色。

TEL. 2455 2499
GF, 12-18 Wing Fung Street, Wan Chai
灣仔永豐街12-18號地下
www.legarconsaigon.com

■ PRICE 價錢
Lunch 午膳
Monday to Friday set
週一至週五套餐 $ 198
à la carte 點菜 $ 200-300
Dinner 晚膳
à la carte 點菜 $ 300-400

■ OPENING HOURS 營業時間
Lunch 午膳 12:00-14:30 (L.O.)
Saturday lunch 週六午膳 12:00-15:00 (L.O.)
Dinner 晚膳 18:00-22:45 (L.O.)
Sunday 週日 12:00-21:00 (L.O.)

Le Souk

Le Souk brings a little exotic spice to the streets of SoHo and is owned by two friendly and hospitable Egyptian brothers who make time to ensure that everyone is having a good time. Trinkets, jewels and lanterns add plenty of colour to the intimate room, while the kitchen prepares Moroccon and Middle Eastern cuisine with care and attention. Tender and aromatic lamb tagine is a standout dish, as is the roasted fig salad.

由兩位友善好客的埃及兄弟開設的Le Souk坐落於蘇豪內，為區內帶來一點獨特的中東味道。餐廳內的空間以色彩繽紛的小飾物、珠寶和燈籠點綴；大廚則在廚房精心烹調摩洛哥和中東美食。嫩滑又香氣洋溢的羊肉煲是出色之作，香燒無花果沙律亦不可錯過。

TEL. 2522 2128
4 Staunton Street, Central
中環士丹頓街 4號

■ PRICE 價錢
Dinner 晚膳
à la carte 點菜 $ 200-400

■ OPENING HOURS 營業時間
Dinner 晚膳 17:00-23:30 (L.O.)

Lei Garden (Central)
利苑酒家 (中環)

16

Forward planning is advisable here – not only when booking but also when selecting certain roast meat dishes and some of their famous double-boiled soups which require advance notice. The extensive menu features specialist seafood dishes and the lunchtime favourites include shrimp and flaky pastries filled with shredded turnip. All this is served up by an efficient team, in clean, contemporary surroundings.

這間利苑分店於2018年剛完成翻新，採用了白色雲石的牆身予餐室潔淨明亮的外觀。菜單上可找到種類繁多的粵菜，其中以海鮮炮製的佳餚最具特色，午市時段的巧製點心如銀蘿千層酥值得一試。燒味和燉湯尤受歡迎，須提早預訂。一如其他分店，這裏常常座無虛席，建議訂座。

TEL. 2295 0238
Shop 3008-3011, 3F, IFC Mall,
1 Harbour View Street, Central
中環港景街1號國際金融中心商場3樓
3008-3011號舖
www.leigarden.com.hk

SPECIALITIES TO PRE-ORDER 預訂食物
Dried abalone in oyster sauce 蠔皇乾鮑 / Baked chicken with sea salt in casserole 古仿鹽甗雞

■ PRICE 價錢
Lunch 午膳
à la carte 點菜 $ 150-300
Dinner 晚膳
à la carte 點菜 $ 200-600

■ OPENING HOURS 營業時間
Lunch 午膳 11:30-14:30 (L.O.)
Dinner 晚膳 18:00-22:30 (L.O.)

■ ANNUAL AND WEEKLY CLOSING 休息日期
Closed 3 days Lunar New Year
農曆新年休息3天

Lei Garden (Kowloon Bay)
利苑酒家 (九龍灣)

P 40

The health conscious can pre-order any of the 10 different double-boiled tonic soups in advance. Other specialities include crispy roast pork, sautéed scallops with macadamia nuts and yellow fungus, and braised boneless spare-ribs with sweet and sour sauce. Reservations are recommended at lunch; if you vacate your table by 12:45pm you get a discount. This branch is conveniently located near an MTR station and boasts thoughtful, friendly service.

這家利苑分店鄰近地鐵站，地理位置佔優，服務也相當周到。招牌菜包括米網黃耳夏果炒帶子、宮庭醬烤骨，和多款須提前預訂的燉湯；大受歡迎的冰燒三層肉亦建議預訂。餐廳為中午12:45前離席的顧客提供折扣優惠；午膳時段人流眾多，若未有提前訂座可能會掃興。

TEL. 2331 3306
Shop F2, Telford Plaza 1,
33 Wai Yip Street, Kowloon Bay
九龍灣偉業街33號德福廣場一期F2號舖
www.leigarden.com.hk

SPECIALITIES TO PRE-ORDER 預訂食物
Dried abalone in oyster sauce 蠔皇乾鮑 / Braised whole fish maw 蠔皇香扣原隻鱉肚公 / Braised goose web with Kanto spiky sea cucumber 關東遼參扣玉掌 / Baked chicken with sea salt in casserole 古仿鹽甑雞

■ PRICE 價錢
Lunch 午膳
à la carte 點菜 $ 100-400
Dinner 晚膳
à la carte 點菜 $ 150-750

■ OPENING HOURS 營業時間
Lunch 午膳 11:30-15:00 (L.O.)
Dinner 晚膳 18:00-23:00 (L.O.)

■ ANNUAL AND WEEKLY CLOSING 休息日期
Closed 3 days Lunar New Year
農曆新年休息 3 天

Lei Garden (Kwun Tong)
利苑酒家 (觀塘)

XX

P 20

The décor is similar to other branches and the atmosphere is just as frantic, even though it is partitioned into different seating areas. The menu is also the same – Cantonese fare reliably cooked with fresh ingredients. On top of the main menu, specials change daily and feature prime ingredients such as king crab and giant lobster served in smaller portions for smaller parties.

如你曾光顧利苑集團的其他分店，對此店絕不會感到陌生，這裏同樣可找到可靠的廣東美食及新鮮的材料，當然也同樣擠滿集團的忠實顧客。餐廳特別設計了每天不同的特色菜單，選用諸如阿拉斯加蟹等大型生猛海鮮分拆饗客，不妨與三兩知己共享。簡潔的屏風巧妙地將餐廳分隔成不同用餐區域。

TEL. 2365 3238
L5-8, 5F, apm, Millennium City 5,
418 Kwun Tong Road, Kwun Tong
觀塘觀塘道 418號創紀之城第 5期
apm 5樓 L5-8
www.leigarden.com.hk

SPECIALITIES TO PRE-ORDER 預訂食物
Dried abalone in oyster sauce 蠔皇乾鮑 / Braised whole fish maw 蠔皇香扣原隻鮝肚 / Braised goose web with Kanto spiky sea cucumber 關東遼參扣玉掌 / Baked chicken with sea salt in casserole 古仿鹽甑雞

■ PRICE 價錢
Lunch 午膳
à la carte 點菜 $ 100-400
Dinner 晚膳
à la carte 點菜 $ 150-750

■ OPENING HOURS 營業時間
Lunch 午膳 11:30-15:00 (L.O.)
Dinner 晚膳 18:00-23:00 (L.O.)

■ ANNUAL AND WEEKLY CLOSING 休息日期
Closed 3 days Lunar New Year
農曆新年休息 3 天

Lei Garden (Mong Kok)
利苑酒家 (旺角)

30

This is the original Lei Garden, which opened back in the 1970s; it's still as busy as ever so it's always worth booking ahead. The contemporary restaurant is spread over two floors and the upper space has views out onto the busy street. The long and varied Cantonese menu certainly represents good value; recommendations include tonic soups like double-boiled teal with Cordyceps militaris and fish maw.

由於這家餐廳太受歡迎，食客必須預先訂座。此店是利苑總店，開業於七十年代。富時代感的餐廳共分為兩層，樓上可看到旺角繁華的街景。以廣東菜為主的菜單花樣多變令人目不暇給，絕對物有所值。特別推薦各式燉品如蛹蟲草鬚燉花膠水鴨。

TEL. 2392 5184
121 Sai Yee Street, Mong Kok
旺角洗衣街 121號
www.leigarden.com.hk

SPECIALITIES TO PRE-ORDER 預訂食物
Dried abalone in oyster sauce 蠔皇乾鮑 / Braised whole fish maw 蠔皇香扣原隻鰵肚公 / Baked chicken with sea salt in casserole 古仿鹽甑雞

■ PRICE 價錢
Lunch 午膳
à la carte 點菜 $ 150-500
Dinner 晚膳
à la carte 點菜 $ 300-850

■ OPENING HOURS 營業時間
Lunch 午膳 11:30-15:00 (L.O.)
Dinner 晚膳 18:00-22:30 (L.O.)

■ ANNUAL AND WEEKLY CLOSING 休息日期
Closed 3 days Lunar New Year
農曆新年休息 3 天

Lei Garden (North Point)
利苑酒家 (北角)

16

Discreetly tucked away on the first floor of a residential block and overlooking a pleasant courtyard garden is this branch of the popular chain. Things here can certainly get quite frenetic as it accommodates up to 200 people. The lengthy Cantonese menu mirrors what's available at other branches, but particular dishes worth noting here are the double-boiled soups and the daily seafood specialities.

這家深受歡迎的連鎖酒家分店，隱藏在住宅大廈一樓。從酒家外望是屋苑的翠綠庭園，寬敞的空間可容納多達二百人，氣氛往往極為熱鬧。這裏的菜單與其他利苑分店大致相同，除了各式燉湯之外，亦可嘗試每日海鮮精選。

TEL. 2806 0008
1F, Block 9-10, City Garden, North Point
北角城市花園 9-10座 1樓
www.leigarden.com.hk

SPECIALITIES TO PRE-ORDER 預訂食物
Dried abalone in oyster sauce 蠔皇乾鮑 / Braised whole fish maw 蠔皇香扣原隻鰵肚公 / Braised goose web with Kanto spiky sea cucumber 關東遼參扣玉掌 / Baked chicken with sea salt in casserole 古仿鹽甑雞

■ PRICE 價錢
Lunch 午膳
à la carte 點菜 $ 80-200
Dinner 晚膳
à la carte 點菜 $ 150-750

■ OPENING HOURS 營業時間
Lunch 午膳 11:30-14:30 (L.O.)
Dinner 晚膳 18:00-22:30 (L.O.)

■ ANNUAL AND WEEKLY CLOSING 休息日期
Closed 3 days Lunar New Year
農曆新年休息 3 天

Lei Garden (Sha Tin)
利苑酒家 (沙田)

P 60

Regular refurbishment has kept this 20-year-old branch feeling fresh. It's set in a shopping mall connected to an MTR station and gets busy at weekends when everyone needs refuelling after a day of shopping. The menu is basically the same as other branches; always ask for the catch of the day. Peking duck, char siu, and rice in seafood soup made with lobster, prawns and crabs are also great options. Reservations are recommended at lunch time.

屹立沙田逾二十年，這家利苑分店憑着精心烹調的正宗粵菜及舒適的室內環境，成為區內居民的熱門聚腳點，午市建議訂座。大受歡迎的海鮮湯泡飯選用龍蝦、蝦及蟹等多款海鮮做湯底，每啖都充溢濃郁海鮮味道。其他熱門菜式包括當日推介海鮮、片皮鴨、叉燒及老火湯，建議於訂座時一併預訂。

TEL. 2698 9111
Shop 628, 6F, Phase I, New Town Plaza, Sha Tin
沙田新城市廣場第1期6樓628號舖
www.leigarden.com.hk

SPECIALITIES TO PRE-ORDER 預訂食物
Dried abalone in oyster sauce 蠔皇乾鮑 / Braised whole fish maw 蠔皇香扣原隻鱉肚公 / Braised goose web with Kanto spiky sea cucumber 關東遼參扣玉掌 / Baked chicken with sea salt in casserole 古仿鹽甑雞

■ PRICE 價錢
Lunch 午膳
à la carte 點菜 $ 100-750
Dinner 晚膳
à la carte 點菜 $ 150-750

■ OPENING HOURS 營業時間
Lunch 午膳 11:30-14:45 (L.O.)
Dinner 晚膳 18:00-23:00 (L.O.)

■ ANNUAL AND WEEKLY CLOSING 休息日期
Closed 3 days Lunar New Year
農曆新年休息 3 天

Lei Garden (Wan Chai)
利苑酒家 (灣仔)

18

An inventory of restaurants in Wan Chai wouldn't be complete without a Lei Garden. This branch is bigger than most and boasts a busy, bustling atmosphere, particularly at lunchtime. It follows the group's tried-and-tested formula by offering an extensive menu of dishes with luxurious dishes alongside less elaborate but classic Cantonese specialities. Seafood enthusiasts should consider pre-ordering the Alaskan king crab or Brittany blue lobster.

論灣仔區的出色食肆，當然少不了利苑的份兒。菜單包含珍饈百味與經典粵式小菜，種類繁多，加上巧手精製的點心和便利的地點，難怪總是座無虛席。食客可於訂位時跟店方預訂特別海鮮如亞拉斯加蟹和法國藍龍蝦等。

TEL. 2892 0333
1F, CNT Tower, 338 Hennessy Road,
Wan Chai
灣仔軒尼詩道 338號北海中心 1樓
www.leigarden.com.hk

SPECIALITIES TO PRE-ORDER 預訂食物
Dried abalone in oyster sauce 蠔皇乾鮑 / Braised whole fish maw 蠔皇香扣原隻鰵肚公 / Braised goose web with Kanto spiky sea cucumber 關東遼參扣玉掌 / Baked chicken with sea salt in casserole 古仿鹽甑雞

■ PRICE 價錢
Lunch 午膳
à la carte 點菜 $ 150-600
Dinner 晚膳
à la carte 點菜 $ 200-800

■ OPENING HOURS 營業時間
Lunch 午膳 11:30-15:00 (L.O.)
Dinner 晚膳 18:00-22:30 (L.O.)

■ ANNUAL AND WEEKLY CLOSING 休息日期
Closed 3 days Lunar New Year
農曆新年休息 3 天

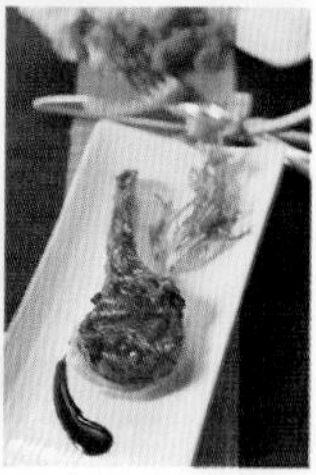

Lin Heung Kui
蓮香居

This huge two-floor eatery opened in 2009 with the aim of building on the success of the famous Lin Heung Tea House in Wellington Street. It's modest inside but hugely popular and the dim sum trolley is a must, with customers keen to be the first to choose from its extensive offerings. The main menu offers classic Cantonese dishes with specialities such as Lin Heung special duck. Don't miss the limited offered pig lungs soup with almond juice. The pastry shop below is worth a look on the way out.

蓮香居於2009年開業，樓高兩層，延續威靈頓街蓮香樓的輝煌成績。樸素的內部裝潢掩不住鼎沸的人氣，以傳統點心車盛載着各式各樣經典點心，讓人急不及待從中選擇心頭好，限量供應的川貝杏汁白肺湯不能錯過。菜單上羅列了傳統廣東菜及懷舊小菜，如蓮香霸王鴨。離開時不妨逛逛樓下的中式餅店。

TEL. 2156 9328
2-3F, 40-50 Des Voeux Road West,
Sheung Wan
上環德輔道西 40-50號 2-3樓

SPECIALITIES TO PRE-ORDER 預訂食物
Lin Heung special duck 蓮香霸王鴨 / Roast suckling pig 乳豬 / Three-treasure soup 三寶湯

■ PRICE 價錢
Lunch 午膳
à la carte 點菜 $ 60-150
Dinner 晚膳
à la carte 點菜 $ 100-400

■ OPENING HOURS 營業時間
06:00-22:00 (L.O.)

Liu Yuan Pavilion
留園雅敘

XX

24

Authentic Shanghainese specialities served in a room where you'll hear plenty of Shanghainese speakers really will make you think you're in Shanghai. You shouldn't miss the stir-fried shrimps, braised meatballs with vegetables and braised pig knuckle. The braised abalone with pork belly is worth pre-ordering. The renovation in 2018 has given the restaurant a look of understated elegance; the booths are the prized seats.

開業多年的留園雅敘擁有不少忠心顧客，當中不乏一眾老上海，侍應亦會親切地以流利上海話為客人點菜。菜單上可找到各式正宗滬菜，不論是清炒蝦仁、松子桂魚或紅燒元蹄等經典小菜，還是需預訂的鮑魚紅燒肉和小米刺參雞湯均值得一試。餐廳於2018年完成翻新，環境素淨優雅，靠窗的卡座尤為舒適。

TEL. 2804 2000
3F, The Broadway,
54-62 Lockhart Road, Wan Chai
灣仔駱克道 54-62號博匯大廈 3樓

SPECIALITIES TO PRE-ORDER 預訂食物
Smoked pomfret with tea leaves 煙燻鯧魚 / Braised abalone with pork belly 鮑魚紅燒肉 / Sea cucumber and chicken soup 小米刺參雞湯

■ PRICE 價錢
Lunch 午膳
à la carte 點菜 $ 200-250
Dinner 晚膳
à la carte 點菜 $ 250-750

■ OPENING HOURS 營業時間
Lunch 午膳 12:00-14:30 (L.O.)
Dinner 晚膳 18:00-22:30 (L.O.)

■ ANNUAL AND WEEKLY CLOSING 休息日期
Closed 3 days Lunar New Year
農曆新年休息 3 天

Loaf On
六福菜館

70

It may not have the large displays of seafood that its promenade rivals boast but this restaurant stands out because of its cooking. Wonderfully fresh seafood is prepared using traditional home recipes that let the quality of the ingredients speak for themselves. Must-try dishes include fish soup, mantis shrimp with chilli and garlic and their steamed fish with sea salt. Traditional Cantonese dishes are also done well, like deep-fried tofu.

這家小菜館佔地三層，藏身於西貢海鮮餐廳一帶後街，門口並未見一般海鮮餐館常設的大魚缸，僅以出色的烹調技巧便吸引了不少食客。以生猛海鮮炮製的小菜選料高質，每一口都散發着鮮味。魚湯、椒鹽瀨尿蝦和鹽水蒸西貢魚仔是必吃菜式，傳統粵式小菜如椒鹽奇脆豆腐也值得一試。

TEL. 2792 9966
49 See Cheung Street, Sai Kung
西貢市場街 49號

SPECIALITIES TO PRE-ORDER 預訂食物
Crispy skin chicken 脆皮風沙雞 / Fish soup with potatoes and tomatoes 西貢地道魚湯 / Minced fish in pumpkin soup 金湯魚蓉羹 / Grilled chicken mixed with grapefruit 六福柚子雞

■ PRICE 價錢
à la carte 點菜 $ 200-500

■ OPENING HOURS 營業時間
11:00-22:30 (L.O.)

■ ANNUAL AND WEEKLY CLOSING 休息日期
Closed 2 days Lunar New Year
農曆新年休息 2 天

Locanda dell' Angelo Ⓝ

Tucked away on a quiet lane, this 28-seater restaurant boasts a clean modern look and a homely feel. The owner-chef has nearly 30 years of experience and grew up on the island of Sicily, hence the ocean-themed logo and seafood-biased menu. The 5-course tasting menu showcases some culinary highlights, such as risotto 'Acquerello' with sea urchin, and linguine 'Mancini' with Boston lobster. It's only open for dinner and reservations are advised.

生於西西里島的主廚曾於世界各地餐廳工作，最後選擇於跑馬地一條寧靜街道上開設名下餐廳。他採用源自本地、西班牙及法國的海鮮及西西里島的乾貨製作正宗意大利菜。拿手之作包括北海道海膽意大利飯；以及用全隻波士頓龍蝦製成且限量供應的龍蝦濃湯扁意粉。五道菜的品嘗菜單可體驗主廚的招牌菜。座位不多，建議訂座。

TEL. 3709 2788
12 Yuen Yuen Street, Happy Valley
跑馬地源遠街12號

SPECIALITIES TO PRE-ORDER 預訂食物
Linguine "Mancini" with Boston lobster, bisque and fresh tarragon 龍蝦濃湯扁意粉

■ PRICE 價錢
Dinner 晚膳
set 套餐 $1,080
à la carte 點菜 $550-1,100

■ OPENING HOURS 營業時間
Dinner 晚膳 18:30-22:30 (L.O.)

■ ANNUAL AND WEEKLY CLOSING 休息日期
Closed 4 days Lunar New Year and Monday
農曆新年 4 天及週一休息

Lucky Indonesia
好運印尼餐廳

One's first impression of this small dining room, with its wooden furniture and traditional wall hangings, is that it's a little dated, but you'll soon feel as though you have been transported to the Indonesian countryside. The Middle Java cuisine is not unlike the décor – there's no fancy presentation, just authentic and tasty flavours. Satay is charcoal roasted which creates a lovely aroma; also try the Nasi Kuming and Mee Goreng.

細小的用膳區、木製的傢具及傳統的掛牆吊飾，室內裝潢予人點點懷舊感覺，令食客感到身處印尼郊區。一如其裝潢，此店的食物不賣弄花巧，只用真材實料炮製出正宗美味的爪哇中部菜式。炭燒沙嗲烤肉風味特別，而印尼黃薑飯和印尼炒麵更不容錯過。

TEL. 2389 3545
46 Tung Ming Street, Kwun Tong
觀塘通明街 46號

■ PRICE 價錢
à la carte 點菜 $ 55-85

■ OPENING HOURS 營業時間
11:00-21:00 (L.O.)

■ ANNUAL AND WEEKLY CLOSING 休息日期
Closed 10 days Lunar New Year
農曆新年休息 10 天

Luk Yu Tea House
陸羽茶室

14

Large numbers of both regulars and tourists come to Luk Yu Tea House for the traditionally prepared and flavoursome dim sum, and its three floors fill up quickly. The animated atmosphere and subtle colonial decoration are appealing but no one really stays too long; the serving team in white jackets have seen it all before and go about their work with alacrity. Popular dishes are fried prawns on toast and fried noodles with sliced beef.

陸羽茶室以傳統方法製作的美味點心，不光招徠本地常客，更令不少外地遊客慕名而至，所以樓高三層的茶室經常滿座。生氣盎然的環境和帶點殖民地色彩的裝潢別具特色，穿着白色外套的侍應敏捷而專注地工作。除點心外，其他菜式如鍋貼蝦及乾炒牛河也值得一試。

TEL. 2523 5464
24-26 Stanley Street, Central
中環士丹利街 24-26號

■ PRICE 價錢
Lunch 午膳
à la carte 點菜 $ 200-300
Dinner 晚膳
à la carte 點菜 $400-600

■ OPENING HOURS 營業時間
07:00-21:30 (L.O.)

■ ANNUAL AND WEEKLY CLOSING 休息日期
Closed 4 days Lunar New Year
農曆新年休息 4 天

Lung King Heen
龍景軒

12

For many, the roast Peking duck alone is reason enough to dine here. However, Chef Chan Yan Tak is a master of Cantonese cuisine and his repertoire is extensive, so consider ordering the Chef's Tasting Menu; wok-fried wagyu with morels and peppers and simmered lobster in crystal sauce are just two specialities. Superb ingredients, flawless cooking and tantalizing flavour combinations are his hallmarks. Ask for a window table for harbour views.

行政總廚陳恩德的一道北京片皮烤鴨廣受稱頌，然而其經典名菜豈止於此？頂級優質食材、無可挑剔的烹調手法、配搭得天衣無縫的味道，盡皆是其菜式標記。羊肚菌爆澳洲特級和牛柳粒、上海焗龍蝦球只是其匠心之作中的少數，品嘗菜單將是體驗主廚手藝的最佳選擇。美食當前，即使面朝維港絕景大概也無暇細賞。

TEL. 3196 8880
4F, Four Seasons Hotel,
8 Finance Street, Central
中環金融街 8號四季酒店 4樓
www.fourseasons.com/hongkong

■ PRICE 價錢
Lunch 午膳
set 套餐 $ 640-1,650
à la carte 點菜 $ 600-2,400

Dinner 晚膳
set 套餐 $ 1,980-2,980
à la carte 點菜 $ 600-2,400

■ OPENING HOURS 營業時間
Lunch 午膳 12:00-14:30 (L.O.)
Weekend and Public Holiday lunch
週末及公眾假期午膳 11:30-15:00 (L.O.)
Dinner 晚膳 18:30-22:00 (L.O.)

Mak Man Kee
麥文記

No one is here for the no-frills interior, typical of any noodle shop in Hong Kong. This 60-year-old establishment is all about Cantonese wonton soup noodles – firm and bouncy prawns, visible through the paper-thin translucent skin, with springy duck egg noodles swimming in a flavourful broth. The serving size isn't the most filling so you may want to order their pork knuckles braised in red taro curd on the side.

麵店已有六十年歷史，裝潢簡單樸素，是典型港式麵食店的陳設。鮮蝦雲吞是這兒最具人氣的食物，薄薄的雲吞皮內包着的就只有滿滿的蝦肉，用料十足，吃起來很爽口。南乳豬手同樣是必吃之選。店家用的生麵並非用雞蛋而是鴨蛋製作，蛋味香而麵質爽彈。

TEL. 2736 5561
51 Parkes Street, Jordan
佐敦白加士街 51號
www.mmk.hk

■ PRICE 價錢
à la carte 點菜 $50-100

■ OPENING HOURS 營業時間
12:00-00:30 (L.O.)

Man Wah
文華廳

Birdcage-inspired lamps, ornate silk paintings and rosewood panels complement each other in this striking dining room. Elegant but bustling at the same time, it is always full whatever the time of day. A new chef has helmed the kitchen since 2018 and his emphasis on precision, finesse and robust flavours are reflected in his dim sum, barbecue meats and stir-fries. Specialities include abalone and chicken with sand ginger in a clay pot.

一盞盞仿鳥籠中式吊燈、牆上古色古香的絲綢畫，與紫檀木的運用為文華廳帶來了雅致的古中國情調。不論午市或晚市，餐廳均座無虛席，氣氛熱鬧卻不失高雅。廚師團隊稍有變更，但各道菜式依然經過精細處理，不論點心、燒味或各款小菜，皆展露扎實的傳統粵菜烹調技巧，不妨一試紅燒鮮沙薑鮑魚雞煲。

TEL. 2825 4003
25F, Mandarin Oriental Hotel,
5 Connaught Road Central, Central
中環干諾道中 5號文華東方酒店 25樓
www.mandarinoriental.com/hongkong

■ PRICE 價錢
Lunch 午膳
set 套餐 $ 628-748
à la carte 點菜 $ 500-1,600
Dinner 晚膳
set 套餐 $ 1,488
à la carte 點菜 $ 500-1,600

■ OPENING HOURS 營業時間
Lunch 午膳 12:00-14:30 (L.O.)
Dinner 晚膳 18:30-22:00 (L.O.)

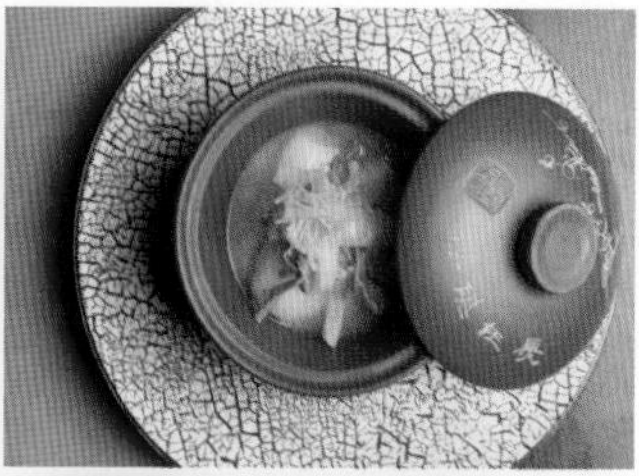

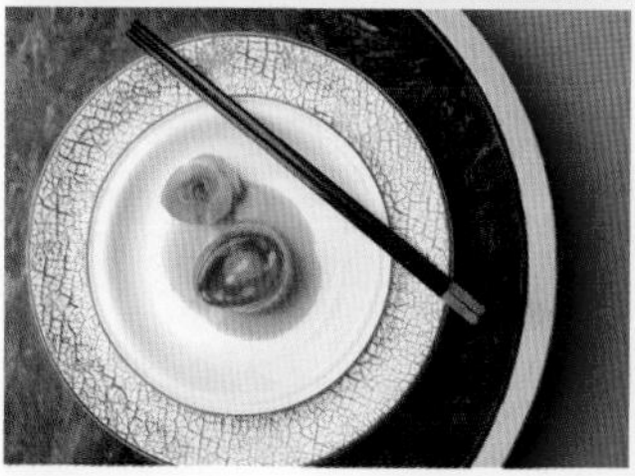

Mandarin Grill + Bar
文華扒房+酒吧

14

Grill restaurants are seldom seen these days, but it would seem very strange for the Mandarin Oriental not to have one. The sophisticated and stylish interior, designed by Sir Terence Conran, includes a feature glass fronted kitchen from where you can expect modern European cooking. It's not just the simpler cooked meat and fish that gets all the attention – starters and desserts show imagination and a lighter hand from the well-versed team.

這家典雅明亮的餐廳是著名室內設計師Sir Terence Conran的作品，注重舒適與休閒。廚房的玻璃窗設計讓你可看到廚房團隊用心烹調時的風姿。菜單上是一道道令人垂涎三尺的歐陸時尚菜式；除了多款烤製肉類和魚類外，頭盤和甜品也充分反映出廚房的創意和功架。

TEL. 2825 4004
1F, Mandarin Oriental Hotel,
5 Connaught Road Central, Central
中環干諾道中5號文華東方酒店1樓
www.mandarinoriental.com/hongkong

■ PRICE 價錢
Lunch 午膳
set 套餐 $ 588-688
à la carte 點菜 $ 930-2,100
Dinner 晚膳
à la carte 點菜 $ 930-2,100

■ OPENING HOURS 營業時間
Lunch 午膳 12:00-14:30 (L.O.)
Dinner 晚膳 18:30-22:00 (L.O.)

■ ANNUAL AND WEEKLY CLOSING 休息日期
Closed Saturday lunch 週六午膳休息

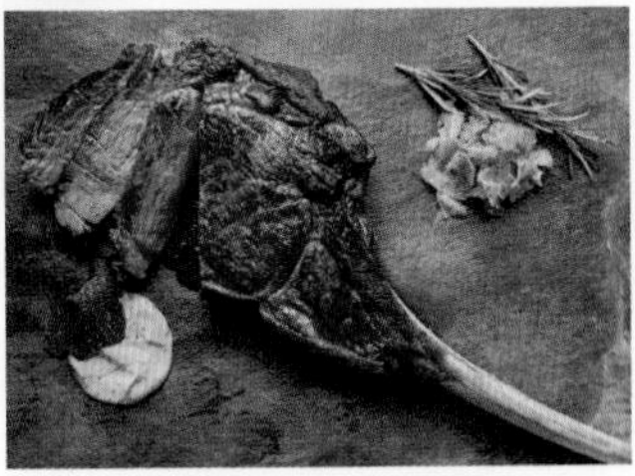

Megan's Kitchen
美味廚

32

Those who like a little privacy while they eat will appreciate the booth seating with sliding screens – the restaurant underwent a renovation in 2016. The choice of Cantonese dishes is considerable and includes specialities like steamed minced beef with dried mandarin peel – and all dishes come with complimentary rice, soup and dessert. The restaurant is also known for its hotpots, which are made with good quality ingredients.

在廣東菜和火鍋中難以選擇？美味廚讓你不再苦惱。這兒除了有各式廣東小菜如陳皮蒸手剁牛肉和美味煲仔飯外，火鍋亦同樣聞名，更有海鮮、和牛、不同口味的自製肉丸等火鍋配料。點選小菜奉送湯、白飯和甜品，經濟實惠。餐廳內的卡座設備齊全，拉下布幕即成私密度高的私人廂座。

TEL. 2866 8305
5F, Lucky Centre,
165-171 Wan Chai Road, Wan Chai
灣仔灣仔道 165-171號樂基中心 5樓
www.meganskitchen.com

■ PRICE 價錢
Lunch 午膳
set 套餐 $ 60-150
à la carte 點菜 $ 200-500
Dinner 晚膳
à la carte 點菜 $ 200-500

■ OPENING HOURS 營業時間
Lunch 午膳 12:00-14:30 (L.O.)
Dinner 晚膳 18:00-23:00 (L.O.)

Mic Kitchen

Helmed by a chef who formerly worked at Bo Innovation, the food here is a little more straightforward, but still provides expressive flavours, balanced textures and manifest Asian influences. Counter seats surround the open kitchen and encourage plenty of interaction. Ingredients are sourced from all over the world and only a set menu is offered. The restaurant moved here from its previous location in Kwun Tong.

從觀塘遷至中環，新址內高椅和櫃枱位置圍繞着開放式廚房，氣氛舒適友善，讓你能與廚師暢談交流，同時近距離欣賞烹調過程的每一個細節。餐廳採用源自世界各地的食材，糅合亞洲風味炮製成各種創意菜式，味道與口感均發揮得宜。套餐每季更換，常客如想轉換口味，可於訂座時作查詢。

TEL. 3758 2239
26F, Stanley 11, 11 Stanley Street, Central
中環士丹利街 11號 Stanley 11 26樓
www.mickitchen.com.hk

■ PRICE 價錢
Dinner 晚膳
set 套餐 $ 800-1,188

■ OPENING HOURS 營業時間
Dinner 晚膳 19:00-21:45 (L.O.)

■ ANNUAL AND WEEKLY CLOSING 休息日期
Closed 2 days Lunar New Year and Sunday
農曆新年 2 天及週日休息

Ming Court
明閣

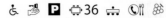

36

There are two distinct dining areas in this elegant Cantonese restaurant on the 6th floor of the Cordis hotel: if you want a cosy, more intimate setting ask for Ming Sun, with its collection of Ming Dynasty bronzes; if you're coming in a larger group go for Ming Moon. Drunken sea prawns with Shao Xing wine, and roasted crispy chicken are among the specialities. The impressive wine list includes suggested pairings for your barbecued meat or abalone.

位於康得思6樓、裝潢典雅的明閣分為兩個截然不同的餐室：擺設着青銅器、充滿古風的明日適合小型聚餐，一大班朋友相聚則可選擇裝潢較現代時髦的明月。此店提供多種餐酒，侍應還會協助顧客揀選適當佳釀配合菜餚佐吃。其招牌菜太白醉翁蝦、明閣炸子雞不容錯過。

TEL. 3552 3028
6F, Cordis Hotel, 555 Shanghai Street, Mong Kok
旺角上海街 555號康得思酒店 6樓
www.cordishotels.com/en/hong-kong

SPECIALITIES TO PRE-ORDER 預訂食物
Suckling pig, roasted 即燒化皮乳豬 /
Chef's soy sauce chicken 生浸豉油雞

■ PRICE 價錢
Lunch 午膳
set 套餐 $ 458-558
à la carte 點菜 $ 480-1,200
Dinner 晚膳
set 套餐 $ 1,088-1,288
à la carte 點菜 $ 480-1,200

■ OPENING HOURS 營業時間
Lunch 午膳 11:00-14:30 (L.O.)
Saturday lunch 週六午膳 11:00-15:00 (L.O.)
Sunday and Public Holiday lunch
週日及公眾假期午膳 10:30-15:00 (L.O.)
Dinner 晚膳 18:00-22:30 (L.O.)

New Punjab Club Ⓝ

This tandoor grill restaurant serving cuisine from Northern India is named after a social club founded during the British era – the owner's father is still a member. The décor is also reminiscent of that era with red leather banquettes and the owner's art collection. Lamb tomahawk is the signature dish on the menu, along with samosa chaat (crushed samosa with yoghurt and crispy noodles) and paneer kulcha (an Indian cheese).

這家餐廳供應北印度美食，嗜肉的饕客會找到眾多以Tandoor土窯爐烤製的菜式，咖喱則只屬配角。選用斧頭扒炮製的羊扒是招牌菜，以乳酪混和咖喱蓉及脆麵而成的咖喱角亦不俗；更有由印度進口的芝士。菜式分量較大，適合多人分享。紅色皮沙發及掛畫盡顯英式風格。建議網上訂座，須以信用卡確認。

TEL. 2368 1223
GF, World Wide Commercial Building,
34 Wyndham Street, Central
中環雲咸街34號世界商業大廈地下
www.newpunjabclub.com

■ PRICE 價錢
Lunch 午膳
à la carte 點菜 $ 300-400
Dinner 晚膳
à la carte 點菜 $ 600-800

■ OPENING HOURS 營業時間
Thursday and Friday lunch
週四及週五午膳 12:00-14:00 (L.O.)
Dinner 晚膳 18:00-22:30 (L.O.)
Wednesday to Saturday dinner
週三至週六晚膳 18:00-23:30 (L.O.)
Sunday dinner 週日晚膳
17:00-22:30 (L.O.)

New Shanghai
新滬坊

Glass walls and Chinese art add some strikingly contemporary flair as the dim sum chefs flaunt their skills in the open kitchen. The menu features light and healthy Shanghainese cooking that mixes the traditional with the innovative. Try their stir-fried barley with dried pork in a rice cracker cone and braised duck stuffed with glutinous rice. Fried pork knuckle in spiced salt is big enough for six people to share and needs to be pre-ordered.

位於會議展覽中心一樓的新滬坊，以精緻的中國藝術襯托玻璃牆設計，營造出時尚的風格。廚師在店中央的開放式廚房內為食客製作各式點心。菜單上的上海菜以輕盈健康為主，糅合傳統和創新意念，且每兩個月會推出時令菜式。馳名菜包括豐年藏珍寶和江南八寶鴨，而可供六位享用的椒鹽元蹄更值得一試，但必須預訂。

TEL. 2582 7332
1F, Hong Kong Convention and Exhibition Centre, 1 Harbour Road, Wan Chai
灣仔港灣道 1號香港會議展覽中心 1樓

SPECIALITIES TO PRE-ORDER 預訂食物
Braised duck stuffed with glutinous rice 江南八寶鴨 / Baked beggar chicken 宮庭富貴雞 / Steamed fresh shad 清蒸鰣魚 / Pork trotter in peppered salt 椒鹽元蹄

■ PRICE 價錢
Lunch 午膳
à la carte 點菜 $ 200-400
Dinner 晚膳
à la carte 點菜 $ 300-500

■ OPENING HOURS 營業時間
Lunch 午膳 12:00-15:00 (L.O.)
Dinner 晚膳 18:30-22:00 (L.O.)

■ ANNUAL AND WEEKLY CLOSING 休息日期
Closed 2 days Lunar New Year
農曆新年休息 2 天

The symbol 🍇 denotes a particularly interesting wine list.

🍇 這個標誌表示該餐廳提供一系列優質餐酒。

Enjoy good food without spending a fortune! Look out for the Bib Gourmand symbol ☺ to find restaurants offering good food at great prices!

既想省錢又想品嘗美食，便要留心注有這個 ☺ 車胎人標誌的餐廳，她們提供的是價錢實惠且高質素的美食。

Nishiki
錦

Despite opening over 20 years ago, the bustling atmosphere and tasty grill dishes of this izakaya-style place still shine. The Japanese owner-chef teaches his kitchen team the tricks for perfect barbeque – his famous tsukune, for example, is made with boneless chicken thigh from Japan and Brazil in a specific ratio. Grilled chicken liver from local farms is another speciality. Reservations are recommended; ask for counter seats to get close to the action.

典型居酒屋格局多年來始終如一，熱鬧非常；開放式廚房旁邊的座位能觀賞烹調過程，氣氛更佳。一向大受歡迎的燒烤由師承日籍老闆的年輕主廚負責，其中免治雞肉棒用上日本及巴西的雞扒肉，按特定比例搓成，深得食客熱愛；生燒本地雞肝亦為鎮店之寶，此外雞肉丸豆腐鍋也不容錯過。建議訂座。

TEL. 2723 8660
Shop 103, 1F, Regal Kowloon Hotel,
71 Mody Road, Tsim Sha Tsui
尖沙咀麼地道 71號富豪九龍酒店 1樓 103室

■ PRICE 價錢
Lunch 午膳
set 套餐 $ 85-110
à la carte 點菜 $ 200-450
Dinner 晚膳
set 套餐 $ 360-380
à la carte 點菜 $ 200-450

■ OPENING HOURS 營業時間
Lunch 午膳 12:00-14:00 (L.O.)
Dinner 晚膳 18:00-22:00 (L.O.)

Octavium

This dining concept from the renowned chef of 8½ Otto e Mezzo Bombana is set in a cosy and minimalistic room. Detail is everything, from handmade Venetian glasses and a wall covered in Norwegian tree bark to the cool Italian furniture. But the décor and tableware don't outshine the food – just try the roasted 'Te Mana' lamb and grand cru chocolate soufflé with hazelnut gelato. Italian seafood soup is only available on Wednesdays and must be pre-ordered.

意籍主廚Bombana新開設的餐廳，以簡約歐陸風格，營造溫暖的歐陸式家庭感覺。主要由意大利人組成的團隊確保風味正宗，佳餚包括各款手製意粉。以十種海鮮熬製、二人分量的意大利海鮮湯只在週三供應，喝不完的話更可用作意粉配汁。菜單每週轉換三至四次，招牌菜有烤Te Mana羊扒、榛子意式雪糕等。

TEL. 2111 9395
8F, One Chinachem Central,
22 Des Voeux Road Central, Central
中環德輔道中 22號華懋中心一期 8樓

SPECIALITIES TO PRE-ORDER 預訂食物
Italian seafood soup (available on Wednesday only) 意大利海鮮湯（僅於週三供應）

■ PRICE 價錢
set 套餐 $ 380-1,180
à la carte 點菜 $ 800-1,100
Dinner 晚膳
set 套餐 $ 1,180-1,580
à la carte 點菜 $ 800-1,100

■ OPENING HOURS 營業時間
Lunch 午膳 11:00-14:30 (L.O.)
Dinner 晚膳 18:30-22:30 (L.O.)

■ ANNUAL AND WEEKLY CLOSING 休息日期
Closed Sunday 週日休息

ON

Its 29th floor location in the heart of Central means that views from the cocktail bar and its terrace are quite something – the perfect spot for a pre-dinner drink. Afterwards, head downstairs to the small restaurant, where you'll find owner-chef Philippe Orrico at work in his open kitchen. His dishes are classically French, full of flavour and use luxury ingredients. Try the 'Discovery' or 'Chef's Menu' to experience his full repertoire.

位處中環心臟地帶的29樓，餐前你可先到雞尾酒吧或陽台小酌一杯，欣賞迷人景觀。餐廳是開放式廚房設計，你會看到經驗豐富的大廚Philippe Orrico和團隊在預備食物時的用心和專注。法國經典菜式以豪華食材烹調而成，味道豐厚濃郁。推介能充分體驗大廚技藝的Discovery菜單或廚師精選。

TEL. 2174 8100
29F, 18 On Lan Street, Central
中環安蘭街18號29樓
www.ontop.hk

■ PRICE 價錢
Lunch 午膳
set 套餐 $ 388-428
à la carte 點菜 $ 650-1,200
Dinner 晚膳
set 套餐 $ 1,288
à la carte 點菜 $ 650-1,200

■ OPENING HOURS 營業時間
Lunch 午膳 12:00-14:30 (L.O.)
Dinner 晚膳 18:00-22:30 (L.O.)

■ ANNUAL AND WEEKLY CLOSING 休息日期
Closed 4 days Lunar New Year
農曆新年休息4天

One Harbour Road
港灣壹號

24

One Harbour Road may be set in a hotel, but its graceful ambience will make you think you're on the terrace of an elegant 1930s Taipan mansion. Split-level dining adds to the airy feel, there are views of the harbour, and the sound of the fountain softens the bold statement of the huge pillars. Cantonese menus offer a wide variety of well-prepared meat and fish dishes. Private parties should consider booking the Chef's Table.

這裏的氣氛，令你恍如置身三十年代的優雅大班府第。分層用餐，空間感較大，且能飽覽維港景色。大型蓮花池及潺潺的流水聲，使感覺硬朗的大柱子變得柔和。這裏的粵菜包括精心準備、種類繁多的肉類和魚類菜式。如想一睹烹調過程，可考慮預訂「廚師餐桌」。

TEL. 2584 7722
8F, Grand Hyatt Hotel,
1 Harbour Road, Wan Chai
灣仔港灣道1號君悅酒店8樓
www.hongkong.grand.hyatt.com

■ PRICE 價錢
Lunch 午膳
set 套餐 $ 538-738
à la carte 點菜 $ 300-800

Dinner 晚膳
set 套餐 $ 1,068-1,588
à la carte 點菜 $ 450-800

■ OPENING HOURS 營業時間
Lunch 午膳 12:00-14:30 (L.O.)
Sunday and Public Holiday lunch
週日及公眾假期午膳 11:30-15:00 (L.O.)
Dinner 晚膳 18:30-22:30 (L.O.)

8 1/2 Otto e Mezzo - Bombana

Italian films are the second passion, after cooking, of owner-chef Umberto Bombana, which is why he named his restaurant after a Fellini film. Everything they do here oozes Italian charm and passion. Ingredients are the best available and the cooking showcases their true flavours; this, along with the personable and professional service, makes for an unforgettable experience.

店東兼主廚Umberto Bombana熱衷的首推烹飪，其次就是電影，是以餐廳亦以意大利著名導演費里尼的作品「八部半」為名。餐廳無一細節不在展露意大利的熱情和魅力，一絲不苟的選材令菜餚的風味和多變得以完美顯展。無懈可擊的服務，色、香、味俱全的佳餚構成令人難以忘懷的饗宴。

TEL. 2537 8859
Shop 202, 2F, Alexandra House,
18 Chater Road, Central
中環遮打道 18號歷山大廈 2樓 202號舖
www.ottoemezzobombana.com

■ PRICE 價錢
Lunch 午膳
set 套餐 $ 580-1,380
à la carte 點菜 $ 760-1,060

Dinner 晚膳
set 套餐 $ 1,380
à la carte 點菜 $ 760-1,060

■ OPENING HOURS 營業時間
Lunch 午膳 12:00-14:30 (L.O.)
Dinner 晚膳 18:30-22:30 (L.O.)

■ ANNUAL AND WEEKLY CLOSING 休息日期
Closed Sunday 週日休息

Pak Loh Chiu Chow (Hysan Avenue)
百樂潮州 (希慎道)

16

There are now four branches of this Chiu Chow restaurant in Hong Kong, but this is the original – which was founded in 1967. For lunch try the baby oyster congee or the fried noodle with sugar and vinegar; in the evening you can go for something a little heavier like soyed goose liver. It's also worth pre-ordering a speciality, like deep-fried king prawn with bread noodles, and finishing with the classic Chiu Chow dessert of fried taro with sugar.

自1967年於銅鑼灣開業，發展至今已有多間分店，而希慎道這間老店的受歡迎程度始終如一。食客最愛的菜式包括各式滷水食物如鵝肝及鵝，還有高質凍蟹，或者預訂特別菜式如子母龍鬚蝦、薑米乳鴿及荷包豬肚雞湯等等。

TEL. 2576 8886
GF, 23-25 Hysan Avenue, Causeway Bay
銅鑼灣希慎道 23-25號地下

■ PRICE 價錢
Lunch 午膳
à la carte 點菜 $ 100-200
Dinner 晚膳
à la carte 點菜 $ 200-400

■ OPENING HOURS 營業時間
11:00-22:30 (L.O.)

Pang's Kitchen
彭慶記

A household name since 2001, this restaurant wins the hearts of many with its traditional and homely Cantonese cooking. Try the baked fish tripe in a clay pot or stir-fried glutinous rice. Unlike places that serve snake soup in autumn and winter only, here it's available all year round. Fried fish head in clay pot with scallion and ginger uses the lower jaws of bighead carp, available in a limited quantity daily. Reservations are recommended.

彭慶記自2001年開業以來一直服務跑馬地居民，並以家常小菜和傳統菜式打響名堂，家喻戶曉的菜式包括缽仔焗魚腸、生炒糯米飯及太史五蛇羹等。以大魚下巴配以薑葱烹煮、名為「薑葱魚鰾煲」的菜式為特別之作，食材由老闆每天親自採購，限量供應。食店座位數量不多，建議提前訂座。

TEL. 2838 5462
25 Yik Yam Street, Happy Valley
跑馬地奕蔭街 25號

■ PRICE 價錢
Lunch 午膳
Monday to Friday set
週一至週五套餐 $ 93
à la carte 點菜 $ 250-500
Dinner 晚膳
à la carte 點菜 $ 250-500

■ OPENING HOURS 營業時間
11:00-22:30 (L.O.)

■ ANNUAL AND WEEKLY CLOSING 休息日期
Closed 3 days Lunar New Year
農曆新年休息 3 天

Peking Garden (Central)
北京樓 (中環)

12

The signature Peking duck is not to be missed – they serve upwards of 60 of them here every night. They arrive plump and glossy at the table, where they are carved with some ceremony by a waiter in white gloves. The restaurant is comprised of two rooms: the more traditional one is best, as it's here the noodle-making demonstration happens each night at 8:30; the more modern dining room, next to the private rooms, is aimed at bigger groups.

毫無疑問，精心炮製的北京填鴨是這兒的招牌菜，每天售出超過六十隻！戴上白手套的服務員以純熟手法為填鴨切割片肉，不消一會便完成，並整齊排好在客人面前。餐廳劃分為兩個大廳：風格較為傳統的一邊，每晚八時半設拉麵製作示範；較為時尚的一邊則適合大伙兒聚餐。服務員更可為客人挑選美酒。

TEL. 2526 6456
Shop B1, Basement 1,
Alexandra House, 18 Chater Road,
Central
中環遮打道 18號歷山大廈地庫首層 B1
www.maximschinese.com.hk

SPECIALITIES TO PRE-ORDER 預訂食物
Beggar's chicken 常熟富貴雞

■ PRICE 價錢
Lunch 午膳
à la carte 點菜 $ 200-1,000
Dinner 晚膳
à la carte 點菜 $ 200-1,000

■ OPENING HOURS 營業時間
Lunch 午膳 11:30-14:30 (L.O.)
Dinner 晚膳 18:00-22:00 (L.O.)

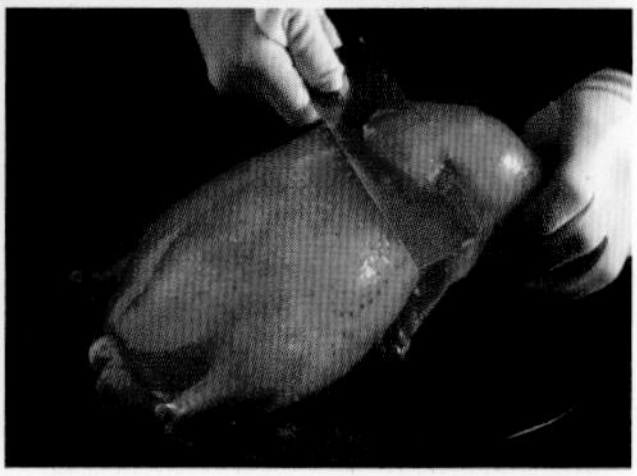

Petrus
珀翠

Heavy drapes at the windows, thick carpets and elegantly laid tables give this restaurant the look of a grand Parisian salon – but here you also get fabulous harbour views. The French cooking, however, shows a certain modernity; the menu is ingredient-led with the luxury ingredients coming from as far as France or sometimes no further than Hong Kong Island. The wine cellar is notable too and includes 45 vintages of Château Pétrus dating back to 1928.

璀璨奪目的水晶吊燈、高貴的絨布簾幕與一絲不苟的餐桌佈置，讓餐廳披上了奢華的巴黎沙龍外觀，窗外美不勝收的海景更是錦上添花。餐單上供應的是經典法國菜，主廚採用來自法國及全球各地的名貴材料，並以現代手法演繹。酒窖內的佳釀多不勝數，包括自1928年起產自珀翠酒莊的多個年份葡萄酒。

TEL. 2820 8590
56F, Island Shangri-La Hotel, Pacific Place, Supreme Court Road, Admiralty
金鐘法院道太古廣場
港島香格里拉酒店 56樓
www.shangri-la.com/island

■ PRICE 價錢
Lunch 午膳
set 套餐 $ 528-618
Dinner 晚膳
set 套餐 $ 980-1,480
à la carte 點菜 $ 800-1,200

■ OPENING HOURS 營業時間
Lunch 午膳 12:00-14:30 (L.O.)
Dinner 晚膳 18:30-22:30 (L.O.)

Pierre

This rather chic and stylish room sits very comfortably on the top floor of the Mandarin Oriental Hotel. It offers stunning harbour views and provides the perfect environment to showcase the unique and intricate cuisine of legendary chef Pierre Gagnaire. The menu includes many of his time-honoured signatures, including the elaborate and multi-faceted Grand Dessert. Come in the evening for a more complete experience.

文華東方酒店頂樓景觀迷人，室內裝潢更是甚有現代感，在舒適的燈光下享用法國廚師Pierre Gagnaire的驚豔菜式，帶來滿足味蕾與視覺的愉悅體驗。菜單網羅了各式各樣歷久不衰的廚師巧手之作，其中少不了包含多款甜品的「Grand Dessert」。侍應團隊殷勤細心，晚膳光臨將能體會更完整的用餐經驗。

TEL. 2825 4001
25F, Mandarin Oriental Hotel,
5 Connaught Road Central, Central
中環干諾道中5號文華東方酒店25樓
www.mandarinoriental.com/hongkong

■ PRICE 價錢
Lunch 午膳
set 套餐 $ 558-1,798
à la carte 點菜 $ 1,800-2,100
Dinner 晚膳
set 套餐 $ 1,398-1,798
à la carte 點菜 $ 1,800-2,100

■ OPENING HOURS 營業時間
Lunch 午膳 12:00-14:30 (L.O.)
Dinner 晚膳 18:30-22:00 (L.O.)

■ ANNUAL AND WEEKLY CLOSING 休息日期
Closed Saturday lunch and Sunday
週六午膳及週日休息

Po Kee
波記

Po Kee is familiar to anyone who's lived in Western District as it's been a feature here for over 40 years and for many local residents a bowl of rice noodles (Lai Fan) with roasted duck leg remains a cherished childhood memory. To prepare his own roast meats, the owner built a factory behind the shop when he moved to the current address. Regulars know to come before 2pm which is about the time the pork sells out each day. Pre-ordering is allowed.

波記在西環屹立四十多年，一碗美味的燒鴨腿瀨粉是不少居民的童年回憶。店內多款燒味均在店鋪後的自家工場製作，很受區內居民歡迎，燒肉往往在下午二時前售罄；而要一嘗其燒鵝，最好在四時前到達，否則可能會掃興。客人亦可預訂各款燒味，店主會因應取貨時間而燒製。

TEL. N/A
425P Queen's Road West,
Western District
西環皇后大道西 425P號

■ PRICE 價錢
à la carte 點菜 $ 40-90

■ OPENING HOURS 營業時間
11:30-19:30 (L.O.)

■ ANNUAL AND WEEKLY CLOSING 休息日期
Closed Sunday 週日休息

Putien (Causeway Bay)
莆田 (銅鑼灣)

P 12

The original restaurant was founded in Singapore in 2000 and named after a coastal city in Fujian province – the owner's home town. This branch comes with an easy-going atmosphere and its Fujian cuisine is respectful of tradition, with the focus on natural flavours. There's much to recommend, like stewed yellow croaker, seaweed with shrimps, and braised pig intestine; and don't miss their homemade chilli sauce – a perfect match for fried bean curd.

莆田於2000年在新加坡開業，後擴展至香港，老闆以其家鄉福建內的城市為餐廳命名，堅守忠於原味、鮮味自然的原則，做出一道道美味菜式；無論是清鮮嫩滑的燜黃花魚、回味悠長的九轉小腸，以至香酥的炒芋頭等都令人留下深刻印象，自家秘製的辣椒醬更是非試不可。

TEL. 2111 8080
Shop A, 7F, Lee Theatre Plaza,
99 Percival Street, Causeway Bay
銅鑼灣波斯富街99號利舞臺廣場 7樓 A號舖

■ PRICE 價錢
Lunch 午膳
à la carte 點菜 $ 150-300
Dinner 晚膳
à la carte 點菜 $ 150-300

■ OPENING HOURS 營業時間
Lunch 午膳 11:30-14:45 (L.O.)
Dinner 晚膳 17:30-21:40 (L.O.)

Qi (Tsim Sha Tsui)
呇 (尖沙咀)

12

Before you taste the creative Sichuanese fare, feast your eyes on the dining room itself – a dragon mural, carved wood panels and red accents are juxtaposed with Hong Kong's electric skyline. Guests can also opt to dine al fresco on the rooftop terrace. Must-try dishes include sugar-glazed ginger beef, and fish fillet in chilli oil soup. New items are added to the menu regularly, such as Sichuanese seafood stone pot rice.

裝潢以深啡色刻花木飾板和飛龍壁畫，配上仿辣椒燈飾，外觀已顯四川風味；食客可坐在玻璃窗旁飽覽維港景致，或登上天台露天區用膳。這裏的新派川菜賣相吸引，蘊含甜、酸、麻、辣、苦、香、鹹等多種滋味。除了必試菜式薑牛及油潑香水魚外，團隊亦不時研發新菜式，其中四川風味的海鮮石鍋飯就是一例。

TEL. 2799 8899
20F, Prince Tower, 12A Peking Road,
Tsim Sha Tsui
尖沙咀北京道12號A太子集團中心20樓
www.qi-ninedragons.hk

SPECIALITIES TO PRE-ORDER 預訂食物
Chili Dungeness crab 霸王辣蟹

■ PRICE 價錢
Lunch 午膳
Monday to Friday set 週一至週五套餐
$ 120-165
à la carte 點菜 $ 250-800
Dinner 晚膳
à la carte 點菜 $ 250-800

■ OPENING HOURS 營業時間
Lunch 午膳 12:00-14:15 (L.O.)
Dinner 晚膳 18:00-22:15 (L.O.)

■ ANNUAL AND WEEKLY CLOSING 休息日期
Closed 1 day Lunar New Year
農曆新年休息1天

Qi (Wan Chai)
呇 (灣仔)

10

Its name means 'shining star' and was inspired by the shape of star-anise, commonly used in Sichuan cooking. The red-and-black colour scheme and atmospheric lighting contrast with a menu deeply rooted in tradition. Offerings slightly differ each season and spices are shipped from Sichuan, including the much-priced dried bird's eye chillies. Items such as deep-fried wontons, and braised eggplant with minced pork are available in vegan versions.

呇解作明亮的星星，亦意指川菜常用的香料八角。餐室以對比鮮明的紅黑色為主調，配上川劇壁畫，隱隱透出中式韻味。廚師採用來自四川的香料入饌，其中辣椒乾不惜選用價格較高的小米椒，取其鮮明色彩，同時提高辣度，以求做出兼具麻、辣、鮮、香的正宗風味。餐單按季節更改，並添加素食元素。

TEL. 2527 7117
2F, J Senses, 60 Johnston Road,
Wan Chai
灣仔莊士敦道 60號 J Senses 2樓
www.qi-sichuan.hk

SPECIALITIES TO PRE-ORDER 預訂食物
Chili Dungeness crab 霸王辣蟹

■ PRICE 價錢
Lunch 午膳
set 套餐 $ 120-240
à la carte 點菜 $ 200-750
Dinner 晚膳
à la carte 點菜 $ 200-750

■ OPENING HOURS 營業時間
Lunch 午膳 12:00-14:15 (L.O.)
Dinner 晚膳 18:00-22:15 (L.O.)

■ ANNUAL AND WEEKLY CLOSING 休息日期
Closed 1 day Lunar New Year
農曆新年休息 1 天

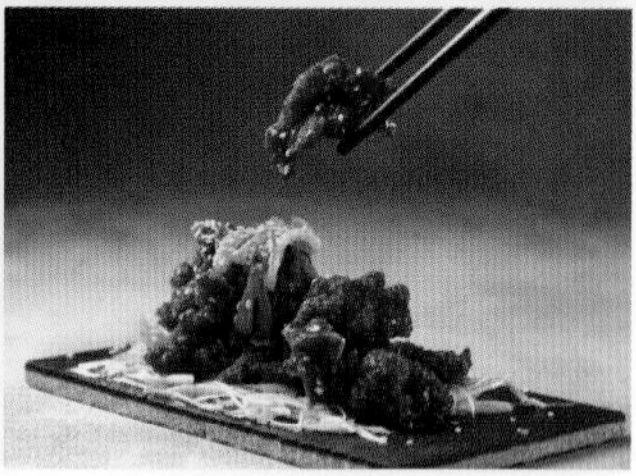

Ramen Jo (Causeway Bay)
拉麵Jo (銅鑼灣)

Named after the owner's favourite manga character, this lively noodle joint serves pork char siu ramen in 10 different flavours alongside gyoza dumplings and other specials. Try the ox's tongue with scallion. From the mild miso-based variety to the fiery spicy type, the rich and flavourful pork bone broth simmered for over 16 hours is the soul of every bowl. Those ordering dipping noodles are given a card illustrating the dipping steps in comic form.

店子名稱源自東主心愛的漫畫人物。餐單內提供十款拉麵及餃子等小食，不妨試試新菜式葱花牛舌。其豬骨湯底花上十六小時熬製而成，濃而不膩，配上特製的麵條和醬汁，令人回味無窮。若點選沾麵，服務員會給你一張「沾麵食法」卡片，其上是以漫畫形式展示的正確沾麵進食方法。

TEL. 2885 0638
3 Caroline Hill Road, Causeway Bay
銅鑼灣加路連山道 3號

■ PRICE 價錢
Lunch 午膳
à la carte 點菜 $ 85-120
Dinner 晚膳
à la carte 點菜 $ 85-120

■ OPENING HOURS 營業時間
Lunch 午膳 12:00-14:30 (L.O.)
Dinner 晚膳 18:00-22:00 (L.O.)
Weekends 週末 12:00-22:00 (L.O.)

■ ANNUAL AND WEEKLY CLOSING 休息日期
Closed 2 days Lunar New Year
農曆新年休息 2 天

Rech

The famous Parisian seafood restaurant was acquired by the world-famous chef Alain Ducasse in 2007 and this is its first international outpost. The modern space with unobstructed harbour views complements the fresh fish on the menu, mostly shipped from France. Classics like seafood platter, raw oysters, and sole meunière are served alongside creative offerings such as marinated raw fish and shrimps with nuts, herbs and seaweed.

於1925年在法國開業的Rech是巴黎有名的海鮮餐館，自2007年後由Alain Ducasse接手經營，此店是海外首家分店。採用的海產全由法國進口，每星期三至四次直送到店，確保食材質素。從生蠔、生醃海鮮冷盤至香煎牛油龍脷柳，一應俱全。明媚的維港景色，讓眼福跟肚腹同等滿足。

TEL. 2313 2323
1F, InterContinental Hotel,
18 Salisbury Road, Tsim Sha Tsui
尖沙咀梳士巴利道18號洲際酒店1樓
www.hongkong-ic.intercontinental.com

■ PRICE 價錢
Lunch 午膳
set 套餐 $ 588
Dinner 晚膳
set 套餐 $ 1,188
à la carte 點菜 $ 700-1,200

■ OPENING HOURS 營業時間
Weekend lunch 週末午膳
12:00-14:30 (L.O.)
Dinner 晚膳 18:00-23:00 (L.O.)

Sabah (Wan Chai)
莎巴 (灣仔)

Sabah is one of the few Malaysian restaurants to have served authentic Malaysian food for many years. It may have an unremarkable façade, but at least it's easy to find thanks to the huge horizontal neon sign. The kitchen staff are all Malaysian and the care they take is palpable, as is the skill they show in preparing the dishes. Satay, king prawns with butter and deep-fried egg yolk, beef Rendang and Hainanese chicken rice are some of the highlights.

這家餐廳的外觀也許毫不起眼，但是靠着巨大的霓虹燈招牌，我們可輕易找到它。內部裝潢與外觀一樣平凡，但吸引眾多食客的並不是餐廳的室內設計，而是正宗的馬拉菜。精選菜式包括沙嗲、金絲奶油大蝦、巴東牛肉與海南雞飯。主廚秘方炮製的炸香蕉也十分惹味。

TEL. 2143 6626
98-102 Jaffe Road, Wan Chai
灣仔謝斐道 98-102號

■ PRICE 價錢
Lunch 午膳
set 套餐 $ 75
à la carte 點菜 $ 100-150
Dinner 晚膳
à la carte 點菜 $ 150-350

■ OPENING HOURS 營業時間
Lunch 午膳 11:00-17:00 (L.O.)
Dinner 晚膳 18:00-22:30 (L.O.)
Sunday and Public Holidays
週日及公眾假期 12:00-21:30 (L.O.)

■ ANNUAL AND WEEKLY CLOSING 休息日期
Closed 4 days Lunar New Year
農曆新年休息 4 天

Sai Kung Sing Kee
勝記

36

At first sight, this brightly coloured seafood restaurant may not seem too dissimilar to others in Sai Kung. However, there is something special here and that's the abalone menu. The abalone are prepared in various ways, from deep-fried to steamed; try the stewed abalone in oyster sauce. The building has 12 variously sized dining rooms spread over its three floors, all differently decorated; the most contemporary are on the 1st and 2nd floors.

這棟建築物樓高三層，備有十二個大小不一、裝飾各異的房間，一樓和二樓的餐室裝潢較時尚，驟眼看來，跟西貢其他餐廳並沒兩樣。但是，它真正特別的地方，在於扣鮑魚菜式。這裏提供多種以不同方式烹調的鮑魚菜式，由酥炸到蒸煮式式俱備，特別推介古法扣兩頭鮑魚。

TEL. 2791 9887
39 Sai Kung Tai Street, Sai Kung
西貢西貢大街 39號
www.singkee.ecomm.hk

SPECIALITIES TO PRE-ORDER 預訂食物
Crispy chicken 金牌炸子雞 / Stewed abalone in oyster sauce 古法扣鮑魚

■ PRICE 價錢
Lunch 午膳
à la carte 點菜 $ 300-950
Dinner 晚膳
à la carte 點菜 $ 400-950

■ OPENING HOURS 營業時間
11:00-22:00 (L.O.)

■ ANNUAL AND WEEKLY CLOSING 休息日期
Closed 2 days Lunar New Year
農曆新年休息 2 天

Samsen
泰麵

Adam Cliff, who once worked for the Aussie chef David Thompson, opened this casual Thai noodle shop next to the historic Blue House. Aptly named after an area in Bangkok where the Chinese traded with the Thais, the restaurant emulates the authentic street-stall vibe and flavours. Rattan blinds, bare concrete walls and distressed wood furniture add to the old-time charm. Most ingredients are shipped from Thailand daily.

Samsen是過去華人在泰國與泰國人做貿易生意和會面之地，在泰文中有三麵之意。在著名的藍屋旁邊，以復古風格裝飾：舊傢具、古老泰國小販檔陳設、泰國鐵標牌，充滿懷舊與泰風情。熱愛泰菜的主廚旨在透過湯河及泰國街頭小吃，讓香港人品嘗地道泰國風味。超過六成食材每天由泰國直送到店。

TEL. 2234 0001
68 Stone Nullah Lane, Wan Chai
灣仔石水渠街 68號地下

■ PRICE 價錢
Lunch 午膳
set 套餐 $ 118-128
Dinner 晚膳
à la carte 點菜 $ 200-400

■ OPENING HOURS 營業時間
Lunch 午膳 12:00-14:30 (L.O.)
Dinner 晚膳 18:30-23:00 (L.O.)

Sang Kee
生記

Having stood here proudly for over 40 years, Sang Kee is a true symbol of Wan Chai and remains refreshingly impervious to modernisation. The owner insists on buying the seafood herself each day and the Cantonese dishes are prepared using traditional methods. You'll find yourself thinking about their classic dishes like fried snapper, fried minced pork with cuttlefish, and braised fish with bitter melon long after you've sampled them.

現在許多粵菜餐廳都以雷同的裝潢和新派菜單作招徠，令生記這類傳統酒家讓人感到特別親切！開業逾四十年，店主一直堅持每天親自採購優質海鮮，以傳統烹調方式製作一道道經典廣東菜：用時令材料炮製的乾煎海鱸，家常菜如土魷煎肉餅和涼瓜燜魚等，令人回味無窮。

TEL. 2575 2236
1-2F, Hip Sang Building,
107-115 Hennessy Road, Wan Chai
灣仔軒尼詩道 107-115號協生大廈 1-2樓
www.sangkee.com.hk

SPECIALITIES TO PRE-ORDER 預訂食物
Fried snapper 乾煎海鱸 / Baked fish intestine 焗魚腸

■ PRICE 價錢
Lunch 午膳
set 套餐 $ 68-82
à la carte 點菜 $ 100-200
Dinner 晚膳
à la carte 點菜 $ 200-500

■ OPENING HOURS 營業時間
Lunch 午膳 12:00-14:15 (L.O.)
Dinner 晚膳 18:00-22:15 (L.O.)

■ ANNUAL AND WEEKLY CLOSING 休息日期
Closed first Monday of each month
每月第一個週一休息

Seventh Son
家全七福

There was a change of venue for this Cantonese restaurant in 2016 – it is now housed on the 3rd floor of the Wharney Guang Dong Hotel. Its new surroundings are smart and contemporary, with gold and yellow colours adding warmth to the comfortable room. The standard of the traditional Cantonese cuisine remains as was, with the kitchen making good use of quality ingredients. The specialities are barbecued suckling pig and crispy chicken.

餐廳名稱包含了東主父親的名字及其在兄弟中的排序，也有傳承父親廚藝之意。從杜老誌道遷至華美粵海酒店，新店以深色木地板配金黃色的日式裝潢，感覺時尚。自十四歲隨父習廚、擅長高級功夫粵菜的東主，以時令食材、最少的調味料和精細的烹調，帶出食物真味。大紅片皮乳豬和炸子雞是招牌菜。

TEL. 2892 2888
3F, The Wharney Guang Dong Hotel,
57-73 Lockhart Road, Wan Chai
灣仔駱克道 57-73號華美粵海酒店 3樓
www.seventhson.hk

SPECIALITIES TO PRE-ORDER 預訂食物
Steamed duck stuffed with various fillings 蛋黃八寶鴨

■ PRICE 價錢
Lunch 午膳
à la carte 點菜 $ 200-600
Dinner 晚膳
à la carte 點菜 $ 350-1,000

■ OPENING HOURS 營業時間
Lunch 午膳 11:30-14:30 (L.O.)
Dinner 晚膳 18:00-22:30 (L.O.)

■ ANNUAL AND WEEKLY CLOSING 休息日期
Closed 1 day Lunar New Year
農曆新年休息 1 天

Shang Palace
香宮

Chandeliers and Sung-style paintings create an impressive backdrop for some sophisticated cooking that has changed little over the years, even with the arrival of a new chef. His signature dishes include steamed garoupa with egg white sauce and sautéed giant green crab with peppercorns in clay pot. This elegant restaurant in the Kowloon Shangri-La has been a reliable favourite for classic Cantonese cooking for over 35 years.

位處九龍香格里拉酒店、開業逾三十五年的香宮，一直是老饕心目中享用傳統粵菜的可靠選擇。用餐區裝潢華麗古雅，水晶吊燈與宋代風格油畫多年來一直點綴餐室，用餐環境更添韻味。新大廚上任後，食物維持一定水準，招牌菜有錦繡星斑件及胡椒焗大肉蟹。

TEL. 2733 8754
Lower Level 1, Kowloon Shangri-La Hotel,
64 Mody Road, East Tsim Sha Tsui
尖東麼地道 64號九龍香格里拉酒店地庫 1樓
www.shangri-la.com/kowloon

■ PRICE 價錢
Lunch 午膳
set 套餐 $ 398-498
à la carte 點菜 $ 350-1,000
Dinner 晚膳
set 套餐 $ 738-1,388
à la carte 點菜 $ 350-1,000

■ OPENING HOURS 營業時間
Lunch 午膳 12:00-14:00 (L.O.)
Weekend & Public Holiday lunch
週末及公眾假期午膳 10:30-14:30 (L.O.)
Dinner 晚膳 18:30-22:00 (L.O.)

Shanghai Yu Yuan Ⓝ
豫園

Named after the famous garden in Shanghai, this restaurant uses a classic vase motif borrowed from the lattice windows there. A hand-painted mural depicting Yu Garden and Old Shanghai takes centre stage, and contrasts nicely with the gorgeous harbour views. Shanghainese classics such as steamed Reeves shad with distillers grains, fried pine nut fish, and braised whole pork ribs are recommended. Cantonese dim sum is also served.

一如其名，餐廳以上海豫園為主題，裝潢中也不難發現其蹤影：屏風上的花瓶圖案與上海豫園的窗花同出一轍，而大廳壁畫描繪的是豫園和老上海人物風貌。餐廳各個細節都別出心裁，碟具更是專程於景德鎮訂造。推薦菜式包括清蒸酒糟鰣魚、招牌松子鮮魚，以及較少見的豫園豬全骨；除了傳統滬菜，也供應粵式點心。

TEL. 2156 1688
26F, V Point, 18 Tang Lung Street,
Causeway Bay
銅鑼灣登龍街18號 V Point 26樓
www.yu-yuan.hk

■ PRICE 價錢
Lunch 午膳
à la carte 點菜 $ 200-300
Dinner 晚膳
à la carte 點菜 $ 200-500

■ OPENING HOURS 營業時間
11:30-22:30 (L.O.)

She Wong Yee
蛇王二

Their signature snake soup has long been renowned and on a typical winter's day over 1,000 bowls are served. Regulars are quick to occupy one of the few tables for this memorable experience and it is no surprise that the recipe has remained unchanged for years. These days, those regulars come also for the famed barbecued meats and homemade liver sausages; the roast goose and double-boiled soups are good too.

位於銅鑼灣中心地帶的蛇王二，多年來以傳統方法烹調蛇羹，一直口碑載道，深受食客歡迎，秋冬高峰期更每日出售逾千碗。其自製膶腸也同樣令食客趨之若鶩，而每日鮮製的盅頭滋補燉湯是不少本地市民的最愛。店內氣氛熱鬧，座無虛席，需與其他人拼桌用膳。

TEL. 2831 0163
24 Percival Street, Causeway Bay
銅鑼灣波斯富街 24號

■ PRICE 價錢
set 套餐 $ 72-110
à la carte 點菜 $ 60-160

■ OPENING HOURS 營業時間
11:00-22:45 (L.O.)

■ ANNUAL AND WEEKLY CLOSING 休息日期
Closed 3 days Lunar New Year
農曆新年休息 3 天

Shek Kee Kitchen
石記廚房

10

It serves ordinary Cha Chaan Teng fare during the day, but turns into a dining hotspot specialising in home-style Cantonese dishes at night. The owner-chef sources the freshest ingredients from wet markets daily. Regulars also call him directly to pre-order certain dishes, including the signature fried chicken with toasted garlic that needs to be ordered one day ahead. The menu changes regularly to reflect the seasonal produce available.

餐廳在日間供應普通茶餐廳食物，而晚間卻是人氣鼎盛、主打家庭式廣東小菜的菜館。大廚兼東主每天會親自往街市選購最新鮮的食材，部分熟客更會直接致電預訂當晚的菜式，石記風沙雞需要提前一天預訂。菜單經常更新，例如每日精選小炒，冬日更少不了合時的煲仔飯。

TEL. 2571 3348
GF, 15-17 Ngan Mok Street, Tin Hau
天后銀幕街 15-17號地下

SPECIALITIES TO PRE-ORDER 預訂食物
Crispy chicken 炸子雞 / Roast chicken with fermented bean curd 南乳吊燒雞 / Fried chicken with toasted garlic 石記風沙雞

■ PRICE 價錢
Lunch 午膳
set 套餐 $ 50-58
à la carte 點菜 $ 80-100
Dinner 晚膳
à la carte 點菜 $ 100-400

■ OPENING HOURS 營業時間
Lunch 午膳 11:30-15:00 (L.O.)
Dinner 晚膳 18:00-23:00 (L.O.)

Sheung Hei Claypot Rice
嚐囍煲仔小菜

Claypot rice is cooked to order over a charcoal stove here and this gives it a characteristic smokiness and a crispy crust at the bottom. Order the one with eel and pork ribs for a rich fish aroma and luscious pork grease that coats every grain. The owner also runs a dim sum shop next door where you can order Cantonese bite-size munchies on the side. New items are added to the menu monthly; claypot rice and dishes are available after 6pm.

即點即煮並非這兒的特別之處，倒是其炭烤煲仔飯的方法使人印象深刻。以炭火烹煮米飯時香氣已撲鼻而來，煮熟後的飯焦更加香味誘人。推介白鱔排骨飯，能吃到鱔的香味之餘，排骨內的油分滲進飯內令米飯更香軟。煲仔小菜及煲仔飯只在晚上六時後供應，款式每月增加。食客可從隔鄰的姊妹店選些點心佐餐。

TEL. 2819 6190
GF, 25 North Street, Western District
西環北街 25號地下

■ PRICE 價錢
Lunch 午膳
set 套餐 $ 40-50
à la carte 點菜 $ 40-60
Dinner 晚膳
à la carte 點菜 $ 80-100

■ OPENING HOURS 營業時間
Lunch 午膳 11:00-15:00 (L.O.)
Dinner 晚膳 18:00-22:00 (L.O.)

■ ANNUAL AND WEEKLY CLOSING 休息日期
Closed 4 days Lunar New Year
農曆新年休息 4 天

Sheung Hei Dim Sum
嚐囍點心皇

Standouts here include shrimp dumplings, steamed chicken and mushroom bun, turnip cake and Cantonese sponge cake. The set lunch is available from 11am to 3pm, while dinner with claypot rice and stir-fries is served from 6 to 10pm. It prides itself on MSG-free dim sum made from scratch and steamed to order; it can also be packed to go. Pre-packaged layered ginger cake, taro cake and the like also make great Chinese New Year gifts.

簡約的店子以全天候供應點心作招徠，點心全是自家製作，即點即蒸，全無味精，價錢相宜。推介水晶鮮蝦餃和各式糕點，特色點心懷舊雞大包也值得一試。除點心外，早上11時至下午3時還供應午市套餐，晚上6時至10時更有煲仔飯和小菜可供選擇。另設外賣點心，新年期間更有各款自製糕點禮盒出售。

TEL. 2817 0838
GF, 25 North Street, Western District
西環北街 25號地下

■ PRICE 價錢
Lunch 午膳
set 套餐 $ 42-50
à la carte 點菜 $ 40-60
Dinner 晚膳
à la carte 點菜 $ 40-60

■ OPENING HOURS 營業時間
06:00-16:00 (L.O.) / 18:00-06:00 (L.O.)

■ ANNUAL AND WEEKLY CLOSING 休息日期
Closed 4 days Lunar New Year
農曆新年休息 4 天

Shugetsu Ramen (Central)
麵鮮醬油房周月 (中環)

The queues form early for the ramen here, with many of the customers coming for the Tsukemen ramen, as well as the Abura and special soup ramen. The shop makes its own noodles – which you can have thick or thin – but it is the sauce at the base of the slow-cooked soup that really makes the difference: it's fermented for 18 months in a 100-year-old wooden basket and adds richness and depth.

周月與別不同之處，在其以醬油為湯底的神髓：採用逾一百四十年歷史的愛媛縣梶田商店特製的醬油，配合沙丁魚粉、鯖魚粉及海帶長時間慢火熬製，味道更醇厚豐富。與日本店一樣，香港店設有製麵房，每天新鮮製造兩款粗幼不同的麵條。除了湯拉麵外，還供應沾麵。

TEL. 2850 6009
5 Gough Street, Central
中環歌賦街 5號
www.shugetsu.com.hk

■ PRICE 價錢
à la carte 點菜 $ 90-150

■ OPENING HOURS 營業時間
11:30-20:50 (L.O.)
Sunday 週日 12:00-19:00 (L.O.)
Sunday before Public Holiday
公眾假期前週日 11:30-20:50 (L.O.)

■ ANNUAL AND WEEKLY CLOSING 休息日期
Closed New Year's Day and 1 day Lunar New Year 元旦及年初一休息

Shugetsu Ramen (Quarry Bay)
麵鮮醬油房周月 (鰂魚涌)

This was the second branch of Shugetsu to open in Hong Kong. It's the freshly made noodles and the soy sauce base that make them so popular. The broth is prepared with sardines, mackerel and kelp, and soy sauce that is produced by a longstanding factory in Ehime. The popular choice is Tsukemen, for which they use thick noodles to absorb the sauce's taste more easily – you decide how large a portion you want.

這是周月在香港的第二間分店，以鮮製麵條和醬油湯為賣點，湯底用放在百年木桶內經十八個月發酵而成的醬油，加上沙丁魚粉、鯖魚粉及海帶煮成，美味且味道特別。除了湯拉麵外，沾麵也頗受歡迎，選用的麵條較粗但掛湯力強，能盡吸醬汁精華。食客可選擇麵的分量。

TEL. 2336 7888
30 Hoi Kwong Street, Quarry Bay
鰂魚涌海光街 30號
www.shugetsu.com.hk

■ PRICE 價錢
à la carte 點菜 $ 90-120

■ OPENING HOURS 營業時間
11:30-20:50 (L.O.)
Sunday 週日 12:00-19:00 (L.O.)
Sunday before Public Holiday
公眾假期前週日 11:30-20:50 (L.O.)

■ ANNUAL AND WEEKLY CLOSING 休息日期
Closed New Year's Day and 1 day
Lunar New Year 元旦及年初一休息

Sing Kee (Central)
星記 (中環)

16

The second branch of Sing Kee is a bright, tidy spot serving classic Cantonese food – something that's proving increasingly hard to find in Central. You'll find only traditional recipes using chicken, pork and seafood here, free of gimmicks or fancy presentation. Many specialities need pre-ordering, like chicken with ginger in clam sauce, or almond juice with fish maw and pig's lung. Come at lunch to take advantage of some reasonable prices.

想在中環區找到提供樸實高質的傳統粵菜且環境乾淨整潔的餐館，星記便是你的選擇。選用新鮮肉類如豬、雞及生猛海鮮等食材，加上扎實的烹調技術，自然不乏支持者。午市提供一系列價錢實惠的小菜，甚得中環人士歡心。建議預訂燉湯如杏汁花膠燉豬肺。

TEL. 2970 0988
2F, 1 Lyndhurst Tower,
1 Lyndhurst Terrace, Central
中環擺花街1號一號廣場2樓
www.singkeedining.com

SPECIALITIES TO PRE-ORDER 預訂食物
Roasted crispy chicken 脆皮炸子雞 / Salt baked chicken in secret sauce 秘製鹽焗雞

■ PRICE 價錢
Lunch 午膳
set 套餐 $ 85
à la carte 點菜 $ 100-200
Dinner 晚膳
à la carte 點菜 $ 200-400

■ OPENING HOURS 營業時間
Lunch 午膳 11:30-14:15 (L.O.)
Dinner 晚膳 18:00-22:15 (L.O.)

Sister Wah (Tin Hau)
華姐清湯腩 (天后)

The legendary Sister Wah is no longer at the helm but her sons are running the shop just like she used to. Its signature beef brisket in clear soup uses fresh local beef which is braised in a stock with over 10 different herbs. Other items on the brief menu include homemade dumplings with pork and white cabbage, drunken chicken and Dan Dan noodles. With only six tables, it gets filled up as soon as it opens.

這間家庭式經營的小店，現由華姐大兒子主理，招待工作則由弟弟打點。馳名牛腩的製作每天早上八時便開始，用上150斤肉味香濃的本地新鮮牛腩燜煮；清湯底以十種以上香料秘製，難怪營業時間剛到就吸引了不少食客光顧。除了清湯牛坑腩，也不要錯過大白菜菜肉雲吞及以白滷水浸上幾小時的醉雞。

TEL. 2807 0181
Shop A1, 13 Electric Road, Tin Hau
天后電氣道 13號 A1號舖

■ PRICE 價錢
à la carte 點菜 $ 40-70

■ OPENING HOURS 營業時間
11:00-23:00 (L.O.)

■ ANNUAL AND WEEKLY CLOSING 休息日期
Closed 6 days Lunar New Year
農曆新年休息 6 天

Siu Shun Village Cuisine (Kowloon Bay)
肇順名匯河鮮專門店 (九龍灣)

32

Fish is shipped daily from Shun Tak County while the cooking also follows the Shun Tak regional style. Recommendations include fried giant prawns with ginger and spring onion, stir-fried beef tenderloin strips with mushrooms in XO sauce, and braised fish lips casserole. After some meticulous preparation and cooking, those live river fish swimming in the tanks at the entrance can also end up on your dining table.

餐廳位於交通不算便利的商場一隅，可鼎沸的人聲足證其菜式甚具水準。各式各樣的生猛河鮮在門外大大小小的魚缸內游來游去，彷彿要提醒客人這裏的河鮮不能錯過。招牌菜包括薑葱大蝦球、XO醬雙菇牛柳條和瓦罉煎焗魚嘴等。河鮮每天由順德新鮮運到，確保鮮活度。

TEL. 2798 9738
Shop 6, 7F, MegaBox,
38 Wang Chiu Road, Kowloon Bay
九龍灣宏照道 38號 MegaBox 7樓 6號舖

■ PRICE 價錢
Lunch 午膳
à la carte 點菜 $ 80-300
Dinner 晚膳
à la carte 點菜 $ 100-300

■ OPENING HOURS 營業時間
Lunch 午膳 09:00-16:15 (L.O.)
Dinner 晚膳 18:00-22:15 (L.O.)

Snow Garden
雪園

16

Established in 1992 at this sleek business address and known for its traditional Shanghainese cuisine, this is a restaurant that operates like clockwork and whose staff are warm and attentive. The long-standing chef's specialities are steamed herring and deep-fried chicken skin with four spices; braised sea cucumber with shrimp roe; and yellow fish with sweet and sour sauce. Dishes arrive carefully prepared and bursting with flavour.

以精心烹調上海菜馳名的雪園於1992年在此商業區開始營業，員工態度親切熱誠，多年以來累積了不少捧場客。餐廳每道菜式都經過精心製作，色香味俱全，歷久不衰的廚師精選包括清蒸鰣魚、四寶片皮雞、蝦籽大烏參及糖醋黃魚。每逢大閘蟹季節，更不缺太湖大閘蟹的餐點。

TEL. 2881 6837
2F, China Taiping Tower,
8 Sunning Road, Causeway Bay
銅鑼灣新寧道 8號中國太平大廈 2樓

■ PRICE 價錢
Lunch 午膳
à la carte 點菜 $ 150-250
Dinner 晚膳
à la carte 點菜 $ 250-700

■ OPENING HOURS 營業時間
Lunch 午膳 11:30-14:30 (L.O.)
Dinner 晚膳 18:00-22:00 (L.O.)

■ ANNUAL AND WEEKLY CLOSING 休息日期
Closed 3 days Lunar New Year
農曆新年休息 3 天

Spring Moon
嘉麟樓

✗✗✗ 48

It's all about tradition here. Firstly, the room, which is set over two levels, cleverly evokes the spirit of a 1920s Shanghainese dining room thanks to its rugs, teak floors and stained glass windows. Secondly, dishes on the Cantonese menu are prepared in a classic way – don't expect any modern interpretation here. The Tea Bar, which boasts an extensive collection of antique teapots, offers over 30 varieties of tea.

古典風格的柚木地板，配襯東方地氈和帶裝飾藝術風格的彩色玻璃，恍如將二十年代老上海重現眼前。從懷舊的室內設計，以至一道道遵照傳統烹調而成的廣東菜式，處處反映這家餐廳對傳統的重視。菜單上的經典菜式包括千絲官燕羹、北京片皮鴨等等。茗茶櫃台提供超過三十種茶葉，更展出古董茶壺收藏品。

TEL. 2696 6760
1F, The Peninsula Hotel, Salisbury Road, Tsim Sha Tsui
尖沙咀梳士巴利道半島酒店 1樓
http://hongkong.peninsula.com

SPECIALITIES TO PRE-ORDER 預訂食物
Hangzhou beggar's fortune chicken
杭州富貴雞

■ PRICE 價錢
Lunch 午膳
set 套餐 $ 500-800
à la carte 點菜 $ 400-800
Dinner 晚膳
set 套餐 $ 1,000-2,000
à la carte 點菜 $ 500-1,500

■ OPENING HOURS 營業時間
Lunch 午膳 11:30-14:30 (L.O.)
Sunday and Public Holiday lunch
週日及公眾假期午膳 11:00-14:30 (L.O.)
Dinner 晚膳 18:00-22:30 (L.O.)

Steak on Elgin Ⓝ

Grass-fed British and Irish meat is the specialities, the latter being quite hard to find in Hong Kong, such as the Irish John Stone hormone-free beef that is dry-aged for at least 25 days. It's also worth trying the daily specials and other meats from Europe, such as Welsh organic lamb from the Rhug Estate. Starters are in a modern European style. For dessert, try the decadent British classic 'Grandma's boozy trifle'.

棄用普遍的美國牛扒，改為選用英國及北愛爾蘭的優質品牌作貨源，使餐廳顯得與別不同。所採用的草飼牛均來自小型農場，無任何添加物或荷爾蒙，並經至少25天乾式熟成，口感有保證；而羊肉則源自一個威爾斯小農莊，間中亦有來自歐盟其他地區的肉排作是日精選。較少見的傳統英式甜品Grandma's Boozy Trifle不容錯過。

TEL. 2627 0528
59 Elgin Street, Central
中環伊利近街 59號
www.steakonelgin.com

■ PRICE 價錢
Lunch 午膳
set 套餐 $ 500
Dinner 晚膳
à la carte 點菜 $ 800-1,000

■ OPENING HOURS 營業時間
Friday Lunch 週五午膳
12:00-14:30 (L.O.)
Dinner 晚膳 18:00-23:00 (L.O.)

■ ANNUAL AND WEEKLY CLOSING 休息日期
Closed Public Holidays and Sunday
公眾假期及週日休息

Summer Palace
夏宮

XXX

There's a timeless, exotic feel to this room whose decoration of gilt screens, golden silk wall coverings and lattice panels is inspired by the palace in Beijing. The menu is a roll-call of Cantonese classics; double-boiled soups are a speciality; dim sum is a highlight; and signature dishes include marinated pig's trotters, braised '23-head' Yoshihama abalone in oyster sauce, and Peking duck. They also offer a good selection of teas.

高聳的餐室以北京故宮為設計靈感，以華麗的水晶吊燈、大紅色餐桌，配以傳統中國屏風、金色絲綢畫作及雕塑，營造了迷人的情調。菜譜羅列各款傳統廣東名菜，招牌菜包括沙薑豬腳仔、蠔皇吉品鮑魚、北京片皮鴨等，燉湯也是其專長，部分需提早預訂。午市時點心是不俗的選擇。可供選擇的茶飲也很多。

TEL. 2820 8552
5F, Island Shangri-La Hotel, Pacific Place, Supreme Court Road, Admiralty
金鐘法院道太古廣場港島香格里拉酒店 5樓
www.shangri-la.com/island

SPECIALITIES TO PRE-ORDER 預訂食物
Beggar's chicken 富貴雞 / Double-boiled soups 燉湯 / Eight treasure duck 夏宮八寶鴨 / Poached fresh sliced sea-whelk 堂灼響螺片

■ PRICE 價錢
Lunch 午膳
à la carte 點菜 $ 350-1,500
Dinner 晚膳
à la carte 點菜 $ 350-1,500

■ OPENING HOURS 營業時間
Lunch 午膳 11:30-14:30 (L.O.)
Sunday and Public Holiday lunch
週日及公眾假期午膳 11:00-15:00 (L.O.)
Dinner 晚膳 18:00-22:00 (L.O.)

Sun Fook Kee
新福記

18

This restaurant prides itself on labour-intensive, traditional Fujian dishes that are hard to find elsewhere, such as a shredded vegetable pancake that uses 12 different ingredients, and deep-fried longans stuffed with minced shrimp and pork that are only available in summer. The chef shops for produce daily from the market to ensure freshness. Ask about the new dishes that are not on the menu and those that require pre-ordering when you book.

高級懷舊福建菜館不多，新福記是其中之一。菜單上有不少難得一見的功夫菜，例如只在夏天供應的傳統菜東壁龍珠，取新鮮龍眼肉去核後釀入蝦膠豬肉，再油炸而成。為取得新鮮食材，廚師每天都會從市場採購。不少新創作並不列於菜單之上，建議訂座時查詢時令或推介菜式。

TEL. 2566 5898
1F, Circle Court, 3-5 Java Road,
North Point
北角渣華道 3-5 號永光閣 1樓

■ PRICE 價錢
Lunch 午膳
à la carte 點菜 $ 350-500
Dinner 晚膳
à la carte 點菜 $ 500-700

■ OPENING HOURS 營業時間
Lunch 午膳 11:00-14:30 (L.O.)
Dinner 晚膳 18:00-22:00 (L.O.)

Sun Tung Lok
新同樂

20

Having moved to this new location after 40 glorious years in Happy Valley, this contemporary dining room comes with hand-painted wallpaper with a flower and bird theme. Must-tries include the abalone, braised beef ribs in house gravy, stuffed crab shell, and roast suckling pig. Local chicken dishes are also not to be missed. The dim sum menu changes every season to include new items.

開業逾四十年，新同樂從跑馬地來到尖沙咀，鳥語花香為題的手繪牆紙使餐室更別緻優雅。粵菜是菜單中的主角，當中不乏用本地新鮮雞隻烹煮的菜式，而用於烹調的雞湯更是每日新鮮熬煮。推薦菜式包括燒汁乾煏牛肋骨、鮮蘑菇焗釀蟹蓋及燒乳豬件，鮑魚是必試之選。點心每隔三個月會更換款式。

TEL. 2152 1417
Shop 401, L4, FoodLoft, Mira Place One,
132 Nathan Road, Tsim Sha Tsui
尖沙咀彌敦道 132號
美麗華廣場一期食四方 4樓 401號舖
www.suntunglok.com.hk

■ PRICE 價錢
Lunch 午膳
set 套餐 $ 298-438
à la carte 點菜 $ 300-500
Dinner 晚膳
à la carte 點菜 $ 800-1,200

■ OPENING HOURS 營業時間
Lunch 午膳 11:30-15:00 (L.O.)
Dinner 晚膳 18:00-22:30 (L.O.)

Sun Yuen Hing Kee
新園興記

Located next to Sheung Wan market, this traditionally styled, simple but well maintained barbecue shop has been run by the same family since the mid-1970s. Over the years they've built up an appreciative following so the small place fills quickly. The appetising looking suckling pigs are not the only draw: roast pork, duck and pigeon all have their followers, as do the soft-boiled chicken, the homemade sausages and the preserved meats.

位於上環街市旁邊，這間格調傳統簡單的燒味店自七十年代中一直由同一家族經營。多年來，累積了不少忠實顧客，小小的地方往往座無虛席。這裏受歡迎的不僅是掛在廚房旁邊，賣相令人垂涎欲滴的乳豬，燒肉、烤鴨和乳鴿都各有忠實擁躉。白切雞、臘腸及臘肉亦十分吸引。

TEL. 2541 2207
327-329 Queen's Road Central,
Sheung Wan
上環皇后大道中 327-329號

■ PRICE 價錢
à la carte 點菜 $ 40-150

■ OPENING HOURS 營業時間
08:00-19:30 (L.O.)

■ ANNUAL AND WEEKLY CLOSING 休息日期
Closed 3 days Lunar New Year
農曆新年休息 3 天

Sushi Masataka

Named after its executive chef, the former Sushi Rozan reopened with a wood-clad interior that reflects the roots of its cuisine. The nine seats in front of an open counter allow diners to watch the chefs in action. Only fixed price omakase menus are available, featuring quality seafood flown straight from Japan daily, such as golden-eye snapper and white sea urchin. Lunch is by reservation only and requires a minimum of 4 people.

從原來的名字鮨魯山(Sushi Rozan)易名後，店子亦重新裝修過。淺啡色木板裝潢，極有日本風味。從十二個櫃枱座位減至九個座位，容納的人數少了，但廚師能更專注地服務每位客人。菜單仍是只供應廚師發辦套餐，食材和分量會按食客的需求調整。金目鯛和白海膽等高級食材每天從日本直送到店。

TEL. 2574 1333
GF, The Oakhill, 18 Wood Road, Wan Chai
灣仔活道 18號萃峯地下

■ PRICE 價錢
Dinner 晚膳
set 套餐 $ 2,080-2,980

■ OPENING HOURS 營業時間
Dinner 晚膳 18:00-20:00 / 20:30-22:30

■ ANNUAL AND WEEKLY CLOSING 休息日期
Closed 3 days Lunar New Year and Monday
農曆新年 3 天及週一休息

Sushi Mori Tomoaki

8

The young Chinese-Japanese chef has years of experience under his belt and an eye for fine details. He uses only the freshest seafood shipped daily from Kyushu and Hokkaido. His sushi rice is dressed in a unique blend of red and rice vinegar – and each piece is seasoned differently, such as yuzu pepper on nodoguro, garlic soy on engawa. A sushi set is offered at lunch, but only omakase at dinner – omakase at lunch is by appointment only.

中日混血兒主廚年紀輕輕卻具多年製作傳統壽司經驗，且喜愛鑽研烹調技法，其壽司以每日由日本運到之新鮮食材，加上以特定比例新舊米混和赤醋及米醋的壽司飯製成。午市只設一個時段，除有套餐供應，亦可預訂廚師發辦套餐。餐廳環境雅淨，適合放慢節奏，好好享受高質素的壽司美饌。

TEL. 2979 5977
Shop D, GF, 9-23 Shell Street, Tin Hau
天后蜆殼街 9-23號地下 D舖

■ PRICE 價錢
Lunch 午膳
set 套餐 $ 750-1,500
Dinner 晚膳
set 套餐 $ 2,200

■ OPENING HOURS 營業時間
Lunch 午膳 12:00-13:30 (L.O.)
Dinner 晚膳 18:30-22:30 (L.O.)

■ ANNUAL AND WEEKLY CLOSING 休息日期
Closed Mid-August, late December to early January and Sunday
八月中、十二月尾至一月初及週日休息

Sushi Saito
鮨 · 齋藤

Famed chef Takashi Saito and his team artfully and masterfully craft each Edomae-style sushi with the finest seasonal seafood. Rice from Akita is cooked in spring water from Kagoshima and dressed in a special blend of vinegar. But before you get to taste his divine creations at the cypress counter, you must first get a seat – and this exclusive sushi-ya seats just 16 guests. Telephone reservations are only accepted on specific days and at specific times.

要一嘗日本大廚齋藤孝司的江戶前壽司，你得先打通只於特定日子開放的訂座熱線。成功的十六位幸運兒，將於以日本柏木鑄造的壽司櫃枱前就座。結合最頂級時令海產、秋田稻米、鹿兒島泉水、特製醬醋和大師熟練技巧的壽司，將逐一登場，每一件都儼如藝術品，讓人禁不住細細端詳品味。

TEL. 2527 0811
45F, Four Seasons Hotel, 8 Financial Street, Central
中環金融街 8號四季酒店 45樓
www.fourseasons.com/hongkong

■ PRICE 價錢
Lunch 午膳
set 套餐 $ 1,480
Dinner 晚膳
set 套餐 $ 3,280

■ OPENING HOURS 營業時間
Lunch 午膳 12:00-13:30 (L.O.)
Dinner 晚膳 18:00-22:15 (L.O.)

Sushi Shikon
志魂

The owner wants his Hong Kong customers to enjoy the same superb quality sushi that he serves in his Tokyo restaurant – so the fish arrives daily from Japan and the rice comes from Niigata. The secret is in the vinegar, made from two kinds of sake sediment and aged for four years. The tiger prawn, the tender octopus and the egg custard with blue crab are just some of the stand-outs. Lunch is reservation only for a minimum of four people. The restaurant will be relocated in the second quarter of 2019.

志魂堅持提供優質食物的宗旨多年保持不變，繼續每天由日本漁市場運來鮮魚及選用由新潟運來的頂級日本米。這兒的壽司烹調秘訣是以兩種熟成度達四年的清酒糟製造的醋入饌，鮮魚的鮮與米飯的醋香配搭出完美的味道。午市時段只接受四人或以上的預訂。餐廳將於2019年第二季搬遷。

TEL. 2643 6800
Citadines Mercer, 29 Jervois Street, Sheung Wan
上環蘇杭街 29號馨樂庭尚圜服務公寓
www.sushi-shikon.com

■ PRICE 價錢
Dinner 晚膳
set 套餐 $ 3,500

■ OPENING HOURS 營業時間
Dinner 晚膳 18:00-20:00 / 20:30-22:30

■ ANNUAL AND WEEKLY CLOSING 休息日期
Closed Christmas; New Year's Day; Lunar New Year; Easter and Sunday
聖誕節、元旦、農曆新年、復活節及週日休息

Sushi Tokami

The owner-chef not only runs the original Tokami in Tokyo but is also the founder of a speciality tuna supplier in Japan, so the quality of the ingredients that he gets flown in daily to his Hong Kong branch is a given. For the Edomae sushi he uses Tanada rice from Yamagata, cooked with red vinegar from sake lees in a traditional claypot, to accompany the various cuts of tuna which comes from Oma, Aomori and Uchiura Bay.

來自銀座，以吞拿魚壽司享負盛名，店主在日本兼營吞拿魚專門店，每日均獲得優質新鮮的吞拿魚，在食材上佔盡優勢。廚師依照江戶前傳統方法製作壽司，選用礦物質豐富的山形縣和鹿兒島溫泉水，配以傳統土鍋烹煮米飯，再混入以酒粕發酵的赤醋，醋味特別香醇。以頸部製作的吞拿魚手卷非試不可。廚師發辦套餐每月更新。

TEL. 2771 3938
Shop 216A, 2F, Ocean Centre,
Harbour City, 17 Canton Road,
Tsim Sha Tsui
尖沙咀廣東道17號
海港城海洋中心2樓216A號舖
www.tokami.com.hk

■ PRICE 價錢
Lunch 午膳
set 套餐 $ 800-1,200
Dinner 晚膳
set 套餐 $ 2,200

■ OPENING HOURS 營業時間
Lunch 午膳 12:00-13:30 (L.O.)
Dinner 晚膳 18:00-20:30 (L.O.)

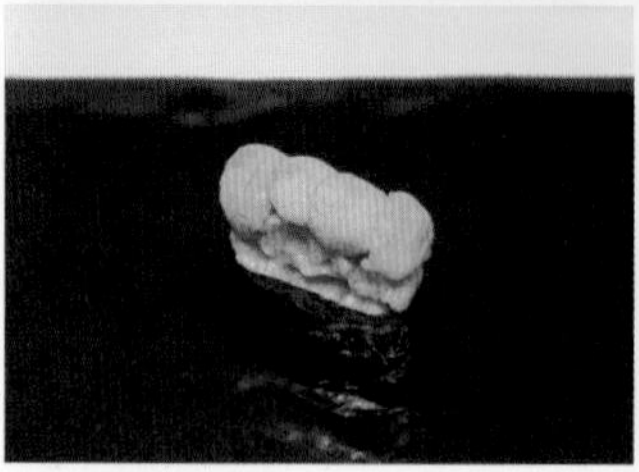

Sushi Wadatsumi

8

Formerly an outpost of Ginza Iwa, Sushi Wadatsumi cut ties with the Tokyo sushiya and changed its name after establishing its foothold. That said, nigiri sushi is still made the traditional way, using top quality fish shipped daily from Toyosu market. The head chef is of Chinese descent, so makes the locals feel right at home. The omakase dinner menus showcase over 10 different seasonal ingredients.

夥拍銀座知名壽司店助店子奠定了穩紮的根基，雖然現改由香港廚師主理，但水準始終如一。每日從日本新鮮直送到店的漁獲，加上山形縣的米，配合廚師特別調配的日本米醋，加起來就是貫徹傳統風格的手握壽司。晚上的廚師發辦套餐可一次過嘗到十多款新鮮時令食材。

TEL. 2619 0199
Shop 201, 2F,
Grand Millennium Plaza,
181 Queen's Road Central,
Sheung Wan
上環皇后大道中 181號新紀元廣場
2樓 201室

■ PRICE 價錢
Lunch 午膳
set 套餐 $ 480-1,380
Dinner 晚膳
set 套餐 $ 2,000-2,800

■ OPENING HOURS 營業時間
Lunch 午膳 12:00-14:00 (L.O.)
Dinner 晚膳 18:30-22:00 (L.O.)

■ ANNUAL AND WEEKLY CLOSING 休息日期
Closed 5 days Japanese New Year and Sunday
日本新年 5 天及週日休息

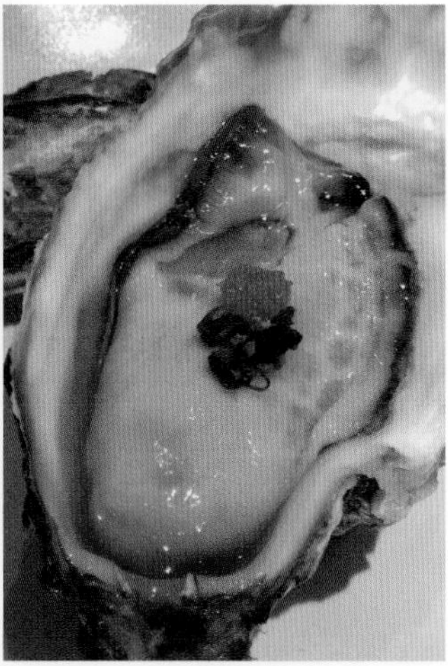

Ta Vie
旅

The mantra of chef Hideaki Sato is "pure, simple and seasonal". He has a passion for the ingredients and flavours of his native Japan which he brings together with French cooking techniques to create original, creative and sophisticated dishes. His charming wife Hiromi delivers the 10-course tasting menu, which is accompanied by an interesting collection of Asian wine and sake. This sweet little restaurant is hidden in the boutique Pottinger hotel.

面積不大的旅藏身於中環・石板街酒店內。日籍大廚佐藤秀明謹遵「純粹、簡約、時令」的信條，以法式烹調手法帶出日本食材的原始滋味，配合創意和精湛純熟的技巧，將之炮製成味道、質感獨特的佳餚。品嘗菜單包含十道菜，並佐以由其妻子精心挑選的亞洲餐酒及日本清酒。

TEL. 2668 6488
2F, The Pottinger Hotel,
21 Stanley Street, Central
中環士丹利街 21號中環・石板街酒店 2樓
www.tavie.com.hk

■ PRICE 價錢
Dinner 晚膳
set 套餐 $ 2,080

■ OPENING HOURS 營業時間
Dinner 晚膳 18:30-21:30 (L.O.)

■ ANNUAL AND WEEKLY CLOSING 休息日期
Closed Sunday 週日休息

Tai Wing Wah
大榮華

♿ 30

A refit in 2016 resulted in this Cantonese restaurant, located in the north of New Territories, looking a little brighter and feeling a little fresher. It serves dim sum and 'Walled Village' cuisine, alongside assorted classic Cantonese dishes. Try the roast duck with bean paste and coriander; claypot rice with lard and premium soy sauce; and, above all, the steamed sponge cake. A seasonal menu is available and changes every month.

光顧大榮華是很多人長途跋涉來到元朗的主要原因。此酒家除了供應點心外，還提供近百款圍村小菜及經典粵式名菜，如香茜燒米鴨、缽仔豬油頭抽撈飯及鹹水檸蒸烏頭等，更少不了奶黃馬拉糕。大廚亦每月更新時令菜式。餐廳用上五彩繽紛的地氈和明亮的燈光，配上傳統裝飾，感覺煥然一新。

TEL. 2476 9888
2F, 2-6 On Ning Road, Yuen Long
元朗安寧路 2-6號 2樓

SPECIALITIES TO PRE-ORDER 預訂食物
Pork lung soup with almond juice and milk 杏汁鮮奶燉白肺 / Roast suckling pig stuffed with glutinous rice 玻璃皮糯米豬 / Braised chicken liver with pork belly 冰肉燒鳳肝

■ PRICE 價錢
à la carte 點菜 $ 80-300

■ OPENING HOURS 營業時間
07:00-22:30 (L.O.)

Tai Woo (Causeway Bay)
太湖海鮮城 (銅鑼灣)

24

One of the district's most famous names, Tai Woo moved to these more comfortable surroundings in 2011 and, while the restaurant may be smaller than before, business is better than ever, with over 1,000 customers served every day. What hasn't changed is the quality of the service or the cooking – along with a menu of Cantonese seafood dishes, such as crunchy shrimp ball and mini lobster casserole, are favourites like sesame chicken baked in salt.

自八十年代開業，太湖一直是區內馳名的酒家。2011年遷到更舒適的現址後，食物質素和服務依然維持一貫的高水準，難怪每天有逾千食客光臨。餐館精於烹調海鮮菜式，更設有不同時令海鮮優惠，讓饕客能大飽口福；此外廣東菜式亦值得細味，招牌菜包括芝麻鹽焗雞、奇脆明珠伴金龍及薑米鮮魚炒飯等。

TEL. 2893 0822
9F, Causeway Bay Plaza 2,
463-483 Lockhart Road, Causeway Bay
銅鑼灣駱克道 463-483號
銅鑼灣廣場第二期 9樓
www.taiwoorestaurant.com

■ PRICE 價錢
Lunch 午膳
set 套餐 $ 428-568
à la carte 點菜 $ 100-250

Dinner 晚膳
set 套餐 $ 428-568
à la carte 點菜 $ 300-500

■ OPENING HOURS 營業時間
10:30-02:30 (L.O.)

■ ANNUAL AND WEEKLY CLOSING 休息日期
Closed 1 day Lunar New Year
農曆新年休息 1 天

Tak Kee
德記

16

It started out as a street-side hawker stall in the 1990s and still retains the casual, vibrant vibe. The second-generation hands-on owner shops for groceries every day and sometimes helps the experienced chefs with kitchen chores. Pork tripe and peppercorn soup is a culinary highlight, using peppers from Malaysia and Indonesia. Regulars also come for its spiced marinated goose liver, crispy chitterlings stuffed with glutinous rice and oyster omelette.

於1990年開業，早期為大牌檔，現由第二代經營。店東凡事親力親為，每天親自到菜市場採購新鮮食材，間或會在廚房幫忙潮州老師傅打點廚務。這兒的胡椒豬肚湯獨特之處是採用馬來西亞和印尼兩種胡椒，滷水大鵝肝、脆皮糯米釀大腸及馳名蠔仔餅深得食客喜愛。傳統荷包鱔，需最少八位或以上才接受預訂。

TEL. 2819 5568
GF, 3G Belcher's Street,
Western District
西環卑路乍街 3號 G地舖

SPECIALITIES TO PRE-ORDER 預訂食物
Double-boiled preserved mustard wrapped eel soup 荷包鱔 / Double-boiled pork lung soup with almond milk 杏汁白肺湯 / Joyful dumplings 繡球藏白玉

■ PRICE 價錢
Lunch 午膳
à la carte 點菜 $ 100-150
Dinner 晚膳
à la carte 點菜 $ 150-300

■ OPENING HOURS 營業時間
Lunch 午膳 11:00-15:00 (L.O.)
Dinner 晚膳 17:30-22:30 (L.O.)

■ ANNUAL AND WEEKLY CLOSING 休息日期
Closed Monday 週一休息

Takeya
竹家

The Japanese owner-chef was originally posted to Hong Kong as an engineer but, having settled here and married a local girl, he switched careers and together they opened this little yakitori shop in Hung Hom. Seating just 15, it's an intimate spot, made warmer with lots of bamboo. There's extensive choice, with seasonal specialities available. Try the special selections of Japanese wine or the high quality homemade umeshu.

日籍店主兼大廚在香港工作多年，其後與太太定居香港並展開新生活，一起經營這間以竹子為主題的串燒小店，小小的店子只有十五個座位卻予人親密溫暖的感覺。店內串燒種類繁多，時有特別食物推介。供應的日本酒較別的店子獨特，尤以自家浸製的梅酒更是不俗。

TEL. 2365 8878
Shop 1, On Wah Building,
31C1 Tak Man Street, Whampoa Estate,
Hung Hom
紅磡黃埔新村德民街 31C1安華樓 1號舖

■ PRICE 價錢
Dinner 晚膳
à la carte 點菜 $ 250-400

■ OPENING HOURS 營業時間
Dinner 晚膳 18:30-22:30 (L.O.)

■ ANNUAL AND WEEKLY CLOSING 休息日期
Closed 14 days Lunar New Year and Monday 農曆新年 14 天及週一休息

Takumi by Daisuke Mori

Revamped and renamed after its executive chef from Japan, this restaurant features greyish-blue panelling, a dark marble counter and soft lighting. Chef Mori specialises in French haute cuisine made with seasonal Japanese produce. The prix-fixe 9-course menu includes his acclaimed chargrilled Hida beef tenderloin, and can be accompanied by excellent wine pairings. There are only 11 counter seats around the open kitchen and reservations are recommended.

以灰藍色牆板與黑底白紋雲石吧枱配搭柔和燈光，時尚中帶點西化，與櫃枱座位相連的開放式廚房屹立於店中央，全店十一個座位均可目睹烹調過程。來自日本的時令食材經處理後成為帶日籍主廚個人風格的菜式；晚市套餐重點在炭燒飛驒和牛。餐酒質素尤佳。建議訂座。

TEL. 2574 1299
GF, The Oakhill, 16 Wood Road, Wan Chai
灣仔活道 16號萃峯地下

■ PRICE 價錢
Lunch 午膳
set 套餐 $ 880-1,280
Dinner 晚膳
set 套餐 $ 2,080-2,680

■ OPENING HOURS 營業時間
Lunch 午膳 12:00-14:00 (L.O.)
Dinner 晚膳 18:00-21:30 (L.O.)

■ ANNUAL AND WEEKLY CLOSING 休息日期
Closed 3 days Lunar New Year, Monday lunch and Sunday 農曆新年 3 天、週一午膳及週日休息

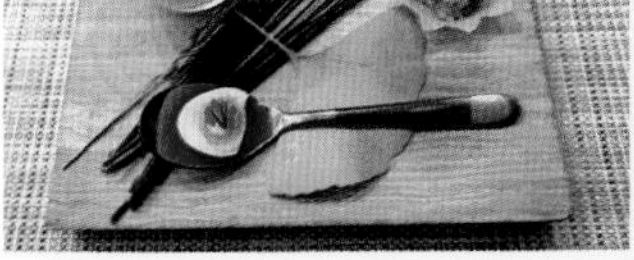

T'ang Court
唐閣

It's easy to see why this restaurant remains so popular and is soon to celebrate its 30th birthday. Comfort and luxury are factors, thanks to the plush fabrics, beautifully dressed tables and Chinese art. But it is the ability and experience of the head chef and his kitchen that plays the greatest part. Their classic and accomplished Cantonese cuisine includes dishes like Peking duck, lobster with onions and shallot, and baked stuffed crab shell with onion.

這家常客眾多的食府即將踏入三十週年，其超凡水準不言而喻。高雅的布藝裝飾、一絲不苟的餐桌佈置和一系列藝術品均引人入勝，然而最教人叫好的要數其由經驗豐富廚房團隊所呈獻的傳統粵式珍饈佳餚。北京片皮鴨、三葱爆龍蝦和釀焗鮮蟹蓋等，巧奪天工的擺盤、無可挑剔的精細處理，叫人再三回味。

TEL. 2132 7898
1-2F, The Langham Hotel,
8 Peking Road, Tsim Sha Tsui
尖沙咀北京道8號朗廷酒店1-2樓
www.langhamhotels.com/hongkong

■ PRICE 價錢
Lunch 午膳
set 套餐 $ 360-1,380
à la carte 點菜 $ 400-1,700
Dinner 晚膳
set 套餐 $ 1,080-1,380
à la carte 點菜 $ 400-1,700

■ OPENING HOURS 營業時間
Lunch 午膳 12:00-14:30 (L.O.)
Weekend and Public Holiday lunch
週末及公眾假期午膳 11:00-14:30 (L.O.)
Dinner 晚膳 18:00-22:30 (L.O.)

Tasty (Central)
正斗粥麵專家 (中環)

Be prepared to queue and share a table because over 1,000 customers a day, many of whom work in IFC, crowd into this Tasty. They mostly come for the trademark shrimp wonton or the much-loved beef and rice noodle stir fry; congee with prawns and dim sum are also recommended from the vast choice on offer. The last redecoration left the interior looking a lot more contemporary.

坐落於機鐵站上蓋，這家繁忙的店子每天接待逾千個顧客，當中除了在IFC工作的上班族，也有不少是為了一嘗港式風味而來的遊客。繁忙時間到訪，便要做好排隊和拼桌的準備。招牌鮮蝦雲吞麵和乾炒牛河都是店內受歡迎之選。此外，生猛大蝦粥及精美點心亦值得一試。

TEL. 2295 0101
Shop 3016-3018, 3F, IFC Mall,
1 Harbour View Street, Central
中環港景街 1號國際金融中心商場 3樓
3016-3018號舖
www.tasty.com.hk

■ PRICE 價錢
à la carte 點菜 $ 60-200

■ OPENING HOURS 營業時間
11:00-22:45 (L.O.)

Tate

12

The ground floor houses 'Poem', a cake shop, while the top floor boasts a sensuous dining room furnished in soft greys, muted pinks and brushed gold. Rather than sticking to the French-Japanese fusion she once championed, the owner-chef revamped the menu to use local ingredients such as osmanthus, Pu-er tea and kumquat – and her dishes exude a certain feminine delicacy. The solely French wine list is also hand-picked by an experienced female sommelier.

遷址後佔地兩層，下層是餅店，上層餐室以柔和灰褐、淡粉紅和磨沙金三種色調拼湊出優雅的氣氛。主廚以女性的細膩觸覺設計菜單，菜式以法國菜為本，獨特之處是糅合了大量中式元素，薑、桂花、普洱等見於菜式、汁醬製作和雞尾酒中。完美體驗，何不來一杯同由女葡萄酒大師挑選的法國餐酒？

TEL. 2555 2172
210 Hollywood Road, Sheung Wan
上環荷李活道 210號
www.tate.com.hk

■ PRICE 價錢
Dinner 晚膳
set 套餐 $ 1,680

■ OPENING HOURS 營業時間
Dinner 晚膳 19:00-22:00 (L.O.)

■ ANNUAL AND WEEKLY CLOSING 休息日期
Closed Sunday 週日休息

Tenku RyuGin
天空龍吟

The views are breathtaking, especially at sunset, and the interior is gracefully understated – but neither outshine the food created by chef Hidemichi Seki. He was born to a family that ran a Chinese restaurant and Chinese influences manifest themselves in some of his dishes, such as anago cooked in Shaoxing wine. The 10- to 12-course Kaiseki menu changes every season; most ingredients are shipped from Japan while the rest are sourced from local organic farms.

天空龍吟坐落於環球貿易廣場101樓，雄偉景色扣人心弦，早點到埗可以在夕照餘暉下進餐。懷石料理套餐包含十道精緻菜餚，日籍主廚生於經營中菜餐館的家庭，令其菜式滲入中國元素，招牌菜海鰻菜式就加入了中國酒烹調。上等食材八成來自日本，其餘採購自本地有機農場。菜單每季更換。

TEL. 2302 0222
Shop B1, 101F,
International Commerce Centre,
1 Austin Road West, Tsim Sha Tsui
尖沙咀柯士甸道西 1號環球貿易廣場 101樓 B1舖
www.ryugin.com.hk

■ PRICE 價錢
Dinner 晚膳
set 套餐 $ 2,380

■ OPENING HOURS 營業時間
Dinner 晚膳 18:00-21:30 (L.O.)

■ ANNUAL AND WEEKLY CLOSING 休息日期
Closed 2 days Lunar New Year
農曆新年休息 2 天

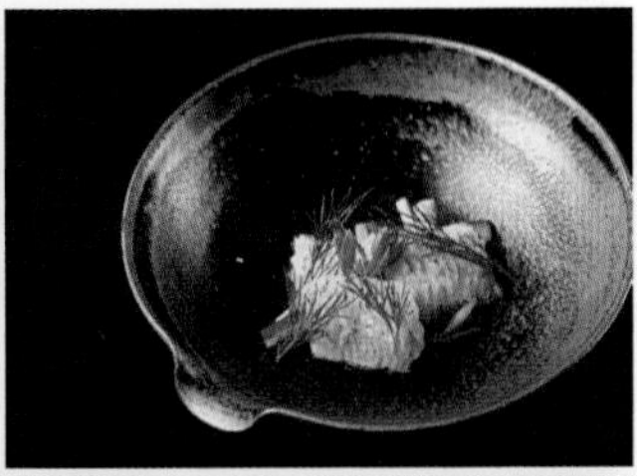

Thai Chiu (Sham Shui Po)
泰潮 (深水埗)

The all-Thai kitchen team is a strong statement regarding the authenticity of the food, while the vibrant green and yellow colour scheme of the dining room gets you in the mood. Obviously, you don't come here for the plastic tables and stools, but for the no-frills Thai food, like Hainanese chicken, tom yum seafood soup, fried egg with herbs, and various different styles of curry – which all taste great and are priced competitively.

亮綠及黃色的裝潢令這家小餐廳充滿生氣，配以膠桌子和小板凳，感覺樸實自然。要一嘗價錢相宜的泰國風味，這兒是不錯的選擇，連廚師在內的整個廚房出品部都是泰國人，自然味道正宗。菜單選擇琳琅滿目，包括泰式海南雞、香草煎蛋、冬蔭功海鮮湯，更少不了一系列咖喱菜式。

TEL. 2314 3333
101 Fuk Wing Street, Sham Shui Po
深水埗福榮街 101號

■ PRICE 價錢
à la carte 點菜 $ 60-150

■ OPENING HOURS 營業時間
11:30-22:30 (L.O.)

The Chairman
大班樓

30

The Chairman looks to small suppliers and local fishermen for its ingredients and much of the produce used is also organic. Showing respect for the provenance of ingredients and using them in homemade sauces and flavoursome dishes – such as steamed crab with aged Shaoxing, crispy chicken stuffed with shrimp paste and almond sweet soup – has attracted a loyal following. The restaurant is divided into four different sections and service is pleasant and reassuringly experienced.

大班樓的食材來自小型供應商和本地漁民，大部分都是有機材料，且將精挑細選的材料用來製作醬料和烹調美味菜式，如雞油花雕蒸大花蟹、香煎百花雞件配魚露、生磨杏仁茶等，吸引不少忠實擁躉。餐廳分成四個不同用餐區，服務令人賓至如歸。

TEL. 2555 2202
18 Kau U Fong, Central
中環九如坊 18號
www.thechairmangroup.com

SPECIALITIES TO PRE-ORDER 預訂食物
Crabmeat sticky rice 蟹肉糯米飯 / Pan fried crispy chicken stuffed with shrimp pasta 香煎百花雞件配魚露

■ PRICE 價錢
Lunch 午膳
set 套餐 $ 208-228
à la carte 點菜 $ 500-800
Dinner 晚膳
à la carte 點菜 $ 500-800

■ OPENING HOURS 營業時間
Lunch 午膳 12:00-14:00 (L.O.)
Dinner 晚膳 18:00-22:00 (L.O.)

■ ANNUAL AND WEEKLY CLOSING 休息日期
Closed 3 days Lunar New Year
農曆新年休息 3 天

The Ocean

Warm birch with turquoise accents and an ocean theme with unobstructed sea views set the mood for a dining experience by the sea, from the sea. Renowned French chef Olivier Bellin's first venture outside Brittany cooks up seafood such as langoustine, sea urchin and scallops as creatively as he does back home. Five- and eight-course prix fixe aside, an à la carte menu also offers pigeon as well as fish. Blue lobster in curry sauce is a must-try.

尊重食材、還原食材的味道，是主廚的理念。透過食物和服務帶給客人歡樂是餐廳的宗旨。五道菜和八道菜的套餐以海洋為主題，每道菜式的食材均以海洋食材組合配搭如Brittany龍蝦、海膽、帶子等，乳鴿是店內唯一非海產類食材。Ocean breeze及great reef是招牌菜。

TEL. 2889 5939
Shop 303-304, 3F, The Pulse,
28 Beach Road, Repulse Bay
淺水灣海灘道 28號
The Pulse 3樓 303-304號舖
www.theocean.hk

■ PRICE 價錢
Lunch 午膳
set 套餐 $ 988
Dinner 晚膳
set 套餐 $ 1,088-1,288
à la carte 點菜 $ 900-1,200

■ OPENING HOURS 營業時間
Weekend and Public Holiday lunch
週末及公眾假期午膳 12:00-14:30 (L.O.)
Dinner 晚膳 18:30-21:15 (L.O.)

■ ANNUAL AND WEEKLY CLOSING 休息日期
Closed Monday 週一休息

The Steak House winebar + grill

One of the most sophisticated grill rooms in town comes with its own colourful wine bar and an impressive wine list – it's 70% American and includes a large number of top Californian wines. The ingredients used here are unimpeachable: beef sourced from Australia, the U.S. and Japan is supplemented by great seafood. You even get to choose your knife from 10 different models. Service is professional but also has personality.

作為城中最著名的扒房之一，它擁有出色的酒吧及令人眼花繚亂的餐酒名單，當中70%產自美國，更包括了許多頂級加州葡萄酒。這裏採用的全是一流食材：來自澳洲、美國與日本的牛肉，配合鮮美的海鮮。你還可以從十種餐刀中挑選最心儀的款式作餐具！服務專業友善。

TEL. 2313 2323
LF, InterContinental Hotel,
18 Salisbury Road, Tsim Sha Tsui
尖沙咀梳士巴利道18號洲際酒店地庫1樓
www.hongkong-ic.intercontinental.com

■ PRICE 價錢
Lunch 午膳
set 套餐 $ 698-898
Dinner 晚膳
set 套餐 $ 888
à la carte 點菜 $ 1,000-2,500

■ OPENING HOURS 營業時間
Weekend lunch 週末午膳 12:00-14:30 (L.O.)
Dinner 晚膳 18:00-22:30 (L.O.)

The Swiss Chalet
瑞士餐廳

12

It was relocated next door, but you may not have noticed, because with its wood furniture and beams set against whitewashed walls, it has retained the same quaint Alpine chalet ambiance. The menu is classic Swiss with a variety of cured meats and sausages, over 20 different cheeses, and of course the unmissable fondue made with five cheeses and kirsch, to be paired with their extensive selection of Swiss wines.

遷到隔鄰舖位後，裝潢仍然保留原店的樣子：木傢具、小窗戶，像極了瑞士高山上的小木屋。店東兼主廚與全店職員共事二十年，食物和服務水準一直維持不變。選用的瑞士香腸、芝士、醃肉和小牛肉等質素都很好。牛面沙律、炸牛仔肉和五種芝士混合櫻桃酒而成的芝士火鍋不可錯過。多款瑞士美酒任你挑選。

TEL. 2191 9197
GF, 8 Hart Avenue, Tsim Sha Tsui
尖沙咀赫德道 8號地下

■ PRICE 價錢
Lunch 午膳
set 套餐 $ 118-168
à la carte 點菜 $ 250-650
Dinner 晚膳
à la carte 點菜 $ 250-650

■ OPENING HOURS 營業時間
Lunch 午膳 12:00-14:30 (L.O.)
Dinner 晚膳 18:00-22:30 (L.O.)

■ ANNUAL AND WEEKLY CLOSING 休息日期
Closed Sunday 週日休息

Tim Ho Wan (North Point)
添好運 (北角)

The residents of North Point appear mighty glad that Tim Ho Wan finally opened a branch on Hong Kong Island. The soberly furnished dining room is always packed and at peak hours there'll even be a queue outside. The atmosphere is typical of a local tea house and hums with general contentment. There are over twenty different dim sum choices, along with a few desserts, and the menu changes each month.

添好運自從在港島區開設分店以來，一直深受北角區街坊喜愛；裝修雖簡約但客源不絕，每逢繁忙時段更會大排長龍；店內氣氛與一般本地茶樓無異，熱鬧而略嫌擠逼。餐牌上雖只列有二十多款點心及數款甜品，但餐單上的食物款式會每月更新一次。

TEL. 2979 5608
2-8 Wharf Road, North Point
北角和富道 2-8號

■ PRICE 價錢
à la carte 點菜 $ 30-50

■ OPENING HOURS 營業時間
10:00-21:30 (L.O.)

■ ANNUAL AND WEEKLY CLOSING 休息日期
Closed 3 days Lunar New Year
農曆新年休息 3 天

Tim Ho Wan (Sham Shui Po)

添好運 (深水埗)

20

The second branch of this famous dim sum chain is roomier than the original, but don't be surprised to still find a queue of expectant diners at the entrance. Over 20 different dim sum are on offer, all skilfully made and reasonably priced. Some items rotate every two to three months to keep the menu fresh. Don't miss their shrimp dumplings, baked buns with barbecue pork filling and steamed beef balls. Two rooms on the first floor offer more privacy.

一如添好運其他分店，這家店子的二十多款精美點心全由廚師巧手製作，且價錢相宜，加上選址於人口稠密的住宅區內，受食客歡迎乃屬意料之中。由於不設訂座，要有排隊輪候的準備。不可不試的點心包括蝦餃、酥皮焗叉燒包和陳皮牛肉球。店家每隔兩至三個月會轉換點心款式。一樓設兩間小型貴賓房。

TEL. 2788 1226
9-11 Fuk Wing Street, Sham Shui Po
深水埗福榮街 9-11號

■ PRICE 價錢
à la carte 點菜 $ 30-50

■ OPENING HOURS 營業時間
10:00-21:30 (L.O.)
Weekends 週末 09:00-21:30 (L.O.)

■ ANNUAL AND WEEKLY CLOSING 休息日期
Closed 3 days Lunar New Year
農曆新年休息 3 天

Tim Ho Wan (Tai Kwok Tsui)
添好運 (大角咀)

The first and original shop of the chain moved into this shopping mall from Mong Kok. Crowds still flock in like before, but this place is much more spacious and airy, thanks to the high ceiling and a light colour scheme. Most of the regulars care more about the food – over 20 handmade dim sum are on the menu, along with a few exclusive items not available at other branches. The ingredients are fresh and the prices are more than reasonable.

添好運的旺角總店遷至大角咀現址後更見寬敞舒適，高聳的樓底配搭白色主調的裝潢感覺明淨清新。二十多款廣式點心不賣弄外形或配搭，而是以傳統手藝配上新鮮食材取勝。這裏更設有本店限定的點心，每隔數月轉換，食客每次到訪都有驚喜。滋味十足且價錢相宜，說明了何以總是座無虛席。

TEL. 2332 2896
Shop 72A-C, GF, Olympian City 2,
18 Hoi Ting Road, Tai Kwok Tsui
大角咀海庭道 18號
奧海城 2期地下 G72A-C舖

■ PRICE 價錢
à la carte 點菜 $ 30-50

■ OPENING HOURS 營業時間
10:00-21:30 (L.O.)

■ ANNUAL AND WEEKLY CLOSING 休息日期
Closed 3 days Lunar New Year
農曆新年休息 3 天

Tim's Kitchen (Sheung Wan)
桃花源小廚 (上環)

26

Founded in 1999 and moved to this location in 2010, this restaurant spans across two floors and accommodates more than 100 guests at one time. Owner-chef Tim is an avid Cantonese opera lover and that explains the décor and posters on display. Traditional Cantonese fare takes centre stage and includes the hugely popular crystal prawn, pomelo skin and pork stomach, which showcase the kitchen's respect for every ingredient.

桃花源小廚取名自同名粵劇工作舍；色彩豐富而時尚的餐室內亦不乏粵劇元素的裝飾，反映出店主對此傳統藝術的鍾愛。自1999年開業以來，餐廳一直以傳統粵菜侍客，每款食品都證明廚房對優質材料的高度重視，鎮店菜式如玻璃蝦球、柚皮及豬肚皆不容錯過。現址佔地兩層，可容納一百人。

TEL. 2543 5919
84-90 Bonham Strand, Sheung Wan
上環文咸東街 84-90號
www.timskitchen.com.hk

SPECIALITIES TO PRE-ORDER 預訂食物
Steamed whole fresh crab claw with winter melon 冬瓜蒸原隻鮮蟹鉗

■ PRICE 價錢
Lunch 午膳
à la carte 點菜 $ 150-300
Dinner 晚膳
à la carte 點菜 $ 300-1,000

■ OPENING HOURS 營業時間
Lunch 午膳 10:30-16:00 (L.O.)
Dinner 晚膳 18:00-22:30 (L.O.)

■ ANNUAL AND WEEKLY CLOSING 休息日期
Closed 4 days Lunar New Year
農曆新年休息 4 天

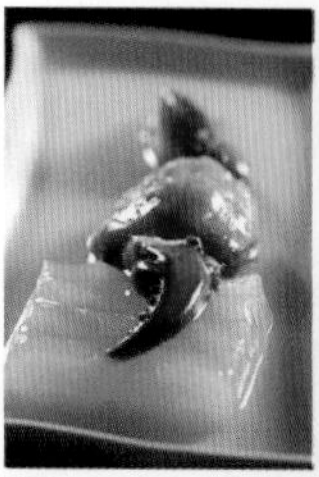

Tin Hung
天鴻燒鵝

Popular with locals since 2001, this shop sells its signature roast geese in specific cuts, halves or whole. Geese are slaughtered daily in a farm in Foshan, China before being shipped here. They are then marinated and roasted to perfection, and served piping hot. Other standouts include honey-glazed char siu pork, roast duck and drunken chicken. Those looking to pair the meats with a local drink should try their homemade herbal tea.

天鴻燒鵝2001年開業，尤為區內居民熟悉。來自佛山養殖場的黑鬃鵝每日直送到店，分批即醃即燒，確保每隻都熱氣騰騰。招牌燒鵝分為全隻、半隻及不同部位發售，高峰期每日售出近百隻，若售罄便會提早關門。除了燒鵝，蜜汁叉燒、燒鴨、花雕醉雞等亦值得一試；店家更出售清熱的自製五花茶。

TEL. 2474 8849
Shop D, GF, Yan Yee Building,
88 Kin Yip Street, Yuen Long
元朗建業街 88號仁義大廈地下 D鋪

■ PRICE 價錢
Lunch 午膳
à la carte 點菜 $ 60-200
Dinner 晚膳
à la carte 點菜 $ 60-200

■ OPENING HOURS 營業時間
Lunch 午膳 11:00-15:00 (L.O.)
Dinner 晚膳 17:00-22:30 (L.O.)

Tin Lung Heen
天龍軒

12

'Dragon in the sky' is a very apposite name as this good looking Cantonese restaurant occupies a large part of the 102nd floor of the Ritz-Carlton hotel. The vast windows bring in plenty of daylight at lunch and make it a good spot from which to watch the sun go down. Among the signature dishes are barbecued Iberian pork with honey, and double-boiled chicken soup with fish maw in coconut. There are also several charming private rooms.

位於香港麗思卡爾頓酒店102樓，這間極具氣派的粵菜餐館以氣勢十足的天龍命名。樓高兩層的設計令餐廳光線充沛，格外舒適，殷勤的服務人員讓你倍感親切。另設有多個精緻的私人包廂。菜單着重傳統菜式，值得一試的有蜜燒西班牙黑豚肉叉燒和原個椰皇花膠燉雞。

TEL. 2263 2150
102F, The Ritz-Carlton Hotel,
1 Austin Road West, Tsim Sha Tsui
尖沙咀柯士甸道西 1號
麗思卡爾頓酒店 102樓
www.ritzcarlton.com/hongkong

■ PRICE 價錢
Lunch 午膳
set 套餐 $ 658-2,098
à la carte 點菜 $ 450-1,300
Dinner 晚膳
set 套餐 $ 1,888-2,098
à la carte 點菜 $ 450-1,300

■ OPENING HOURS 營業時間
Lunch 午膳 12:00-14:30 (L.O.)
Weekend and Public Holiday lunch
週末及公眾假期午膳 11:30-15:00 (L.O.)
Dinner 晚膳 18:00-22:30 (L.O.)

Toritama
西玉

8

There appears to be no end to the number of Tokyo restaurants opening branches in Hong Kong and this time here in LKF it's all about yakitori. Seating is limited so it's worth booking ahead and asking for the bar counter to watch the expert preparation in the semi-open kitchen. 40-day-old chickens are used and 28 different parts of the chicken are offered – all you have to do is decide how many skewers you want.

室內座位數量不多，建議預先訂座。餐廳選用的雞隻只有四十天大，確保肉質鮮嫩，供應超過二十八種由不同部位製作的雞串。由日籍和來自南非的大廚共同主理的串燒，每一件都烤得恰到好處。廚師會因應食客的進食速度預備每一道食物，並會親自送到食客面前。

TEL. 2388 7717
GF, Greenville, 2 Glenealy, Central
中環己連拿利 2號翠怡閣地舖
www.toritama.hk

■ PRICE 價錢
Dinner 晚膳
set 套餐 $ 298-598
à la carte 點菜 $ 200-600

■ OPENING HOURS 營業時間
Dinner 晚膳 18:00-23:00 (L.O.)

■ ANNUAL AND WEEKLY CLOSING 休息日期
Closed 7 days Lunar New Year and Sunday 農曆新年 7 天及週日休息

Tosca

The dining room is airy and striking, with an ultra-high ceiling, a show-stopping chandelier, a water feature, an open kitchen and gigantic windows that afford panoramic views. The menu has changed as the new chef champions a direct and no-frills approach to traditional Italian cooking. Cotoletta alla Milanese (breaded veal cutlet) with green salad and roast potatoes particularly stands out and is big enough for two to share.

闊落的天花、店中央的開放式廚房、巨型穆拉諾吊燈，替這家在102樓層上擁有迷人海景的餐廳錦上添花。新主廚掌舵後，菜單格調稍有調整，以直接簡潔的烹調手法把意大利菜呈現於食客眼前，有意品嘗傳統意式風味的不容錯過。供二人享用、分量十足的炸小牛排值得一試。

TEL. 2263 2270
102F, The Ritz-Carlton Hotel,
1 Austin Road West, Tsim Sha Tsui
尖沙咀柯士甸道西 1號麗思卡爾頓酒店 102樓
www.ritzcarlton.com/hongkong

■ PRICE 價錢
Lunch 午膳
set 套餐 $ 448-698
à la carte 點菜 $ 1,000-1,500
Dinner 晚膳
set 套餐 $ 1,308-1,708
à la carte 點菜 $ 1,000-1,500

■ OPENING HOURS 營業時間
Lunch 午膳 12:00-14:30 (L.O.)
Dinner 晚膳 18:00-22:30 (L.O.)

Town

8

Bryan Nagao, the owner-chef of this chic yet relaxed urban eatery, is a name familiar to Hong Kong food lovers. Here he has created a menu that reflects his international background by using Japanese and Hawaiian influences along with French and Italian flavours, in dishes like suckling pig, and short rib with black garlic, cabbage and miso sweet potato. Lunch is a simpler affair and includes an hors d'oeuvres buffet.

混凝土和紅磚牆、櫟木地板、藍或淺啡色靠背椅與面向繁忙街道的落地玻璃窗塑造出活潑、現代的感覺。主廚兼東主Bryan Nagao設計的菜單帶有日本、夏威夷、法國和意大利風格，並按季節配搭時令食材；拿手菜包括西西里蝦配黑松露魚子醬薄肉片及味噌甜薯牛仔骨。午餐供應較簡約的餐單和自助頭盤。

TEL. 2568 8708
10F, Cubus, 1 Hoi Ping Road,
Causeway Bay
銅鑼灣開平道1號 Cubus 10樓
www.townrestauranthk.com

■ PRICE 價錢
Lunch 午膳
set 套餐 $ 218-288
à la carte 點菜 $ 500-900
Dinner 晚膳
set 套餐 $ 700
à la carte 點菜 $ 500-900

■ OPENING HOURS 營業時間
Lunch 午膳 12:00-14:30 (L.O.)
Dinner 晚膳 18:30-22:30 (L.O.)

TRi

Borrowing its name from the Balinese concept of a balance between man, nature and divinity, this place exudes otherworldly serenity. The show-stopping 10-metre-long century table carved from one piece of wood seats 16 people. Lotus bud-shaped pods over water pools house round booth seating with sea views. Traditional Balinese fare is done with a touch of finesse and slightly less heat here. Try their Sapi Marangi, slow-cooked beef in sweet soy.

人工湖上是以竹竿與木材打造而成的半圓形卡座，傢具全是從峇里運來，10米長的木餐桌，帶着純樸的大自然味道。餐廳供應的峇里菜雖傳統，味道卻並不太辣，餐單上的菜式貴精不貴多。招牌菜Sapi Marangi(慢煮牛肉)經過48個小時慢煮後再以秘製醬汁烹調，值得一試。

TEL. 2515 0577
Shop 302, 3F, The Pulse, 28 Beach Road, Repulse Bay
淺水灣海灘道 28號 The Pulse 3樓 302號舖
www.tri.hk

■ PRICE 價錢
Lunch 午膳
set 套餐 $ 680
à la carte 點菜 $ 450-800
Dinner 晚膳
set 套餐 $ 680
à la carte 點菜 $ 450-1,000

■ OPENING HOURS 營業時間
Lunch 午膳 12:00-15:00 (L.O.)
Dinner 晚膳 18:30-22:00 (L.O.)
Weekends and Public Holidays
週末及公眾假期 11:30-22:00 (L.O.)

■ ANNUAL AND WEEKLY CLOSING 休息日期
Closed Monday 週一休息

Trusty Congee King (Wan Chai)
靠得住 (灣仔)

As suggested by its name, you can really trust the quality of the food served in this long-standing congee shop. The menu has become more versatile in recent years with congee, noodles and snack sets available. All congee is cooked in fish broth that gives an extra dimension of flavour. Many rave about the pork liver and scallop congee, sticky rice dumpling with salted egg yolk and pork, and poached grass carp skin.

位於灣仔多年的靠得住出品一如其名，從不令人失望。其粥品採用魚湯作粥底，是餐廳一大特色，不容錯過的有心肝寶貝粥、鹹肉粽和皇牌魚皮。食物的種類愈來愈多元化，精選套餐有不同的配搭，不妨試試新增的炸雲吞。2017年翻新後餐室簡潔光亮。

TEL. 2882 3268
7 Heard Street, Wan Chai
灣仔克街 7號

■ PRICE 價錢
set 套餐 $ 55-108
à la carte 點菜 $ 50-120

■ OPENING HOURS 營業時間
11:00-22:00 (L.O.)

Trusty Gourmet
信得過

The owner also runs a company supplying pork so he has an edge on sourcing the freshest pork at competitive prices. He believes the quality of the food speaks louder than fame and doesn't allow MSG in the kitchen. The signature stir-fried pork offal with salted mustard greens boasts offal from 12- to 14-month-old pigs for tenderness. Diners also rave about the thickly sliced pork liver and the boiled chicken with Chinese chive.

豬肉供應商的家族背景，令店東在貨源上佔有優勢，確保豬肉新鮮和有質素。店東不僅實行無味精烹調方式，還選用12-14個月大的中豬作豬雜材料，肉質較幼嫩。厚切豬肝是此店的特色食品，較受食客喜愛的有鹹菜炒豬雜、奇妙肚絲蛋缽及萬綠葱中半隻雞。店東特別搜羅特色豬仔器皿作食具，更顯心思。

TEL. 2838 7373
Shop A, Fasteem Mansion,
307-311 Jaffe Road, Wan Chai
灣仔謝斐道 307-311號快添大廈 A舖

■ PRICE 價錢
Lunch 午膳
set 套餐 $ 58-88
à la carte 點菜 $ 100-150
Dinner 晚膳
à la carte 點菜 $ 100-150

■ OPENING HOURS 營業時間
11:30-22:00 (L.O.)

■ ANNUAL AND WEEKLY CLOSING 休息日期
Closed 5 days Lunar New Year
農曆新年休息 5 天

Tsim Chai Kee (Wellington Street)
沾仔記 (威靈頓街)

This highly regarded, simple noodle shop has been here since 1998 and is easy to spot – just look for the lunchtime queues. The staff are as bright as their aprons; the popular side booths are quickly snapped up; and the regulars know to eat outside peak times when the pace is less frenetic. The attraction is the handmade fish balls, the generously filled wontons and the beef; ordering a three topping noodle is the way to go.

享負盛名的沾仔記於1998年開業，裝修簡單但整潔舒適。侍應制服明亮潔淨，設有卡位及經常滿座；熟客會在非繁忙時間光顧，因氣氛較悠閒。著名食品包括自製鮮鯪魚球、餡料豐富的招牌雲吞及鮮牛肉麵；你可以來一碗三拼湯麵，一次過品嘗以上三種美食。

TEL. 2850 6471
98 Wellington Street, Central
中環威靈頓街 98號

■ PRICE 價錢
à la carte 點菜 $25-50

■ OPENING HOURS 營業時間
09:00-22:00 (L.O.)

■ ANNUAL AND WEEKLY CLOSING 休息日期
Closed 4 days Lunar New Year
農曆新年休息 4 天

Tsui Hang Village (Tsim Sha Tsui)
翠亨邨 (尖沙咀)

60

A staple of the Tsim Sha Tsui restaurant scene since 1970s, this place is famous for its authentic Cantonese and Shun Tak fare, namely its bestselling honey-glazed char siu pork, braised beef ribs and shredded chicken, alongside some original creations by the head chef, such as fried king prawns in mango sauce topped with caviar. The dim sum is also good. Watching the chefs work their magic through the large window is all part of the experience.

翠亨邨早於1970年代在尖沙咀開業，菜式以傳統粵菜為主，如醬燒牛肋排、翠亨邨靚一雞及最暢銷的蜜汁叉燒；此外亦不乏順德菜式，以及注入現代元素的新創作，如黑魚子醬芒貴妃蝦球。在這裏，你可以透過大玻璃窗，欣賞廚師烹調各式佳餚，同時滿足視覺和味覺享受。

TEL. 2376 2882
Shop 507, 5F, FoodLoft,
Mira Place One, 132 Nathan Road,
Tsim Sha Tsui
尖沙咀彌敦道132號美麗華廣場一期食四方5樓507號舖
www.miradining.com

SPECIALITIES TO PRE-ORDER 預訂食物
Baked chicken with preserved vegetables, shredded pork and mushroom 宮廷富貴雞

■ PRICE 價錢
Lunch 午膳
à la carte 點菜 $ 150-350
Dinner 晚膳
à la carte 點菜 $ 200-500

■ OPENING HOURS 營業時間
Lunch 午膳 11:30-14:30 (L.O.)
Sunday and Public Holiday lunch
週日及公眾假期午膳 10:30-14:30 (L.O.)
Dinner 晚膳 18:00-22:00 (L.O.)

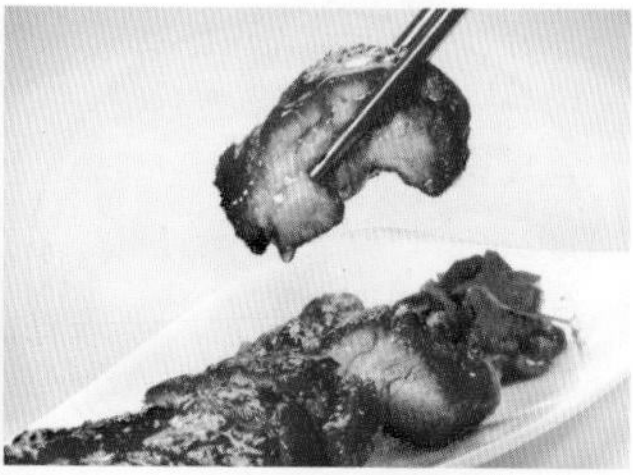

Upper Modern Bistro

The dining room feels fresh and vibrant with different shades of white, grey and blue, and oversized petal-like pieces cascading from the ceiling onto a wall. The food is equally creative and attractive, and shows some Asian influences, such as roast pigeon with Indian spices, and the Okinawa poached egg with shiitake mushrooms, crabmeat and baby spinach. Over 30 French cheeses, including rare 48-month aged Comté, would keep any turophile happy.

純白、銀灰及海藍色的配搭，予人滿有朝氣的感覺，花瓣狀的銀片天花裝飾添了點前衛創新的味道。這兒的法國菜在傳統上滲入了亞洲風味的新元素，例如以印度香料醃製，慢煮再燒烤而成的燒鴿；還有加入了冬菇和蟹肉的沖繩燉蛋。另有超過三十款法國芝士可供挑選，當中包括難得一見、經48個月熟成的Comté。

TEL. 2517 0977
6-14 Upper Station Street,
Sheung Wan
上環差館上街 6-14號
www.upper-bistro.com

■ PRICE 價錢
Lunch 午膳
Monday to Friday set 週一至週五套餐
$ 168-268
à la carte 點菜 $ 420-820

Dinner 晚膳
set 套餐 $ 768
à la carte 點菜 $ 420-820

■ OPENING HOURS 營業時間
Lunch 午膳 12:00-14:30 (L.O.)
Dinner 晚膳 18:00-22:30 (L.O.)

Symbols shown in red indicate particularly charming establishments XXX.

紅色標誌 XXX 表示酒店和餐館在同級別的舒適程度中較優秀。

Read 'How to use this guide' for an explanation of our symbols, classifications and abbreviations.

請細閱「如何使用餐廳 / 酒店指南」，當中的標誌、分類等簡介助你掌握使用本指南的訣竅，作出智慧選擇。

VEA

🏵 10

An impressive counter and open kitchen dominate the room and this is where you'll want to sit to watch chef Cheng and his team in action. An experience it most certainly is, thanks to a 10-course tasting menu that features ingredients from Hong Kong, Taiwan and the provinces of China. The creative and original dishes stimulate all the senses while also paying respect to the history of Hong Kong. Arrive early and enjoy a cocktail in their bar.

開放式廚房和櫃台座位佔據着餐室主要位置，安坐此處將能讓你一睹廚師團隊揮灑自如的烹調過程。十道菜的品嘗菜單採用港台和中國各省份食材，卻以西式手法烹調，菜式設計創意十足，更蘊含了香港文化在其中，為食客帶來耳目一新的味覺體驗。用餐前可先到酒吧淺酌一杯同樣富創意的雞尾酒。

TEL. 2711 8639
30F, The Wellington,
198 Wellington Street, Central
中環威靈頓街 198號 The Wellington 30樓
www.vea.hk

■ PRICE 價錢
Dinner 晚膳
set 套餐 $ 1,480

■ OPENING HOURS 營業時間
Dinner 晚膳 17:00-21:30 (L.O.)

■ ANNUAL AND WEEKLY CLOSING 休息日期
Closed Sunday 週日休息

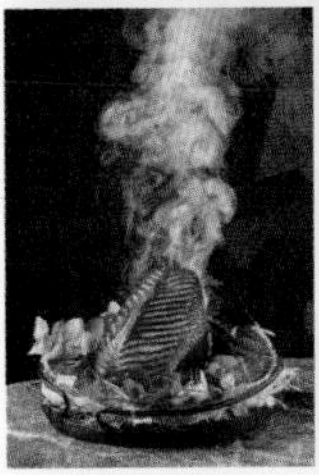

Wang Fu (Central)
王府 (中環)

Wang Fu was one of the first shops to open on Wellington Street and its Pekingese dumplings are renowned. Over ten kinds of freshly hand-made dumplings with different fillings are on offer each day. Don't miss the green onion mutton dumpling or the vegetarian dumpling – the tomato and egg dumpling, which is only available after 2pm, is also good. As well as the dumplings and noodles, assorted hot Sichuan snacks are also offered.

王府是威靈頓街最早期開業的水餃店，其北京水餃遠近馳名，供應的餃子款式超過十種，每天均由人手新鮮包製，羊肉京葱餃和花素餃不可不試。除水餃麵食外，還供應多款京川小食。

TEL. 2121 8006
65 Wellington Street, Central
中環威靈頓街 65號

■ PRICE 價錢
à la carte 點菜 $ 50-100

■ OPENING HOURS 營業時間
11:00-22:00 (L.O.)

■ ANNUAL AND WEEKLY CLOSING 休息日期
Closed 4 days Lunar New Year
農曆新年休息 4 天

What To Eat
吃什麼

The two Taiwanese mums have revived the old name of their first bento shop. The menu is now bigger, but the food is just as good and the service just as warm and homely. The egg crepe roll is made with ingredients imported from Taiwan and the beef shin in the noodle soup is braised for more than five hours in a spiced broth. Taiwanese veggies such as citron daylily and vegetable fern are hard to find elsewhere.

兩位台灣媽媽的食店之路雖經一番波折，但初心依然：希望客人能安然坐下好好享用一頓簡單的餐點，感受當中濃濃的人情味。原班人馬帶來種類更多的食品，猶幸食材和手法不變：燜煮逾五小時的牛肉美味依然；招牌蛋餅的蛋皮始終由台灣進口；麵條經特別調配，在本地現做。多款小吃及時令台灣土產均值得一試。

TEL. 2810 9278
Shop A, GF,
Carfield Commercial Building,
75-77 Wyndham Street, Central
中環雲咸街 75-77號
嘉兆商業大廈地下 A號地舖

■ PRICE 價錢
Lunch 午膳
à la carte 點菜 $65-250
Dinner 晚膳
à la carte 點菜 $65-250

■ OPENING HOURS 營業時間
Lunch 午膳 12:00-15:00 (L.O.)
Dinner 晚膳 18:00-21:00 (L.O.)

■ ANNUAL AND WEEKLY CLOSING 休息日期
Closed 4 days Lunar New Year and Sunday 農曆新年 4 天及週日休息

Whisk

The chef's new-found love of all things Japanese means his cooking now falls into two distinct halves. On the one side you have sharing dishes, like suckling pig and Bretagne lobster, which blend modern European dishes with subtle Asian tones. On the other side you'll find the newer, "infused" Japanese-style dishes where, for example, your lobster comes with uni and kombu. Some may be a work in progress but they certainly show innovation.

熟悉當代歐洲烹調技巧的廚師在歐陸菜基礎上糅合日本元素，令菜式出現了有趣迥異的兩種風格，一方面有適合大伙兒分享的時尚歐陸菜式，如波士頓龍蝦意大利麵和風味烤乳豬；另一方面也有濃濃的日本風菜式，如包括了油甘魚和海膽的龍蝦海鮮籃。酒單羅列超過二百款全球佳釀，在露台享用另有一番風情！

TEL. 2315 5999
5F, The Mira Hotel, 118 Nathan Road, Tsim Sha Tsui
尖沙咀彌敦道 118號 The Mira 5樓
www.themirahotel.com

■ PRICE 價錢
Lunch 午膳
set 套餐 $ 268-398
Dinner 晚膳
à la carte 點菜 $ 900-1,200

■ OPENING HOURS 營業時間
Lunch 午膳 12:00-14:30 (L.O.)
Sunday lunch 週日午膳 12:00-15:00 (L.O.)
Dinner 晚膳 18:30-22:30 (L.O.)

■ ANNUAL AND WEEKLY CLOSING 休息日期
Closed Sunday dinner 週日晚膳休息

Wing Lai Yuen
詠藜園

12

The film business glitterati used to flock to the original shop in San Po Kong for the authentic Sichuan Dan Dan noodles. A decade ago the Yeung family moved it to its current address in Whampoa Garden, where the Dan Dan noodles are still the main attraction, although these days you can decide whether or not you want them spicy. Along with other Sichuan dishes are a few Shanghainese specialities too.

新蒲崗原鋪吸引了無數影星名人，全為了一嘗正宗四川擔擔麵蜂擁而至。隨着社區的發展，楊氏家族決定把店子遷址到現在的黃埔花園。直至今日擔擔麵仍然是其主打麵食，不過，現在你還可以選擇辣或不辣的湯底。另外，店內同時供應多款川菜和上海美食。

TEL. 2320 6430
Shop 102-105, 1F, Gourmet Place,
Whampoa Plaza, Site 8,
Whampoa Garden, Hung Hom
紅磡黃埔花園第 8 期 1 樓
黃埔美食坊 102-105號鋪

■ PRICE 價錢
Lunch 午膳
à la carte 點菜 $ 80-120
Dinner 晚膳
à la carte 點菜 $ 100-180

■ OPENING HOURS 營業時間
Lunch 午膳 11:00-15:30 (L.O.)
Dinner 晚膳 18:00-22:30 (L.O.)

HONG KONG 香港

Wu Kong (Causeway Bay)
滬江 (銅鑼灣)

XX

36

The many customers of this Shanghainese restaurant had reason to celebrate its relocation in 2011 to the upper level of Lee Theatre Plaza as it resulted in better views, more space and a nicer environment in which to eat. An experienced kitchen shows its practised hand in specialities such as braised pig's knuckle with brown sauce and honey ham and crispy bean curd in bread. Do try the hairy crab menu in the autumn season.

於2011年搬到利舞臺高層的滬江飯店，為顧客帶來更佳的景觀、更寬敞的空間和更舒適的環境，讓他們更盡情享用美食。廚藝精湛的廚師為顧客炮製多款巧手小菜，如紅燒元蹄和響鈴火腿夾。於秋季期間，肥美的大閘蟹是必吃的時令佳餚。

TEL. 2506 1018
Shop B, 17F, Lee Theatre Plaza,
99 Percival Street, Causeway Bay
銅鑼灣波斯富街 99號利舞臺廣場 17樓 B號舖
www.wukong.com.hk

■ PRICE 價錢
Lunch 午膳
set 套餐 $ 98
à la carte 點菜 $ 150-450
Dinner 晚膳
à la carte 點菜 $ 150-450

■ OPENING HOURS 營業時間
Lunch 午膳 11:45-14:45 (L.O.)
Dinner 晚膳 17:45-22:45 (L.O.)

■ ANNUAL AND WEEKLY CLOSING 休息日期
Closed 3 days Lunar New Year
農曆新年休息 3 天

Xin Rong Ji (N)

新榮記

15

Taizhou cuisine emphasises the natural flavours of ingredients, which are only sparingly seasoned with aromatics. Wild-caught yellow croaker from the East China Sea is the speciality here; other recommendations include deep-fried conger eel and braised radish and seasonal offerings are also available. The elegant dining room is traditionally styled and decorated with bonsai plants; tables are made from one piece of solid wood.

新榮記秉承待人為本的信念，把台州口味帶來香港。台州菜着重原汁原味，在烹煮過程中毫不添加任何醬料，僅以葱、薑、蒜配合簡單調味料，帶出食材本身的味道。餐廳推崇東海海鮮，堅持採用優質新鮮的食材；推介家燒黃魚、黃金脆帶魚，以及從台州運到香港，經多重功夫烹煮的家燒蘿蔔。另有按季節推出的時令菜式。

TEL. 3462 3518
GF, China Overseas Building,
138 Lockhart Road, Wan Chai
灣仔駱克道138號中國海外大廈地下
www.xinrongji.cc

■ PRICE 價錢
Lunch 午膳
à la carte 點菜 $ 350-600
Dinner 晚膳
à la carte 點菜 $ 600-1,000

■ OPENING HOURS 營業時間
Lunch 午膳 12:00-14:30 (L.O.)
Dinner 晚膳 18:00-22:30 (L.O.)

■ ANNUAL AND WEEKLY CLOSING 休息日期
Closed 3 days Lunar New Year
農曆新年休息 3 天

Yan Toh Heen
欣圖軒

42

Its location on the lower level of the InterContinental hotel may be somewhat concealed but it's well worth seeking out this elegant Cantonese restaurant and that's not just because of the lovely views of Hong Kong Island. The authentic, carefully prepared specialities include stuffed crab shell with crabmeat; wagyu beef with green peppers, mushrooms and garlic; double-boiled fish maw and sea whelk; and wok-fried lobster with crab roe and milk.

酒店經重新規劃後，這家優雅的粵菜酒家現遷至大堂低座，全新裝潢設計仍保留了原有的玉石主題，精緻華美，遠眺窗外更能細賞香港島的美景。經驗豐富的廚師團隊繼續帶來傳統粵式佳餚，精心之作包括脆釀鮮蟹蓋、蒜片青尖椒爆和牛、花膠響螺燉湯及龍皇炒鮮奶等。

TEL. 2313 2243
Lower Level, InterContinental Hotel,
18 Salisbury Road, Tsim Sha Tsui
尖沙咀梳士巴利道18號洲際酒店大堂低座
www.hongkong-ic.intercontinental.com

SPECIALITIES TO PRE-ORDER 預訂食物
Braised fish maw with sea cucumber in oyster jus 蠔皇厚花膠扣遼參 / Barbecued whole suckling pig 金陵脆皮乳豬 / Peking duck 北京片皮鴨 / Hangzhou beggar's fortune chicken 杭州富貴雞

■ PRICE 價錢
Lunch 午膳
à la carte 點菜 $350-2,000
Dinner 晚膳
set 套餐 $2,688
à la carte 點菜 $450-2,000

■ OPENING HOURS 營業時間
Lunch 午膳 12:00-14:30 (L.O.)
Sunday & Public Holiday lunch
週日及公眾假期午膳 11:30-15:00 (L.O.)
Dinner 晚膳 18:00-23:00 (L.O.)

Yat Lok
一樂燒鵝

The signature roast geese glistening behind the window are marinated with a secret recipe and go through over 20 preparatory steps before being chargrilled to perfection. Char siu pork uses pork shoulder from Brazil for melty tenderness. Roast pork belly and soy-marinated chicken are also recommended. Expect to share a table with others. It's been run by the Chus since 1957 and in this location since 2011.

早於1957年開始營業的一樂於2011年遷至現址，一直由店東朱氏夫婦打理。掛在窗前的鎮店招牌燒鵝油光亮澤，乃朱先生以其家族秘方醃製、經過二十多道工序炮製而成，色香味俱佳。由於每次只燒製十隻，要嘗到特定部位就得靠點運氣了。店內燒味均以炭爐燒製，推介燒腩仔，玫瑰油雞也做得不錯。

TEL. 2524 3882
34-38 Stanley Street, Central
中環士丹利街 34-38號

■ PRICE 價錢
à la carte 點菜 $60-360

■ OPENING HOURS 營業時間
10:00-21:00 (L.O.)
Sunday & Public Holidays 週日及公眾假期 10:00-17:30 (L.O.)

■ ANNUAL AND WEEKLY CLOSING 休息日期
Closed 10 days Lunar New Year and Wednesday 農曆新年 10 天及週三休息

Yat Tung Heen (Jordan)
逸東軒 (佐敦)

48

The remodelled dining room boasts dark wood panels and moody lighting, which are refreshingly different from its formerly conventional décor. Since 1990, the kitchen team has been creating traditional but refined Cantonese fare that highlights the ingredients' natural tastes. Barbecued meats, stir-fries and slow-cooked soups are hugely popular. Regulars also order the abalone and bird's nest set menu for their banquet dinners in the private rooms.

經全面裝修後一改以往傳統中菜廳格調，簡約裝潢配上昏黃燈光，更顯年輕型格。自1990年開業至今，廚師團隊一直為食客烹調傳統而精緻的粵菜，沒花巧噱頭卻以扎實的烹調功夫盡顯四時食材真鮮味。燒味、小菜和老火湯深得食客歡迎，不少人更愛於廂房以鮑魚燕窩套餐宴客。

TEL. 2710 1093
B2F, Eaton Hotel, 380 Nathan Road, Jordan
佐敦彌敦道 380號逸東酒店地庫 2樓
www.eatonhongkong.com

SPECIALITIES TO PRE-ORDER 預訂食物
Crispy roasted Peking duck 片皮鴨二食 / Whole roasted marinated suckling pig 金陵醬脆皮燒乳豬

■ PRICE 價錢
Lunch 午膳
set 套餐 $288
à la carte 點菜 $450-1,000
Dinner 晚膳
à la carte 點菜 $450-1,000

■ OPENING HOURS 營業時間
Lunch 午膳 11:00-14:30 (L.O.)
Dinner 晚膳 18:00-22:30 (L.O.)

Yau Yuen Siu Tsui (Jordan)
有緣小敍 (佐敦)

The owner's wife works alone in this shop, serving authentic Shaanxi dishes and snacks from her hometown, like dumplings and baked buns with meat. The most impressive dish is Biang Biang noodles – these long, flat, handmade noodles come with a spicy chilli sauce and are full of flavour. Other specialities include Shaanxi-style noodles with vegetables and pork in spicy and sour soup, and Shaanxi-style bread with stewed pork.

由原來位於西貢街的小店搬至現址後，環境較為舒適且能招待更多客人。來自陝西的店東太太為食客奉上風味獨特的家鄉小食如哨子麵、肉夾饃等，其中最令人難忘的莫過於Biang Biang麵。這款由人手製作，麵身寬長的麵食配上特製醬料，香辣味濃，令人再三回味。店內還提供多款熱葷小菜。

TEL. 5300 2682
GF, 36 Man Yuen Street, Jordan
佐敦文苑街 36號地下

■ PRICE 價錢
à la carte 點菜 $50-100

■ OPENING HOURS 營業時間
12:00-22:00 (L.O.)

Yè Shanghai (Tsim Sha Tsui)
夜上海 (尖沙咀)

80

Drawing not only on Shanghai but also on the neighbouring provinces of Jiangsu and Zhejiang, the cooking here is subtle and expertly balanced. Specialities include sautéed shredded Mandarin fish, baked stuffed crab shell and braised beef ribs with brown sauce. The contemporary décor recalls 1930s Shanghai in its use of dark woods, subdued lighting and semi-private alcoves. This is a busy, sophisticated operation.

餐室以當代風格設計，昏暗的燈光配上深色木材，散發着三十年代老上海的味道。這裏除了供應上海菜，還有江蘇及浙江菜，全由技術精湛的廚師烹調，特色美食包括龍鬚桂魚絲、蟹粉釀蟹蓋及紅燒原條牛肋排。餐廳每月更會以時令食材構思不同的廚師推介菜式，為食客增添新鮮感。

TEL. 2376 3322
6F, Marco Polo Hotel,
3 Canton Road, Tsim Sha Tsui
尖沙咀廣東道3號馬哥孛羅酒店6樓
www.elite-concepts.com

SPECIALITIES TO PRE-ORDER 預訂食物
Beggar's chicken 富貴雞

■ PRICE 價錢
Lunch 午膳
à la carte 點菜 $ 150-300
Dinner 晚膳
à la carte 點菜 $ 250-600

■ OPENING HOURS 營業時間
Lunch 午膳 11:30-14:30 (L.O.)
Dinner 晚膳 18:00-22:30 (L.O.)

Yee Tung Heen
怡東軒

96

The first thing you'll notice is the Chinese ornaments and the second is how well Chinese screens and contemporary lighting go together. This elegant restaurant not only offers traditional Cantonese favourites but also serves specialities of a more creative persuasion. The enthusiastic chef and his team spend much time seeking out the best quality seasonal ingredients, whether that's from local markets or overseas. The restaurant will be closed at the end of March 2019.

踏入怡東酒店內的怡東軒中菜廳，馬上便會給精緻的中式擺設吸引。往內走，會發現四周的中式屏風與現代天花燈，配搭得十分別致。餐廳供應傳統粵菜，廚師及營運團隊充滿熱誠，專程由本地及世界各地搜羅各種高質素及時令食材，時有創新菜式或特別餐單推出。餐廳將於2019年3月底停業。

TEL. 2837 6790
2F, The Excelsior Hotel,
281 Gloucester Road, Causeway Bay
銅鑼灣告士打道 281號怡東酒店 2樓

SPECIALITIES TO PRE-ORDER 預訂食物
Baked traditional salt-crusted chicken with Chinese wine 古法酒香鹽焗雞

■ PRICE 價錢
Lunch 午膳
à la carte 點菜 $ 250-1,000
Dinner 晚膳
à la carte 點菜 $ 400-1,000

■ OPENING HOURS 營業時間
Lunch 午膳 12:00-14:30 (L.O.)
Sunday lunch 週日午膳
10:30-12:30 / 13:00-15:00 (L.O.)
Dinner 晚膳 18:00-22:30 (L.O.)

Ying Jee Club
營致會館

24

Rather than gimmicky promotions, the owner prefers diverting more energy and resources to finding the freshest ingredients and refining the chef's cooking techniques. Diners are greeted by an elegant and contemporary dining hall adorned with marble tables, velvet seats and metallic trims. The menu is traditionally Cantonese with a touch of finesse. Their signature crispy salted chicken is silky and tender without being overly oily.

裝潢運用翡翠、雲石、絲絨、金屬框等物料，典雅時尚。食物亦同樣細緻，廚師沉實地以新鮮食材和熟練烹調技巧炮製細緻傳統的廣東菜來滿足客人，招牌菜脆香貴妃雞皮脆酥香、肉質嫩滑且不油膩；片皮乳豬件亦是水準之作。地下酒吧專售氈酒調製的雞尾酒，也有較特別的選擇如輕井澤威士忌。

TEL. 2801 6882
Shop G05, 107-108, GF & 1F,
Nexxus Building,
41 Connaught Road Central, Central
中環干諾道中41號盈置大廈
地下G05及1樓107-108號舖
www.yingjeeclub.hk

■ PRICE 價錢
Lunch 午膳
set 套餐 $ 380
à la carte 點菜 $ 300-1,000
Dinner 晚膳
à la carte 點菜 $ 500-1,200

■ OPENING HOURS 營業時間
Lunch 午膳 11:30-15:00 (L.O.)
Dinner 晚膳 18:00-23:00 (L.O.)

Yixin
益新

36

North Point was the original location for this family-run restaurant when it opened in the 1950s. It's moved a few times since then but is now firmly ensconced here in Wan Chai. Run by the 3rd generation of the family, a sense of continuity also comes from the head chef who has been with the company over 50 years! The Cantonese food is traditional, with quite a few Shun Tak dishes; specialities include roasted duck Pipa-style, and smoked pomfret.

早於五十年代於港島區開業，輾轉搬至灣仔現址，現由第三代經營。除了地面的主廳和客房外，地庫還有一個裝潢時尚的餐室。益新一向以傳統粵菜馳名，餐單上不乏耗功夫製作的懷舊菜式，吸引不少客人在此舉行宴會。琵琶鴨、金錢雞及煙焗鯧魚等都是常客所愛。另設有預訂菜譜，可向店員查詢。

TEL. 2834 9963
50 Hennessy Road, Wan Chai
灣仔軒尼詩道 50號
www.yixinrestaurant.com

■ PRICE 價錢
Lunch 午膳
à la carte 點菜 $ 200-250
Dinner 晚膳
à la carte 點菜 $ 400-500

■ OPENING HOURS 營業時間
Lunch 午膳 11:30-15:30 (L.O.)
Dinner 晚膳 18:00-22:30 (L.O.)

■ ANNUAL AND WEEKLY CLOSING 休息日期
Closed 2 days Lunar New Year and 1st July lunch 農曆新年 2 天及 7 月 1 日午膳休息

Yuè (Gold Coast)
粵 (黃金海岸)

36

It's not often one can enjoy Cantonese food surrounded by verdant scenery but here on the ground floor of the Gold Coast hotel that's exactly what you get as this comfortable restaurant looks out onto a delightful garden. The menu includes both traditional and more contemporary dishes and it's worth seeking out the chef's specialities such as barbecued pork and chicken liver with honey, and deep-fried chicken with shrimp paste.

位於黃金海岸酒店的地面層，優雅舒適的室內環境，與落地玻璃窗外的園林景致巧妙地配合起來。選擇豐富的餐單提供傳統懷舊及較創新的粵菜，廚師精選菜式如蜜餞金錢雞和星洲蝦醬炸雞件等，值得一試。邊品嘗美味的廣式點心邊欣賞宜人的園林美景，實在是賞心樂事。

TEL. 2452 8668
LG, Gold Coast Hotel,
1 Castle Peak Road, Gold Coast
黃金海岸青山公路1號黃金海岸酒店低層
www.goldcoasthotel.com.hk

■ PRICE 價錢
Lunch 午膳
à la carte 點菜 $ 200-500
Dinner 晚膳
à la carte 點菜 $ 250-700

■ OPENING HOURS 營業時間
Lunch 午膳 11:30-15:15 (L.O.)
Sunday and Public Holiday lunch
週日及公眾假期午膳 09:00-15:45 (L.O.)
Dinner 晚膳 18:30-22:45 (L.O.)

Yuè (North Point)
粵 (北角)

120

It may seem like nothing more than a mezzanine area of the City Garden hotel but it's well worth coming up here for the Cantonese food. The experienced chef's respect for the traditions of Cantonese cuisine is clearly demonstrated in dishes like double-boiled jus of almonds with fish maw, fried rice with prawns and barbecue pork, and seared garoupa with layered egg white. There are a number of different sized private rooms.

看起來只是城市花園酒店的閣層，並不特別，定讓不少人忽略了這間中菜廳，但絕對值得前來一嘗這兒的粵菜。資深大廚對傳統粵菜的尊重完全反映在其製作的各樣菜式上，例如杏汁花膠燉蹄筋、師傅炒飯和雪嶺紅梅映松露等。餐廳設有不同大小的廂房供各類宴會之用。

TEL. 2806 4918
1F, City Garden Hotel,
9 City Garden Road, North Point
北角城市花園道 9號城市花園酒店 1樓
www.citygarden.com.hk

■ PRICE 價錢
Lunch 午膳
à la carte 點菜 $ 280-1,300
Dinner 晚膳
à la carte 點菜 $ 280-1,300

■ OPENING HOURS 營業時間
Lunch 午膳 11:30-14:30 (L.O.)
Weekend and Public Holiday lunch
週末及公眾假期午膳 10:30-14:30 (L.O.)
Dinner 晚膳 18:00-22:15 (L.O.)

Yue Kee
裕記

From humble beginnings as a tiny countryside joint in 1958, this second-generation family business has gone big, but without losing its flair. Geese are sourced from eight farms in China to ensure quality and a steady supply. The owner insists on chargrilling them according to his family recipe, to give them their distinctive smokiness, crispy skin and juicy meat. They're served after 11:45am and the menu also includes seafood and stir-fries.

裕記於1958年開業，現由第二代打理。從鄉村小店到現在的規模，仍保留着傳統食店風味。其招牌燒鵝是店東按家傳秘方以炭火烤製，味道獨特且酥香肉嫩，採用的鵝從內地八個農場合作伙伴中挑選，確保貨源和質素。每天第一爐鵝於11:45出爐，早到埗的食客需稍候。燒鵝以外，亦供應海鮮及特色小菜。

TEL. 2491 0105
9 Sham Hong Road, Sham Tseng
深井深康路 9號
www.yuekee.com.hk

■ PRICE 價錢
à la carte 點菜 $ 150-550

■ OPENING HOURS 營業時間
11:00-22:15 (L.O.)

■ ANNUAL AND WEEKLY CLOSING 休息日期
Closed 3 days Lunar New Year
農曆新年休息 3 天

Yuet Lai Shun
粵來順

Ceiling fans, window grilles, booth seats and faux-marble tables are reminiscent of the good old cha chaan teng in Hong Kong circa 1960s. The décor also chimes with the food it serves – retro Cantonese classics that are well-made and reasonably priced. Chicken poached in honey soy stands out, with juicy velvety meat and well-balanced sauce. Deep-fried shrimp balls with cheese filling and pork lung almond milk soup are among diners' favourites.

吊扇加鐵窗花、帶點茶餐廳味道的雲石方桌卡座，裝潢一如六、七十年代的酒樓，很有老香港風情。與其裝潢一樣，這兒主打的就是懷舊廣東菜。蜂蜜豉油雞，肉質嫩滑，與以蝦膠芝士作餡料的千絲芝心球和生磨杏汁白肺湯同屬鎮店招牌菜。

TEL. 2788 3078
Shop 10-12, GF, Po Hang Building,
2-8 Dundas Street, Mong Kok
旺角登打士街 2-8號寶亨大廈地下 10-12號舖

SPECIALITIES TO PRE-ORDER 預訂食物
Double-boiled pork lung and almond milk soup 生磨杏汁白肺湯 / Steamed crab roe with glutinous rice in lotus leaf 籠仔荷香糯米蒸羔蟹

■ PRICE 價錢
Lunch 午膳
set 套餐 $ 42-52
à la carte 點菜 $ 100-200
Dinner 晚膳
à la carte 點菜 $ 200-300

■ OPENING HOURS 營業時間
11:30-23:00 (L.O.)

■ ANNUAL AND WEEKLY CLOSING 休息日期
Closed 3 days Lunar New Year
農曆新年休息 3 天

Don't confuse the rating X with the Stars ✿! The first defines comfort and service, while Stars are awarded for the best cuisine.

千萬別混淆了餐具 X 和星星 ✿ 標誌！餐具標誌表示該餐廳的舒適程度和服務質素，而星星代表的是食物質素與味道非常出色而獲授為米芝蓮星級餐廳的餐館。

An important business lunch? The symbol ⌂ indicates restaurants with private rooms.

需要一個合適的地點享用商務午餐？可從注有這個 ⌂ 標誌的餐廳中選一間有私人廂房又合你心意的餐館。

Zhejiang Heen
浙江軒

XX 16

At what must be one of the easiest restaurants to find – just look for the huge Zhejiang landscape on the outside of the building – you'll find authentic Zhejiang and Shanghainese specialities made from top quality ingredients, such as smoked fish, shrimps with seaweed, and steamed shad fish. Run by a Zhejiang Fraternity Association, the dining room is spread over two floors and while it may not be particularly lavish, it is comfortable. Vegetarian menu is available.

要數最容易找的酒家，這家必定榜上有名，因為它的外牆有一大幅浙江風景圖。你可在這裏品嘗到採用上等食材烹調的傳統浙江及上海美食，如長江燻魚、苔條蝦仁及廚師引以為傲的清蒸鰣魚。這裏由香港浙江省同鄉會聯合會經營，樓高兩層，雖然裝修並不豪華，但感覺十分舒適，更設有素菜餐單供素食人士選擇。

TEL. 2877 9011
1-3F, Kiu Fu Commercial Building,
300-306 Lockhart Road, Wan Chai
灣仔駱克道 300-306號
橋阜商業大廈 1-3樓
www.zhejiangheen.com

SPECIALITIES TO PRE-ORDER 預訂食物
Crispy deep-fried chicken with 4 treasures 四寶片皮雞 / Braised duck stuffed with 8 treasures 蠔燒八寶鴨

■ PRICE 價錢
Lunch 午膳
set 套餐 $ 450
à la carte 點菜 $ 200-300
Dinner 晚膳
set 套餐 $ 450
à la carte 點菜 $ 400-500

■ OPENING HOURS 營業時間
Lunch 午膳 11:30-14:30 (L.O.)
Dinner 晚膳 18:00-22:30 (L.O.)

■ ANNUAL AND WEEKLY CLOSING 休息日期
Closed 3 days Lunar New Year
農曆新年休息 3 天

Street Food 街頭小吃

Popular places for snack food
馳名小食店

Block 18 Doggie's Noodle 十八座狗仔粉

MAP 地圖 17/C-2
GF, 27A Ning Po Street, Jordan
佐敦寧波街 27A地下

Fried pork fat noodles, pork skin and radish, and roast duck leg.
狗仔粉(豬油渣麵)、豬皮蘿蔔、碗仔翅，還有火鴨髀。

$ 30-50 24 hours 24小時

Butchers Club

MAP 地圖 28/A-2
GF, 2 Landale Street, Wan Chai
灣仔蘭杜街 2號

Burgers made with Australian grain-fed beef and duck fat fries are always the perfect match in here.
澳洲穀飼牛肉漢堡和鴨油薯條是絕配！

$ 100-150 12:00-23:00

Chin Sik 千色車仔麵

MAP 地圖 5/B-1
49 Shiu Wo Street, Tsuen Wan
荃灣兆和街 49號

Choose your own selection of noodles and toppings.
車仔麵。

$ 25-50 11:30-01:00

Durian Land 榴槤樂園 N

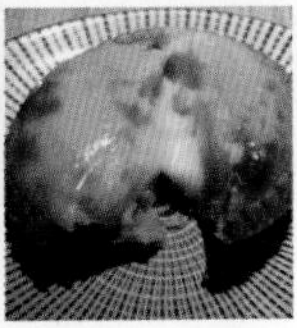

Offers different types of durian from their own farm, as well as durian desserts.

供應產自自置果園的不同品種原個榴槤，及各種榴槤甜品。

$ 25-110 14:00-20:00

MAP 地圖 19/C-1
92 Kimberly Road, Tsim Sha Tsui
尖沙咀金巴利道 92號

Fat Boy 第三代肥仔

Hong Kong style snacks including octopus, pork liver, turkey gizzard marinated in soy sauce.

墨魚、生腸、火雞腎及豬膶等港式小食。

$ 20-40 13:00-00:00

MAP 地圖 19/C-2
3 Hau Fook Street, Tsim Sha Tsui
尖沙咀厚福街 3號

Fork Eat

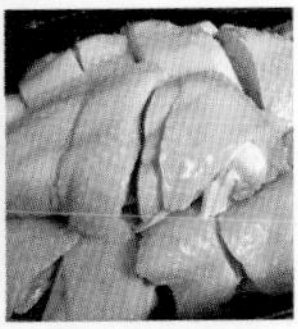

Slow cooked local farm chicken, USDA rib steak.

自家農場雞，真空慢煮美國安格斯小牛排。

$ 50-170 12:00-21:00
Closed Monday 週一休息

MAP 地圖 2/B-2
Shop 10, GF, Yik Fat Building,
11-15 Fung Yau Street North, Yuen Long
元朗鳳攸北街 11-15號益發大廈 10號舖

Hop Yik Tai 合益泰小食

Rice rolls; fish balls and radish.

豬腸粉、魚蛋、豬皮及蘿蔔，每天也人頭湧湧。

$ 10-40 06:30-20:00

MAP 地圖 7/B-2
121 Kweilin Street, Sham Shui Po
深水埗桂林街 121號

I Love You Dessert Bar

MAP 地圖 15/D-3
Shop 3A, GF, Ngai Hing Mansion,
24 Pak Po Street, Mong Kok
旺角白布街 24號藝興大廈地下 3A號舖

Soufflé pancake.
梳乎厘班戟。

$ 30-45 15:00-23:00
13:00-23:00 (Weekend and Public Holiday 週末及公眾假期)
Closed Monday 週一休息

Joyful Dessert House (Mong kok)

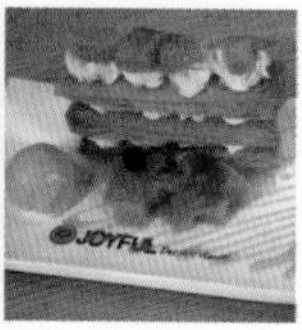

MAP 地圖 15/D-3
Shop 2-3, 74 Hak Po Street, Mong Kok
旺角黑布街 74號 2-3號舖

Western desserts like mango Napoleon, pineapple sherbet.
西式甜品如芒果拿破崙、燒菠蘿雪葩及綠茶心太軟伴雪糕。

$ 55-70 15:00-01:00
15:00-02:00 (Fri , Sat & Public Holiday Eve 週五、六及公眾假期前夕)

Kai Kai 佳佳甜品

MAP 地圖 17/C-2
29 Ning Po Street, Jordan
佐敦寧波街 29號

Offers traditional Chinese sweet soups. Ginkgo and job's tears sweet soup and black sesame soup are worth trying.
售賣傳統中式糖水，白果薏米腐竹糖水和芝麻糊值得一試。

$ 20-30 12:00-04:00

Kei Tsui 奇趣餅家

MAP 地圖 15/D-2
135 Fa Yuen Street, Mong Kok
旺角花園街 135號

Cantonese traditional puddings and pastries like Xiaofeng cake and walnut cookies.
中式餅食如雞仔餅、老婆餅、光酥餅、合桃酥及香蕉糕等。

$ 10-60 07:30-20:00

Kelly's Cape Bop

MAP 地圖 28/B-3
C1, GF, Southorn Mansion,
55-61 Johnston Road, Wan Chai
灣仔莊士敦道 55-61號修頓大廈 C1舖

In addition to its famous kimbop in various flavours, it's worth waiting for the à la minute egg rolls.
除了不同口味的紫菜飯卷，即叫即做的煎蛋卷也值得等待。

$60-150 11:00-21:00

Keung Kee 強記美食

MAP 地圖 29/D-2
382 Lockhart Road, Wan Chai
灣仔駱克道 382號

The glutinous rice with preserved meat is available all year. Rice rolls are cooked-to-order.
全年供應臘味糯米飯及豬骨粥，還有即叫即煎的腸粉。

$ 20-40 12:00-01:00

King of Soyabeans (San Po Kong) 豆漿大王 (新蒲崗) N

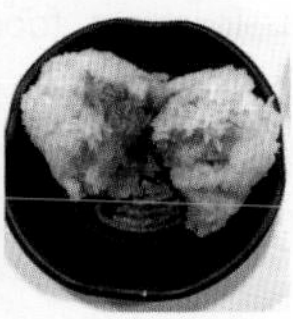

MAP 地圖 8/A-2
Shop 9, GF, New Tech Plaza,
34 Tai Yau Street, San Po Kong
新蒲崗大有街 34號新科技廣場地下 9號舖

Provides freshly made Shanghainese sticky rice rolls, along with soy milk and other bean curd snacks.
粢飯即場製作，口感尤佳；鹹甜豆漿及其他豆製品亦不容錯過。

$ 15-50 08:00-21:00
09:00-21:00 (Sun and Public Holiday 週日及公眾假期)

Kung Wo Tofu 公和荳品廠 N

MAP 地圖 7/B-2
118 Pei Ho Street, Sham Shui Po
深水埗北河街 118號

Besides its reowned tofu pudding, it also offers soy milk and tofu snacks.
除馳名豆腐花，還有各類豆製品和豆漿。

$ 10-30 07:00-21:00

Kwan Kee Store 坤記糕品

Chinese rice pudding; white sugar cake and black sesame roll.

砵仔糕、芝麻糕、白糖糕、馬蹄糕等傳統小食。

$ 20-40　08:00-20:00

MAP 地圖 7/B-2
115-117 Fuk Wa Street, Sham Shui Po
深水埗福華街 115-117號

Mak Kee 麥記美食

Offers daily made Shanghainese buns and cakes. Scallion pancakes are sold from 3pm until they run out.

每天鮮製的上海包點，其中葱油餅只在下午三時開售，售完即止。

$ 30-50　11:00-22:00
11:00-20:00 (Sun 週日)
Closed Monday 週一休息

MAP 地圖 34/B-2
Shop 1, 21 Fort Street, North Point
北角堡壘街 21號 1號鋪

Mammy Pancake 媽咪雞蛋仔

Classic street food cooked in a special egg waffle pan.

經典及創新口味雞蛋仔。

$ 20-40　11:00-22:30

MAP 地圖 19/C-2
8-12 Carnarvon Road, Tsim Sha Tsui
尖沙咀加拿芬道 8-12號

Man Kei Cart Noodles 文記車仔麵

Turnip, minced dace, Chinese chive dumpling, beef tendon, pork trotter, pig intestine and chicken wing.

配菜多樣如蘿蔔、鯪魚肉、韭菜餃、牛孖筋、牛腩、牛肚、豬手、豬大腸等。

$ 25-60　11:00-01:00

MAP 地圖 7/B-2
121 Fuk Wing Street, Sham Shui Po
深水埗福榮街 121號

Owl's

Homemade choux and gelato with different condiments.

手工泡芙及意大利雪糕。

$ 25-60　　15:30-22:30
Closed Monday 週一休息

MAP 地圖　19/C-2
GF, 32 Mody Road, Tsim Sha Tsui
尖沙咀麼地道 32號地下

So Kee 蘇記燉蛋 N

Offers cooked-to-order double-steamed egg white with milk.

只售原味牛奶燉蛋白，以北海道牛乳及鮮蛋白燉製，即叫即做。

$ 30　　15:30-22:30

MAP 地圖　2/B-2
Shop 15, GF, Block A, Ho Shun Yee Building, 9 Fung Yau Street East, Yuen Long
元朗鳳攸東街 9號好順意大廈 A座地下 15號鋪

The Noodle Hive 蜜斗 N

Offers MSG-free cart noodles with toppings that are not commonly available, like rock salt shredded chicken.

標榜無味精的車仔麵，餸菜包括少見的岩鹽雞肉、木魚雞湯浸的牛舌等。

$ 40-60　　12:00-19:00
12:00-22:00 (Thur-Fri 週四至週五)
Closed Sunday 週日休息

MAP 地圖　24/B-2
12A, Elgin Street, Central
中環伊利近街 12A

HOTELS
酒店

HOTELS IN ORDER OF COMFORT
酒店 — 以舒適程度分類

Citadines Mercer
馨樂庭尚圜

Those who need the convenience of a Central location but also want a little space should consider Citadines Mercer. The narrow 31-storey building has just 15 standard bedrooms but 40 one-bedroom suites. Ubiquitous beige tones add to the up-to-date feel and rooms come with large writing desks and a host of free extras which include the minibar and local phone calls.

如果你既愛中環的便利，又需要較多私人空間，馨樂庭尚圜服務公寓絕對適合你。建築外形修長，樓高三十一層，只有十五間標準客房，卻有達四十間單人睡房套間。統一的米白色調散發出時尚感覺，房間設有大型書桌和附送多項免費服務，包括免費本地電話服務和迷你酒吧。

TEL. 2922 9988
29 Jervois Street, Sheung Wan
上環蘇杭街 29號
www.citadines.com

RECOMMENDED RESTAURANTS 餐廳推薦
Sushi Shikon 志魂 ✿✿✿

† = $ 1,350-2,650
†† = $1,500-2,800
Suites 套房 = $ 1,650-2,950

Rooms 客房 15
Suites 套房 40

City Garden
城市花園

You'll find the City Garden in a largely residential area, a short walk from Fortress Hill MTR. The bedrooms would not necessarily win any design awards but they are fair in both size and price. The Garden Café offers an extensive international buffet; Satay Inn on the basement level provides Asian specialities; and Yuè serves authentic Cantonese dishes.

城市花園酒店坐落於寧靜的住宅區內，與炮台山港鐵站只有咫尺，交通網絡非常便利。除了佔盡港島區的優越地勢外，客房空間充裕且收費合理；附屬的綠茵閣餐廳提供豐富的午、晚市環球美食自助餐，開設在一樓的粵中菜廳則提供傳統廣東佳餚。

TEL. 2887 2888
9 City Garden Road, North Point
北角城市花園道 9號
www.citygarden.com.hk

RECOMMENDED RESTAURANTS 餐廳推薦
Yuè (North Point) 粵（北角） ⅠO ✗✗

♦ = $ 2,800-4,200
♦♦ = $ 2,800-4,200
Suites 套房 = $ 5,900
☕ = $ 180

Rooms 客房　602
Suites 套房　11

Conrad
港麗

It's been a feature in Admiralty for almost 30 years now and while this hotel still looks modern from the outside, the interior has more of an understated feel. Choose a Harbour or Peak view room – or a corner suite which offers both. The outdoor pool comes complete with cabanas, and dining options include Italian cuisine in Nicholini's and Cantonese in Golden Leaf.

酒店位處集購物娛樂於一身的太古廣場之上，即使坐落金鐘近三十年，外觀仍歷久常新；大堂設計簡樸古典，配上中式花瓶及銅像擺設，優雅而壯麗。寢室設在40至61樓，套房能讓你盡享海景和山景，而且空間寬敞。室外游泳池坐擁香港全景，池畔設有帷幔。酒店設意大利及粵菜餐館。

TEL. 2521 3838
Pacific Place, 88 Queensway, Admiralty
金鐘道 88號太古廣場
www.conradhongkong.com

= $ 2,300-5,300
= $2,300-5,300
Suites 套房 = $ 5,200-8,600
= $ 285

Rooms 客房 467
Suites 套房 45

Cordis
康得思

The modern, luminous lobby of this 42-storey glass tower features contemporary Chinese paintings and sculptures – part of the collection of 1,500 pieces that you'll find dotted around the hotel. Good-sized rooms with picture windows come with smart marble bathrooms and nice views. There's a pool on the top floor and an all-day buffet restaurant on the lobby floor.

康得思坐落於行人如鯽的旺角心臟地帶，連接地鐵站和購物商場。琉璃塔般的大樓高42層，不僅有科技發燒友夢寐以求的電子產品，還有超過1,500幅畫作、雕塑與裝置藝術品，是一個中國現代美術展覽館。客房的設計含蓄而時髦，窗外是五光十色的繁華市景；天台設有室外恒溫游泳池，並有多間餐廳供客人選擇。

TEL. 3552 3388
555 Shanghai Street, Mong Kok
旺角上海街555號
cordishotels.com/hongkong

RECOMMENDED RESTAURANTS 餐廳推薦
Ming Court 明閣 ✿ XXX

† = $ 1,400-2,200
†† = $1,400-2,200
Suites 套房 = $ 2,400-4,200

Rooms 客房 636
Suites 套房 29

Crowne Plaza
皇冠假日

Upper level bedrooms at this modern, corporate-minded hotel have the best outlooks, which include views of the Happy Valley racetrack on the south side. All of the bedrooms are decently sized and come with glass-walled bathrooms and impressive extras such as a wide choice of pillows. On the top floor you'll find Club@28: a chic bar with a terrace.

這家精心設計的時尚酒店，高層客房坐擁最美麗的港島景觀，南邊客房可飽覽跑馬地馬場全景。所有房間都寬敞舒適，浴室牆壁以玻璃砌成，擴闊了視覺上的空間，設施應有盡有，包括不同款式的枕頭。酒店頂層有為時尚人士而設的Club@28酒吧，還有小型泳池和健身室。

TEL. 3980 3980
8 Leighton Road, Causeway Bay
銅鑼灣禮頓道 8號
www.cphongkong.com

† = $ 2,050-3,600
†† = $ 2,050-3,600
Suites 套房 = $ 4,850-6,400
☕ = $ 238

Rooms 客房 253
Suites 套房 10

Crowne Plaza Kowloon East
九龍東皇冠假日

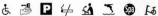

A comfortable, well-equipped hotel in a busy commercial district with good transport links. It boasts one of the largest ballrooms around and dining options include a buffet, a Chinese restaurant and a steakhouse on the roof-top, along with a bar with great views. The contemporary bedrooms are warm and stylish and come with glass-walled bathrooms and a host of extras.

由著名酒店集團管理，坐落於將軍澳鐵路站上蓋，交通便捷。客房設計時尚，色調柔和、簡單的線條和善用空間的設計，平實卻不失優雅。大型多用途宴會廳和會議設施是其一大特色。綠草如茵的露天花園可作婚禮場地。酒店頂層的露天酒吧是一個能讓人放鬆心情的好地方。

TEL. 3983 0388
3 Tong Tak Street, Tseung Kwan O
將軍澳唐德街 3號
www.crowneplaza.com/kowlooneast

= $ 1,300-2,800
= $ 1,300-2,800
Suites 套房 = $ 6,300-8,000
= $ 268

Rooms 客房 354
Suites 套房 5

East
東隅

East is a modern business hotel designed for those who, like the hotel staff, can wear a pair of Converse with their suit. It has an uncluttered lobby, a bright, open plan restaurant serving international cuisine, and a great rooftop terrace bar named 'Sugar', as this was once a sugar factory. Bedrooms are minimalist but well-kept; corner rooms are especially light.

標榜為品味商務酒店。整潔的大堂、時尚的酒吧、提供國際美食的餐廳，加上可觀看迷人維港景色的天台酒吧Sugar——名字靈感源自酒店前身的糖廠，絕對切合你的需要。客房佈置簡約優雅，以大量玻璃與木材塑造出溫暖感覺與品味。位處轉角的客房景觀尤佳。

TEL. 3968 3968
29 Taikoo Shing Road, Taikoo Shing
太古城太古城道 29號
www.east-hongkong.com

🚹 = $ 2,800-3,800
🚹🚹 = $2,800-3,800
Suites 套房 = $ 4,500-6,800
☕ = $ 228

Rooms 客房 339
Suites 套房 6

Four Seasons
四季

Four Seasons hotel not only offers some of the most spacious accommodation in Hong Kong but the bedrooms, which have wall-to-wall windows, also feature an impressive array of extras. Choose between a Western style room and one with a more Asian feel; all have large and luxurious bathrooms. The hotel also boasts two bars, two swimming pools and three world class restaurants.

四季酒店與維港毗鄰，景色壯麗，提供香港最寬敞時尚的客房。客房佈置分為現代風格和東方情調兩種，且設有大型豪華浴室。Blue Bar專為享受雞尾酒和現場音樂演奏而設。水療設施令人印象難忘，更設有兩個溫度不同的泳池。舒適的環境與高質素服務兩者俱備。

TEL. 3196 8888
8 Finance Street, Central
中環金融街 8號
www.fourseasons.com/hongkong

RECOMMENDED RESTAURANTS 餐廳推薦
Caprice ✿✿✿ XXXXX
Lung King Heen 龍景軒 ✿✿✿ XXXX
Sushi Saito 鮨·齋藤 ✿✿ XX

† = $ 4,100-5,500
†† = $ 4,300-5,600
Suites 套房 = $ 11,800-13,500
☕ = $ 340

Rooms 客房 345
Suites 套房 54

Gold Coast
黃金海岸

This beach resort 30 minutes away from the city has undergone a major overhaul. Two-thirds of the rooms were revamped with a few themed around outer space, pirates, princesses and safaris to amuse your little ones. The new ocean-themed play area is also a fun way to burn off energy. Those tying the knot will applaud the indoor garden feel of The Terrace and the solemn grandeur of The Chapel.

酒店三分之二的客房經過翻新，感覺明亮、時尚、舒適。兒童特色主題房間：公主、太空、恐龍、森林等，佈置得色彩繽紛、生動逼真，此外，新增設的鯊魚冒險島，緊張刺激卻有趣。重新設計的婚禮教堂和庭園，是不錯的婚宴場地。毗鄰泳灘，兼有完備的康樂設施和幽美園林，是度假的理想之選。

TEL. 2452 8888
1 Castle Peak Road, Gold Coast
黃金海岸青山公路 1號
www.goldcoasthotel.com.hk

RECOMMENDED RESTAURANTS 餐廳推薦
Yuè (Gold Coast) 粵（黃金海岸）

Single = $ 2,900-4,000
Double = $ 2,900-4,000
Suites 套房 = $ 5,800-16,800
Breakfast = $ 248

Rooms 客房 442
Suites 套房 11

Grand Hyatt
君悅

Towering above its neighbour, the Convention and Exhibition centre, this hotel was refurbished by an Australian design studio and now comes with a smart and contemporary look. The best rooms are between floors 31-36. The pool is long enough for decent lengths and there's an array of restaurants, including Tiffin which brings the lobby alive day and night.

毗鄰香港會議展覽中心，盡享維港兩岸遼闊景色。富麗堂皇的大堂早於1989年酒店開業時便已落成，由澳洲設計師操刀修葺後更見時尚；31-36樓的客房能讓你有更佳享受，並設豪華雲石浴室。大型室外泳池是盡情舒展的好去處。餐廳選擇良多，其中茶園更可欣賞悠揚的即場音樂演奏。

TEL. 2588 1234
1 Harbour Road, Wan Chai
灣仔港灣道 1號
www.hongkong.grand.hyatt.com

RECOMMENDED RESTAURANTS 餐廳推薦
Grand Hyatt Steakhouse XX
One Harbour Road 港灣壹號 XXX

† = $ 2,800-6,000
†† = $2,800-6,000
Suites 套房 = $ 5,800-88,000
☕ = $ 318

Rooms 客房 477
Suites 套房 65

Harbour Grand Kowloon
九龍海逸君綽

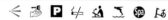

Location is the draw here, thanks to its enviable harbour-side views of both Hong Kong and Kowloon, which are best seen from the rooftop pool and bar. The grand marble staircase remains a feature of the refurbished lobby. Ask for one of the newer rooms opened in 2018 – they also have plans to remodel the original ones.

優越的地段是這家酒店的優勢，位於紅磡海濱、閃閃發亮的玻璃建築物與維港相毗鄰，飽覽無敵的兩岸景色，於天台泳池或酒吧可享最美景觀。大堂金碧輝煌，修葺過後標誌性的白色雲石階梯仍保留其中。房間光潔舒適，設備齊全，建議預訂於2018年夏天翻新過的房間。

TEL. 2621 3188
20 Tak Fung Street, Whampoa Garden, Hung Hom
紅磡黃埔花園德豐街 20號
www.harbourgrand.com/kowloon

† = $ 2,900-4,200
†† = $3,200-4,500
Suites 套房 = $ 5,800-35,000
☕ = $218

Rooms 客房 469
Suites 套房 86

Hyatt Regency Sha Tin
沙田凱悅

Just a minute's walk from University Station is this 26-floor hotel, whose large, well-equipped bedrooms have either harbour or mountain views. It makes clever use of neutral colours and natural materials like stone and wood to create a soothing ambience. It's business-orientated during the week; the impressive leisure facilities appeal to families at weekends.

沙田凱悅於2009年開幕，從港鐵大學站前往僅需步行兩分鐘。酒店設計充滿時代感，巧妙運用中性色彩及天然物料如石材及木材製造出柔和融洽的感覺。酒店平日以接待商務旅客為主，到週末則以出色的休閒設施吸引家庭顧客。

TEL. 3723 1234
18 Chak Cheung Street, Sha Tin
沙田澤祥街18號
hyattregencyhongkongshatin.com

† = $ 1,060-2,800
†† = $1,060-2,800
Suites 套房 = $ 2,260-6,200
☕ = $ 218

Rooms 客房 388
Suites 套房 174

Hyatt Regency Tsim Sha Tsui
尖沙咀凱悅

Occupying floors 10-24 of the impressive K11 skyscraper means that bedrooms here at the Hyatt Regency benefit from impressive views of the city or harbour. The rooms are decorated in a crisp, modern style; anyone choosing the Regency Club level has access to a private lounge. There are dining options galore and an impressive selection of whiskies in the Chin Chin Bar.

尖沙咀凱悅佔據K11摩天大樓的10至24層，並與K11購物藝術館相連，酒店房間能看到城市的繁華景色或醉人的維港景致。房間風格清新時尚，選擇嘉賓軒樓層的住客更可享受專用酒廊服務。酒店提供多種餐飲選擇，請請吧內的威士忌種類之多更是令人歎為觀止。

TEL. 2311 1234
18 Hanoi Road, Tsim Sha Tsui
尖沙咀河內道 18號
www.hongkongtsimshatsui.regency.hyatt.com

RECOMMENDED RESTAURANTS 餐廳推薦
Hugo's 希戈 XXX

= $2,500-4,200
= $2,500-4,200
Suites 套房 = $4,200-22,000
= $228

Rooms 客房 348
Suites 套房 33

Icon
唯港薈

Several of the world's leading designers helped create this rather cool hotel which returns all profits to its owner, the Hong Kong Polytechnic University, to reinvest in the building. Students are actively involved as part of their studies. Rooms have an uncluttered look and features include a living wall garden in the foyer and over 100 pieces from local artists.

這間香港理工大學名下的酒店由著名設計師嚴迅奇、泰倫斯・康藍爵士和林偉而等攜手設計，該院校學生亦著手參與酒店發展，實踐酒店管理知識。房間整潔有序，精美之餘兼具功能性。整所酒店設計風格鮮明，陳設了超過一百件本地藝術家的作品，亦有令人驚歎的現代化樓梯和垂直花園。

TEL. 3400 1000
17 Science Museum Road,
East Tsim Sha Tsui
尖東科學館道17號
www.hotel-icon.com

RECOMMENDED RESTAURANTS 餐廳推薦
Above & Beyond 天外天

= $2,000-5,000
= $2,000-5,000
Suites 套房 = $4,000-15,000
= $218

Rooms 客房 236
Suites 套房 26

Indigo
英迪格

Bordering Tai Yuen Street and its market, so ideally placed for discovering old Hong Kong, Indigo is also a good choice for those who've come to shop – there's even a shopping bag placed in every room! For others, there's always the rooftop bar and infinity pool. The bedrooms come with floor-to-ceiling windows and boast some cute design touches.

這幢外觀獨特的建築物坐落於灣仔商業區及住宅區交界，不光擁有完善的交通網絡，更毗鄰地區色彩濃厚的市集，讓你深入了解本區生活脈搏。全部房間設有落地玻璃窗，傢具擺設均經過精心設計，設施亦十分齊全，文具、購物袋一應俱全。天台玻璃底泳池，前臨山巒，感覺開揚，是放鬆身心的好地方。

TEL. 3926 3888
246 Queen's Road East, Wan Chai
灣仔皇后大道東 246號
www.hotelindigo.com/hongkong

🚹 = $ 1,600-2,600
🚹🚹 = $1,600-2,600
Suites 套房 = $ 3,500-5,000
☕ = $ 180

Rooms 客房 132
Suites 套房 6

InterContinental
洲際

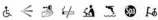

It may be unremarkable from the outside, but this hotel is decidedly impressive once you're in the lobby with its magnificent harbour views. All bedrooms are well-equipped, with spacious marble bathrooms. Relax in either the swimming pool or spa pool, or enjoy a massage in an outside cabana. Options for dining are excellent and service is exemplary.

踏入富麗堂皇的酒店大堂，望着一流海景，絕對令你印象深刻。客房非常寬敞，淺色調的設計感覺寧靜，更設有寬闊的雲石浴室。你可以在優雅的游泳池或水療池鬆弛身心；戶外的池邊小室內有按摩服務。酒店內的餐飲服務非常出色，服務水準一流。

TEL. 2721 1211
18 Salisbury Road, Tsim Sha Tsui
尖沙咀梳士巴利道18號
www.intercontinental.com

RECOMMENDED RESTAURANTS 餐廳推薦
Rech ✿ XXX
The Steak House winebar + grill XXX
Yan Toh Heen 欣圖軒 ✿✿ XXXX

† = $2,000-6,000
†† = $2,000-6,000
Suites 套房 = $3,500-98,000
☕ = $330

Rooms 客房 419
Suites 套房 82

InterContinental Grand Stanford
海景嘉福洲際

After a comprehensive renovation, this 18-storey hotel close to the waterfront is looking much more contemporary in style. The rooms are a decent size; ask for a harbour view. Dining options range from Cantonese to Italian, with over 300 whiskies offered in Tiffany's. The eye-catching lobby is the place for afternoon tea to the accompaniment of either a piano or harp.

經歷全面翻新後，這所樓高18層、毗鄰維港的酒店更見時尚。客房非常寬敞，淺色調的設計予人靜謐之感，謹記選擇有海景的房間。酒店餐廳網羅廣東、意大利等不同菜系；Tiffany's有超過300款威士忌任君選擇。富麗堂皇的酒店大堂伴隨鋼琴或豎琴樂韻，是享受悠閒下午茶的好去處。

TEL. 2721 5161
70 Mody Road, East Tsim Sha Tsui
尖東麼地道 70號
www.hongkong.intercontinental.com

† = $3,300-4,600
†† = $3,300-4,600
Suites 套房 = $7,500-15,000
☕ = $248

Rooms 客房 531
Suites 套房 39

Island Shangri-La
港島香格里拉

In contrast to its modern exterior, the décor inside is a more classic style, with a little glamour thrown in thanks to an array of chandeliers and gilt-framed pictures. A vast Chinese silk painting of mountains and rivers adorns the vast atrium rising up 16 floors. Choose Harbour or Peak views; those on floors 52-55 have exclusive use of the executive lounge.

摩登的外觀內是樸素典雅的裝潢，金光閃爍的吊燈及掛畫更添韻味。大堂掛上延伸至16樓、世上最大幅的中國山水絲綢畫，筆工細膩、構圖錯綜複雜，散發着攝人魅力。住客可在海景及山景房間中任選其一，海景房空間寬敞，更顯時尚。52至55樓豪華閣樓層的住客可享用專屬會客廳和美不勝收的天台庭園。

TEL. 2877 3838
Pacific Place, Supreme Court Road, Admiralty
金鐘法院道太古廣場
www.shangri-la.com/island

RECOMMENDED RESTAURANTS 餐廳推薦
Petrus 珀翠
Summer Palace 夏宮

† = $2,800-5,000
†† = $2,800-5,000
Suites 套房 = $6,800-9,000
☕ = $328

Rooms 客房 531
Suites 套房 34

JW Marriott
JW萬豪

Boasting 608 rooms spread over 35 storeys, this business hotel also offers a number of executive floors which have their own discreet lounge and meeting rooms. The bedrooms are functional but up-to-date and there's a pleasant outdoor pool and a well-equipped fitness centre. Dining options include Cantonese and seafood, along with a wine bar and tea room.

以商務住客為主的萬豪酒店樓高三十五層，客房數量達608間。位於頂樓的一列行政套房，附有素雅的休息室和會議室。房間設計富現代感且十分實用。戶外游泳池環境清幽、健身中心設備齊全，還網羅了各地餐飲美食，廣東菜、海鮮、酒吧、茶室等不同類別的餐室任君選擇。

TEL. 2810 8366
Pacific Place, 88 Queensway, Admiralty
金鐘道88號太古廣場
www.jwmarriotthongkong.com

= $ 2,500-5,000
= $2,500-5,000
Suites 套房 = $ 5,600-8,500
= $ 328

Rooms 客房 581
Suites 套房 27

Kowloon Shangri-La
九龍香格里拉

This is one of Kowloon's most respected hotels, both for its longevity and for the quality of the service. Harbour view bedrooms are the most sought after; choose a Horizon Club room for its luxury. Pick from Japanese cuisine in Nadaman, Italian in Angelini or Cantonese in Shang Palace. Afternoon tea in the lounge, with its fountains and chandeliers, is a special experience.

別具氣派的雲石大堂與三層噴泉水池，都令人對這歷史悠久的酒店留下深刻印象。坐擁維多利亞港迷人景觀，海景客房自然最受歡迎，若入住豪華閣的客房更可享受最奢華的體驗。酒店不乏環球美饌，包括日本餐廳灘萬、提供粵菜的香宮等，在大堂的吊燈下享用下午茶亦是不錯的選擇。

TEL. 2721 2111
64 Mody Road, East Tsim Sha Tsui
尖東麼地道 64號
www.shangri-la.com/kowloon

RECOMMENDED RESTAURANTS 餐廳推薦
Shang Palace 香宮 ✿ XXXX

= $2,200-4,800
= $2,200-4,800
Suites 套房 = $3,780-6,580
= $200

Rooms 客房 646
Suites 套房 42

Lan Kwai Fong
蘭桂坊

A hotel which feels part of the local area and mixes Chinese and contemporary furniture, neutral tones and dark wood veneers to create a relaxing environment. Try to secure one of the deluxe corner bedrooms or a suite with a balcony if you want more space; those higher than the 21st floor have the harbour views. Celebrity Cuisine offers accomplished Cantonese food.

融合了中國傳統與現代品味的傢具，中性色調及深色木間隔，環境舒適。如果你需要更寬敞的空間，建議預訂轉角位置的豪華客房或附設露台的套房。21樓以上的房間可飽覽維港景色。客人可借用房間內的流動電話，方便在外與朋友聯絡。

TEL. 3650 0000
3 Kau U Fong, Central
中環九如坊 3號
www.lankwaifonghotel.com.hk

RECOMMENDED RESTAURANTS 餐廳推薦
Celebrity Cuisine 名人坊 ✿ XX

†† = $1,080-3,080
Suites 套房 = $ 2,880-6,800
☕ = $ 165

Rooms 客房 157
Suites 套房 5

Lanson Place
逸蘭

Despite being ideally located for the shopping malls and restaurants of Causeway Bay, this hotel with its elegant façade is a calming oasis. Its lounge is the perfect place for an evening cocktail before setting out for dinner. Each of the bedrooms is classically furnished and comes with a kitchenette; choose a Premier room on an upper floor for its space and relative quiet.

位於購物及美食集中地的銅鑼灣，逸蘭擁有歐洲風格的典雅外觀，猶如鬧市中一片寧靜的綠洲。休息室設計優雅，裝潢交織古典與現代風格，晚餐前坐下呷杯雞尾酒更添愜意。客房舒適雅致，且都附設小廚房供簡單煮食之用。想要更寧靜舒適的體驗可選擇較高層的房間。

TEL. 3477 6888
133 Leighton Road, Causeway Bay
銅鑼灣禮頓道 133號
www.lansonplace.com

= $ 2,000-3,400
= $2,400-3,800
Suites 套房 = $ 3,200-4,600
= $ 231

Rooms 客房 170
Suites 套房 24

Mandarin Oriental
文華東方

One of Hong Kong's most iconic hotels continues to update itself whilst remaining true to its heritage. The most recent renovation gave the rooms a fresher, more contemporary feel. Suites range from traditional Asian to those that are more eye-catching – like the one dedicated to the late photographer Lord Lichfield. The spa is an oasis of tranquillity and dining options are varied.

開業逾半世紀，這家標誌性的酒店在保留優良傳統之餘，還致力提升其質素。最近的翻新工程為客房賦予更新鮮時尚的感覺，無論是典雅的大班風格或陽台房間的裝潢均非常精緻。套房主題多元，除了傳統亞洲風格，甚至有以攝影師里奇菲德爵士為靈感的設計。附設的水療設施令你猶如置身樂園；更不乏飽餐一頓的餐飲選擇。

TEL. 2522 0111
5 Connaught Road Central, Central
中環干諾道中5號
www.mandarinoriental.com/hongkong

RECOMMENDED RESTAURANTS 餐廳推薦
Man Wah 文華廳 ✿ XXX
Mandarin Grill + Bar 文華扒房 + 酒吧 ✿ XXXX
Pierre ✿✿ XXXX

† = $4,200-7,000
†† = $4,200-7,000
Suites 套房 = $5,500-10,000
☕ = $328

Rooms 客房 434
Suites 套房 67

New World Millennium
千禧新世界

The former Nikko hotel is now run by a different management company but little else has changed here. The hotel is known for its comprehensive banqueting and conference rooms and its impressive number of restaurants providing a wide range of different cuisines. The smart bedrooms come with up-to-the-minute comforts. The harbour-front location adds to the appeal.

日航酒店易名後，酒店完善的宴會及會議設施仍然保留，四間提供不同菜式的餐廳仍然為賓客提供多種選擇，令他們樂在其中；優越的海濱地段及設計現代化的智能客房，為顧客帶來舒適享受，上述種種條件均足以令它躋身國際級酒店之列。

TEL. 2739 1111
72 Mody Road, East Tsim Sha Tsui
尖東麼地道 72號
www.newworldmillenniumhotel.com

† = $ 1,650-4,800
†† = $1,650-4,800
Suites 套房 = $ 3,950-8,950
☕ = $ 275

Rooms 客房 445
Suites 套房 19

Ozo Wesley
遨舍衛蘭軒

You'll find Ozo Wesley sitting pretty between Wan Chai and Admiralty so it's ideally placed whether you're in town for business or just in the mood for shopping and dining. All of the guest rooms are crisply decorated in a bright, fresh and contemporary style and the effective soundproofing ensures a decent night's sleep however busy it is outside.

位於金鐘與灣仔交界，距金鐘的商業金融區只有數分鐘路程，附近的小街道滿佈食店，位置便利，適合商業旅客。大堂設計具時代感。客房均以素色系配搭簡單時尚裝潢，舒適的感覺令你身心放鬆。全部房間都設有大玻璃窗和隔音設備，讓你既能欣賞灣仔的繁華景象，又能享受片刻寧靜。

TEL. 2292 3000
22 Hennessy Road, Wan Chai
灣仔軒尼詩道 22號
www.ozohotels.com

🚹 = $ 1,250-2,950
🚹🚹 = $ 1,250-2,950
Suites 套房 = $ 2,100-3,800
☕ = $ 145

Rooms 客房 235
Suites 套房 16

Sheraton
喜來登

It may not have the prominence and stature of its neighbours but this hotel is much larger than you initially think and offers great harbour views. It appeals mostly to business travellers. The rooftop pool comes with Jacuzzis and in the foyer is an all-day cafe and shops selling wine and cigars. Dining options include oysters in the wine bar and Cantonese cuisine in Celestial Court.

喜來登的外觀可能不如鄰近建築富麗堂皇，但它其實是全港最大的酒店之一。酒店通常接待商務旅客，行政套房的住客可享用進入塔樓酒廊的獨享通道及海景餐廳。天台游泳池設有三個按摩池，更可盡覽維多利亞港景色。大堂有非常舒適的國際咖啡廳、酒舖和雪茄廊。餐廳包括蠔酒吧及粵菜廳。

TEL. 2369 1111
20 Nathan Road, Tsim Sha Tsui
尖沙咀彌敦道 20號
www.sheratonhongkonghotel.com

RECOMMENDED RESTAURANTS 餐廳推薦
Celestial Court 天寶閣

= $4,600-6,200
= $4,600-6,400
Suites 套房 = $ 7,500-16,000
= $ 250

Rooms 客房 691
Suites 套房 91

The Emperor N
英皇駿景

The Emperor not only moved from Happy Valley to Wan Chai but it's now a much smarter, swankier place thanks to the eye-catching contemporary look, courtesy of a Turkish design studio and a French botanist. Rooms may be a touch bijou for some, so ask for an Executive with a little more space. Golden Valley offers Cantonese and Sichuan cuisine; Monkey Café serves international dishes.

從跑馬地遷至灣仔，位置相差不遠，環境卻大有進步；新址經土耳其設計師及法籍植物學家Patrick Blanc聯手建造，酒店環境更為時尚奪目。房間方面同樣時髦，倘若愛好空間感可選擇入住行政客房；套房則減少了間隔以營造空間感。餐飲方面駿景園供應粵川菜式，若對菜系心猿意馬則可到其多國菜餐廳用膳。

TEL. 2893 3693
373 Queen's Road East, Wan Chai
灣仔皇后大道東 373號
www.emperorhotel.com.hk

= $ 2,200
Suites 套房 = $ 8,800-18,000

Rooms 客房 292
Suites 套房 7

The Landmark Mandarin Oriental
置地文華東方

 🚹 P ⚹ 🏊 🖼 Spa 🚴

From the personal airport pick-up to the endless spa choices, this is the hotel for those after a little pampering. Not only are the comfortable, smartly designed bedrooms big on luxury and size but they also come with stylish bathrooms attached; these feature either sunken or circular baths. MO is the cool ground floor bar for all-day dining or night time cocktails.

從專人機場接送服務到設備完善的水療中心，置地文華東方讓你盡享尊貴服務。令人讚歡的不光是設計型格獨特、面積達450至600呎的寬敞客房，還有房內豪華時尚的浴室設備，包括巨型下沉式或圓形浴缸。位於地下的MO Bar是解決一日三餐和品嘗雞尾酒的好去處。

TEL. 2132 0188
15 Queen's Road Central, Central
中環皇后大道中15號
www.mandarinoriental.com/landmark

RECOMMENDED RESTAURANTS 餐廳推薦
Amber ✿✿ ✗✗✗✗

🧍 = $ 4,300-6,300
🧍🧍 = $ 4,300-6,300
Suites 套房 = $ 7,800-19,000
☕ = $ 263

Rooms 客房　98
Suites 套房　13

The Langham
朗廷

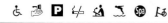

The clamour of Peking Road will seem but a distant memory once you're in the hushed surroundings of this elegant hotel. Its striking lobby, furnished in a classical European style, features some impressive modern art and sculptures, and bedrooms are furnished in a smart, contemporary style. The charm of the hotel is underpinned by modern facilities and attentive service.

進入這幢優雅建築物，讓你立刻忘卻北京道熙來攘往的煩囂。大堂以傳統歐洲風格裝潢，配上當代藝術品及雕塑作點綴，奢華奪目。客房典雅時尚，極具吸引力。迷人之處，盡見於其現代設施及細心周到的服務。

TEL. 2375 1133
8 Peking Road, Tsim Sha Tsui
尖沙咀北京道 8號
www.langhamhotels.com/hongkong

RECOMMENDED RESTAURANTS 餐廳推薦
Bostonian Seafood & Grill XX
T'ang Court 唐閣 ✿✿✿ XXXX

† = $ 2,000-4,100
†† = $2,000-4,100
Suites 套房 = $ 4,500-6,600
☕ = $ 208

Rooms 客房 471
Suites 套房 27

The Mira

It's all about design at this hotel in the heart of Kowloon's main shopping district. The bedrooms may not be the largest but they feature plenty of modern gadgets, including your own transportable wi-fi link. The penthouse is the space for an event, with views overlooking Kowloon Park, and the heated water beds in MiraSpa are perfect for de-stressing.

位於九龍心臟地帶的購物區，客房面積相對不大，但出色的設計彌補了不足，房間設施非常現代化，提供流動無線上網連接；套房裝潢豪華。宴會廳擁有最時尚的音訊設備和巨型入牆顯示屏，適合各種宴會，頂樓更能俯瞰九龍公園園景。水療設施舒適豪華，熱療水床讓您能肆意放鬆。

TEL. 2368 1111
118 Nathan Road, Tsim Sha Tsui
尖沙咀彌敦道 118號
www.themirahotel.com

RECOMMENDED RESTAURANTS 餐廳推薦
Cuisine Cuisine at The Mira
國金軒（尖沙咀）XXX
Whisk XX

† = $ 1,500-2,200
†† = $ 1,700-2,400
Suites 套房 = $ 2,500-3,600
☕ = $ 248

Rooms 客房 436
Suites 套房 56

The Murray Ⓝ
美利

Built in 1969, this former government office got a new lease of life when it was re-designed and re-opened as a stylish, luxury hotel. Popinjays is a relaxed rooftop bar and restaurant with stunning views; Tai Pan offers sophisticated Asian-influenced food. Bedrooms radiate style, with Italian marble, leather and wood. Ask for one with views over Hong Kong Park or the western city districts.

前身為政府辦公室，建於1969年，現改建為集奢華時尚於一身的酒店。室內設計由著名建築師包辦，客房採用意大利大理石、皮革及木材等特製傢具，色調樸實卻不失貴氣，建議選擇面向香港公園或西區的房間。餐飲選擇亦別具特色：天台酒吧Popinjays坐擁迷人景緻；Tai Pan則提供帶亞洲風情的菜餚。

TEL. 3141 8888
22 Cotton Tree Drive, Central
中環紅棉道22號
www.niccolohotels.com/hotels/hongkong/central/the_murray

RECOMMENDED RESTAURANTS 餐廳推薦
Guo Fu Lou 國福樓 ✿ XXX

† = $3,800-51,300
†† = $3,800-51,300
Suites 套房 = $ 6,500-51,300
☕ = $ 332

Rooms 客房 298
Suites 套房 38

The Peninsula
半島

This grand dame of Hong Kong hotels has been welcoming guests since 1928 and does a fine job of blending age old traditions with modern day comforts. Whilst there is not a bad room in the house it's worth taking one higher up for the views across to Hong Kong Island. The host of facilities include a helipad on the roof and a serene spa. The lobby remains the place for afternoon tea.

於1928年開幕的半島，一直把現代舒適標準融入傳統建築之中，於2013年修葺過後，客房更時尚雅致，房內設備全部透過高科技觸控屏操作，高層房間能遠眺香港島景色。作為酒店標誌的大堂保留原來樣式，供顧客享用下午茶。羅馬式泳池及水療服務一應俱全，天台更設直升機場。

TEL. 2920 2888
Salisbury Road, Tsim Sha Tsui
尖沙咀梳士巴利道
www.peninsula.com/hongkong

RECOMMENDED RESTAURANTS 餐廳推薦
Chesa 瑞樵閣
Gaddi's 吉地士
Spring Moon 嘉麟樓

† = $4,180-6,180
†† = $4,180-6,180
Suites 套房 = $ 7,180-128,000
☕ = $360

Rooms 客房 246
Suites 套房 54

The Pottinger
中環・石板街

Standing in the middle of Central, and on one of Hong Kong's oldest 'stone slab streets', is this elegant and stylish hotel. Its location is celebrated through its collection of iconic and historic photographs taken by award-winning artist Fan Ho. The 68 bedrooms are contemporary and graceful and boast all the amenities the modern traveller expects.

位於有過百年歷史的砵甸乍街(又名石板街)旁邊，故以此命名。斜斜的石板路見證了中環百多年來的故事，也為酒店增添了一分魅力。接待廳雖小卻流露着歐陸優雅格調，共有68間客房，面積適中、設備齊全。位處中環心臟地帶，無論往辦公、飲食、娛樂或乘搭交通工具都非常便利，是商務住宿的理想選擇。

TEL. 2308 3188
21 Stanley Street, Central
中環士丹利街 21號
www.thepottinger.com

RECOMMENDED RESTAURANTS 餐廳推薦
Ta Vie 旅 ✿✿ XX

🚹 = $2,200-5,800
🚹🚹 = $2,350-6,800
Suites 套房 = $4,000-10,000

Rooms 客房 61
Suites 套房 7

The Ritz-Carlton
麗思卡爾頓

Occupying the top 16 floors of the International Commerce Centre, this hotel remains, for now, the highest in the world. The spacious, elegant bedrooms have subtle Asian influences in their decoration and most of the suites have harbour and mountain views. The indoor swimming pool is on the 116th floor; the cool Ozone bar is on the 118th!

位於香港最高建築物最頂的16層樓，至今仍是全球最高的酒店。空間偌大的客房裝潢高雅，展現亞洲韻味；套房窗外是宜人的海景或山景，更設有望遠鏡，讓住客居高臨下俯瞰香港景色。時尚酒吧Ozone位於118層，設有戶外露台；泳池亦設於海拔490米高處的116層。

TEL. 2263 2263
International Commerce Centre,
1 Austin Road West, Tsim Sha Tsui
尖沙咀柯士甸道西 1號環球貿易廣場
www.ritzcarlton.com/hongkong

RECOMMENDED RESTAURANTS 餐廳推薦
Tin Lung Heen 天龍軒 ✿✿ XXXXX
Tosca ✿ XXXX

† = $ 3,800-11,100
†† = $3,800-11,600
Suites 套房 = $ 6,600-13,900
☕ = $338

Rooms 客房 262
Suites 套房 50

The Royal Garden
帝苑

This hotel continues to evolve thanks to its newer, more spacious and contemporary bedrooms in the Sky Tower, along with a smart gym and spa. J's Bar is for cocktails and live music and the numerous dining options include Chinese, Vietnamese, Italian and Japanese; there's even a mini food store selling some irresistible cakes and biscuits.

帝苑酒店不斷革新，客房時尚舒適，附有現代化設備，位於16-19樓的天際套房更坐擁維港兩岸景色。餐廳種類繁多，有中菜、越南菜、意大利菜及日本菜任君選擇。J's酒吧提供雞尾酒及現場音樂表演；想在正餐以外來點小吃的話，大堂餅店還有使人無法抗拒的蛋糕和餅乾。水療和健身設施足夠你享受一整天。

TEL. 2721 5215
69 Mody Road, East Tsim Sha Tsui
尖東麼地道 69號
www.rghk.com.hk

RECOMMENDED RESTAURANTS 餐廳推薦
Dong Lai Shun 東來順

† = $4,620-9,240
†† = $4,620-9,240
Suites 套房 = $6,380-75,680
☕ = $275

Rooms 客房 396
Suites 套房 54

The Upper House
奕居

This hotel has one clear focus: the wellbeing of its guests. There are subtle Japanese influences to its decoration thanks to designer Andre Fu, who also sourced the various pieces of art and sculpture seen in the rooms and around the hotel. The garden, whilst small, is still a great feature in the heart of the city; try one of the weekend yoga sessions held there.

奕居由建築師傅厚民精心設計，在客房及酒店四周都放置了不少藝術品，格調時尚且隱隱透出和式風格。酒店希望營造私人居所感覺，住客入住時會給直接帶到房間，由服務員送上飲品，並以平板電腦作簡單登記。六樓的小花園陽台是洗滌繁囂的好去處；住客更可參與逢週末舉行的瑜伽活動。

TEL. 2918 1838
Pacific Place, 88 Queensway, Admiralty
金鐘道 88號太古廣場
www.upperhouse.com

RECOMMENDED RESTAURANTS 餐廳推薦
Café Gray Deluxe

= $5,200-8,000
= $5,200-8,000
Suites 套房 = $17,000-25,000
= $280

Rooms 客房 96
Suites 套房 21

MACAU
澳門

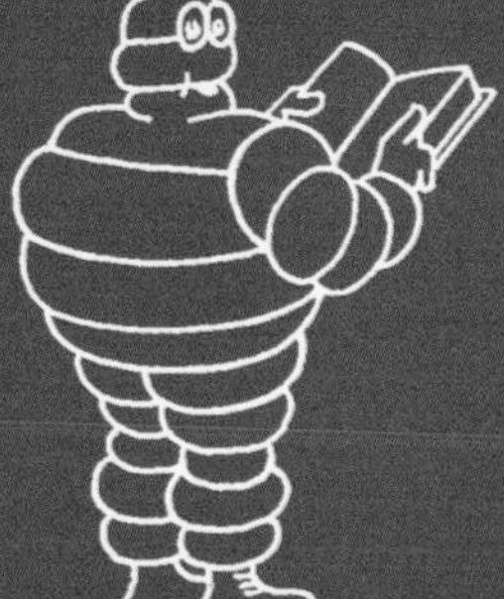

RESTAURANTS
餐廳

STARRED RESTAURANTS
星級餐廳

Within this selection, we have highlighted a number of restaurants for their particularly good cooking. When awarding one, two or three Michelin Stars there are a number of factors we consider: the quality and compatibility of the ingredients, the technical skill and flair that goes into their preparation, the clarity and combination of flavours, the value for money and above all, the taste. Equally important is the ability to produce excellent cooking not once but time and time again. Our inspectors make as many visits as necessary, so that you can be sure of the quality and consistency.

A two or three star restaurant has to offer something very special that separates it from the rest. Three stars – our highest award – are given to the very best.

Cuisines in any style of restaurant and of any nationality are eligible for a star. The decoration, service and comfort levels have no bearing on the award.

在這系列的選擇裏，推薦的是食物質素特別出色的餐廳。給予一、二或三粒米芝蓮星時，我們考慮到以下因素：材料的質素和配搭、烹調技巧和特色、氣味濃度和組合、價錢是否相宜及味道層次。同樣重要的是該餐館的食物恆常保持在高水平。閣下對我們的推薦絕對可以放心！我們的評審員會因應需要多次到訪同一家餐館，以確認其食物品質能恆常保持高水準。

二或三星餐廳必有獨特之處，比同類型其他餐廳更出眾。最高評級——三星——只會給予最好的餐廳。

星級評定不會受到餐廳風格、菜式、裝潢陳設、服務及舒適程度影響。只要烹調技巧出色，食物品質特別優秀，都有機會獲得米芝蓮星星。

Exceptional cuisine, worth a special journey.
卓越的烹調，值得專程到訪。

Our highest award is given for the superlative cooking of chefs at the peak of their profession. The ingredients are exemplary, the cooking is elevated to an art form and their dishes are often destined to become classics.

獲得最高級別的餐館，其廚師的烹調技巧卓絕，選材用料堪稱典範，並將烹飪提升至藝術層次，菜式大多會成為經典。

Jade Dragon 譽瓏軒	XXXX	Cantonese 粵菜	351
Robuchon au Dôme 天巢法國餐廳	XXXXX	French contemporary 時尚法國菜	368
The Eight 8餐廳	XXXX	Chinese 中國菜	372

Excellent cooking, worth a detour.
烹調出色，不容錯過！

The personality and talent of the chef and their team is evident in the refined, expertly crafted dishes.

主廚的個人風格與烹飪天賦及其團隊的優秀手藝完全反映在精巧味美的菜式上。

Alain Ducasse at Morpheus 杜卡斯	N	XXXX	French contemporary 時尚法國菜	329
Feng Wei Ju 風味居		XXX	Hunanese and Sichuan 湘川菜	343
Golden Flower 京花軒		XXXX	Chinese 中國菜	345
Mizumi (Macau) 泓 (澳門)		XXX	Japanese 日本菜	361
The Tasting Room 御膳房		XXXX	French contemporary 時尚法國菜	376

High quality cooking, worth a stop!
優質烹調，不妨一試！

Within their category, these establishments use quality ingredients and serve carefully prepared dishes with distinct flavours.

此名單上的餐館，在同類型餐館中，其食材較具質素，烹調細緻用心、味道出色。

King 帝皇樓	XX	Cantonese 粵菜	353
Lai Heen 麗軒	XXXXX	Cantonese 粵菜	354
8 1/2 Otto e Mezzo - Bombana	XXX	Italian 意大利菜	366
Pearl Dragon 玥龍軒	XXXX	Cantonese 粵菜	367
Shinji by Kanesaka 金坂極上壽司	XX	Sushi 壽司	369
The Golden Peacock 皇雀	XX	Indian 印度菜	373
The Kitchen 大廚	XX	Steakhouse 扒房	374
Tim's Kitchen 桃花源小廚	XXX	Cantonese 粵菜	377
Wing Lei 永利軒	XXXX	Cantonese 粵菜	380
Ying 帝影樓	XXX	Cantonese 粵菜	386
Zi Yat Heen 紫逸軒	XXXX	Cantonese 粵菜	387

BIB GOURMAND RESTAURANTS
車胎人美食推介餐廳

This symbol indicates our inspectors' favourites for good value. These restaurants offer quality cooking for MOP400 or less (price of a 3-course meal excluding drinks).

車胎人標誌表示該餐廳提供具質素且經濟實惠的美食:費用在400元或以下(三道菜但不包括飲品)。

Chan Seng Kei 陳勝記	Cantonese 粵菜	337
Cheong Kei 祥記	Noodles 麵食	338
Din Tai Fung (COD) 鼎泰豐 (新濠天地)	Shanghainese 滬菜	340
Hou Kong Chi Kei 濠江志記美食	Cantonese 粵菜	347
IFT Educational Restaurant 旅遊學院教學餐廳	Macanese 澳門菜	348
Lou Kei (Fai Chi Kei) 老記 (筷子基)	Cantonese 粵菜	356
Luk Kei Noodle 六記粥麵	Noodles and Congee 粥麵	357
O Castiço	Portuguese 葡國菜	365
Tou Tou Koi 陶陶居	Cantonese 粵菜	378

: New entry in the guide 新增推介

: Restaurant promoted to a Bib Gourmand or Star 評級有所晉升的餐廳

RESTAURANTS BY AREA
餐廳 — 以地區分類

Coloane 路環

Macau 澳門

Robuchon au Dôme 天巢法國餐廳	✿✿✿	XXXXX	French contemporary 時尚法國菜	368
The Eight 8餐廳	✿✿✿	XXXX	Chinese 中國菜	372
The Kitchen 大廚	✿	XX	Steakhouse 扒房	374
Tim's Kitchen 桃花源小廚	✿	XXX	Cantonese 粵菜	377
Tou Tou Koi 陶陶居	☺	X	Cantonese 粵菜	378
Wing Lei 永利軒	✿	XXXX	Cantonese 粵菜	380
Wong Kun Sio Kung (Rua do Campo) 皇冠小館 (水坑尾街)	‖O	🍜	Noodles and Congee 粥麵	383

Taipa 氹仔

Alain Ducasse at Morpheus 杜卡斯 Ⓝ	✿✿	XXXX	French contemporary 時尚法國菜	329
António 安東尼奧	‖O	XX	Portuguese 葡國菜	330
Aurora 奧羅拉	‖O	XXX	Italian 意大利菜	331
Banza 百姓	‖O	X	Portuguese 葡國菜	332
Beijing Kitchen 滿堂彩	‖O	XX	Chinese 中國菜	333
Bi Ying 碧迎居	‖O	X	Chinese 中國菜	334
Canton 喜粵	‖O	XXX	Cantonese 粵菜	336
Din Tai Fung (COD) 鼎泰豐 (新濠天地)	☺	X	Shanghainese 滬菜	340
Dynasty 8 朝	‖O	XXX	Cantonese 粵菜	341
Fook Lam Moon 福臨門	‖O	XXX	Cantonese 粵菜	344
Jade Dragon 譽瓏軒 🍷	✿✿✿	XXXX	Cantonese 粵菜	351
Lai Heen 麗軒	✿	XXXXX	Cantonese 粵菜	354
Lei Garden 利苑酒家	‖O	XXX	Cantonese 粵菜	355
Manuel Cozinha Portuguesa 阿曼諾葡國餐	‖O	X	Portuguese 葡國菜	359
Mezza9	‖O	XX	International 國際菜	360
O Castiço	☺	X	Portuguese 葡國菜	365
8 1/2 Otto e Mezzo - Bombana	✿	XXX	Italian 意大利菜	366
Pearl Dragon 玥龍軒	✿	XXXX	Cantonese 粵菜	367
Shinji by Kanesaka 金坂極上壽司	✿	XX	Sushi 壽司	369
Tenmasa 天政	‖O	XX	Japanese 日本菜	370
Terrazza 庭園	‖O	XXX	Italian 意大利菜	371

RESTAURANTS BY CUISINE TYPE
餐廳 — 以菜式分類

Cantonese 粵菜

Canton 喜粵		🍴	XXX	Taipa 氹仔	336
Chan Seng Kei 陳勝記		☺	🍜	Coloane 路環	337
Dynasty 8 朝		🍴	XXX	Taipa 氹仔	341
Fook Lam Moon 福臨門		🍴	XXX	Taipa 氹仔	344
Hou Kong Chi Kei 濠江志記美食		☺	🍜	Macau 澳門	347
Imperial Court 金殿堂		🍴	XXX	Macau 澳門	350
Jade Dragon 譽瓏軒	😋	✿✿✿	XXXX	Taipa 氹仔	351
Kam Lai Heen 金麗軒		🍴	XX	Macau 澳門	352
King 帝皇樓		✿	XX	Macau 澳門	353
Lai Heen 麗軒		✿	XXXXX	Taipa 氹仔	354
Lei Garden 利苑酒家		🍴	XXX	Taipa 氹仔	355
Lou Kei (Fai Chi Kei) 老記 (筷子基)		☺	🍜	Macau 澳門	356
Lung Wah Tea House 龍華茶樓		🍴	🍜	Macau 澳門	358
Pearl Dragon 玥龍軒		✿	XXXX	Taipa 氹仔	367
Tim's Kitchen 桃花源小廚		✿	XXX	Macau 澳門	377
Tou Tou Koi 陶陶居		☺	X	Macau 澳門	378
Wing Lei 永利軒		✿	XXXX	Macau 澳門	380
Wing Lei Palace 永利宮	Ⓝ	🍴	XXXX	Taipa 氹仔	381
Ying 帝影樓		✿	XXX	Taipa 氹仔	386
Zi Yat Heen 紫逸軒		✿	XXXX	Taipa 氹仔	387

Asian contemporary 時尚亞洲菜

Voyages by Alain Ducasse 風雅廚	Ⓝ	🍴	XX	Taipa 氹仔	379

Ⓝ : New entry in the guide 新增推介

😋 : Restaurant promoted to a Bib Gourmand or Star 評級有所晉升的餐廳

Chinese 中國菜

Beijing Kitchen 滿堂彩		🍽	XX	Taipa 氹仔	333
Bi Ying 碧迎居		🍽	X	Taipa 氹仔	334
Golden Flower 京花軒		✿✿	XXXX	Macau 澳門	345
The Eight 8餐廳		✿✿✿	XXXX	Macau 澳門	372

Chinese contemporary 時尚中國菜

Yi 天頤	Ⓝ	🍽	XXX	Taipa 氹仔	385

French 法國菜

The Ritz-Carlton Café 麗思咖啡廳		🍽	XX	Taipa 氹仔	375

French contemporary 時尚法國菜

Alain Ducasse at Morpheus 杜卡斯	Ⓝ	✿✿	XXXX	Taipa 氹仔	329
Robuchon au Dôme 天巢法國餐廳		✿✿✿	XXXXX	Macau 澳門	368
The Tasting Room 御膳房		✿✿	XXXX	Taipa 氹仔	376

Hunanese and Sichuan 湘川菜

Feng Wei Ju 風味居		✿✿	XXX	Macau 澳門	343

Indian 印度菜

The Golden Peacock 皇雀		✿	XX	Taipa 氹仔	373

International 國際菜

Mezza9		🍽	XX	Taipa 氹仔	360

Italian 意大利菜

Aurora 奧羅拉		🍽	XXX	Taipa 氹仔	331
Il Teatro 帝雅廷		🍽	XXXX	Macau 澳門	349
8 1/2 Otto e Mezzo - Bombana		✿	XXX	Taipa 氹仔	366
Terrazza 庭園		🍽	XXX	Taipa 氹仔	371

Japanese 日本菜

Mizumi (Macau) 泓 (澳門)	✿✿	XXX	Macau 澳門	361
Tenmasa 天政	ǁO	XX	Taipa 氹仔	370
Yamazato 山里	ǁO	XXX	Taipa 氹仔	384

Macanese 澳門菜

Café Encore 咖啡廷	ǁO	XX	Macau 澳門	335
IFT Educational Restaurant 旅遊學院教學餐廳	(Bib)	XX	Macau 澳門	348

Noodles 麵食

Cheong Kei 祥記	(Bib)	(bowl)	Macau 澳門	338
99 Noodles 99麵	ǁO	X	Macau 澳門	364

Noodles and Congee 粥麵

Luk Kei Noodle 六記粥麵	(Bib)	(bowl)	Macau 澳門	357
Ngao Kei Ka Lei Chon 牛記咖喱美食	ǁO	(bowl)	Macau 澳門	363
Wong Kun Sio Kung (Broadway) 皇冠小館 (百老匯)	ǁO	(bowl)	Taipa 氹仔	382
Wong Kun Sio Kung (Rua do Campo) 皇冠小館 (水坑尾街)	ǁO	(bowl)	Macau 澳門	383

Portuguese 葡國菜

A Lorcha 船屋	ǁO	X	Macau 澳門	328
António 安東尼奧	ǁO	XX	Taipa 氹仔	330
Banza 百姓	ǁO	X	Taipa 氹仔	332
Clube Militar de Macau 澳門陸軍俱樂部	ǁO	XX	Macau 澳門	339
Espaço Lisboa 里斯本地帶	ǁO	X	Coloane 路環	342
Guincho a Galera 葡國餐廳	ǁO	XXXX	Macau 澳門	346
Manuel Cozinha Portuguesa 阿曼諾葡國餐	ǁO	X	Taipa 氹仔	359
O Castiço	(Bib)	X	Taipa 氹仔	365

Shanghainese 滬菜

Din Tai Fung (COD) 鼎泰豐 (新濠天地)	☺	X	Taipa 氹仔	340

Steakhouse 扒房

The Kitchen 大廚	✻	XX	Macau 澳門	374

Sushi 壽司

Shinji by Kanesaka 金坂極上壽司	✻	XX	Taipa 氹仔	369

Thai 泰國菜

Naam 灆	ıIO	XX	Macau 澳門	362

RESTAURANTS WITH INTERESTING WINE LISTS
供應優質餐酒的餐廳

N : New entry in the guide 新增推介

☺ : Restaurant promoted to a Bib Gourmand or Star 評級有所晉升的餐廳

STREET FOOD
街頭小吃

A Lorcha
船屋

Business is booming at this friendly Portuguese restaurant and that's not just because it's close to Barra Temple. The owner's mother still holds the most important role here – as head chef – and she makes sure the quality of the food remains high. A charcoal grill in the kitchen is used for the barbecue and grill dishes and carefully prepared specialities include Ameijoas "Bulhão Pato", Arroz de marisco à Portuguesa and Macanese coconut and turmeric chicken.

這家位於媽閣廟附近的葡國餐廳，地點便利並非其成功的主要因素，餐廳總廚的要職由東主母親擔任，餐廳開業近三十年一直親力親為，致力保持食品質素和正宗風味。燒烤菜式全部用炭爐烹調。精選推介包括欖油香蒜炒鮮蜆、葡式燴海鮮飯及葡國雞。

TEL. 2831 3193
289 Rua do Almirante Sergio
河邊新街 289號
www.alorcha.com

■ PRICE 價錢
Lunch 午膳
à la carte 點菜 MOP 200-350
Dinner 晚膳
à la carte 點菜 MOP 200-350

■ OPENING HOURS 營業時間
Lunch 午膳 12:30-14:30 (L.O.)
Dinner 晚膳 18:30-22:30 (L.O.)

■ ANNUAL AND WEEKLY CLOSING 休息日期
Closed Tuesday 週二休息

Alain Ducasse at Morpheus
杜卡斯

You'll find renowned French Chef Alain Ducasse's first restaurant in Macau on the third floor of the architecturally striking Morpheus Hotel. Water, glass and polished metal are used to great effect to create a unique environment that is both stylish and intimate. Dishes are intensely flavoured, perfectly balanced and sophisticated. Those who know his other restaurants around the world will recognize some of the signature dishes.

法籍廚師Alain Ducasse在澳門的首間餐廳，選址別具型格的摩珀斯酒店三樓。室內設計巧妙運用水、玻璃及金屬等元素，營造出高雅而親密的格調，與其所在的酒店同樣令人難以忘懷。食物也沒有令人失望，味道濃烈而恰到好處，簡單中盡顯不平凡。在此食客能細味廚師在全球各地的招牌菜。

TEL. 8868 3432
3F, Morpheus, City of Dreams,
Estrada do Istmo, Cotai
路氹連貫公路新濠天地摩珀斯 3樓
www.cityofdreamsmacau.com

■ PRICE 價錢
Dinner 晚膳
set 套餐 MOP 1,888
à la carte 點菜 MOP 1,400-2,100

■ OPENING HOURS 營業時間
Dinner 晚膳 19:00-22:30 (L.O.)

■ ANNUAL AND WEEKLY CLOSING 休息日期
Closed Monday 週一休息

António
安東尼奧

32

António is the head chef, the creator of the menus and the heart and soul of the restaurant. Customers come for the atmosphere as much as the food; António offers everyone a glass of his own label port at the end of the meal and a musician passes by every night except Monday to sing fado. The restaurant occupies a three-storey house and has a charming little terrace. The speciality is seafood stew in a copper pot, and wet seafood rice in a ceramic pot.

安東尼奧現址在離舊店不遠的一座三層高小屋中，餐室主要在地下和二樓，還附有小陽台。為了營造歐陸風情，店家選用了葡式瓷磚及皮椅，並飾以古舊的葡國畫作。店子好客熱情的服務和餐單保持不變，用膳後每位客人會獲贈一杯此店獨家進口的砵酒，並有音樂人獻唱葡國民謠。海鮮雜燴及海鮮燴飯均是招牌菜。

TEL. 2899 9998
7 Rua dos Clerigos, Taipa
氹仔木鐸街 7號
www.antoniomacau.com

■ PRICE 價錢
à la carte 點菜 MOP 350-1,000

■ OPENING HOURS 營業時間
11:30-22:30 (L.O.)

Aurora
奥羅拉

14

A drink on the outdoor terrace affording panoramic city views is a must before a meal in the sophisticated dining room. Luckily, you can behold the same views from all its tables through the floor-to-ceiling windows. Counter seats let guests garner insights into how the chefs work in the open kitchen. Specialities include Mediterranean seafood nage, and suckling pig porchetta – slow-cooked for eight hours before the skin is then crisped up.

位於新濠鋒酒店10樓，落地玻璃窗把只供客人會飲的露台與寬敞時尚的餐室分隔，然而這無礙室內室外的食客盡享澳門醉人夜色。侍應服務貼心專注，特別推介地中海式燴海鮮，以及家傳意式烤乳豬：乳豬先經慢煮八小時，客人下單後才開始烤焗，肉質細嫩，外皮鬆脆。侍酒師可替你配搭餐點與美酒。

TEL. 2886 8868
10F, Altira Hotel,
Avenida de Kwong Tung, Taipa
氹仔廣東大馬路新濠鋒酒店 10樓
www.altiramacau.com

■ PRICE 價錢
Lunch 午膳
set 套餐 MOP 338-418
à la carte 點菜 MOP 500-1,000

Dinner 晚膳
set 套餐 MOP 988
à la carte 點菜 MOP 500-1,000

■ OPENING HOURS 營業時間
Lunch 午膳 12:00-14:00 (L.O.)
Dinner 晚膳 18:00-22:30 (L.O.)

Banza
百姓

Located in a huge apartment complex, Banza boasts a green and white dining room which exudes country chic. The fish dishes are the hero items on the menu, while the popular choices among regulars include clams 'Banza-style' in a spicy tomato, onion and bell pepper sauce. Feel free to ask about their selection of Portuguese wine. The cosy mezzanine seats about six.

位於氹仔的大型屋苑內，餐廳四周環境寧靜，室內裝潢以白、綠色調為主，感覺休閒舒適。菜單上眾多的美食中以魚類最受歡迎，另推介配以甜椒洋葱蕃茄汁的百姓炒蜆。餐廳亦備有多款精心挑選的葡萄牙美酒，嗜杯中物者不容錯過。

TEL. 2882 1519
G-H, GF, Block 5, Edf. Nam San Garden,
154A & 154B, Avenida de Kwong Tung,
Taipa
氹仔廣東大馬路 154A及 154B號
南新花園第 5座地下 G、H座

■ PRICE 價錢
Lunch 午膳
set 套餐 MOP 98
à la carte 點菜 MOP 200-300
Dinner 晚膳
à la carte 點菜 MOP 200-300

■ OPENING HOURS 營業時間
Lunch 午膳 12:00-15:00 (L.O.)
Dinner 晚膳 18:00-22:30 (L.O.)

Beijing Kitchen
滿堂彩

10

'Dinner and a show' at Beijing Kitchen means one and the same, as the cooking is divided between four lively show kitchens which will hold your attention. There's a dim sum and noodle area; a duck section with two applewood-fired ovens; a wok station; and a dessert counter whose bounty is well worth leaving room for. Northern China provides many of the specialities. Ask for one of the tables under the birdcages suspended from the ceiling.

這家店子有四個開放式廚房：點心與粉麵區、烤鴨區、明爐小炒區和甜品區；食客在進餐之餘還能欣賞現場烹飪表演，稱得上集用膳與娛樂於一身。廚房團隊來自北京，招牌菜以北方菜為主，烤鴨區廚房內懸掛着兩座燃木窯爐，甚具特色，因此絕不能錯過這兒的果木烤鴨。

TEL. 8868 1930
1F, Grand Hyatt Hotel, City of Dreams,
Estrada do Istmo, Cotai
路氹連貫公路新濠天地君悅酒店 1樓
macau.grand.hyatt.com

SPECIALITIES TO PRE-ORDER 預訂食物
Traditional Beijing style duck from wood fired oven with classic condiment 老式果木烤鴨

■ PRICE 價錢
Lunch 午膳
set 套餐 MOP 300-1.400
à la carte 點菜 MOP 300-1,400
Dinner 晚膳
set 套餐 MOP 400-800
à la carte 點菜 MOP 300-1,400

■ OPENING HOURS 營業時間
Lunch 午膳 11:30-14:30 (L.O.)
Dinner 晚膳 17:30-23:30 (L.O.)

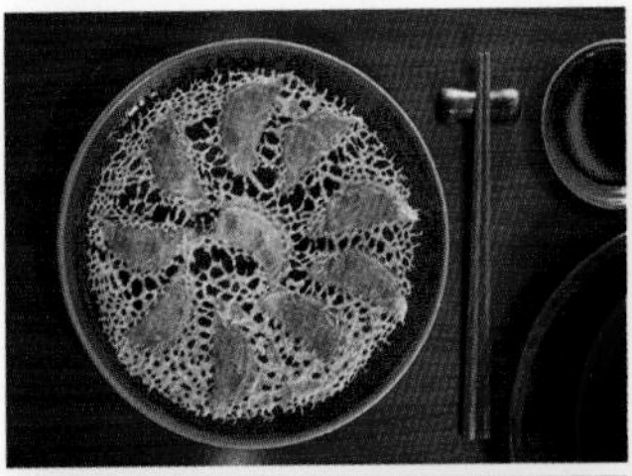

Bi Ying
碧迎居

The name means 'sure win' and it provides the ideal pit-stop if you need a quick break from the gaming tables. It's a buzzy, busy 24-hour operation with its focus on the open kitchen where you can watch noodles being made. The menu offers a culinary journey around China, with plenty of regional specialities, although the wood-roasted dishes are a particular highlight. Finish with one of the desserts made with medicinal herbs.

位處酒店娛樂場所旁的碧迎居，廿四小時提供大江南北美饌，不論你鍾情川式脆椒炒肉蟹、佛跳牆、古法醬燒琵琶鴨，或巧手南北點心，都能盡情滿足口欲。不妨試試其招牌燒味，以靈芝龜苓膏或花旗參冰糖燉官燕作結也不錯。開放式廚房設有果木燒烤爐，食客更有機會觀賞手拉麵條的製作過程。

TEL. 8865 6650
Shop 1182, 1F,
Casino at Studio City Hotel,
Estrada do Istmo, Cotai
路氹連貫公路新濠影匯娛樂場 1樓 1182號舖
www.studiocity-macau.com

■ PRICE 價錢
Lunch 午膳
set 套餐 MOP 180-300
à la carte 點菜 MOP 200-500
Dinner 晚膳
set 套餐 MOP 300-500
à la carte 點菜 MOP 200-500

■ OPENING HOURS 營業時間
24 hours 24 小時

Café Encore
咖啡廷

Café Encore is an elegant restaurant on the ground floor of the Encore hotel. The look is that of a classic European café but one with a strong Italian accent. The menu offers a combination of Macanese and Portuguese cuisine, along with a separate menu of Cantonese dishes, but it is in the Macanese specialities that the kitchen particularly excels. Try dishes like curried crab and baked African chicken.

咖啡廷位於萬利酒店地下，格調高雅。餐廳設計以傳統歐洲餐館裝潢作藍本，並滲入大量意大利藝術元素。菜單以澳門菜與葡國菜為主，另設有粵菜菜單。不過這裏最出色的還是地道澳門菜，例如咖喱蟹與非洲雞。

TEL. 8989 3663
GF, Encore Hotel, Rua Cidade de Sintra, NAPE
外港新填海區仙德麗街萬利酒店地下
www.wynnmacau.com

■ PRICE 價錢
set 套餐 MOP 250-400
à la carte 點菜 MOP 250-600

■ OPENING HOURS 營業時間
06:30-23:45 (L.O.)

Canton
喜粵

XXX

♿ P 12

Modern in design and a deep sensual red in colour, Canton is a stylish restaurant with a sophisticated atmosphere – and is hidden away in a corner of the world's biggest indoor gaming floor. A Kouan-Chiau (gastronomic) version of Cantonese cooking is on offer, with dishes like steamed egg white topped with red bird's nest, and signature crispy chicken. Popular Sichuan dishes are also available.

喜粵位於全球最大室內娛樂場的一角，採用誘人的深紅色作主調，裝潢時尚。菜單以廣州粵菜為主，如太極芙蓉紅燕及金牌炸子雞等。此外，店內亦有提供數款四川名菜，讓食客有更多美食選擇。

TEL. 8118 9930
Shop 1018, 1F, The Venetian Resort,
Estrada da Baia de N. Senhora da
Esperança, s/n, Taipa
氹仔望德聖母灣大馬路
威尼斯人酒店娛樂場 1樓 1018號鋪
www.venetianmacao.com

■ PRICE 價錢
Lunch 午膳
set 套餐 MOP 158
à la carte 點菜 MOP 250-1,000
Dinner 晚膳
set 套餐 MOP 420-1,680
à la carte 點菜 MOP 250-1,000

■ OPENING HOURS 營業時間
Lunch 午膳 11:00-14:45 (L.O.)
Dinner 晚膳 18:00-21:45 (L.O.)
Saturday dinner 週六晚膳
18:00-22:45 (L.O.)

Chan Seng Kei
陳勝記

Chan Seng Kei has stood next to the ancient church for over 70 years and is now run by the 3rd generation of the family. It's well known for its traditional Cantonese food, with seafood supplied daily by local fishermen. The signature dish is stewed duck with tangerine peel but, as the cooking process takes more than 10 hours, only a few are available each day. It's a simple, semi open-air restaurant intertwined with several old banyan trees.

坐落舊教堂旁的陳勝記開業至今已傳至第三代，向以傳統粵菜和海鮮菜式馳名。新鮮野生海鮮每天直接從漁民處採購；而製作工序繁複，需烹調十個小時的陳皮鴨是其招牌菜，每天限量供應。梅菜扣肉及生炒骨也值得一試。半開放式餐室非常樸實，當中數棵樹身粗壯的老榕樹，見證着飯店逾七十載歷史。

TEL. 2888 2021
21 Rua Caetano, Coloane
路環計單奴街 21號

SPECIALITIES TO PRE-ORDER 預訂食物
Stewed duck with tangerine peel
陳皮鴨

■ PRICE 價錢
à la carte 點菜 MOP 150-350

■ OPENING HOURS 營業時間
12:00-22:30 (L.O.)

■ ANNUAL AND WEEKLY CLOSING 休息日期
Closed 2 days Lunar New Year
農曆新年休息 2 天

Cheong Kei
祥記

A family business since the '70s, this tiny noodle shop sticks to its roots and its thin, fine noodles are pressed by bamboo shoots in its own little factory nearby. Their soup uses dried prawns and bonito and is cooked for 8 hours. The noodles with dried shrimp roe are great, but also try the wonton and deep-fried fish ball. Although it's handily placed on Rua de Felicidade, you'll need to weave round shoppers and stalls to get here.

這間家族經營的小麵店於七十年代開業，且在鄰近自設小型廠房製造幼細竹昇麵。湯底以蝦乾和大地魚熬製八小時而成；蝦籽撈麵非試不可，雲吞及鯪魚球亦不容錯過。店內更有頂級蝦籽及秘製辣椒油發售。

TEL. 2857 4310
68 Rua de Felicidade
福隆新街 68號

■ PRICE 價錢
à la carte 點菜 MOP 35-50

■ OPENING HOURS 營業時間
11:30-23:30 (L.O.)

■ ANNUAL AND WEEKLY CLOSING 休息日期
Closed 4 days each month 每月休息 4 天

Clube Militar de Macau
澳門陸軍俱樂部

32

Built in 1870 for the benefit of army officers, this striking pink-hued building was renovated in 1995 when its restaurant was opened to the public; but sadly the delightful sitting room and bar are reserved for its club members. The room has a charming colonial feel, thanks largely to the echoing teak floorboards, netted windows and ceiling fans. The kitchen focuses on traditional Portuguese flavours and hosts occasional food festivals.

這座最初為澳門陸軍軍官而設的粉紅色建築物建於1870年，在1995年完成翻新，並將餐廳對外開放，惟俱樂部內的雅致大廳及酒吧則只限會員使用。大廳內的柚木地板，配上窗紗的大窗及天花板上的吊扇，帶有濃厚的殖民地色彩。俱樂部供應傳統葡萄牙菜式，並會偶爾舉辦美食節。

TEL. 2871 4000
975 Avenida da Praia Grande
南灣大馬路975號

■ PRICE 價錢
Lunch 午膳
buffet 自助餐 MOP 198
à la carte 點菜 MOP 250-550
Dinner 晚膳
set 套餐 MOP 198
à la carte 點菜 MOP 250-550

■ OPENING HOURS 營業時間
Lunch 午膳 12:30-15:30 (L.O.)
Weekend lunch 週末午膳 12:00-15:00 (L.O.)
Dinner 晚膳 19:00-23:00 (L.O.)

■ ANNUAL AND WEEKLY CLOSING 休息日期
Closed Christmas dinner and New Year's Day 聖誕節晚膳及元旦休息

Din Tai Fung (COD)
鼎泰豐 (新濠天地)

The second floor of COD plays host to a plethora of casual eateries – and in the corner you'll find this sizeable branch of the international chain. Din Tai Fung is rightly known for its exquisite Xiao Long Bao but also special here is the steamed crab roe and pork dumpling. Other notables from the 70-odd Shanghainese dishes on offer include the excellent braised beef noodle soup. To finish, try the red bean glutinous rice cake.

這是鼎泰豐的第一間澳門分店，位於新濠天地的蘇濠區內，特高的樓底搭配一貫的雅淨裝潢。菜單包羅逾七十款涼菜、麵食、小炒、湯品及甜點等，焦點是玲瓏的小籠包，香濃味美的紅燒牛肉麵會給你不少驚喜，正宗上海甜點如赤豆鬆糕亦不容錯過。

TEL. 8868 7348
SOHO, 2F, City of Dreams,
Estrada do Istmo, Cotai
路氹連貫公路新濠天地 2樓・蘇濠
www.dintaifung.com.hk

■ PRICE 價錢
Lunch 午膳
set 套餐 MOP 170-190
à la carte 點菜 MOP 150-350
Dinner 晚膳
set 套餐 MOP 180-200
à la carte 點菜 MOP 150-350

■ OPENING HOURS 營業時間
Lunch 午膳 12:00-16:00 (L.O.)
Dinner 晚膳 18:00-22:00 (L.O.)

Dynasty 8
朝

12

Inspired by the eight dynasties of ancient China, the intricately carved wood chairs, red lanterns and classic Chinese eaves provide plenty of old-world charm. From a menu that changes every six months come traditional Cantonese dishes made with top-quality gourmet ingredients. It's worth pre-ordering their double-boiled soups in smoked coconut. A variety of dim sum is available at lunch and wine lovers will want to check out the cellar.

雕花木椅、木地板、紅燈籠，濃濃中國古風的裝潢意念來自中國古代八個皇朝，亦與店名同出一轍。餐廳選用名貴高質的新鮮食材，製作出一道道色香味美的傳統廣東小菜。特別推介原個椰皇燉湯，選用新鮮原個椰皇燉製逾四小時，建議預訂。餐牌菜式每半年會更換一次，午市亦有點心供應；另設有酒窖，適合愛酒人士。

TEL. 8113 8920
1F, Conrad Hotel, Estrada do Istmo, Cotai
路氹連貫公路康萊德酒店 1樓
www.sandscotaicentral.com

■ PRICE 價錢
Lunch 午膳
set 套餐 MOP 688-1,288
à la carte 點菜 MOP 250-1,250
Dinner 晚膳
set 套餐 MOP 688-1,288
à la carte 點菜 MOP 250-1,250

■ OPENING HOURS 營業時間
Lunch 午膳 11:00-15:00 (L.O.)
Weekend lunch 週末午膳 10:00-15:00 (L.O.)
Dinner 晚膳 18:00-23:00 (L.O.)

Espaço Lisboa
里斯本地帶

The owner has created a homely 'Lisbon space' within this two-storey house in this Chinese village. The decorative style comes straight out of Portugal, as do the influences behind many of the home-style dishes. Don't miss the presunto pata negra and if you fancy something a little different then try the African chicken from Mozambique with its coconut flavour. Ask for a table on the veranda when the weather is right.

Espaço意謂空間，店主有意在東方這臨海小鎮營造一個充滿葡國情調的空間。不論是鋪地板的石塊、擺設以至烹調用的陶缽，全部從葡國運抵。葡籍廚師用家鄉材料與傳統食譜炮製多款家常菜。源自莫桑比克食譜的非洲雞，啖啖椰汁香，美味無窮；風味絕佳的黑蹄火腿亦不能錯過。

TEL. 2888 2226
8 Rua das Gaivotas, Coloane
路環水鴨街 8號

SPECIALITIES TO PRE-ORDER 預訂食物
Lobster rice 龍蝦飯 / Suckling pig (whole) 乳豬(全隻) / Lamb leg bakery style 烤羊腿

■ PRICE 價錢
Lunch 午膳
à la carte 點菜 MOP 250-500
Dinner 晚膳
à la carte 點菜 MOP 250-500

■ OPENING HOURS 營業時間
Lunch 午膳 12:00-15:00 (L.O.)
Dinner 晚膳 18:30-22:00 (L.O.)
Weekends 週末 12:00-22:30 (L.O.)

■ ANNUAL AND WEEKLY CLOSING 休息日期
Closed Wednesday 週三休息

Feng Wei Ju
風味居

Gold and red are the traditional festive hues for the Chinese and also the colour scheme of this opulent restaurant. Along with Sichuan classics, such as sautéed chicken with peanuts and chilli, are Hunanese favourites like steamed carp fish head with chilli. The hand-pulled noodles are also worth trying – watching the chefs pulling them in the display kitchen adds to the entertainment.

當大紅配上金，整個餐室都給映襯得金光閃爍；紅色就像與餐廳提供的湘川菜互相呼應似的。由剁椒魚頭到宮保雞丁，味道全都鮮辣刺激！此外，還有多款手製麵條和餃子。隔着玻璃，你還能夠看到廚師團隊在忙着準備食物。

TEL. 8290 8668
5F, StarWorld Hotel, Avenida da Amizade
友誼大馬路星際酒店 5樓
www.starworldmacau.com

■ PRICE 價錢
Lunch 午膳
set 套餐 MOP 150-200
à la carte 點菜 MOP 350-550
Dinner 晚膳
set 套餐 MOP 250-350
à la carte 點菜 MOP 350-550

■ OPENING HOURS 營業時間
11:00-22:30 (L.O.)

Fook Lam Moon
福臨門

One of the most famous restaurant names in Hong Kong has long been celebrated for its traditional Cantonese menu. It is also known for its clientele of high-rollers and decision makers, so it was perhaps inevitable that a branch would eventually appear in Macau. You'll find local lobster on the menu, along with their famous crispy chicken; many regulars opt for the chicken stuffed with bird's nest – even though it isn't always listed on the menu.

門外懸掛着的一副對聯和橢圓形的水晶吊燈為餐廳營造了別具一格的氣派。福臨門是香港享負盛名的粵菜酒家，熟客都懂得預訂餐牌上沒有的鳳吞燕，當紅炸子雞則是廚師得意之作，此外，選用本地BB龍蝦製作的油泡龍蝦球亦值得一試。食客更可向品酒師請教配搭美酒佳餚的心得，專業的服務態度讓人賓至如歸。

TEL. 2888 0888
Shop 2008, 2F, Galaxy Macau Phase 2 Shopping Mall, Cotai
路氹城澳門銀河綜合渡假城二期商場2樓 2008號舖
www.fooklammoon-grp.com

SPECIALITIES TO PRE-ORDER 預訂食物
Steamed duck stuffed with various fillings 蓮子霸皇鴨 / Barbecued whole suckling pig 大紅片皮乳豬全體 / Traditional baked chicken in rock salt 正宗鹽焗雞

■ PRICE 價錢
Lunch 午膳
à la carte 點菜 MOP 200-500
Dinner 晚膳
à la carte 點菜 MOP 500-1,000

■ OPENING HOURS 營業時間
Lunch 午膳 11:00-14:30 (L.O.)
Dinner 晚膳 18:00-22:30 (L.O.)

Golden Flower
京花軒

Within the Encore hotel is this elegant and sophisticated restaurant, whose kitchen is noted for its dextrous use of superb ingredients in the preparation of three different cuisines: Sichuan, Lu and Tan – along with a few Cantonese dishes. The room is adorned with the colours of gold and orange and the booths are the prized seats, but wherever you sit you'll receive charming service from the strikingly attired ladies, including the 'tea sommelier'.

京花軒坐落於澳門萬利酒店內，以金色和橙色裝潢，既典雅又獨特。店內設有圓形白色皮卡座，不管安坐何處，都能享受端莊的女侍應的悉心服務，包括「調茶」。廚房最出色之處，除了選料上乘，還能俐落地烹調出川菜、魯菜、譚家菜三款不同菜系的菜式，同時供應少量廣東菜。

TEL. 8986 3663
GF, Encore Hotel. Rua Cidade de Sintra, NAPE
外港新填海區仙德麗街萬利酒店地下
www.wynnmacau.com

■ PRICE 價錢
Lunch 午膳
à la carte 點菜 MOP 250-2,000
Dinner 晚膳
à la carte 點菜 MOP 250-2,000

■ OPENING HOURS 營業時間
Weekend lunch 週末午膳
11:30-14:15 (L.O.)
Dinner 晚膳 18:00-22:15 (L.O.)

■ ANNUAL AND WEEKLY CLOSING 休息日期
Closed Monday 週一休息

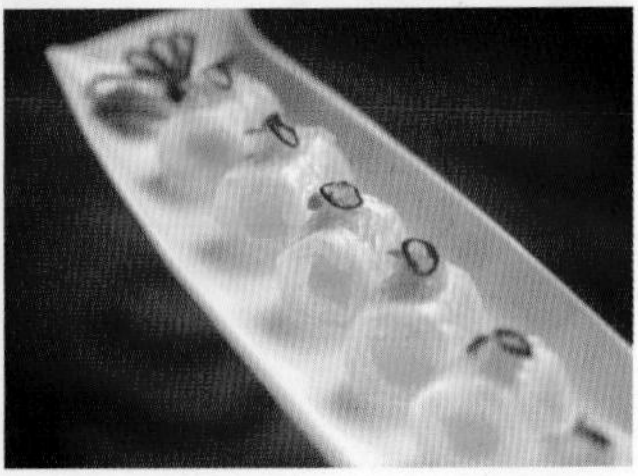

Guincho a Galera
葡國餐廳

Portuguese 'fine dining' comes to Macau in the form of this branch of Fortaleza do Guincho restaurant in Cascais, near Lisbon. It occupies the room in the Lisboa hotel that was formerly used by Joël Robuchon. The atmosphere is refined, the decoration vivid and the service attentive. The Portuguese food is polished and classical and is occasionally accompanied by subtle French notes; it is also complemented by a very impressive wine list.

來自鄰近里斯本的卡斯凱什，Fortaleza do Guincho餐廳的分店正式登陸澳門，帶來葡式高級餐飲享受。它位處葡京酒店內，餐廳格調高雅、裝潢精緻，服務亦十分周到。它供應的葡式佳餚製作精美、味道正宗，偶爾亦會滲入些許法國風味。餐廳還提供種類繁多的美酒。

TEL. 8803 7676
3F, Lisboa Tower, Hotel Lisboa,
2-4 Avenida de Lisboa
葡京路 2-4號葡京酒店西座 3樓
www.hotelisboa.com

■ PRICE 價錢
Lunch 午膳
set 套餐 MOP 310-380
à la carte 點菜 MOP 530-1,200
Dinner 晚膳
set 套餐 MOP 580-980
à la carte 點菜 MOP 530-1,200

■ OPENING HOURS 營業時間
Lunch 午膳 12:00-14:30 (L.O.)
Dinner 晚膳 18:30-22:30 (L.O.)

Hou Kong Chi Kei
濠江志記美食

It's not easy to find and the ambiance isn't much to speak of, but what keeps regulars coming back are the Cantonese dishes that reflect owner-chef Chan's passion for food. The baby oyster and salted radish omelette on a sizzling iron plate literally bursts with eggy flavour. Barbecued fish and deep-fried taro fish balls are also excellent choices. Certain seafood dishes, such as steamed crab on sticky rice, need to be pre-ordered in advance.

要找到這家位置隱蔽的餐廳確是個小小的挑戰，其環境亦非十分出眾；但你所獲得的回報，就是一嘗東主兼廚師陳先生主理的廣式佳餚，並感受他如何用心烹調每一道菜式。個別海鮮美食如蒸糯米蟹飯，需致電預訂；其他推介菜式還有燒魚及香芋炸魚球，以鐵板奉上並充滿蛋香的蠔仔菜脯蛋亦是不二之選。

TEL. 2895 3098
GF, Block 3, Lai Hou Garden,
Praça de Luís de Camões
白鴿巢前地麗豪花園第三座地舖
佳樂園石級上

SPECIALITIES TO PRE-ORDER 預訂食物
Steamed crab on sticky rice 蒸糯米蟹飯 /
Grilled fish or prawns 燒魚或蝦

■ PRICE 價錢
Dinner 晚膳
à la carte 點菜 MOP 100-200

■ OPENING HOURS 營業時間
Dinner 晚膳 19:00-23:00 (L.O.)

■ ANNUAL AND WEEKLY CLOSING 休息日期
Closed the 15th & 16th of each month
每月 15 及 16 日休息

IFT Educational Restaurant
旅遊學院教學餐廳

XX

12

Being part of the Institute for Tourism Studies means that while the head chef is a professional, some of his brigade and front of house team are students – and the pride they have in their work is palpable. The menu is a mix of European and Macanese dishes – presented in a modern style using herbs from their own garden. There's even the occasional Scandinavian touch (they cure their own salmon). On Friday nights they offer a Macanese buffet.

這家旅遊學院教學餐廳的廚房由專業廚師主理，部分團隊成員則由學生組成，供應多款歐陸及澳葡美食。其特色是採用多種自家種植的有機香草和蔬菜作食材，並以廚餘作肥料。非洲雞和乾炒免治肉碎都是推介菜式，別忘了試試這兒的甜品。團隊友善而專業，是遠離賭場喧囂的用膳好去處。逢週五供應澳葡自助晚餐。

TEL. 8598 3077
Pousada de Mong-Há,
Colina de Mong-Há
望廈山望廈迎賓館
www.ift.edu.mo

■ PRICE 價錢
Lunch 午膳
set 套餐 MOP 220
à la carte 點菜 MOP 300-700
Dinner 晚膳
set 套餐 MOP 390
à la carte 點菜 MOP 300-700

■ OPENING HOURS 營業時間
Lunch 午膳 12:30-14:30 (L.O.)
Dinner 晚膳 19:00-22:00 (L.O.)

■ ANNUAL AND WEEKLY CLOSING 休息日期
Closed weekends and Public Holidays
週末及公眾假期休息

Il Teatro
帝雅廷

⊙20

The name, which means 'the theatre', makes perfect sense as you can watch the fire, water and light show from most tables in the restaurant. Equally spectacular is the family-style cuisine given a modern edge, which includes homemade pasta, pizza and seafood. Try their Fassone milk-fed veal chop and make sure you save room for the divine Il Teatro tiramisu. The menu offers seasonal dishes which update every two to three months and service is slick and smooth.

餐廳大部分的座位都能飽覽表演湖景致，湖上每晚上演噴泉表演，音樂水柱與激光穿梭，蔚為奇觀。這兒主要提供帶現代元素的意大利家庭菜，如奶飼牛仔扒伴巴馬火腿及意大利軟芝士餅，亦有意粉、即製薄餅及高級海鮮可供選擇。餐牌上的時令菜式每兩至三個月會更新一次。年輕團隊服務殷勤周到。

TEL. 8986 3663
1F, Wynn Hotel, Rua Cidade de Sintra, NAPE
外港新填海區仙德麗街永利酒店 1樓
www.wynnmacau.com

■ PRICE 價錢
Dinner 晚膳
à la carte 點菜 MOP 500-1,000

■ OPENING HOURS 營業時間
Dinner 晚膳 17:30-23:00 (L.O.)

■ ANNUAL AND WEEKLY CLOSING 休息日期
Closed Monday 週一休息

Imperial Court
金殿堂

36

On the same floor as the hotel's VIP lobby, this sleek and contemporary dining room wows guests with its vividly carved Chinese dragon coiling around a marble pillar. The food is Cantonese, with standouts like sautéed prawns with chilli and shallot, and barbecued duck liver and pork skewers. Chef's recommendations are updated monthly, with specific themes like old-time Cantonese classics. The impressive wine list includes over 2,000 labels.

如欲品嘗傳統廣東菜，位於貴賓大堂同一樓層的金殿堂是尚佳選擇。餐廳每月推出不同主題的推介菜單，例如懷舊廣東菜。萬勿錯過大千爆蝦球，而吊燒鴨肝金錢雞以鴨肝代替雞肝，同樣出色。餐廳格調高貴優雅而不失時尚，氣勢十足的雕龍雲石柱更是標誌，巧奪天工值得駐足欣賞。

TEL. 8802 2361
GF, MGM Macau, Avenida Dr. Sun Yat Sen, NAPE
外港新填海區孫逸仙大馬路澳門美高梅酒店地下
www.mgm.mo

■ PRICE 價錢
Lunch 午膳
set 套餐 MOP 188-1,080
à la carte 點菜 MOP 200-800
Dinner 晚膳
set 套餐 MOP 500-1,080
à la carte 點菜 MOP 500-1,500

■ OPENING HOURS 營業時間
Lunch 午膳 11:00-15:00 (L.O.)
Weekend and Public Holiday lunch
週末及公眾假期午膳 10:00-15:00 (L.O.)
Dinner 晚膳 18:00-23:00 (L.O.)

Jade Dragon
譽瓏軒

XXXX 24

Chinese art is set against ebony, crystal, gold and silver to create a contemporary and lavish feel. Carved jade chopstick stands and the glass-clad wine cellar are also quite stunning. The food is equally amazing – first-rate ingredients are deftly prepared in dishes like lychee wood-barbecued meat. Try too their double-boiled tonic soups based on herbal medicine. The immaculate service also makes the meal unforgettable.

烏木、金、銀和水晶的運用，揉合了現代設計與中國傳統美學的精髓，透明方柱酒窖、豪華廂房，或是餐桌上的玉雕筷子座，都給人留下深刻印象。由歐陽師傅帶領的團隊以精心烹製的粵菜擄獲一眾食客歡心，除了一貫出色的荔枝木燒味外，多款滋補燉湯也不容錯過。細心的服務令用餐經驗錦上添花。

TEL. 8868 2822
2F, The Shops at the Boulevard,
City of Dreams, Estrada do Istmo, Cotai
路氹連貫公路新濠天地新濠大道 2樓
www.cityofdreamsmacau.com

SPECIALITIES TO PRE-ORDER 預訂食物
Steamed herbal chicken wrap 藥膳紙包雞 /
Whole supreme fish maw 原隻廣肚花膠公

■ PRICE 價錢
Lunch 午膳
set 套餐 MOP 380-780
à la carte 點菜 MOP 300-2,000
Dinner 晚膳
set 套餐 MOP 1,180-1,880
à la carte 點菜 MOP 300-2,000

■ OPENING HOURS 營業時間
Lunch 午膳 11:00-15:00 (L.O.)
Dinner 晚膳 18:00-23:00 (L.O.)

Kam Lai Heen
金麗軒

60

The dining room exudes understated elegance thanks to its eye-catching lights and subtle Chinese design motifs. The long-standing kitchen team attracts a loyal Macanese following thanks to its classic Cantonese dishes prepared in traditional ways. An array of exquisitely crafted dim sum are on offer, along with other signature dishes.

酒店大堂的上方正是金麗軒所在之處，餐室天花上的燈飾華麗奪目，配以牆上富中國韻味的圖案和裝飾，格調高貴優雅。廚師團隊經驗十足，烹調手法熟練，精於傳統技法同時亦不忘為菜式注入本土元素。菜單上除了一系列富澳門特色的粵菜，亦不乏經典的廣東菜餚及點心。

TEL. 8793 3821
2F, Grand Lapa Hotel,
956-1110 Avenida da Amizade, Macau
澳門友誼大馬路 956-1110號
金麗華酒店 2樓
www.grandlapa.com

SPECIALITIES TO PRE-ORDER 預訂食物
Braised Boston lobster with vermicelli and black pepper in clay pot 黑椒波士頓龍蝦粉絲煲 / Steamed rice in lotus leaf with prawns and mud crab 鮮蝦荷葉蒸蟹飯 / Stir-fried sole fish with honey beans and bell peppers 蜜椒龍脷球 / Fire beggar's chicken 火焰富貴雞

■ PRICE 價錢
Lunch 午膳
set 套餐 MOP 166
à la carte 點菜 MOP 200-2,300
Dinner 晚膳
set 套餐 MOP 204
à la carte 點菜 MOP 200-2,300

■ OPENING HOURS 營業時間
Lunch 午膳 11:00-15:00 (L.O.)
Dinner 晚膳 18:00-22:00 (L.O.)

■ ANNUAL AND WEEKLY CLOSING 休息日期
Closed Tuesday 週二休息

King
帝皇樓

P 24

Though discreetly tucked away in a commercial building, it hasn't stopped the regulars coming for their Cantonese dishes. The signature dishes include crispy young pigeon, and baked chicken with Shaoxing wine; the homemade dim sum also comes highly recommended. Being sufficiently removed from the casinos means the atmosphere is comparatively sedate.

這家隱藏在商業大樓內的餐廳並不顯眼，但卻有不少捧場熟客。此酒家的招牌菜有原隻脆皮妙齡鴿及花雕焗飛天雞，後者製作需時，建議預訂。午市供應的自製點心即點即蒸，亦值得一試。酒家位置與各大賭場之間有一段距離，環境較為寧靜。

TEL. 2875 7218
G05-07, GF, AIA Tower,
251A-301 Avenida Commercial de Macau
澳門商業大馬路友邦廣場地下 G05-07

SPECIALITIES TO PRE-ORDER 預訂食物
Whole duck stuffed with eight goodies 八子全鴨 / Steamed crab claw in egg white 蛋白蒸蟹拑 / Deep-fried crab claw with peppered salt 椒鹽蟹拑

■ PRICE 價錢
Lunch 午膳
à la carte 點菜 MOP 150-300
Dinner 晚膳
à la carte 點菜 MOP 250-500

■ OPENING HOURS 營業時間
Lunch 午膳 11:30-15:30 (L.O.)
Dinner 晚膳 18:00-22:30 (L.O.)

Lai Heen
麗軒

If you're looking to impress then you can't fail with this Cantonese restaurant on the top floor of the Ritz-Carlton hotel. The stunning room is richly decorated and supremely comfortable, as are the numerous private dining rooms which can be opened out and enlarged. The ambition of the kitchen is apparent in the Cantonese specialities – they are presented in a modern way and are a match for the sumptuous surroundings.

麗軒位處麗思卡爾頓酒店51樓，居高臨下，盡賞窗外秀麗景色。富麗堂皇的裝潢與造型時尚精緻的傳統粵菜，同時滿足視覺與味覺的需求。館內設有五間裝飾同樣華美，能隨時將木板牆移開騰出更多空間的私人廂房，適合舉行大小宴會。專業的服務團隊態度親切，令食客有賓至如歸之感！

TEL. 8886 6742
51F, The Ritz-Carlton, Galaxy, Estrada da Baia da N. Senhora da Esperança, Cotai
路氹城望德聖母灣大馬路銀河綜合渡假城麗思卡爾頓酒店 51樓
www.ritzcarlton.com

SPECIALITIES TO PRE-ORDER 預訂食物
Peking duck 片皮鴨 / Shrimp flambé 火焰醉翁蝦 / Pacific garoupa 老鼠斑

■ PRICE 價錢
Lunch 午膳
set 套餐 MOP 428-2,088
à la carte 點菜 MOP 300-800
Dinner 晚膳
set 套餐 MOP 1,888-2,088
à la carte 點菜 MOP 500-1,500

■ OPENING HOURS 營業時間
Lunch 午膳 12:00-14:30 (L.O.)
Weekend and Public Holiday lunch
週末及公眾假期午膳 11:30-15:00 (L.O.)
Dinner 晚膳 18:00-22:30 (L.O.)

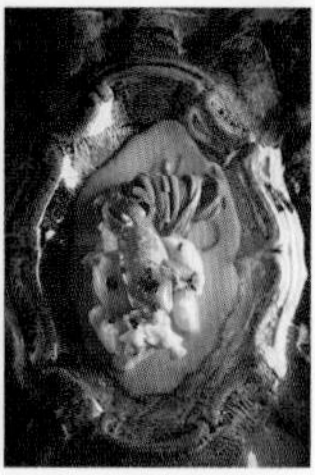

Lei Garden
利苑酒家

A smart restaurant set amongst the canals of this vast hotel's third floor. A comprehensive range of traditional Cantonese dishes are delivered by an efficient and well-organised team of servers. The best place to be seated is in one of the cosy booths. Pre-order the popular crispy roasted pork and various double-boiled soups.

餐廳設於三樓，佔據此大型酒店運河旁的位置，雄據地利。服務效率非常高，但以這家餐廳的受歡迎程度，食客到此用膳，建議預先訂座。餐廳的熱門菜式如冰燒三層肉及各式燉湯均值得一試，建議預訂。

TEL. 2882 8689
Shop 855, 3F, Grand Canal Shoppes,
The Venetian Resort,
Estrada da Baia de N. Senhora da
Esperança, Taipa
氹仔望德聖母灣大馬路威尼斯人酒店
大運河購物中心 3樓 855號舖
www.venetianmacao.com

SPECIALITIES TO PRE-ORDER 預訂食物
Crispy roasted pork 冰燒三層肉 / Double-boiled soups 燉湯

■ PRICE 價錢
Lunch 午膳
à la carte 點菜 MOP 200-1,000
Dinner 晚膳
à la carte 點菜 MOP 250-1,000

■ OPENING HOURS 營業時間
Lunch 午膳 11:30-14:15 (L.O.)
Dinner 晚膳 18:00-22:15 (L.O.)

■ ANNUAL AND WEEKLY CLOSING 休息日期
Closed 3 days Lunar New Year
農曆新年休息 3 天

Lou Kei (Fai Chi Kei)
老記 (筷子基)

If you're looking for a simple, good value supper then Lou Kei may well fit the bill. Granted, it may not be in the centre of town, but every local and cab driver knows this lively place. It has been renowned for over 20 years for its sizeable selection of tasty noodles, congee and Cantonese dishes; frogs' legs in a clay pot and sea crab congee are both highly recommended. The interior is bright and neat while the service is polite and attentive.

若然你想品嘗價廉物美的美食，老記便是不二之選。儘管餐廳並非位於市中心，但是所有本地人和的士司機皆知這間馳名食府的位置。老記二十多年來提供美味粥品麵食及廣東菜式，其田雞腿煲及水蟹粥更備受食客推崇，店內光猛潔淨，侍應親切有禮。店子營業至凌晨，專門照顧吃宵夜的食客。

TEL. 2856 9494
Shop H&M, GF,
12 Avenida Da Concõrdia N
和樂大馬路 12號宏基大廈第 4座 H及 M鋪

■ PRICE 價錢
à la carte 點菜 MOP 120-250

■ OPENING HOURS 營業時間
18:00-04:30 (L.O.)

Luk Kei Noodle
六記粥麵

This busy shop next to the pier still kneads the noodles with a bamboo pole just like old times and the flavourful broth is simmered with an array of seasonal fish. The owner's wife insists on making wonton wrappers and cooking noodles by herself and she's very specific about both the cooking time and the consistency of the noodles. Other popular dishes include crab congee, tossed noodles with dried prawn roe, and deep-fried wontons with crispy dace balls.

店子位於碼頭旁邊的街道上，廣受食客歡迎。第二代店主堅持以傳統手法製作竹昇麵，並由其太太親手烹煮，她對時間控制及麵條質感的要求十分嚴謹。湯底以時令的鮮魚熬製，鮮味十足；而雲吞皮更是用手打造。小小的餐牌上附有特色食品的照片，包括蝦籽撈麵、炸鴛鴦（炸雲吞及米通鯪魚球）及水蟹粥等。

TEL. 2855 9627
1-D Travessa da Saudade
沙梨頭仁慕巷 1號 D

■ PRICE 價錢
à la carte 點菜 MOP 40-70

■ OPENING HOURS 營業時間
18:30-02:30 (L.O.)

■ ANNUAL AND WEEKLY CLOSING 休息日期
Closed 4 days Lunar New Year
農曆新年休息 4 天

Lung Wah Tea House
龍華茶樓

Little has changed from when this old-style Cantonese tea house, up a flight of stairs, opened in the 1960s: the large clock still works, the boss still uses an abacus to add the bill and you still have to refill your own pot of tea at the boiler. The owner buys fresh produce, including chicken for their most popular dish, from the market across the road. Get here early for the freshly made dim sum.

這家有一列樓梯的傳統廣東茶樓自1962年開業以來，變化不大，古老大鐘依然在擺動，老闆依然用算盤結算帳單，你依然要自行到熱水器前沖茶。店主從對面街市選購新鮮食材烹調美食，包括茶樓名菜葱油雞。建議早上前來享用新鮮點心。

TEL. 2857 4456
3 Rua Norte do Mercado Aim-Lacerda
提督市北街 3號

■ PRICE 價錢
à la carte 點菜 MOP 50-150

■ OPENING HOURS 營業時間
07:00-14:00 (L.O.)

■ ANNUAL AND WEEKLY CLOSING 休息日期
Closed 4 days Lunar New Year, 4 days May and 4 days October 農曆新年、五月及十月各休息4天

Manuel Cozinha Portuguesa
阿曼諾葡國餐

Authenticity and hospitality are what draw customers to this cosy little corner restaurant. Newcomers will find themselves welcomed by the owner-chef just as warmly as if they were regulars. His traditional Portuguese cooking uses quality ingredients and many of the dishes are cooked in the old-fashioned barbecue way. He makes his own cheese and the two specialities of which he is most proud are grilled codfish, and fried rice with squid ink.

離開氹仔舊城區的熱鬧街道，從施督憲正街向飛能便度街方向走，便會找到位於路口這家小店。在這兒你能吃到美味正宗的葡國菜。葡籍店東兼主廚親切好客。他堅持選用本地和葡國優質食材，且以炭火燒烤食物，還在店內自製芝士。燒馬介休和墨魚汁炒飯是他最引以為傲的菜式。

TEL. 2882 7571
GF, 90 Rua de Femão Mendes Pinto, Taipa
氹仔飛能便度街 90號

SPECIALITIES TO PRE-ORDER 預訂食物
Roasted piglet "Manuel style" 原隻阿曼諾燒乳豬 / Baked lobster "Manuel style" 阿曼諾焗龍蝦 / Seafood rice (except Saturday) 海鮮飯（週六除外）

■ PRICE 價錢
Lunch 午膳
à la carte 點菜 MOP 130-340
Dinner 晚膳
à la carte 點菜 MOP 130-340

■ OPENING HOURS 營業時間
Lunch 午膳 12:00-15:00 (L.O.)
Dinner 晚膳 18:00-22:00 (L.O.)

■ ANNUAL AND WEEKLY CLOSING 休息日期
Closed Wednesday 週三休息

Mezza9

XX

♿ ☂ 🍸 P ⊡12 ✆

This is a gastronomic paradise for those wanting to sample various world cuisines in one place. The vast and striking interior encompasses several show kitchens with varied choices from sushi and Cantonese stir-fries to grilled meats and South Asian noodles. Diners can opt for the 'dining from the kitchen' dinner buffet to interact with chefs during a meal tailored to their preferences. It is hugely popular and reservations are recommended six months ahead.

Mezza9供應多國菜式，從廣東小炒、澳門特色菜、南亞麵食，以至壽司、烤肉等應有盡有，定能滿足心猿意馬的食客。也可體驗「與廚共饗」自助晚餐，與各大廚互動，親自決定烹調方式和口味。餐廳面積寬敞，設有數個開放式廚房，讓食客一睹廚師的烹調過程。餐廳經常滿座，務必提前訂座。

TEL. 8868 1920
3F, Grand Hyatt Hotel, City of Dreams,
Estrada do Istmo, Cotai
路氹連貫公路新濠天地君悅酒店 3樓
macau.grand.hyatt.com

■ PRICE 價錢
set 套餐 MOP 599-699

■ OPENING HOURS 營業時間
18:00-23:00 (L.O.)

Mizumi (Macau)
泓 (澳門)

16

The lucky colours of gold and red were incorporated into the latest redecoration – and it's certainly a strikingly bright room now. Three consultants are involved, including Chef Shimamiya from Sushi Zen in Hokkaido. The fish comes from Japan; the beef from a private ranch on Ishigaki Island, south of Okinawa. Go for the 'Taste of Mizumi'.

裝修後的餐室，地氈、牆身和裝飾均換上金、紅兩色，加上入口的銅鑄日本摺紙工藝雕塑，奪目且煥然一新。食物方面，不論是魚生、壽司、鐵板燒或天婦羅均選用高質食材，包括每週由日本運到的新鮮海產及精心搜購的沖繩和牛，加上精細的烹調，令人回味無窮。點選泓之風味套餐能一次品嘗各式料理。

TEL. 8986 3663
GF, Wynn Hotel, Rua Cidade de Sintra, NAPE
外港新填海區仙德麗街永利酒店地下
www.wynnmacau.com

■ PRICE 價錢
Dinner 晚膳
set 套餐 MOP 1,300-1,680
à la carte 點菜 MOP 250-1,800

■ OPENING HOURS 營業時間
Dinner 晚膳 17:30-23:00 (L.O.)

■ ANNUAL AND WEEKLY CLOSING 休息日期
Closed Tuesday 週二休息

Naam
灆

The name of Grand Lapa's Thai restaurant translates as 'water', which seems appropriate as it overlooks the pool and tropical garden and features a small fountain in the middle of the room, which adds to the calm and peaceful atmosphere. The majority of the kitchen and service team are Thai and the food is attractively presented and the spicing is well-judged. The menu also features a section of Royal Thai cuisine dishes.

Naam在泰文中是水的意思。餐廳位於泳池旁邊，中央位置設有一個水池，天然光線從其頂上透射而下，整個環境寧靜而優雅。這兒的泰國菜味道較為柔諧，更設有一系列的宮廷菜式，友善的泰國侍應亦會給予客人合適的推介。

TEL. 8793 4818
GF, Grand Lapa Hotel,
956-1110 Avenida da Amizade, Macau
澳門友誼大馬路956-1110號
金麗華酒店地下
www.grandlapa.com

■ PRICE 價錢
Lunch 午膳
set 套餐 MOP 158
à la carte 點菜 MOP 350-850
Dinner 晚膳
set 套餐 MOP 260
à la carte 點菜 MOP 350-850

■ OPENING HOURS 營業時間
Lunch 午膳 12:00-14:30 (L.O.)
Dinner 晚膳 18:30-22:30 (L.O.)

■ ANNUAL AND WEEKLY CLOSING 休息日期
Closed Monday 週一休息

Ngao Kei Ka Lei Chon
牛記咖喱美食

Don't judge a book by its cover because the broken neon signs outside do not reflect the quality of food and service at this friendly, well-run noodle shop. The key draw is the swimmer crab congee – crabs are dressed à la minute and burst with seafood flavours, while the creamy congee imparts a rich aroma of rice. Other recommendations include braised E-fu noodles with crab roe, beef brisket in clear broth, and curry chicken with coconut milk.

位於大街一角的小巷內，這小麵店被老舊的建築物包圍，卻不減其吸引力，全因店家管理有序，職員態度友善，服務使人稱心滿意。店子以水蟹、蟹黃燜伊麵和蟹粥聞名，所用的蟹均即叫即劏；粥底香綿且帶蟹肉鮮甜味。此外，清湯牛腩、牛筋麵和椰汁咖喱雞也值得一試。

TEL. 2895 6129
GF, 1 Rua de Cinco de Outubro
十月初五街 1號地下

■ PRICE 價錢
à la carte 點菜 MOP 40-90

■ OPENING HOURS 營業時間
08:00-00:30 (L.O.)

■ ANNUAL AND WEEKLY CLOSING 休息日期
Closed 3 days Lunar New Year, Mid-autumn Festival and National Day
農曆新年 3 天、中秋節及國慶日休息

99 Noodles
99麵

Noodle lovers will need a few visits to this stylish pit-stop at the Encore hotel to work their way through the huge choice of Chinese noodles – there's everything from Beijing la mian to Shanxi knife-shaved, tip-ended and one string noodles, all served with various broths and garnishes, along with specialities from Northern China. The colours of the room are vivid; the jumbo chopsticks on the walls are striking; and the atmospheregolden is buzzy.

細小的餐室以鮮艷的紅色作主調，牆上懸着一雙雙色彩繽紛的巨型筷子，華麗且充滿活力，與四周的賭場環境風格一致。顧名思義，這裏是嘗麵的好地方：北京拉麵、山西刀削麵、轉盤剔尖及一根麵等多款麵食，配以各式湯底和澆頭，令人食指大動。餃子和北方點心當然也不能錯過。

TEL. 8986 3663
GF, Encore Hotel, Rua Cidade de Sintra, NAPE
外港新填海區仙德麗街萬利酒店地下
www.wynnmacau.com

■ PRICE 價錢
set 套餐 MOP 150
à la carte 點菜 MOP 150-500

■ OPENING HOURS 營業時間
10:00-00:30 (L.O.)

O Castiço

Ownership of this simple, unassuming little place with just five tables has now passed to the late owner's son – though his spirit is still honoured in the atmosphere of the restaurant, which is as friendly and as intimate as it ever was. The food is also just as good – the home-style dishes are authentic and carefully prepared, with recommendations being the stewed pork with clams and the oven-roasted bacalhau with potatoes.

這家隱藏於氹仔舊城區大街附近的小店陳設簡約樸實，只有五張餐桌。店子由已故葡籍廚師的兒子掌管，女友則負責掌廚。從清早到深夜，她就在細小的開放式廚房，以原店主的食譜繼續烹調家庭式葡國美食，店子待客如親人、收費合理的作風貫徹不變，推介菜有豬肉粒炒蜆。

TEL. 2857 6505
65B Rua Direita Carlos Eugénio, Taipa
氹仔施督憲正街 65號 B

SPECIALITIES TO PRE-ORDER 預訂食物
Leitao assado Á "Xiolas" (roasted suckling pig xiolas style) 烤乳豬

■ PRICE 價錢
à la carte 點菜 MOP 130-250

■ OPENING HOURS 營業時間
11:00-22:30 (L.O.)

■ ANNUAL AND WEEKLY CLOSING 休息日期
Closed Thursday 週四休息

8 1/2 Otto e Mezzo - Bombana

18

Chef Umberto Bombana offers the same menu here as he does at the Hong Kong original; the wine list – of mostly Italian and French bottles – is also of equal breadth and depth. Since day one, the same kitchen team have been meticulously preparing every course here, including the particularly good desserts. The manager ensures service is attentive and thoughtful, and the elegant, chic dining room comes with a striking central bar.

與香港店同由意籍廚師Bombana帶領，餐單及食物風格亦與香港店如出一轍。穩定的廚師團隊使出品維持一貫的高水準，從頭盤到甜品每一道都經精心烹調，讓人回味無窮。酒單羅列的美酒種類豐富，包括眾多來自意大利及法國的佳釀。室內佈置美輪美奐，位於餐廳中央的雞尾酒吧也甚為吸引。

TEL. 8886 2169
Shop 1031, 1F, Galaxy, The Promenade, Avenida de Cotai
路氹城澳門銀河綜合渡假城 1樓 1031號舖
www.ottoemezzobombana.com

■ PRICE 價錢
Lunch 午膳
set 套餐 MOP 488-988
à la carte 點菜 MOP 900-1,200

Dinner 晚膳
set 套餐 MOP 1,380-2,180
à la carte 點菜 MOP 900-1,200

■ OPENING HOURS 營業時間
Lunch 午膳 12:00-14:00 (L.O.)
Dinner 晚膳 18:00-22:30 (L.O.)

■ ANNUAL AND WEEKLY CLOSING 休息日期
Closed Monday to Thursday lunch and Wednesday 週一至週四午膳及週三休息

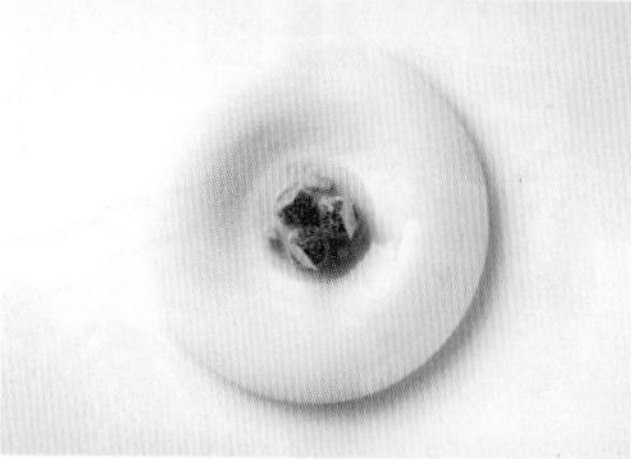

Pearl Dragon
玥龍軒

12

No expense has been spared at this elegant and luxurious Cantonese restaurant on the 2nd floor of Studio City. The menu offers a range of refined Cantonese dishes: soy-braised dishes from the lychee wood barbecue are a speciality. Other highlights are double-boiled chicken soup with matsutake and sea conch; stir-fried lobster with caviar; and seafood rice with fish maw and sea cucumber. The tea counter offers a choice of over 50 premium teas.

這家位於新濠影滙酒店的粵菜餐廳裝潢時尚高雅，細節中盡顯心思。香茗選擇逾五十款，酒櫃內放滿陳年佳釀，餐桌上的擺設及用具以龍和珍珠設計，別致而雍雅豪華。餐單選擇繁多，招牌菜包括果木燒烤和滷水菜式，油泡龍蝦球伴黑魚子和上品海皇泡飯均值得一試。貼心周到的服務，令用餐過程更添美滿。

TEL. 8865 6560
Shop 2111, 2F, Star Tower,
Studio City Hotel, Estrada do Istmo, Cotai
路氹連貫公路新濠影匯酒店
巨星匯 2樓 2111號
www.studiocity-macau.com

■ PRICE 價錢
Lunch 午膳
set 套餐 MOP 688-1,488
à la carte 點菜 MOP 350-1,300
Dinner 晚膳
set 套餐 MOP 1,288-1,488
à la carte 點菜 MOP 350-1,300

■ OPENING HOURS 營業時間
Lunch 午膳 12:00-14:30 (L.O.)
Weekend and Public Holiday lunch
週末及公眾假期午膳 11:00-14:30 (L.O.)
Dinner 晚膳 18:00-22:30 (L.O.)

Robuchon au Dôme
天巢法國餐廳

Its lofty position atop the Grand Lisboa Hotel lets diners take in breathtaking views over Macau and is a great setting for Joël Robuchon's renowned contemporary French cuisine. Choose the 7-course 'Menu Aux Crustacés' or an 8-course seasonal menu; the dishes are intricate, beautifully presented and deliver an array of intense flavours, with the stunning dessert trolley providing a fitting finale. The restaurant boasts one of the best wine lists in Asia.

Joël Robuchon的天巢法國餐廳位於新葡京酒店頂樓，大型水晶吊燈引人矚目，食客更能俯瞰令人屏息的360度澳門全景，是品味時尚法式美饌的絕佳舞台。可選擇七道菜的海鮮菜單或八道菜的季節菜單。菜式艷麗如畫，入口濃郁可口，各菜單均以精緻甜品作結。餐酒選擇過萬種，大概在亞洲數一數二。

TEL. 8803 7878
43F, Grand Lisboa Hotel,
Avenida de Lisboa
葡京路新葡京酒店 43樓
www.grandlisboahotels.com

■ PRICE 價錢
Lunch 午膳
set 套餐 MOP 688-1,288
à la carte 點菜 MOP 1,250-3,400
Dinner 晚膳
set 套餐 MOP 2,188-3,088
à la carte 點菜 MOP 1,250-3,400

■ OPENING HOURS 營業時間
Lunch 午膳 12:00-14:30 (L.O.)
Dinner 晚膳 18:30-22:30 (L.O.)

Shinji by Kanesaka
金坂極上壽司

⊕6

This is as authentic as it gets when it comes to a Japanese dining experience: a solid wood counter made from a 220-year-old cypress tree, Japanese servers, Japanese rice dressed in pale red vinegar and fish shipped straight from Japan. Apart from the various set menus, you may order omakase at lunch and dinner, for mostly sushi alongside some sashimi and stews. Watching the chefs masterfully preparing the catch adds to the experience.

由享齡逾二百歲的柏木打造的日式壽司枱、牆上的日本漢字、日籍服務團隊，餐廳的日本氣息濃厚。琳瑯滿目的時令鮮魚從日本直送，鮮味十足。喜歡壽司的可從「江戶前壽司」挑選手握紅醋飯壽司，欲先品嘗刺身請從「真」或「和」餐單上挑選。午、晚市均提供的廚師發辦套餐則可一次嘗到壽司、刺身和煮物。

TEL. 8868 7300
1F, Nüwa, City of Dreams,
Estrada do Istmo, Cotai
路氹連貫公路新濠天地頤居 1樓
www.cityofdreamsmacau.com

■ PRICE 價錢
Lunch 午膳
set 套餐 MOP 738-1,688
Dinner 晚膳
set 套餐 MOP 1,688-2,988

■ OPENING HOURS 營業時間
Lunch 午膳 12:00-15:00 (L.O.)
Dinner 晚膳 18:00-22:00 (L.O.)

■ ANNUAL AND WEEKLY CLOSING 休息日期
Closed Tuesday lunch and Monday
週二午膳及週一休息

Tenmasa
天政

This outpost of its renowned namesake in Tokyo that opened in 1937 boasts a sushi bar, a tempura counter, a tatami area, and decked walkways over golden pebble filled ponds that connect to the private rooms. Two Japanese chefs take turns to make tempura with fresh, seasonal ingredients. Besides watching the culinary magic unfold, you can also enjoy dazzling firework displays from the restaurant. Set menus are available at lunch.

天政總店早於1937年在東京開業，澳門店則位於新濠鋒酒店內，榻榻米地板、鋪板走廊和金石水池使人感覺猶如身處日本！天婦羅料理採用新鮮時令食材，由兩位日籍大廚輪替為客人炮製；廚師就在眼前大顯身手，視覺同時得到滿足。餐廳設有壽司吧、天婦羅櫃枱及私人廂房，臨窗的座位有機會觀賞到煙花美景。

TEL. 2886 8868
11F, Altira Hotel,
Avenida de Kwong Tung, Taipa
氹仔廣東大馬路新濠鋒酒店 11樓
www.altiramacau.com

■ PRICE 價錢
Lunch 午膳
set 套餐 MOP 268-900
à la carte 點菜 MOP 338-900
Dinner 晚膳
set 套餐 MOP 680-1,780
à la carte 點菜 MOP 680-1,680

■ OPENING HOURS 營業時間
Lunch 午膳 11:00-14:15 (L.O.)
Dinner 晚膳 18:00-22:15 (L.O.)

Terrazza
庭園

30

The menu covers the culinary traditions of every region in Italy and is updated every three months to keep it fresh. Guests get to see how the food is prepared through the glass wall. Pizza dough, tagliatelle, ravioli and tagliolini are made from scratch in-house and the extensive wine list is well worth exploring. Add in exceedingly comfy chairs and warm, welcoming service and you have a great place for a relaxing meal.

古典優雅的設計、柔軟舒適的座椅、友善熱情的服務，使你身心放鬆；透過玻璃窗觀看廚房團隊的烹調過程更是饒有趣味。菜單涵蓋意大利全國美食，讓你總能挑選到合心意的；部分食材是自家製，包括薄餅及數款意粉。餐牌每三個月按季節變更菜式，讓食客保持新鮮感。而其種類繁多的酒單，更是使人驚喜。

TEL. 8883 2221
Shop 201, 2F, Galaxy Hotel, Estrada da Baia de Nossa Senhora da Esperanca, Cotai
路氹城望德聖母灣大馬路
澳門銀河綜合渡假城銀河酒店 2樓 201號舖
www.galaxymacau.com

SPECIALITIES TO PRE-ORDER 預訂食物
The "Secret" pork 秘製豬肉 / Grilled tenderloin "Tagliata" steak 烤牛里脊肉

■ PRICE 價錢
Dinner 晚膳
à la carte 點菜 MOP 350-650

■ OPENING HOURS 營業時間
Dinner 晚膳　18:00-22:30 (L.O.)

The Eight
8餐廳

The lavish interior uses the traditional Chinese elements of the goldfish and the number eight to ensure good fortune for all who dine here. The cuisine is a mix of Cantonese and Huaiyang, but the kitchen also adds its own innovative touches to some dishes. Specialities include steamed crab claw with ginger and Chinese wine, and stir-fried lobster with egg, minced pork and black bean. At lunchtime, over 40 kinds of dim sum are served.

豪華的內部裝潢採用了傳統中國元素，如金魚及數目字「8」，寓意所有到訪的客人都會遇上好運。菜式融合了廣東及淮揚風味，部分美食更滲入了創新點子。推介菜式有薑米酒蒸鮮蟹拑及廣東式炒龍蝦。午餐時段供應逾四十款點心。

TEL. 8803 7788
2F, Grand Lisboa Hotel,
Avenida da Lisboa
葡京路新葡京酒店 2樓
www.grandlisboahotels.com

SPECIALITIES TO PRE-ORDER 預訂食物
Buddha jumping over the wall 蟲草當歸佛跳牆

■ PRICE 價錢
Lunch 午膳
set 套餐 MOP 1,000-2,500
à la carte 點菜 MOP 410-3,080
Dinner 晚膳
set 套餐 MOP 1,000-2,500
à la carte 點菜 MOP 410-3,080

■ OPENING HOURS 營業時間
Lunch 午膳 11:30-14:30 (L.O.)
Dinner 晚膳 18:30-22:30 (L.O.)

The Golden Peacock
皇雀

It's in the vast Venetian complex so you may need a map to find this contemporary Indian restaurant – just look out for the bright neon peacock. The chef is a native of Kerala but the menu covers all parts of India. Spices are ground in-house and everything from paneer to pickles is made from scratch. At lunch they offer an extensive buffet; come for dinner and you'll experience dishes that are flamboyant in presentation and rich in flavour.

嚴謹認真的印度主廚會自製各種醬料、乳酪、芝士、腰果蓉等，加上每週由印度空運而到的食材和新鮮研磨的香料，炮製出色香味俱全的印度美食。印式石榴烤雞肉串、印式洋葱燴羊小腿和各款素菜均值得一試。午市供應自助餐，價格相宜。店內陳設簡約時尚，以印度國鳥孔雀作裝飾，具濃濃的印度風情。

TEL. 8118 9696
Shop 1037, 1F, The Venetian Resort,
Estrada de Baia de N. Senhora da Esperança, Taipa
氹仔望德聖母灣大馬路威尼斯人酒店
大運河購物中心 1樓 1037號舖
www.venetianmacao.com

■ PRICE 價錢
Lunch 午膳
buffet 自助餐 MOP 198
Dinner 晚膳
à la carte 點菜 MOP 250-600

■ OPENING HOURS 營業時間
Lunch 午膳 11:00-15:00 (L.O.)
Dinner 晚膳 18:00-22:30 (L.O.)

The Kitchen
大廚

12

Beef is the star of the show at this handsome, masculine dining room which also houses a sushi bar, a salad bar and a live fish tank. Choose from prime cuts from the U.S. and Wagyu from Kagoshima and Australia; then have it seared on an open flame to your desired 'doneness' and pair it with one of the 16,800-plus wine labels from around the world. Bread is baked daily and appetisers are made in the open kitchen à la minute.

融匯西式扒房、日式壽司吧及海鮮魚缸於一室，餐廳裝潢亦別樹一格。廚師會在開放式廚房即席製作麵包和各款頭盤，確保提供最新鮮的美食佳餚予食客。來自美國、澳洲及日本等地的頂級牛肉放於肉櫃內供挑選，食客可選取不同部位與分量，亦可從魚缸中點選新鮮海產。酒單備有逾萬款來自世界各地的名酒佳釀。

TEL. 8803 7777
3F, Grand Lisboa Hotel,
Avenida de Lisboa
葡京路新葡京酒店 3樓
www.grandlisboahotels.com

■ PRICE 價錢
Lunch 午膳
set 套餐 MOP 430-630
à la carte 點菜 MOP 450-1,650
Dinner 晚膳
set 套餐 MOP 950-1,550
à la carte 點菜 MOP 450-1,650

■ OPENING HOURS 營業時間
Lunch 午膳 12:00-14:30 (L.O.)
Dinner 晚膳 18:30-22:30 (L.O.)

The Ritz-Carlton Café
麗思咖啡廳

Tiles, mirrors and marble have all been used to great effect to create a chic French brasserie here at the Ritz-Carlton. There's a tasting menu along with the à la carte and set menus so, whether you're here for a full meal of classic French dishes or a quick bite or afternoon tea after shopping, you'll find there's plenty of choice. You can also expect live music, mime artists and even a caricaturist.

意大利白色雲石地、長長的真皮沙發和圓形雲石面餐桌、典雅的水滴形吊燈、精緻的長鏡，營造出高雅、舒適的環境。來自法國里昂的主廚擅長烹調法國住家菜，許多食客到此是為了品嘗帶有住家風味的法國菜。除了美食，餐廳內每天都有不同的藝術表演如音樂演奏、默劇等演出。

TEL. 8886 6696
GF, The Ritz-Carlton, Galaxy, Estrada da Baia da N. Senhora da Esperança, Cotai
路氹城望德聖母灣大馬路澳門銀河綜合渡假城麗思卡爾頓酒店地下
www.ritzcarlton.com/macau

■ PRICE 價錢
Lunch 午膳
set 套餐 MOP 258-338
à la carte 點菜 MOP 350-1,000
Dinner 晚膳
à la carte 點菜 MOP 350-1,000

■ OPENING HOURS 營業時間
Lunch 午膳 11:30-14:30 (L.O.)
Dinner 晚膳 17:30-22:30 (L.O.)
Sunday Dinner 週日晚膳
18:00-22:30 (L.O.)

The Tasting Room
御膳房

14

Ingredients sourced directly from France underpin cuisine that is classically based and a reflection of Chef Fabrice Vulin's extensive experience. Beautifully presented, with vegetables a feature, the combinations and flavours are sophisticated and modern, yet light and well judged. The impressive glass wine cellar supports a wine list strong on French producers. The view from this restaurant is particularly impressive, especially when darkness falls.

路氹城的風光在玻璃窗前一覽無遺，夜幕低垂時別具氣氛。廚師Fabrice Vulin每週兩次從法國直接引入高級食材，以其豐富經驗與精湛技術，炮製出一道道傳統法國菜式，材料配搭講究而恰到好處，賣相美不勝收。酒單種類繁多，大都是法國佳釀。輕鬆的用餐經驗，精心細密的服務團隊功不可沒。

TEL. 8868 6681
3F, Nüwa, City of Dreams,
Estrada do Istmo, Cotai
路氹連貫公路新濠天地頤居 3樓
www.cityofdreamsmacau.com

■ PRICE 價錢
Lunch 午膳
set 套餐 MOP 488-788
à la carte 點菜 MOP 1,100-2,000
Dinner 晚膳
set 套餐 MOP 1,788-2,638
à la carte 點菜 MOP 1,100-2,000

■ OPENING HOURS 營業時間
Lunch 午膳 12:00-14:30 (L.O.)
Dinner 晚膳 18:00-22:30 (L.O.)

■ ANNUAL AND WEEKLY CLOSING 休息日期
Closed Wednesday 週三休息

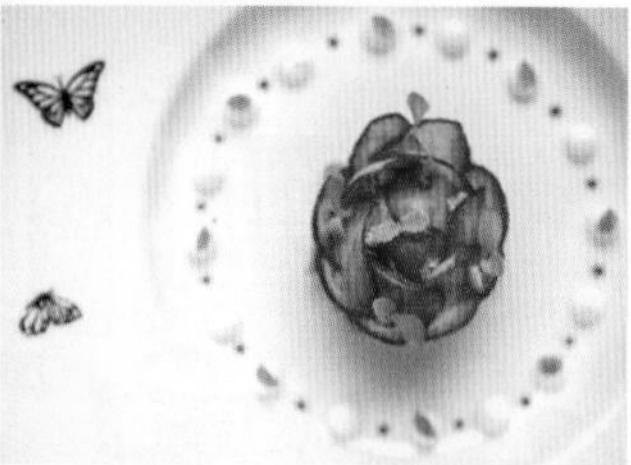

Tim's Kitchen
桃花源小廚

Hong Kong foodies make special pilgrimages here and it's easy to see why: the Cantonese dishes may appear quite simple but they are very skilfully prepared. Among the highlights are poached and sliced pork stomach in wasabi sauce, and sweet & sour pork ribs. Do make sure you try the crystal prawn and, during the winter, the tasty snake ragout. The restaurant is decorated with a variety of operatic costumes and photos.

香港食家喜歡專程到此朝聖，原因十分簡單：此食店的廣東菜式看似簡單，卻實在是經過精心巧手炮製。推介菜式包括涼拌爽肚片及京都骨。此外，萬勿錯過玻璃蝦球及冬瓜蒸原隻蟹鉗，而冬天的重點推介則離不開美味的太史五蛇羹。餐廳放滿戲曲照片和戲服裝飾，散發出淡淡的藝術氣息。

TEL. 8803 3682
Shop F25, GF, East Wing, Hotel Lisboa,
2-4 Avenida de Lisboa
葡京路 2-4號葡京酒店東翼地下 F25號舖
www.hotelisboa.com

SPECIALITIES TO PRE-ORDER 預訂食物
De-boned 'Eight Treasure' duck 八寶鴨 / Deep-fried scallops on mashed taro 香酥荔芋帶子 / Deep-fried king prawn roll with liver sausage and spring onion 網油明蝦卷

■ PRICE 價錢
Lunch 午膳
set 套餐 MOP 200-500
à la carte 點菜 MOP 250-1,600
Dinner 晚膳
set 套餐 MOP 300-800
à la carte 點菜 MOP 250-1,600

■ OPENING HOURS 營業時間
Lunch 午膳 12:00-14:30 (L.O.)
Dinner 晚膳 18:30-22:30 (L.O.)

Tou Tou Koi
陶陶居

24

As this 80-year-old restaurant is always packed, it's vital to book ahead; at the same time why not also pre-order the duck? It's dim sum during the day and Cantonese cuisine at night and among the favourites are deep-fried dumplings stuffed with prok, shrimp and crabmeat, crispy US beef chuck and fish from the tank in the dining room. Service is sufficiently swift to accommodate the non-stop flow of customers. A refurbishment has left the restaurant looking much more contemporary.

有八十多年歷史的陶陶居總是賓客如雲，必須訂座，你亦可順道預訂八寶鴨。日間以點心為主，晚上則提供粵菜，受歡迎菜式包括鮮蝦金錢蟹盒和脆皮美國牛肩肉，還有新鮮烹調的海魚。為了應付絡繹不絕的客人，侍應生的工作效率十分高。早上九時開始有早茶供應，吸引不少茶客前來一聚。

TEL. 2857 2629
6-8 Travessa do Mastro
爐石塘巷 6-8號

SPECIALITIES TO PRE-ORDER 預訂食物
Braised duck stuffed with eight treasures 八寶霸王鴨 / Signature deep-fried dumplings stuffed with pork, shrimp and crabmeat 鮮蝦金錢蟹盒

■ PRICE 價錢
Lunch 午膳
à la carte 點菜 MOP 100-300
Dinner 晚膳
à la carte 點菜 MOP 250-800

■ OPENING HOURS 營業時間
Lunch 午膳 11:00-15:00 (L.O.)
Dinner 晚膳 17:00-23:15 (L.O.)

Voyages by Alain Ducasse
風雅廚

Located on the 3F of the striking Morpheus hotel, this restaurant is a much more relaxed option from famed French chef Alain Ducasse and, with its trendy design, cocktail bar and lounge, it's a fashionable spot. The menu is an eclectic mix of dishes informed by his travels around the world, so expect Thai, Chinese, Indian and even Middle Eastern influences. Start with a Negroni from the cocktail trolley and then share the dishes.

位於摩珀斯酒店三樓，風雅廚是法國廚師Alain Ducasse名下另一家餐廳。氣氛相對輕鬆，裝潢時尚休閒，附設酒吧及廂房。大廚將其在世界各地遊歷時所構思的菜式放於菜單之內，故不難發現中國、泰國、印度，甚至中東風味元素。用餐前先呷一口內格羅尼雞尾酒，再品嘗各種美食，倍添滋味。

TEL. 8868 3432
3F, Morpheus, City of Dreams,
Estrada do Istmo, Cotai
路氹連貫公路新濠天地摩珀斯 3樓
www.cityofdreamsmacau.com

■ PRICE 價錢
Lunch 午膳
à la carte 點菜 MOP 400-600
Dinner 晚膳
à la carte 點菜 MOP 400-600

■ OPENING HOURS 營業時間
Lunch 午膳 12:00-14:30 (L.O.)
Dinner 晚膳 18:00-22:00 (L.O.)

Wing Lei
永利軒

✗✗✗✗ ♿ 🍴 Ⓟ ⌷52 ◐🍴 ⅋

The bright yellow look gives the room an airy feel, while the tassel lamps hanging from the ceiling cast a romantic glow. The centrepiece of the room, however, remains the three-dimensional flying dragon made up of 100,000 sparkling Swarovski crystals. At lunch over 40 dim sum are available, while the à la carte offers a great range of refined Cantonese classics. The 'Signature Menu' is a good way of trying the chef's best dishes.

明亮的黃色裝潢營造出輕鬆悠閒的氣氛，大型燈籠透出浪漫燈光，襯托以十萬片水晶製成的立體飛龍，盡展豪華氣派；舒適寬敞的座椅讓人生出好感。餐廳裝潢一流，服務也親切周到。傳統粵菜，菜式選擇良多，大廚精髓菜譜是一嘗其手藝的最佳選擇。午市的手工點心叫人眼花繚亂，不妨點選自選點心套餐。

TEL. 8986 3663
GF, Wynn Hotel, Rua Cidade de Sintra, NAPE
外港新填海區仙德麗街永利酒店地下
www.wynnmacau.com

SPECIALITIES TO PRE-ORDER 預訂食物
Barbecued suckling pig with black pepper
即烤黑椒小乳豬 / Barbecued Beijing duck
京烤片皮鴨

■ PRICE 價錢
Lunch 午膳
à la carte 點菜 MOP 200-2,000
Dinner 晚膳
set 套餐 MOP 1,180
à la carte 點菜 MOP 200-2,000

■ OPENING HOURS 營業時間
Lunch 午膳 11:30-14:45 (L.O.)
Sunday and Public Holiday lunch
週日及公眾假期午膳 10:30-14:45 (L.O.)
Dinner 晚膳 18:00-22:45 (L.O.)

Wing Lei Palace
永利宮

The appointment of chef Tam led to a rejuvenation of Wing Lei Palace, with many of his signature and seasonal dishes added to the menu. Don't miss the lychee wood roasted meats or braised fish broth with fish maw and vegetables. At lunch, dim sum options are also available. The room features spacious table settings and floor to ceiling windows which also provide fantastic views of the Performance Lake show.

金碧輝煌的餐室以碧玉及孔雀為題，一邊以落地玻璃環繞，讓食客享受美食的同時能欣賞窗外的音樂噴泉表演。新上任的行政總廚譚師傅為菜單加入了不少巧手菜式及時令佳餚，感覺煥然一新。萬勿錯過各款以荔枝木炮製的燒味，以及精緻味美的花膠魚蓉羹。中午時段少不了各式精美點心。

TEL. 8889 3663
West Esplanade, GF, Wynn Palace,
Avenida da Nave Desportiva, Cotai
路氹城體育路大馬路
永利皇宮西名店街地面層
www.wynnpalace.com

■ PRICE 價錢
Lunch 午膳
set 套餐 MOP 428
à la carte 點菜 MOP 400-1,000
Dinner 晚膳
set 套餐 MOP 1,488
à la carte 點菜 MOP 400-1,500

■ OPENING HOURS 營業時間
Lunch 午膳 11:30-14:45 (L.O.)
Sunday and Public Holiday lunch
週日及公眾假期午膳 10:30-15:15 (L.O.)
Dinner 晚膳 17:30-22:15 (L.O.)

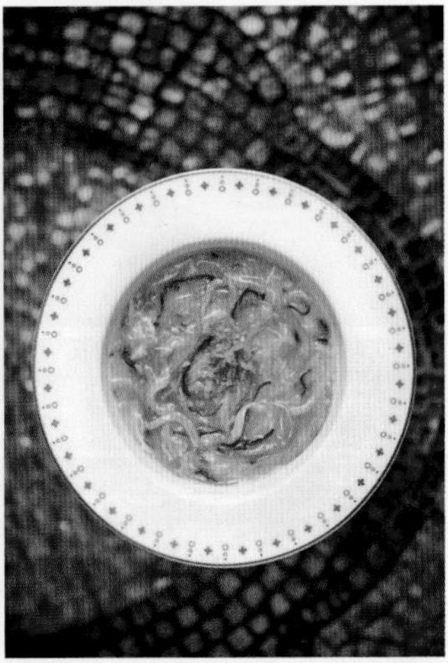

Wong Kun Sio Kung (Broadway)
皇冠小館 (百老匯)

If you're looking for a quick bite after watching all the street entertainment on Broadway then try this simple noodle and congee shop. The menu is slightly smaller than the original branch but it still has the same focus on handmade noodles using the traditional bamboo method and served with dried shrimp roe. The congee is smooth and satisfying and has a delicate aftertaste and there are also a few other hot dishes available.

百老匯酒店後面的食街，雲集多間澳門本地知名食店，非常熱鬧。作為本地代表之一，皇冠小館以古法竹竿炮製的彈牙麵配大頭蝦籽及以新鮮原隻海蟹及瑤柱熬製的蟹粥馳名。另外還有其他粥麵小食和數款小炒。環境簡樸乾淨。

TEL. 8883 3338
Shop A-G017, Broadway Food Street,
Broadway Macau,
Avenida Marginal Flor de Lotus, Cotai
路氹城蓮花海濱大馬路澳門百老匯
百老匯美食街 A-G017舖
www.broadwaymacau.mo

■ PRICE 價錢
Lunch 午膳
set 套餐 MOP 55-68
à la carte 點菜 MOP 50-600
Dinner 晚膳
set 套餐 MOP 68
à la carte 點菜 MOP 50-600

■ OPENING HOURS 營業時間
11:00-23:45 (L.O.)

Wong Kun Sio Kung (Rua do Campo)
皇冠小館 (水坑尾街)

Owner Mr. Cheng, who is native Macanese, has over 30 years of experience when it comes to making noodles using the traditional bamboo pressing method. His shop opened back in 2000 but such was its popularity that he later expanded into next door. A selection of traditional Cantonese dishes is offered but most come here for the sea crab congee and the bamboo noodles with dried shrimp roe (which is also sold in bottles in the shop).

澳門土生土長的東主鄭先生，已有逾三十年以傳統竹竿手打方法製麵的經驗。餐廳早於2000年開業，大受歡迎下擴充至隔鄰舖位。他的店子提供一系列傳統廣東美食，但慕名而來的食客，通常會點遠近馳名的竹昇蝦籽撈麵及海蟹粥。店內亦有出售瓶裝蝦籽及辣椒油。

TEL. 2837 2248
308-310A Rua do Campo
水坑尾街 308-310號 A
www.wongkun.com.mo

■ PRICE 價錢
à la carte 點菜 MOP 30-120

■ OPENING HOURS 營業時間
10:00-02:00 (L.O.)

Yamazato
山里

12

A few contemporary flourishes are enough to make this minimalist dining room warm and welcoming. The sweeping garden views also set the mood for a lavish and delectable meal. The Japanese and Macanese kitchen team has been working with the hotel group for years and is well-versed and well-honed in a variety of Japanese cooking styles, from sashimi and sushi, to tempura, grill and even shabu shabu… almost any Japanese dish you can think of.

除了壽司和刺身兩款主打食物外，山里還供應各式日本料理：懷石料理、天婦羅、燒物、日本火鍋……大概你能想到的菜式都能在這兒品嘗。廚師團隊來自日本及澳門本土，曾於大倉集團服務多年，經驗十足。金黃色的牆身、時尚的水晶吊燈和淺啡色的木製傢具，瑰麗雅致，巨幅玻璃窗讓你盡賞動人園景。

TEL. 8883 5127
28F, Hotel Okura, Galaxy,
Avenida Marginal Flor de Lotus, Cotai
路氹城蓮花海濱大馬路澳門銀河綜合渡假城
大倉酒店 28樓
www.hotelokuramacau.com

SPECIALITIES TO PRE-ORDER 預訂食物
Omakase menu 廚師發辦套餐

■ PRICE 價錢
Lunch 午膳
set 套餐 MOP 280-580
à la carte 點菜 MOP 430-3,700
Dinner 晚膳
set 套餐 MOP 1,580
à la carte 點菜 MOP 430-3,700

■ OPENING HOURS 營業時間
Lunch 午膳 12:00-14:30 (L.O.)
Dinner 晚膳 17:30-21:30 (L.O.)

■ ANNUAL AND WEEKLY CLOSING 休息日期
Closed Monday 週一休息

Yi
天頤

Located on a Sky Bridge on the 21st floor, Yi's impressive position is matched by stunning views, impressive architecture and exotic interiors. With a Hong Kong chef at the helm, the menu is a unique blend of Chinese and Japanese flavours, with sommeliers providing tea-pairing suggestions. Along with local ingredients, you can also expect Australian wagyu, Vietnamese prawns, Hakka chili and Chiu Chow Puning sauces from China.

天頤位於摩珀斯二十一樓的高架天橋，食客不單被迷人景色環抱，更可從另一角度欣賞酒店獨特的建築風格。包含八道菜的品嘗菜單以廚師發辦形式上場，生於香港的主廚按當日新鮮材料構思菜式，並糅合全球各地和中國各省份的特色食材及調料，菜式兼具創意和精緻賣相。茶藝師更可為客人配對茶飲。用餐區內的龍形屏風閃閃生輝，別具氣派。

TEL. 8868 3443
21F, Morpheus, City of Dreams,
Estrada do Istmo, Cotai
路氹連貫公路新濠天地摩珀斯 21樓
www.cityofdreamsmacau.com

■ PRICE 價錢
Dinner 晚膳
à la carte 點菜 MOP 1,388-1,688

■ OPENING HOURS 營業時間
Dinner 晚膳 18:00-22:00 (L.O.)

Ying
帝影樓

XXX 18

It's not just the breathtaking views looking north to Macau that set this restaurant apart – the beautifully styled interior has been designed with taste and verve; the beaded curtains, which feature gold cranes and crystal trees, are particularly striking. The Cantonese dishes are prepared with contemporary twists and much flair. Try the flambé Iberico pork char siu, and stir-fried Boston lobster with black beans and spring onions.

帝影樓北望海港及澳門繁華景色，環境宜人。餐廳設計品味獨特，風格絢麗；珠簾上飾有金鶴和水晶樹圖案，使裝潢更添神采。餐廳的粵菜融入了新口味，大廚的烹調技藝精湛。專業的服務態度令人賓至如歸。值得一試的有果木火焰黑豚叉燒和蒜豉葱爆波士頓龍蝦。

TEL. 2886 8868
11F, Altira Hotel,
Avenida de Kwong Tung, Taipa
氹仔廣東大馬路新濠鋒酒店 11樓
www.altiramacau.com

■ PRICE 價錢
Lunch 午膳
set 套餐 MOP 244
à la carte 點菜 MOP 200-1,000
Dinner 晚膳
set 套餐 MOP 588
à la carte 點菜 MOP 200-1,300

■ OPENING HOURS 營業時間
Lunch 午膳 11:00-14:45 (L.O.)
Dinner 晚膳 18:00-22:15 (L.O.)

Zi Yat Heen
紫逸軒

XXXX ♿ P 24

This spacious, elegant yet intimate restaurant boasts a glass-clad wine cellar at its centre. The chef champions a cooking style with reduced amounts of seasoning so as to allow the true flavours of the first-rate ingredients to come through. Recommendations include baked stuffed crab shell, baked lamb chops in coffee sauce and egg white milk custard with sweetened mashed taro.

巨型玻璃餐酒庫佔據餐廳的正中位置，具空間感的設計令紫逸軒洋溢着高雅格調。精於烹調傳統粵菜的廚師着重選材用料，堅持採用最新鮮食材與最少的調味料，經他處理的菜式鮮味清新，推介有傳統的焗釀鮮蟹蓋和具創意的咖啡汁焗羊排；甜品芋蓉燉鮮奶更是不容錯過。

TEL. 2881 8888
GF, Four Seasons Hotel, Estrada da Baia de N. Senhora da Esperanca, Cotai
路氹望德聖母灣大馬路
四季酒店地下
www.fourseasons.com/macau

■ PRICE 價錢
Lunch 午膳
set 套餐 MOP 1,800-3,000
à la carte 點菜 MOP 300-3,000
Dinner 晚膳
set 套餐 MOP 1,800-3,000
à la carte 點菜 MOP 300-3,000

■ OPENING HOURS 營業時間
Lunch 午膳 12:00-14:15 (L.O.)
Dinner 晚膳 18:00-22:15 (L.O.)

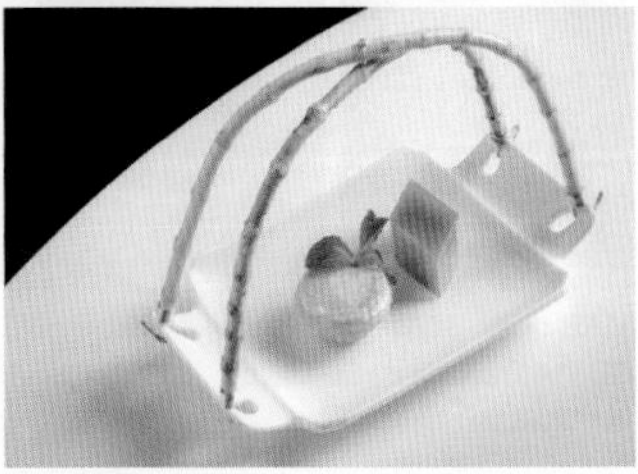

Street Food 街頭小吃

Popular places for snack food
駎名小食店

Chong Shing 昌盛

MAP 地圖 38/B-2
GF, 11 Tomé Pires, Macau
澳門新橋道咩啤利士街 11號地下

Cantonese dim sum and steamed buns. Sponge cakes and sticky rice rolls are recommended.

粵式點心及包點，推介馬拉糕和糯米卷。

MOP 10-20 07:00-20:30

Fong Kei 晃記餅家

MAP 地圖 44/B-2
14 Rua do Cunha, Taipa
氹仔官也街 14號

Almond cakes; egg rolls.

老字號餅店，推介杏仁餅及蛋捲。

MOP 30-50 09:00-21:00

KIKA

MAP 地圖 38/B-3
GF, 11A Travessa da Sé, Macau
澳門大堂巷 11A號地下

Japanese gelato. It specializes in matcha flavour with different levels of richness.

售賣日式雪糕，抹茶雪糕有不同濃度可供選擇。

MOP 30-50 10:00-22:00

LemonCello (Macau) 檸檬車露 (澳門)

Daily-made fresh gelato.
每日新鮮製造的意大利雪糕。

MOP 30-50　　11:00-23:00

MAP 地圖　38/B-3
GF, 11 Travessa da Sé, Macau
澳門大堂巷 11號地下

Leong Heng Kei 梁慶記 N

Springy fresh egg noodles.
每日鮮製的全蛋麵爽滑帶蛋香。

MOP 23-35　　07:00-19:00
Closed 7 days Lunar New Year
農曆新年休息 7天

MAP 地圖　38/A-3
GF, 51 Rua de Cinco de Outubro, Macau
澳門十月初五日街 51號地舖

Lord Stow's Bakery (Rua do Tassara) 安德魯餅店 (戴紳禮街)

Portuguese egg tarts.
鬆脆而香甜軟滑的葡撻。

MOP 20-30　　07:00-22:00

MAP 地圖　45/A-1
1 Rua do Tassara, Coloane Town Square
路環市中心戴紳禮街 1號

Mok Yee Kei 莫義記

Durian ice cream; mango ice cream.
榴槤雪糕及芒果雪糕。

MOP 25-70　　09:00-22:30

MAP 地圖　44/B-2
9 Rua do Cunha, Taipa
氹仔官也街 9號

Looking for a taste of local life? Check out our top street food picks.
到哪兒尋找本土特色小食？請翻閱本年度的街頭小吃推介。

Enjoy good food without spending a fortune! Look out for the Bib Gourmand symbol to find restaurants offering good food at great prices!
既想省錢又想品嘗美食，便要留心注有這個 車胎人標誌的餐廳，她們提供的是價錢實惠且高質素的美食。

Sei Kee Café (Rua da Palha) 世記咖啡 (賣草地街) N

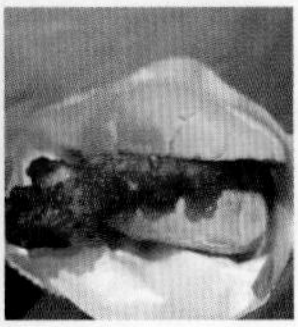

Crispy buns and juicy meat make up the delicious pork chop buns.

秘製豬扒包外層鬆脆，肉味香濃多汁。

MOP 15-30 11:00-19:00
Closed 3 days Lunar New Year, National Day and Tuesday
農曆新年 3天、國慶日及週二休息

MAP 地圖 38/B-3
15D, Patio da Palha, Rua da Palha, Macau
澳門賣草地街乾草圍 15號 D

Ving Kei (Macau) 榮記荳腐 (澳門)

Tofu products and noodles.

豆腐、豆腐花及麵食。

MOP 20-40 08:00-18:30

MAP 地圖 38/B-3
GF, 47 Rua da Tercena, Macau
澳門果欄街 47號地下

Yi Shun (Macau) 義順鮮奶 (澳門)

Fresh milk custard; milk custard with ginger juice.

雙皮燉奶、薑汁撞奶。

MOP 30-40 11:00-21:00

MAP 地圖 38/A-3
381 Avenida de Almeida Ribeiro, Macau
澳門新馬路 381號

HOTELS
酒店

HOTELS IN ORDER OF COMFORT
酒店 — 以舒適程度分類

Altira
新濠鋒

High quality design, a serene atmosphere and wondrous peninsula views produce something quite spectacular here. Guests arrive at the stylish lobby on the 38th floor and the luxury feel is enhanced by a super lounge and terrace on the same level. Bedrooms face the sea and merge tranquil tones with a contemporary feel. There's also a great spa and a pool-with-a-view.

酒店設計獨特，舒適典雅，位置優越，澳門半島的環迴美景盡入眼簾。38樓的大堂時尚尊貴，同層的天宮備有室內酒廊及露天陽台，豪華瑰麗。客房位於較高的樓層，海景一望無際，寧靜的環境與現代設計相互交織，氣派超凡。顧客享用附設的豪華水療設施時可飽覽美景。

TEL. 2886 8888
Avenida de Kwong Tung, Taipa
氹仔廣東大馬路
www.altiramacau.com

RECOMMENDED RESTAURANTS 餐廳推薦
Aurora 奧羅拉 XXX
Tenmasa 天政 XX
Ying 帝影樓 XXX

= MOP 1,100-2,600
Suites 套房 = MOP 4,500-7,500
= MOP 298

Rooms 客房 188
Suites 套房 28

Banyan Tree
悅榕庄

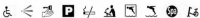

Forming part of Galaxy Macau, this luxurious resort comprises 246 suites, as well as 10 villas which come with their own private gardens and swimming pools. The very comfortable bedrooms all have large baths set by the window and the array of services includes a state-of-the-art spa – the biggest in the group. Guests enjoy full access to all of Galaxy's facilities.

作為路氹城澳門銀河綜合渡假城的一部分及毗鄰澳門國際機場，澳門悅榕庄共有246間套房和10間擁有私人花園和泳池的別墅。所有寬敞套房內均設有私人悅心池，酒店提供一系列貼心服務，當中包括集團最大及最頂級的水療中心。住客更可享用銀河綜合渡假城內所有設施。

TEL. 8883 6888
Galaxy Macau,
Avenida Marginal Flor de Lotus, Cotai
路氹城蓮花海濱大馬路澳門銀河綜合渡假城
www.banyantree.com/en/cn-china-macau

Suites 套房 = MOP 2,999-7,899

Suites 套房 256

Conrad
康萊德

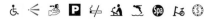

The largest of all the Conrad hotels is on the Cotai Strip and its guests have access to an abundance of shopping, gaming, dining and entertainment opportunities. The Himalayan and Chinese inspired décor creates a relaxing environment; anyone requiring extra stress reduction should book a restorative session in one of the ten treatment rooms in the luxurious spa.

坐落於路氹金光大道上的康萊德，是該集團規模最大的酒店，這裏有為數不少的購物、賭博、餐飲及娛樂場所。陳設靈感取材自喜瑪拉雅和中國地區，感覺悠閒舒適。豪華水療中心內設有十間套房，客人可盡情享受水療服務，令壓力和疲勞一掃而空。客房空間寬敞，設計時尚。

TEL. 2882 9000
Estrada do Istmo, Cotai
路氹連貫公路
www.conradmacao.com

RECOMMENDED RESTAURANTS 餐廳推薦
Dynasty 8 朝

† = MOP 1,498-6,098
†† = MOP 1,748-6,348
Suites 套房 = MOP 2,098-6,698
☕ = MOP 208

Rooms 客房 430
Suites 套房 224

Encore
萬利

For VIPs wanting an even more exclusive resort experience than the Wynn, there is Encore – their luxury brand. The word 'standard' certainly does not apply here as the choice is between suites or villas, all of which are lavishly decorated. You also get an exceptional spa offering bespoke treatments and Bar Cristal: as small as a jewellery box and just as precious.

欲享受比永利更獨特尊貴的服務，可考慮同集團旗下更豪華的萬利。酒店提供豪華套房及渡假別墅，兩者均以紅色與金色裝潢，特顯富麗堂皇。貴賓級水療中心為你提供度身訂造的療程，酒店內的Bar Cristal一如其名，像珠寶盒般嬌小高貴。賭場內附設多間貴賓娛樂房。

TEL. 2888 9966
Rua Cidade de Sintra, NAPE
外港新填海區仙德麗街
www.wynnmacau.com

Suites 套房 = MOP 2,688-22,000
☕ = MOP 160

Suites 套房 414

RECOMMENDED RESTAURANTS 餐廳推薦
Café Encore 咖啡廷 XX
Golden Flower 京花軒 ✿✿ XXXX
99 Noodles 99 麵 X

Four Seasons
四季

The luxurious Four Seasons fuses East and West by blending Colonial Portuguese style with Chinese traditions. The lobby acts as a living room, with its fireplace, Portuguese lanterns and Chinese lacquer screens. The hotel also has a luxury shopping mall and connects to The Venetian and Plaza Casino. If you want peace, simply escape to the spa or one of the five pools and the charming garden.

2008年開幕的四季酒店融合了東西方元素，將葡萄牙風格與中國傳統融為一體。大堂設有壁爐、葡國燈籠和中國雕漆屏風，猶如置身家中客廳。酒店設有豪華購物商場，直通威尼斯人酒店及百利沙娛樂場。想離開五光十色稍作喘息，可享用酒店的水療設備和五個泳池，還有迷人的花園。

TEL. 2881 8888
Estrada da Baia de N. Senhora da Esperanca, Cotai
路氹望德聖母灣大馬路
www.fourseasons.com/macau

RECOMMENDED RESTAURANTS 餐廳推薦
Zi Yat Heen 紫逸軒 ✿ XXXX

† = MOP 2,088-10,888
†† = MOP 2,088-10,888
Suites 套房 = MOP 4,088-64,588
☕ = MOP 258

Rooms 客房 276
Suites 套房 84

Galaxy
銀河

The striking exterior of Galaxy is one of the most recognisable landmarks of Taipa. The guestrooms are very spacious and impressively well equipped. Another of the attractions of the hotel is its 2,000sqm artificial beach and the world's largest wave pool; there also are cinemas and assorted restaurants. It's just a few minutes' walk from the Old Town.

外觀金碧輝煌的銀河渡假城是氹仔的地標。作為渡假城內其中一間酒店，銀河酒店予人國際化的印象。每間客房都裝潢時尚、空間寬敞、設備齊全兼現代化。最吸引的設施是佔地二千平方米的人造沙灘及大型衝浪泳池。戲院和餐飲設施一應俱全，與舊城區只有一條馬路之隔，便於觀光購物。

TEL. 2888 0888
Estrada da Baia de N. Senhora da Esperanca, Cotai
路氹望德聖母灣大馬路
www.galaxymacau.com

RECOMMENDED RESTAURANTS 餐廳推薦
Terrazza 庭園

= MOP 1,398-4,988
= MOP 1,598-5,188
Suites 套房 = MOP 2,398-6,488
= MOP 148

Rooms 客房 1,307
Suites 套房 142

Grand Hyatt
君悅

With its striking 22m ceiling and fabulous artwork, the lobby sets the tone – the droplets appear to be falling from a cloud. The contemporary bedrooms are split between two towers. Along with contemporary and luxurious suites, the Grand Club on the top floor provides a dining service where customers can order any kind of cuisine they choose.

君悅酒店的大堂設計獨特，從22米天花上空墜下的吊飾，配合藝術設計營造出水珠從雲層落下再匯聚一起的壯觀景象。設計時尚的房間分佈在兩幢大樓內。位於頂層的嘉賓軒裝潢高雅，有多間貴賓廂房，按客人喜好提供不同餐飲服務，是舉辦私人商務聚會的理想場地。

TEL. 8868 1234
City of Dreams, Estrada do Istmo, Cotai
路氹連貫公路新濠天地
www.macau.grand.hyatt.com

RECOMMENDED RESTAURANTS 餐廳推薦
Beijing Kitchen 滿堂彩 Ⅰ○ XX
Mezza9 Ⅰ○ XX

🛉 = MOP 1,299-5,499
🛉🛉 = MOP 1,299-5,499
Suites 套房 = MOP 1,599-5,799
☕ = MOP 258

Rooms 客房 503
Suites 套房 288

Grand Lapa
金麗華

Plenty of Portuguese character and a relaxing, peaceful atmosphere set this hotel apart. There is also a lovely tropical garden behind the main building, along with a swimming pool and spa. Bedrooms come with large windows and face either the harbour or the city – ask for one with a balcony on floors 16-18. Prices are reasonable and the staff are eager to please.

於1984年建成，是澳門早期的豪華酒店之一。大堂面貌多年來改變不大，頗富葡國色彩且有一種寧靜優雅的感覺。房間裝潢並不時髦，然方正寬敞，16至18樓的客房更設有露台可觀賞海景。大樓後的熱帶園林邊設有水療中心及露天泳池，是澳門鬧市中少有的休閒設施。

TEL. 2856 7888
956-1110 Avenida da Amizade
友誼大馬路 956-1110號
www.grandlapa.com

RECOMMENDED RESTAURANTS 餐廳推薦
Kam Lai Heen 金麗軒
Naam 灆

= MOP 1,000- 2,000
= MOP 1,000- 2,000
Suites 套房 = MOP 2,500-3,500
= MOP 198

Rooms 客房 390
Suites 套房 26

Grand Lisboa
新葡京

Impossible to miss, the Grand Lisboa can be seen from miles away with its eye-popping, brightly-lit lotus design atop a shining diamond. Opulent soundproofed bedrooms feature Asian paintings, and offer grand sea or city vistas. If you have a corner room or a suite, you'll get the added bonus of a sauna; if you have neither, you can make use of the sumptuous spa.

2008年12月開幕的新葡京外形像一片耀目的黃蓮葉，坐落於一顆閃爍的鑽石之上，遠處可見。客房隔音設備完善，擁有典型的棕色牆壁、紅色扶手椅和亞洲油畫，並坐擁豪華海景或澳門的秀麗風光。角位客房及套房設有桑拿設施，其他客房亦可享用豪華的水療設施。

TEL. 2828 3838
Avenida de Lisboa
葡京路
www.grandlisboahotels.com

RECOMMENDED RESTAURANTS 餐廳推薦
Robuchon au Dôme
天巢法國餐廳 ✱✱✱ ✗✗✗✗✗
The Eight 8 餐廳 ✱✱✱ ✗✗✗✗
The Kitchen 大廚 ✱ ✗✗

♦ = MOP 2,400-3,200
♦♦ = MOP 2,400-3,200
Suites 套房 = MOP 4,480-48,000
☕ = MOP 150

Rooms 客房 331
Suites 套房 50

JW Marriott
JW萬豪

A soaring lobby forms the centrepiece of this impressive hotel within Galaxy Macau. The Grand Ballroom can host up to 1,600 and the hotel offers every service you'd expect in a resort. The well-equipped bedrooms may lack a little personality but they make up for it in square footage. Restaurants include the contemporary 'Urban Kitchen' with its international buffet.

宏偉的酒店大堂和完備的休閒設施如水療按摩及健身中心等服務，令你怦然心動！偌大的客房裝潢風格一致，設備齊全，雖稱不上別致，卻不失明亮整潔。酒店內的大宴會廳能容納千六人，不論是大型私人宴會或業務交流會議，都不愁找不到場地。設計時尚雅致的名廚都匯提供早、午、晚國際自助餐。

TEL. 8886 6888
Galaxy Macau, Estrada da Baia da Nossa Senhora da Esperança, Cotai
路氹望德聖母灣大馬路澳門銀河綜合渡假城
www.jwmarriottmacau.com

= MOP 1,488-4,488
Suites 套房 = MOP 3,388-7,288
= MOP 208

Rooms 客房 944
Suites 套房 71

Lisboa
葡京

Thanks largely to its 1970s style façade, The Lisboa sports a relatively sober look for Macau, and so stands in stark contrast to the glitzier Grand Lisboa. There are ten types of guestroom available and the decoration is a mix of Chinese and Portuguese styles; it's worth asking for a Royal Tower room, as these are larger and more luxurious than those in the east wing.

仍然保留着七十年代外觀的葡京酒店，帶出澳門較為樸實的一面，與閃閃生輝的新葡京酒店可謂相映成趣。酒店共有十種客房，其陳設融合了中葡兩國的風格與特色；當中尊尚客房比東翼的客房更大更豪華。酒店設有多家餐廳，提供多國菜式。

TEL. 2888 3888
2-4 Avenida de Lisboa
葡京路 2-4號
www.hotelisboa.com

RECOMMENDED RESTAURANTS 餐廳推薦
Guincho a Galera 葡國餐廳 XXXX
Tim's Kitchen 桃花源小廚 XXX

†† = MOP 990-1,880
Suites 套房 = MOP 2,890-4,880
☕ = MOP 154

Rooms 客房 861
Suites 套房 65

Mandarin Oriental
文華東方

The Mandarin Oriental is a non-gaming hotel but that's not the only reason it stands out – it is also a model of taste and discretion. Local artists' work adds a sense of locale to the bedrooms which come in muted, contemporary tones and offer great views – even from the tub! Those in search of further relaxation can choose between a very serene spa and a slick bar.

於2010年開業的澳門文華東方，除了不經營賭場外，更是品味的典範。本地藝術家的創作，為色調柔和時尚的客房添上韻味，即使在浴室裏也能欣賞醉人景觀。想進一步放鬆身心，可到幽靜的水療中心或雅致的酒吧。此外，服務質素保持極高水準。

TEL. 8805 8888
945 Avenida Dr. Sun Yat Sen, NAPE
外港新填海區孫逸仙大馬路945號
www.mandarinoriental.com/macau

† = MOP 1,888-5,000
†† = MOP 1,888-5,000
Suites 套房 = MOP 3,288-9,300
☕ = MOP 251

Rooms 客房 186
Suites 套房 27

MGM Cotai
美獅美高梅

Sister to MGM Macau, this hotel boasts the world's largest indoor LED wall, which is part of its impressive central atrium. As well as shops it offers a comprehensive choice of dining options. Take a break from the casino and relax by the appealing pool or be invigorated in Tria spa. Gaze over Cotai from Resort bedrooms that offer luxury and all the latest technology.

澳門美高梅旗下的新酒店，附設獨立購物商場及娛樂場所，多家餐廳讓你能盡享各地美饌，從牛扒到川菜，以至澳門首間日式秘魯菜餐廳，應有盡有。酒店中庭的視博廣場設有全球最大型室內LED牆，帶來不同感官藝術體驗。客房極盡奢華，備有先進科技設施，滿足住客需求；亦可到泳池或禪潺水療放鬆身心。

TEL. 8806 8888
Avenida da Nave Desportiva, Cotai
路氹體育館大馬路
www.mgm.mo

= MOP 1,488-6,000
= MOP 1,588-6,500
Suites 套房 = MOP 3,288-9,000
= MOP 218

Rooms 客房 1,291
Suites 套房 99

MGM Macau
澳門美高梅

Its iconic, wave-like exterior makes MGM one of Macau's more instantly recognisable hotels. The interior is pretty eye-catching too: topped by a vast glass ceiling, the Grande Praça covers over 1,000 square metres and is where you'll find an assortment of bars and restaurants. Spread over 35 floors, bedrooms are suitably luxurious and have glass-walled bathrooms.

標誌性的波浪形建築設計讓美高梅成為澳門最矚目酒店之一。店內設計同樣出色：巨型玻璃天幕下的天幕廣場佔地逾一千平方米，設有多間酒吧和餐廳。如果看膩了浮華的裝潢，不妨前往恬靜的水療中心。酒店有35層，客房華麗得恰到好處，景觀優美，浴室採用玻璃間隔，感覺寬敞。

TEL. 8802 8888
Avenida Dr. Sun Yat Sen, NAPE
外港新填海區孫逸仙大馬路
www.mgm.mo

RECOMMENDED RESTAURANTS 餐廳推薦
Imperial Court 金殿堂

= MOP 1,688-6,000
= MOP 1,688-6,000
Suites 套房 = MOP 3,488-18,000
= MOP 190

Rooms 客房 483
Suites 套房 99

Morpheus
摩珀斯

This hotel, part of the City of Dreams, is set to become a landmark in Cotai. It's architecturally stunning exterior was designed by the late Dame Zaha Hadid. Its interior is no less striking with a rooftop pool, a spa and numerous eateries, including two restaurants from Alain Ducasse. Bedrooms are luxurious, beautifully styled and equipped with the latest technology.

摩珀斯由已故建築師札哈·哈蒂女爵士設計，其縱橫交錯的外觀別樹一格，目光難以從中移離，勢將成為區內新的地標建築。客房同樣時尚奢華，先進科技設施應有盡有。酒店餐飲選擇良多，包括兩家法國大廚Alain Ducasse名下的餐廳，以及各式環球美食。欲肆意享受怎能錯過天台泳池及水療設施？

TEL. 8868 8888
City of Dreams, Estrada do Istmo, Cotai
路氹連貫公路新濠天地
www.cityofdreamsmacau.com

RECOMMENDED RESTAURANTS 餐廳推薦
Alain Ducasse at Morpheus 杜卡斯 ✿✿ XXXX
Voyages by Alain Ducasse 風雅廚 🍴O XX
Yi 天頤 🍴O XXX

👥 = MOP 2,998-5,298
Suites 套房 = MOP 10,998-16,998
☕ = MOP 288

Rooms 客房 604
Suites 套房 168

Okura
大倉

Looking for sanctuary from the outside world? Try this tasteful, discreet and elegant hotel, which is part of Galaxy Macau resort. Charming staff provide excellent service; bedrooms are up-to-the-minute; and all suites have private saunas and steam showers. Dining options include Japanese and international fare.

裝修典雅與品味並重的大倉酒店讓賓客感覺如遠離了凡塵的一切。身穿日本和服的服務員服務親切貼心，時尚的酒店客房寬敞舒適，套房內設有私人桑拿及蒸氣浴。

TEL. 8883 8883
Galaxy Macau, Avenida Marginal Flor de Lotus, Cotai
路氹城蓮花海濱大馬路澳門銀河綜合渡假城
www.hotelokuramacau.com

RECOMMENDED RESTAURANTS 餐廳推薦
Yamazato 山里

† = MOP 1,498-4,998
†† = MOP 1,498-4,998
Suites 套房 = MOP 2,698-6,498
☕ = MOP 209

Rooms 客房 429
Suites 套房 59

If you are looking for particularly pleasant accommodation, book a hotel shown in red: 🏠... 🏠🏠🏠.
欲享受特別舒適的留宿體驗，請選擇注有此 🏠…… 🏠🏠🏠 紅色酒店標誌的推介酒店。

Symbols shown in red indicate particularly charming establishments 🏠🏠🏠 XXX.
紅色標誌 🏠🏠🏠 XXX 表示酒店和餐館在同級別的舒適程度中較優秀。

Sheraton
喜來登

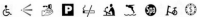

Currently the biggest hotel in Macau, Sheraton Macau forms part of the resort complex of Sands Cotai Central and is connected to a huge shopping mall. Needless to say, the facilities are comprehensive and include a varied choice of restaurant, three outdoor pools with private cabanas and an impressive spa. There are Family suites and special amenities for children.

作為全澳門最大規模、位於金沙城中心的喜來登酒店，連接大型購物商場，便於閒逛購物。酒店內設備亦相當完善：設有數間餐館、三個戶外泳池及舒適的水療設施，吃喝玩樂與休憩，一網打盡。酒店還設有家庭套房和兒童遊樂設施，適合一家大小住宿。

TEL. 2880 2000
Estrada do Istmo, Cotai
路氹連貫公路
www.sheratongrandmacao.com

† = MOP 1,098-5,838
†† = MOP 1,098-5,838
Suites 套房 = MOP 1,988-7,138
☕ = MOP 228

Rooms 客房 3,640
Suites 套房 361

St. Regis
瑞吉

Starwood are relative newcomers to Macau but their very comfortable St. Regis hotel is a worthy addition to the Cotai Strip. The spacious bedrooms, on floors 8-37, have good views and are well-appointed in an understated, contemporary style; they have floor-to-ceiling windows and white marble bathrooms. The Manor restaurant offers a wide-ranging international menu.

這家Starwood麾下的酒店位於路氹金光大道，地點優越。1樓的雅舍餐廳明亮而富現代氣息，可品嘗各式國際菜餚美饌。客房位處8-37樓，寬敞時尚的室內陳設透着點點東方韻味，配上落地玻璃窗，予人舒適靜謐之感，記着預訂能眺望金光大道美景的房間。水療中心的寶石按摩讓人感官愉悅。

TEL. 2882 8898
Estrada do Istmo, Cotai
路氹連貫公路
www.stregismacao.com

= MOP 1,648-7,338
= MOP 1,848-7,538
Suites 套房 = MOP 2,948-8,638
= MOP 248

Rooms 客房 278
Suites 套房 122

StarWorld
星際

Opened in 2006, StarWorld Macau is a comfortable, well-managed hotel in a good location. Its bedrooms are bright and contemporary and the bathrooms are smart and well-equipped. Along with various restaurants and assorted gaming, the hotel also offers comprehensive entertainment and leisure facilities and these include a bar with live music every night.

在2006年開業的星際酒店地點便利之餘，亦是一間管理完善的酒店。光猛的房間設計風格前衛，時髦的浴室設施相當完備。除了各式餐館和娛樂場所外，酒店內還附設各種休閒設施，例如每天晚上都有現場音樂演奏的酒吧。

TEL. 2838 3838
Avenida da Amizade
友誼大馬路
www.starworldmacau.com

RECOMMENDED RESTAURANTS 餐廳推薦
Feng Wei Ju 風味居 ✿✿ XXX

† = MOP 1,460-2,360
†† = MOP 1,460-2,360
Suites 套房 = MOP 2,920-4,720
☕ = MOP 98

Rooms 客房 465
Suites 套房 40

Studio City
新濠影滙

Even by Macau standards, this immense, art deco styled hotel made quite a statement when it opened in 2015. It aims to offer the complete leisure experience and that means extensive gaming facilities, a 5,000 seater arena, a 4D Batman experience, a magic show, shopping malls, spas, numerous restaurants and a nightclub! Bedrooms have floor-to-ceiling windows and good views.

這家耗資逾三十億美元興建、裝飾派藝術風格的酒店於2015年開業，目標是提供一站式的綜合娛樂，設有娛樂場、大型表演場地、4D影院、購物商場、水療中心等等，還有號稱高度冠絕全球、達130米的8字形摩天輪，讓你流連忘返。時尚而設備完善的客房分佈於兩幢大樓內，落地玻璃窗外是金光大道的醉人景致。

TEL. 8865 6868
Estrada do Istmo, Cotai Strip
路氹連貫公路
www.studiocity-macau.com

RECOMMENDED RESTAURANTS 餐廳推薦
Bi Ying 碧迎居
Pearl Dragon 玥龍軒

= MOP 1,888-3,888
= MOP 1,888-3,888
Suites 套房 = MOP 3,888-28,888
= MOP 150

Rooms 客房 979
Suites 套房 621

The Parisian
巴黎人

Building a half-scale recreation of the Eiffel Tower in front of your hotel is certainly one way of getting it noticed. It opened in 2016 and the hotel's interior also makes much of French history – the reception area is inspired by Louis XIV. Bedrooms, in contrast, are more neutral in tone. Dining options include La Chine, a fusion restaurant within the replica Eiffel Tower.

在酒店外重塑一個只有半個規模的艾菲爾鐵塔，絕對有助吸引遊客的焦點。於2016年開業的巴黎人酒店，裝潢帶有路易十四時期的巴洛克風格，客房的布置卻較為素淨。位於酒店外的仿艾菲爾鐵塔內的餐廳，供應自助餐、法國菜或多國菜的都有，不妨挑一間坐下來，邊享用餐點邊欣賞窗外景色。

TEL. 2882 8833
Estrada do Istmo, Lote 3, Cotai Strip
路氹金光大道連貫公路
www.parisianmacao.com

† = MOP 1,493-6,325
†† = MOP 1,665-6,900
Suites 套房 = MOP 2,183-9,200
☕ = MOP 252

Rooms 客房 2,429
Suites 套房 571

The Ritz-Carlton
麗思卡爾頓

All bedrooms are suites at the exclusive Ritz-Carlton hotel, which is located on the upper floors at Galaxy Macau. They are impeccably dressed and come with particularly luxurious marble bathrooms. They also provide great views of Cotai, as does the outdoor pool. Along with a state-of-the-art spa is an elegant bar and stylish, very comfortable lounges.

講究的裝潢、精緻的藝術擺設、舒適的座椅，甫踏進設在51樓的接待處，心已給融化！風格典雅的套房除了設有舒適奢華的大理石浴室外，還能俯瞰欣賞銀河渡假村景觀或遠眺市內風光。與接待處同層的麗思酒廊設計優雅，且能飽覽氹仔景致，是與摯愛親朋把酒談心的好地方。

TEL. 8886 6868
Galaxy Macau, Estrada da Baia da Nossa Senhora da Esperança, Cotai
路氹城望德聖母灣大馬路
澳門銀河綜合渡假城
www.ritzcarlton.com/macau

Suites 套房 = MOP 3,388-28,488
☕ = MOP 380

Suites 套房 236

RECOMMENDED RESTAURANTS 餐廳推薦
Lai Heen 麗軒 ✿ XXXXX
The Ritz-Carlton Café 麗思咖啡廳 XX

The Venetian
威尼斯人

One thing you'll need at Asia's largest integrated resort is a map to find your way around. Expect vast shopping malls and even canals with singing gondoliers; there are frescoes, colonnades and sculptures everywhere – it's easy to get caught up in the sheer scale and exuberance of it all. Identikit luxury is assured in a towering bedroom skyscraper with 3,000 rooms.

你需要一張地圖才能環遊這間全亞洲最大型綜合渡假酒店！在這裏你會找到大型購物商場，更有貢多拉船夫一邊撐船一邊唱歌。遍佈各處的壁畫、柱廊和雕塑裝飾，具規模且色彩繽紛，令人目不暇給。高聳的摩天大樓設有三千間套房，全部房間都很寬敞。

TEL. 2882 8888
Estrada da Baia de Nossa Senhora da Esperança, Taipa
氹仔望德聖母灣大馬路
www.venetianmacao.com

Suites 套房 = MOP 1,950-8,050
☕ = MOP 198

Suites 套房 3,000

RECOMMENDED RESTAURANTS 餐廳推薦
Canton 喜粵 XXX
Lei Garden 利苑酒家 XXX
The Golden Peacock 皇雀 ✿ XX

Wynn
永利

The Wynn's easy-on-the-eye curving glass façade is enhanced by a lake and dancing fountains, while the classically luxurious interior includes Murano glass chandeliers, plush carpets and much marble. An attractively landscaped oasis pool forms the centrepiece to corridors lined with famous retail names. Comfortable bedrooms display a considerable degree of taste.

弧形的玻璃外牆十分奪目，更設有表演湖及噴水池。酒店內部散發着經典豪華氣息：穆拉諾穆玻璃吊燈、豪華的地氈，觸目所及皆是大理石。走廊中心設有一個造型迷人的綠洲池，而兩旁滿是名店。客房融合了傳統與現代兩種設計風格，盡顯卓越品味。其吉祥樹同樣令你印象深刻。

TEL. 2888 9966
Rua Cidade de Sintra, NAPE
外港新填海區仙德麗街
www.wynnmacau.com

RECOMMENDED RESTAURANTS 餐廳推薦
Il Teatro 帝雅廷
Mizumi (Macau) 泓 (澳門)
Wing Lei 永利軒

† = MOP 1,888-13,500
†† = MOP 1,888-13,500
Suites 套房 = MOP 3,988-17,000
☕ = MOP 210

Rooms 客房 460
Suites 套房 134

Wynn Palace
永利皇宮

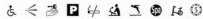

Opened in 2016, with a striking flower motif and impressive pieces of art scattered around the vast hotel. Luxurious bedrooms are uncluttered, large and bright, with a Mandarin, Peacock or Gold colour theme; the caramel-coloured suites are also impressive. There's a host of dining choices, from noodles to steaks; show kitchens are a feature of several of the restaurants.

於2016年開業，以上萬朵花卉製作的巨型花卉雕塑、隨處可見的藝術作品，寬敞的酒店，典雅高貴。以柑橘、孔雀和金作主題陳設的豪華客房感覺整潔、寬敞及明亮，橙棕色作主調的套房尤為使人印象深刻。酒店內餐廳種類很廣，從簡單的麵食到高級的牛扒，一應俱全，開放式廚房似乎是這裏的餐廳特色。

TEL. 8889 8889
Avenida da Nave Desportiva, Cotai
路氹體育館大馬路
www.wynnpalace.com

RECOMMENDED RESTAURANTS 餐廳推薦
Wing Lei Palace 永利宮 XXXX

† = MOP 1,888-13,888
†† = MOP 2,388-13,888
Suites 套房 = MOP 2,888-15,888
☕ = MOP 220

Rooms 客房 845
Suites 套房 861

MAPS
地圖

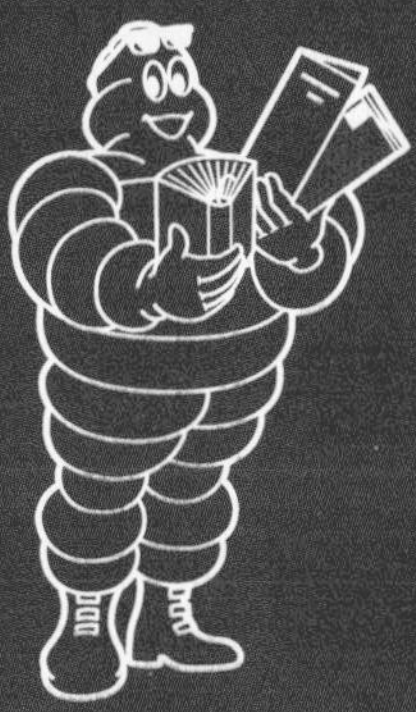

蔗園市
米埔
Mai Po
落馬洲
Lok Ma Chau
古洞
Kwu Tung
流浮山
Lau Fau Shan
錦繡花園
Fairview Park
天水圍
Tin Shui Wai
2
元朗
YUEN LONG
八鄉
Pat Heung
錦田
Kam Tin
白泥
Pak Nai
稔灣
Nim Wan
藍地
LAM TEI
大棠
Tai Tong
新界
NEW TERR
內伶仃島
龍鼓洲
LUNG KWU CHAU
龍鼓灘
Lung Kwu Tan
屯門
TUEN MUN
1
踏石角
Tap Shek Kok
黃金海岸
HK Gold Coast
大欖涌
Tai Lam Chung
深井
Sham Tseng
3
荃灣
TSUEN W
馬灣
MA WAN
青衣
TSING YI
香港國際機場
HONG KONG INTERNATIONAL AIRPORT
欣澳
Sunny Bay
香港迪士尼樂園
HK Disneyland
愉景灣
DISCOVERY BAY
沙螺灣
Sha Lo Wan
東涌
TUNG CHUNG
大嶼山
LANTAU ISLAND
(TAI YUE SHAN)
大水坑
Trappist Haven
Peng Chau
交椅洲
昂坪
NGONG PING
大澳
Tai O
鳳凰山
Lantau Peak
周公島
喜靈洲
Hei Ling Chau
貝澳
Pui O
長沙
Cheung Sha
塘福
Tong Fuk
芝麻灣半島
CHI MA WAN PENINSULA
二澳
Yi O
石壁
Shek Pik
West Lamma Channel
分流
FAN LAU
長洲
Cheung Chau
石鼓洲
Shek Kwu Chau
索罟群島
Soko Islands

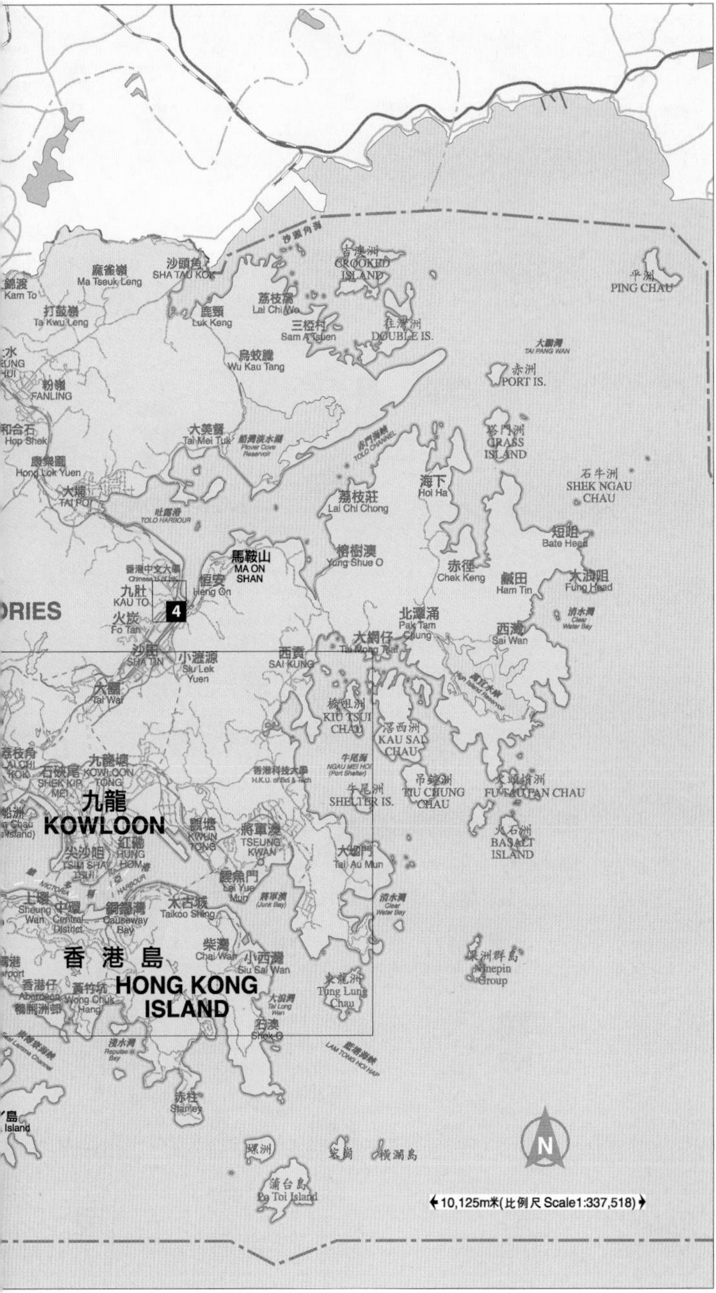

沙頭角海
吉澳洲
CROOKED ISLAND
平洲
PING CHAU
麻雀嶺
Ma Tseuk Leng
沙頭角
SHA TAU KOK
錦渡
Kam To
打鼓嶺
Ta Kwu Leng
荔枝窩
Lai Chi Wo
鹿頸
Luk Keng
三椏村
Sam A Tsuen
往灣洲
DOUBLE IS.
大鵬灣
TAI PANG WAN
烏蛟騰
Wu Kau Tang
粉嶺
FANLING
赤洲
PORT IS.
和合石
Hop Shek
大美督
Tai Mei Tuk
船灣淡水湖
Plover Cove Reservoir
赤門海峽
TOLO CHANNEL
滘門洲
GRASS ISLAND
康樂園
Hong Lok Yuen
大埔
TAI PO
海下
Hoi Ha
石牛洲
SHEK NGAU CHAU
荔枝莊
Lai Chi Chong
吐露港
TOLO HARBOUR
短咀
Bate Head
馬鞍山
MA ON SHAN
榕樹澳
Yung Shue O
香港中文大學
赤徑
Chek Keng
鹹田
Ham Tin
大浪咀
Fung Head
九肚
KAU TO
恒安
Heng On
4
清水灣
Clear Water Bay
ORIES
火炭
Fo Tan
北潭涌
Pak Tam Chung
西灣
Sai Wan
大網仔
Tai Mong Tsai
沙田
SHA TIN
小瀝源
Siu Lek Yuen
西貢
SAI KUNG
萬宜水庫
High Island Reservoir
大圍
Tai Wai
橋咀洲
KIU TSUI CHAU
滘西洲
KAU SAI CHAU
牛尾海
NGAU MEI HOI
(Port Shelter)
九龍塘
KOWLOON TONG
石硤尾
SHEK KIP MEI
香港科技大學
牛尾洲
SHELTER IS.
吊鐘洲
TIU CHUNG CHAU
火頭擔洲
FU TAU PAN CHAU
九龍
KOWLOON
觀塘
KWUN TONG
將軍澳
TSEUNG KWAN
火石洲
BASALT ISLAND
尖沙咀
TSIM SHA TSUI
紅磡
HUNG HOM
大坳門
Tai Au Mun
鯉魚門
Lei Yue Mun
將軍澳
(Junk Bay)
清水灣
Clear Water Bay
上環
Sheung Wan
中環
Central District
銅鑼灣
Causeway Bay
太古城
Taikoo Shing
柴灣
Chai Wan
小西灣
Siu Sai Wan
果洲群島
Ninepin Group
香港島
HONG KONG ISLAND
香港仔
Aberdeen
黃竹坑
Wong Chuk Hang
東龍洲
Tung Lung Chau
大浪灣
Tai Long Wan
石澳
Shek O
淺水灣
Repulse Bay
藍塘海峽
LAM TONG HOI HAP
赤柱
Stanley
螺洲
蒲台島
Po Toi Island
N
10,125m米(比例尺 Scale1:337,518)

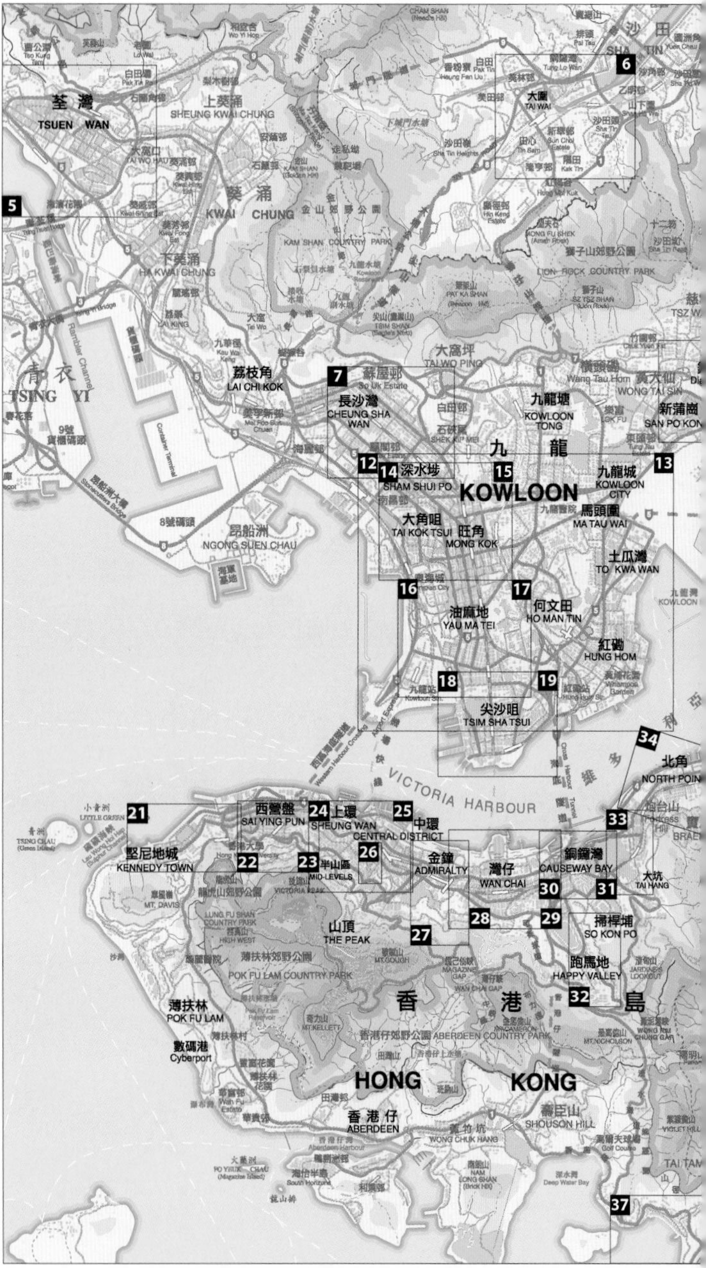

荃灣
TSUEN WAN
上葵涌
SHEUNG KWAI CHUNG
葵涌
KWAI CHUNG
下葵涌
HA KWAI CHUNG
金山郊野公園
KAM SHAN COUNTRY PARK
獅子山郊野公園
LION ROCK COUNTRY PARK
大窩坪
TAI WO PING
大圍
TAI WAI
SHA TIN
青衣
TSING YI
Rambler Channel
Container Terminal
荔枝角
LAI CHI KOK
長沙灣
CHEUNG SHA WAN
深水埗
SHAM SHUI PO
九龍塘
KOWLOON TONG
九龍
KOWLOON
九龍城
KOWLOON CITY
馬頭圍
MA TAU WAI
大角咀
TAI KOK TSUI
旺角
MONG KOK
昂船洲
NGONG SUEN CHAU
土瓜灣
TO KWA WAN
何文田
HO MAN TIN
油麻地
YAU MA TEI
紅磡
HUNG HOM
新蒲崗
SAN PO KONG
黃大仙
WONG TAI SIN
尖沙咀
TSIM SHA TSUI
VICTORIA HARBOUR
北角
NORTH POINT
西營盤
SAI YING PUN
上環
SHEUNG WAN
中環
CENTRAL DISTRICT
堅尼地城
KENNEDY TOWN
半山區
MID-LEVELS
金鐘
ADMIRALTY
灣仔
WAN CHAI
銅鑼灣
CAUSEWAY BAY
大坑
TAI HANG
掃捍埔
SO KON PO
跑馬地
HAPPY VALLEY
山頂
THE PEAK
薄扶林郊野公園
POK FU LAM COUNTRY PARK
香港仔郊野公園
ABERDEEN COUNTRY PARK
薄扶林
POK FU LAM
數碼港
Cyberport
香港島
HONG KONG
香港仔
ABERDEEN
壽臣山
SHOUSON HILL
黃竹坑
WONG CHUK HANG
5
6
7
12
13
14
15
16
17
18
19
21
22
23
24
25
26
27
28
29
30
31
32
33
34
37

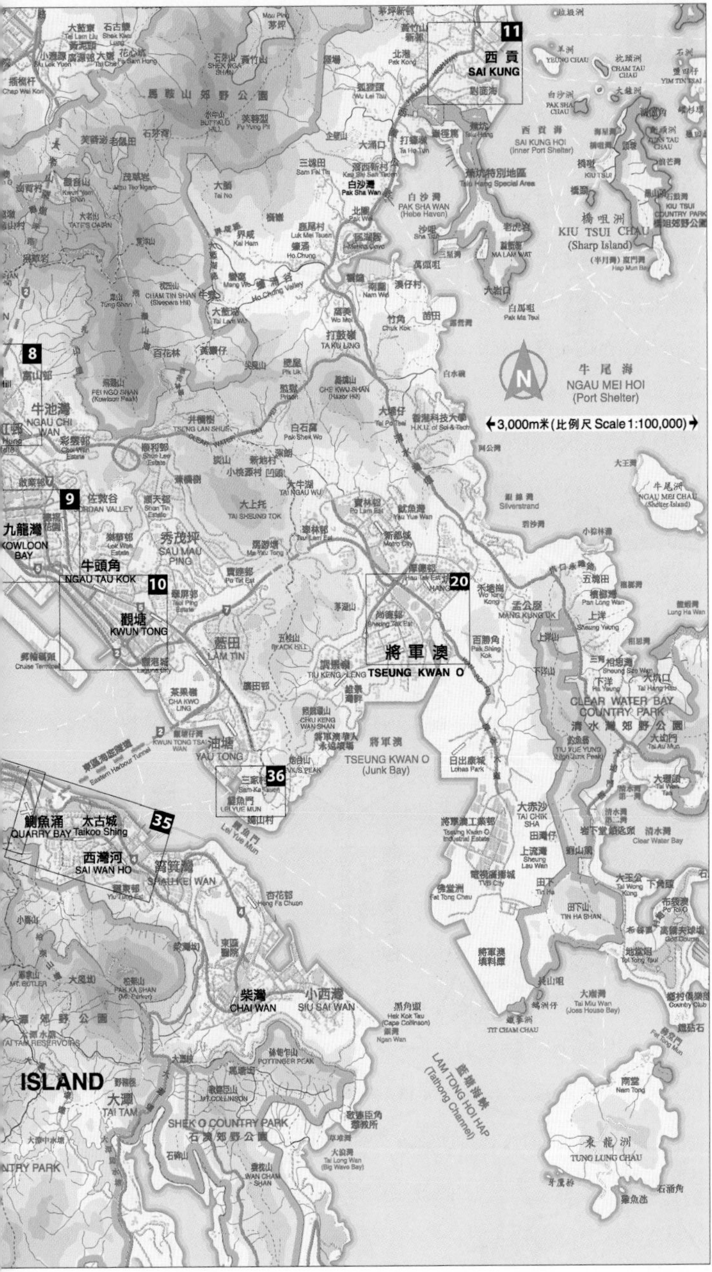

11
西貢
SAI KUNG
8
9
10
20
35
36
牛池灣
NGAU CHI WAN
九龍灣
KOWLOON BAY
牛頭角
NGAU TAU KOK
秀茂坪
SAU MAU PING
觀塘
KWUN TONG
藍田
LAM TIN
油塘
YAU TONG
將軍澳
TSEUNG KWAN O
將軍澳
TSEUNG KWAN O
(Junk Bay)
鰂魚涌
QUARRY BAY
太古城
Taikoo Shing
西灣河
SAI WAN HO
筲箕灣
SHAU KEI WAN
柴灣
CHAI WAN
小西灣
SIU SAI WAN
ISLAND
大潭
TAI TAM
SHEK O COUNTRY PARK
石澳郊野公園
牛尾海
NGAU MEI HOI
(Port Shelter)
←3,000m米(比例尺 Scale 1:100,000)→
橋咀洲
KIU TSUI CHAU
(Sharp Island)
SAI KUNG HOI
(Inner Port Shelter)
PAK SHA WAN
(Hebe Haven)
CLEAR WATER BAY
COUNTRY PARK
清水灣郊野公園
LAM TONG HOI HAP
(Tathong Channel)
東龍洲
TUNG LUNG CHAU
Eastern Harbour Tunnel
N

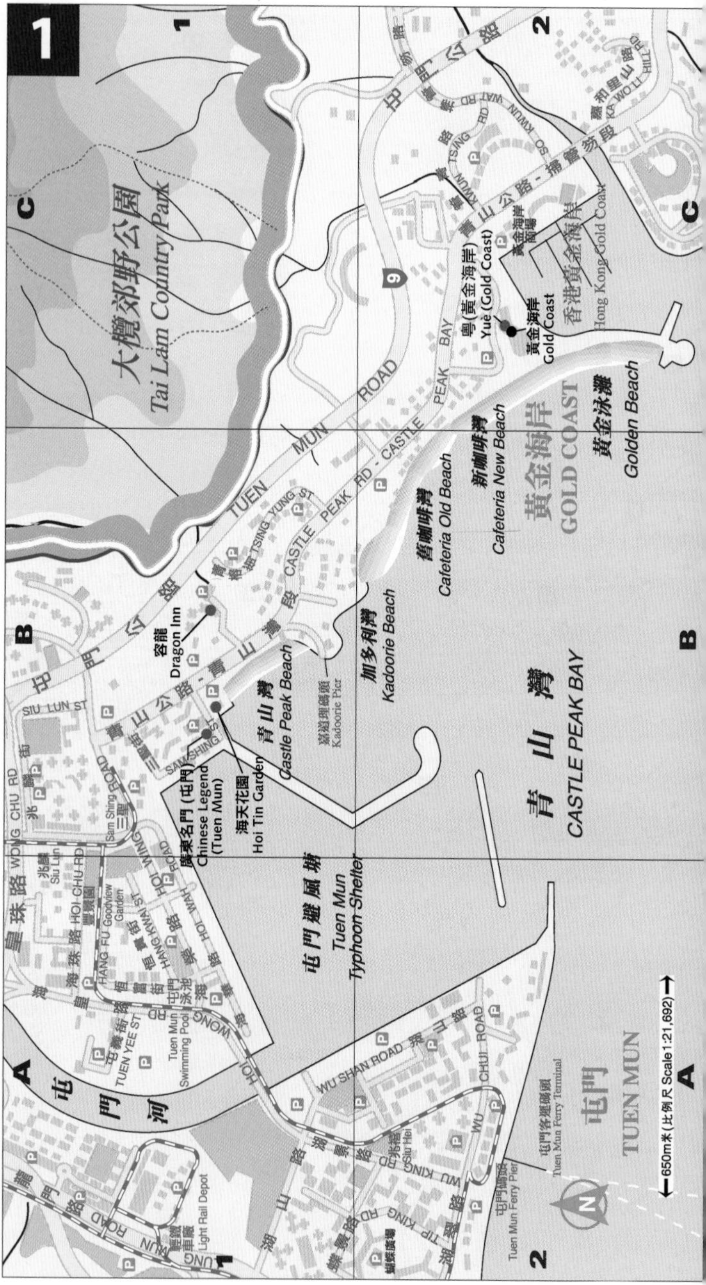
1
大欖郊野公園
Tai Lam Country Park
TUEN MUN ROAD
屯門公路
CASTLE PEAK RD - CASTLE PEAK BAY
青山公路 - 青山灣段
Dragon Inn
容龍
Chinese Legend (Tuen Mun)
廣東名門 (屯門)
Hoi Tin Garden
海天花園
Castle Peak Beach
青山灣
Kadoorie Pier
Kadoorie Beach
加多利灣
Cafeteria Old Beach
舊咖啡灣
Cafeteria New Beach
新咖啡灣
GOLD COAST
黃金海岸
Golden Beach
黃金泳灘
Yue (Gold Coast)
粵 (黃金海岸)
Gold Coast
黃金海岸
Hong Kong Gold Coast
香港黃金海岸
CASTLE PEAK BAY
青山灣
Tuen Mun Typhoon Shelter
屯門避風塘
TUEN MUN
屯門
Tuen Mun Ferry Terminal
屯門客運碼頭
Tuen Mun Ferry Pier
屯門碼頭
Light Rail Depot
輕鐵車廠
Tuen Mun Swimming Pool
屯門泳池
Goodview Garden
豐景園
Siu Lun
兆麟
Siu Hei
兆禧
屯門河
SIU LUN ST
SAM SHING ST
Sam Shing
三聖
WONG CHU RD
HOI CHU RD
HANG FU
HANG KWAI ST
HOI WING ROAD
HOI WAH ROAD
WONG CHU ROAD
TUEN YEE ST
WU SHAN ROAD
WU CHUI ROAD
TIP KING RD
WU KING RD
LUNG MUN ROAD
TSING YUNG ST
KWUN TSING RD
KWUN WAT RD
KA WO LI HILL RD
嘉和里山路
9
650m米 (比例尺 Scale 1:21,692)
A
B
C
1
2

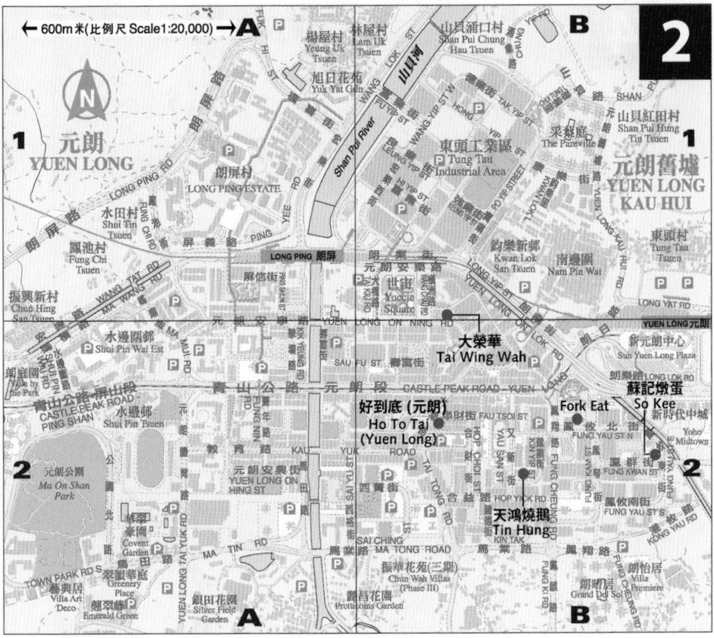

2
600m 米(比例尺 Scale1:20,000)
A
B
1
2
N
元朗
YUEN LONG
元朗舊墟
YUEN LONG KAU HUI
大榮華
Tai Wing Wah
好到底 (元朗)
Ho To Tai (Yuen Long)
Fork Eat
蘇記燉蛋
So Kee
天鴻燒鵝
Tin Hung
LONG PING 朗屏
楊屋村
Yeung Uk Tsuen
林屋村
Lam Uk Tsuen
山貝涌口村
Shan Pui Chung Hau Tsuen
旭日花苑
Yuk Yat Gdn
Shan Pui River
山貝河
東頭工業區
Tung Tau Industrial Area
山貝紅田村
Shan Pui Hung Tin Tsuen
采葉庭
The Pareville
朗屏邨
LONG PING ESTATE
水田村
Shui Tin Tsuen
鳳池村
Fung Chi Tsuen
振興新村
Chun Hing San Tsuen
鈞樂新邨
Kwan Lok San Tsuen
南邊圍
Nam Pin Wai
東頭村
Tung Tau Tsuen
世街
Yuccie Square
新元朗中心
Sun Yuen Long Plaza
新時代中城
Yoho Midtown
水邊圍邨
Shui Pin Wai Est
朗庭園
Villa by the Park
青山公路-屏山段
CASTLE PEAK ROAD PING SHAN
水邊邨
Shui Pin Tsuen
青山公路元朗段
CASTLE PEAK ROAD - YUEN LONG
元朗公園
Ma On Shan Park
華翠豪園
Covent Garden
翠韻華庭
Greenery Place
藝典居
Villa Art Deco
翹翠峰
Emerald Green
銀田花園
Silver Field Garden
振華花苑(三期)
Chun Wah Villas (Phase III)
豐昌花園
Prettycoins Garden
朗晴居
Grand Del Sol
朗怡居
Villa Premiere
LONG PING RD
YUEN LONG ON NING RD
CASTLE PEAK ROAD - YUEN LONG
MA TIN RD
MA TONG ROAD
KAU YUK ROAD
YUEN LONG ON HING ST
HOP YICK RD
FUNG YAU ST N
FUNG KWAN ST
FUNG YAU ST S
KONG YAU RD
LONG YAT RD
YUEN LONG 元朗

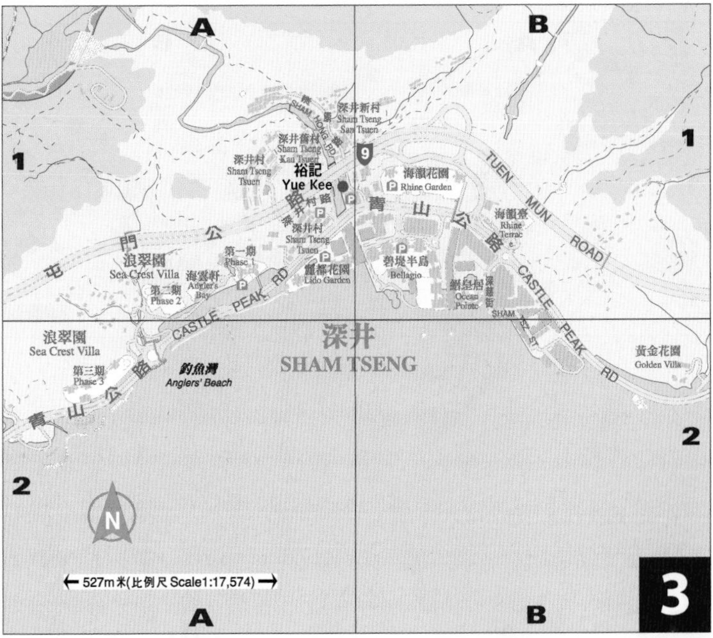

A
B
1
2
N
527m 米(比例尺 Scale1:17,574)
3
深井
SHAM TSENG
裕記
Yue Kee
9
深井新村
Sham Tseng San Tsuen
深井舊村
Sham Tseng Kau Tsuen
深井村
Sham Tseng Tsuen
海韻花園
Rhine Garden
海韻臺
Rhine Terrace
碧堤半島
Bellagio
瓏璽
Ocean Pointe
麗都花園
Lido Garden
第一期
Phase 1
第二期
Phase 2
海雲軒
Anglers' Bay
浪翠園
Sea Crest Villa
第三期
Phase 3
釣魚灣
Anglers' Beach
黃金花園
Golden Villa
TUEN MUN ROAD
屯門公路
青山公路
CASTLE PEAK RD
SHAM HONG RD

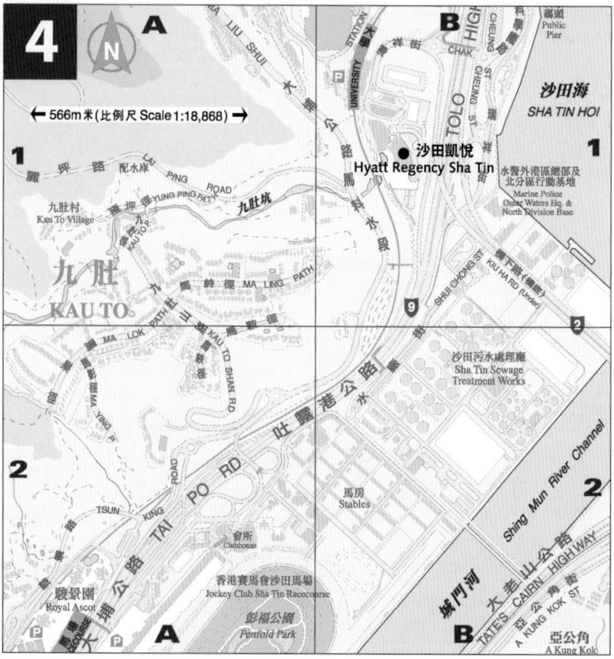
4
566m米(比例尺 Scale1:18,868)
沙田凱悅
Hyatt Regency Sha Tin
沙田海
SHA TIN HOI
九肚
KAU TO
九肚村
Kau To Village
沙田污水處理廠
Sha Tin Sewage Treatment Works
馬房
Stables
會所
Clubhouse
香港賽馬會沙田馬場
Jockey Club Sha Tin Racecourse
彭福公園
Penfold Park
駿景園
Royal Ascot
吐露港公路
TAI PO RD
Shing Mun River Channel
城門河
TATE'S CAIRN HIGHWAY
A KUNG KOK ST
亞公角
A Kung Kok
水警外港區總部及北分區行動基地
Marine Police Outer Waters Hq. & North Division Base

5
740m米(比例尺 Scale1:24,655)
千色車仔麵
Chin Sik
荃灣
TSUEN WAN
荃景花園
TSUEN KING GARDEN
荃德花園
TSUEN TAK GARDENS
柴灣角
Chai Wan Kok
福來邨
FUK LOI ESTATE
綠楊新邨
LUK YEUNG SUN CHUEN
白田壩
Pak Tin Pa
石圍角邨
SHEK WAI KOK EST
大窩口
TAI WO HAU
大窩口邨
TAI WO HAU EST
如心廣場
Nina Tower
萬景峰
Vision City
御凱
The Dynasty
爵悅庭
Chelsea Court
海濱花園
Riviera Gardens
葵盛西邨
Kwai Shing W. Est
青山公路
CASTLE PEAK RD
TSUEN WAN RD
TEXACO ROAD NORTH
ROUTE TWISK

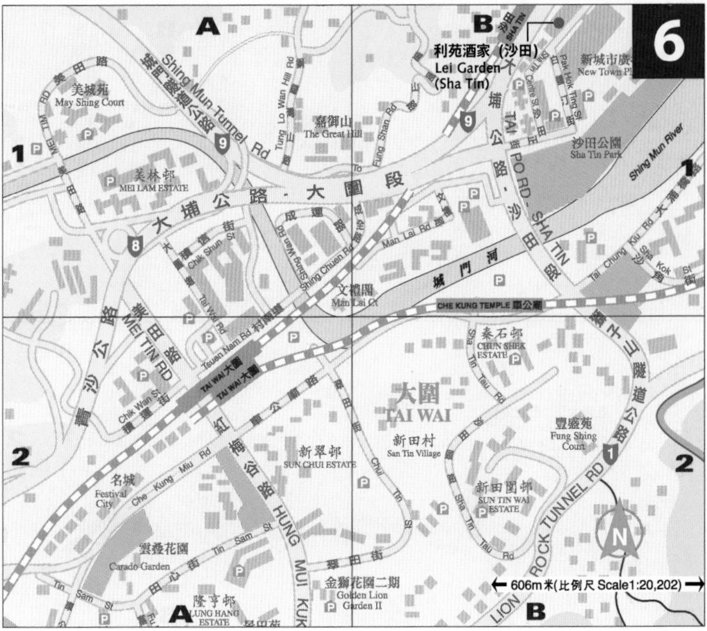
6
A
B
1
2
利苑酒家 (沙田)
Lei Garden
(Sha Tin)
美城苑
May Shing Court
嘉御山
The Great Hill
新城市廣場
New Town Plaza
沙田公園
Sha Tin Park
Shing Mun River
美林邨
MEI LAM ESTATE
大埔公路 - 大圍段
Shing Mun Tunnel Rd
Tung Lo Wan Hill Rd
Fung Shan Rd
TAI PO RD - SHA TIN
Pak Hok Ting St
Man Lai Rd
城門河
Chik Shun St
Shing Chuen Rd
Sheung Wan Rd
文禮閣
Man Lai Ct
CHE KUNG TEMPLE 車公廟
Tai Chung Kiu Rd
Sha Kok St
Tsuen Nam Rd
TAI WAI 大圍
秦石邨
CHUN SHEK ESTATE
Sha Tin Tau Rd
MEI TIN RD
Chik Wan St
大圍
TAI WAI
新田村
San Tin Village
豐盛苑
Fung Shing Court
新翠邨
SUN CHUI ESTATE
名城
Festival City
Che Kung Miu Rd
HUNG MUI KUK
新田圍邨
SUN TIN WAI ESTATE
Chui Tin St
LION ROCK TUNNEL RD
雲疊花園
Carado Garden
Tin Sam St
翠田街
金獅花園二期
Golden Lion Garden II
隆亨邨
LUNG HANG ESTATE
606m 米(比例尺 Scale1:20,202)
N

7
A
B
1
2
樂仁學校
Lok Yan School
蘇屋邨 So Uk Est
CHING CHEUNG RD
荔枝角
LAI CHI KOK
LUNG CHEUNG RD
南華中學
Nam Wah Secondary School
善導小學
Good Counsel Catholic Primary School
WING HONG ST
CASTLE PEAK RD
大同中學
Tai Hung College
聖公會基愛小學
SKH Kei Oi Primary School
澤安邨
Chak On Est
CHEUNG WAH ST
CHEUNG FAT ST
FAT TSEUNG ST
KWONG LEE RD
李鄭屋邨
Lei Cheng Uk Est
李鄭屋游泳池
Lei Cheng Uk Swimming Pool
TONKIN ST
TAI PO RD
CHEUNG SHA WAN RD
HING WAH ST
坤記竹昇麵 (長沙灣)
Kwan Kee Bamboo Noodles
(Cheung Sha Wan)
深水埗運動場
Sham Shui Po Sports Ground
元洲邨
UN CHAU ESTATE
WING LUNG ST
PRATAS ST
545m 米(比例尺 Scale1:18,155)
幸俊苑
Hang Chun Court
幸福邨
FORTUNE EST
WEST KOWLOON CORRIDOR
宇晴軒
The Pacifica
CAMP ST
劉森記麵家 (福榮街)
Lau Sum Kee
(Fuk Wing Street)
文記車仔麵
Man Kei Cart Noodles
石硤尾邨
泰潮 (深水埗)
Thai Chiu
(Sham Shui Po)
怡閣苑
Yee Kok Court
麗閣邨
LAI KOK ESTATE
LAI CHI KOK RD
怡靖苑
Yee Ching Court
公和荳品廠
Kung Wo Tofu
坤記糕品
Kwan Kee Store
順德聯誼總會
Tsung Tsin Christian Academy
Ching Girls' Secondary School
深水埗公園游泳池
Sham Shui Po Park Swimming Pool
麗安邨
LAI ON ESTATE
YEN CHOW ST
SHAM SHUI PO 深水埗
聖瑪加利中小學
St.Margaret's
深水埗公園
Sham Shui Po Park
合益泰小食
Hop Yik Tai
添好運 (深水埗)
Tim Ho Wan
(Sham Shui Po)
KWEILIN ST
PEI HO ST
N

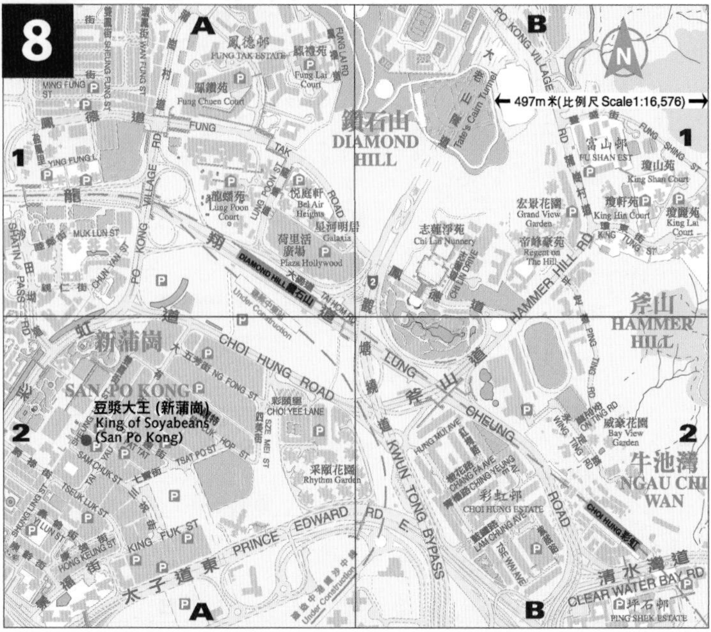
8
A
B
1
2
497m 米(比例尺 Scale1:16,576)
鑽石山
DIAMOND HILL
斧山
HAMMER HILL
新蒲崗
SAN PO KONG
牛池灣
NGAU CHI WAN
豆漿大王 (新蒲崗)
King of Soyabeans (San Po Kong)
鳳德邨
FUNG TAK ESTATE
鳳禮苑
Fung Lai Court
鳳鑽苑
Fung Chuen Court
龍蟠苑
Lung Poon Court
悅庭軒
Bel Air Heights
星河明居
Galaxia
荷里活廣場
Plaza Hollywood
志蓮淨苑
Chi Lin Nunnery
富山邨
FU SHAN EST
瓊山苑
King Shan Court
宏景花園
Grand View Garden
瓊軒苑
King Hin Court
瓊麗苑
King Lai Court
帝峰豪苑
Regent on The Hill
威豪花園
Bay View Garden
彩頤里
CHOI YEE LANE
采頤花園
Rhythm Garden
彩虹邨
CHOI HUNG ESTATE
坪石邨
PING SHEK ESTATE
Tate's Cairn Tunnel
DIAMOND HILL 鑽石山
CHOI HUNG 彩虹
Under Construction
FUNG
TAK
CHOI HUNG ROAD
LUNG CHEUNG ROAD
KWUN TONG BYPASS
PRINCE EDWARD RD E.
太子道東
清水灣道
CLEAR WATER BAY RD
HAMMER HILL RD
PO KONG VILLAGE RD
SHATIN PASS RD
KING FUK ST
NG FONG ST
TSAT PO ST
SZE MEI ST
HUNG MUI AVE
CHANG FA AVE
CHING YEUNG AVE
LAM CHUNG AVE
TSE WAN AVE
MUK LUN ST
CHUN YAN ST
YING FUNG L
MING FUNG ST
SAM CHUK ST
TSEUK LUK ST
HONG KEUNG ST
YI LUN ST
SHUNG LING ST
ON TING RD
PING TING RD
FUNG SHING ST
KING TUNG ST

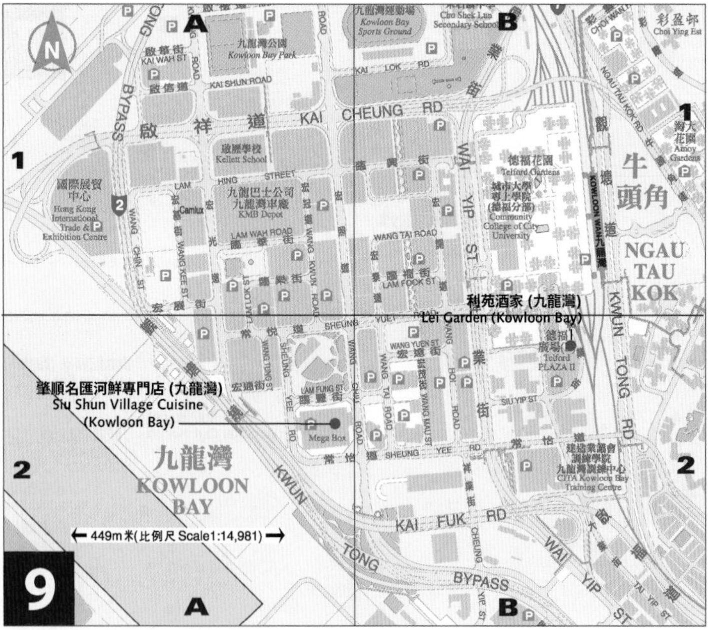
9
A
B
1
2
449m 米(比例尺 Scale1:14,981)
九龍灣
KOWLOON BAY
牛頭角
NGAU TAU KOK
利苑酒家 (九龍灣)
Lei Garden (Kowloon Bay)
肇順名匯河鮮專門店 (九龍灣)
Siu Shun Village Cuisine (Kowloon Bay)
九龍灣公園
Kowloon Bay Park
九龍灣運動場
Kowloon Bay Sports Ground
Cho Shek Lun Secondary School
彩盈邨
Choi Ying Est
啟廈學校
Kellett School
國際展貿中心
Hong Kong International Trade & Exhibition Centre
九龍巴士公司九龍灣車廠
KMB Depot
德福花園
Telford Gardens
城市大學專上學院(德福分部)
Community College of City University
德福廣場II
Telford PLAZA II
淘大花園
Amoy Gardens
Mega Box
建造業議會訓練學院九龍灣訓練中心
CITA Kowloon Bay Training Centre
Camlux
KAI CHEUNG RD
KAI WAH ST
KAI SHUN ROAD
KAI LOK RD
HING STREET
LAM WAH ROAD
WANG TAI ROAD
LAM FOOK ST
WANG CHIN ST
WANG KEE ST
WANG KWUN ROAD
SHEUNG YUET RD
WANG YUEN ST
WANG TUNG ST
LAM FUNG ST
SIU YIP ST
SHEUNG YEE RD
KAI FUK RD
WAI YIP ST
KWUN TONG BYPASS
KWUN TONG RD
NGAU TAU KOK RD
KOWLOON WAN 九龍灣
TAI YIP ST

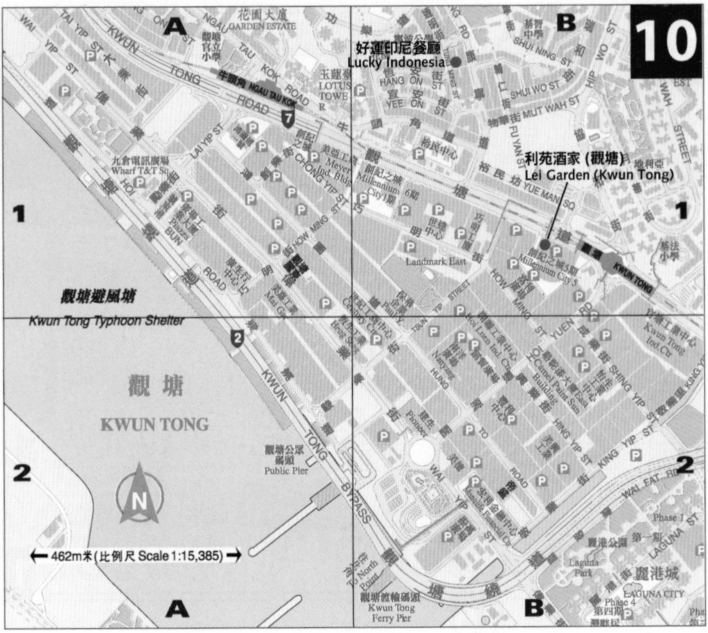
10
好運印尼餐廳
Lucky Indonesia
利苑酒家 (觀塘)
Lei Garden (Kwun Tong)
花園大廈
GARDEN ESTATE
牛頭角 NGAU TAU KOK
KWUN TONG ROAD
九倉電訊廣場
Wharf T&T Sq
創紀之城6期
Millennium City 6
Landmark East
創紀之城5期
Millennium City 5
觀塘避風塘
Kwun Tong Typhoon Shelter
觀塘
KWUN TONG
觀塘公眾碼頭
Public Pier
KWUN TONG BYPASS
觀塘渡輪碼頭
Kwun Tong Ferry Pier
麗港公園
Laguna Park
麗港城
LAGUNA CITY
462m米(比例尺 Scale 1:15,385)

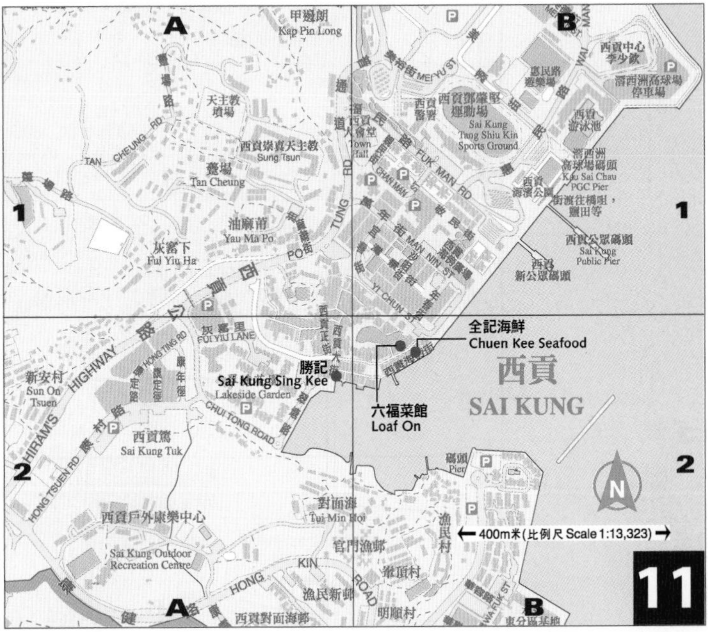
甲邊朗
Kap Pin Long
天主教
墳場
西貢崇真天主教
Sung Tsun
躉場
Tan Cheung
油麻莆
Yau Ma Po
灰窰下
Fui Yiu Ha
西貢警署
西貢鄧肇堅
運動場
Sai Kung
Tung Shiu Kin
Sports Ground
西貢中心
李少欽
西貢
海濱公園
滘西洲高球場碼頭
Kau Sai Chau
PGC Pier
西貢公眾碼頭
Sai Kung
Public Pier
西貢
新公眾碼頭
全記海鮮
Chuen Kee Seafood
勝記
Sai Kung Sing Kee
Lakeside Garden
六福菜館
Loaf On
西貢
SAI KUNG
新安村
Sun On
Tsuen
HIRAM'S HIGHWAY
西貢篤
Sai Kung Tuk
對面海
Tui Min Hoi
西貢戶外康樂中心
Sai Kung Outdoor
Recreation Centre
官門漁邨
碼頭
Pier
400m米(比例尺 Scale 1:13,323)
11

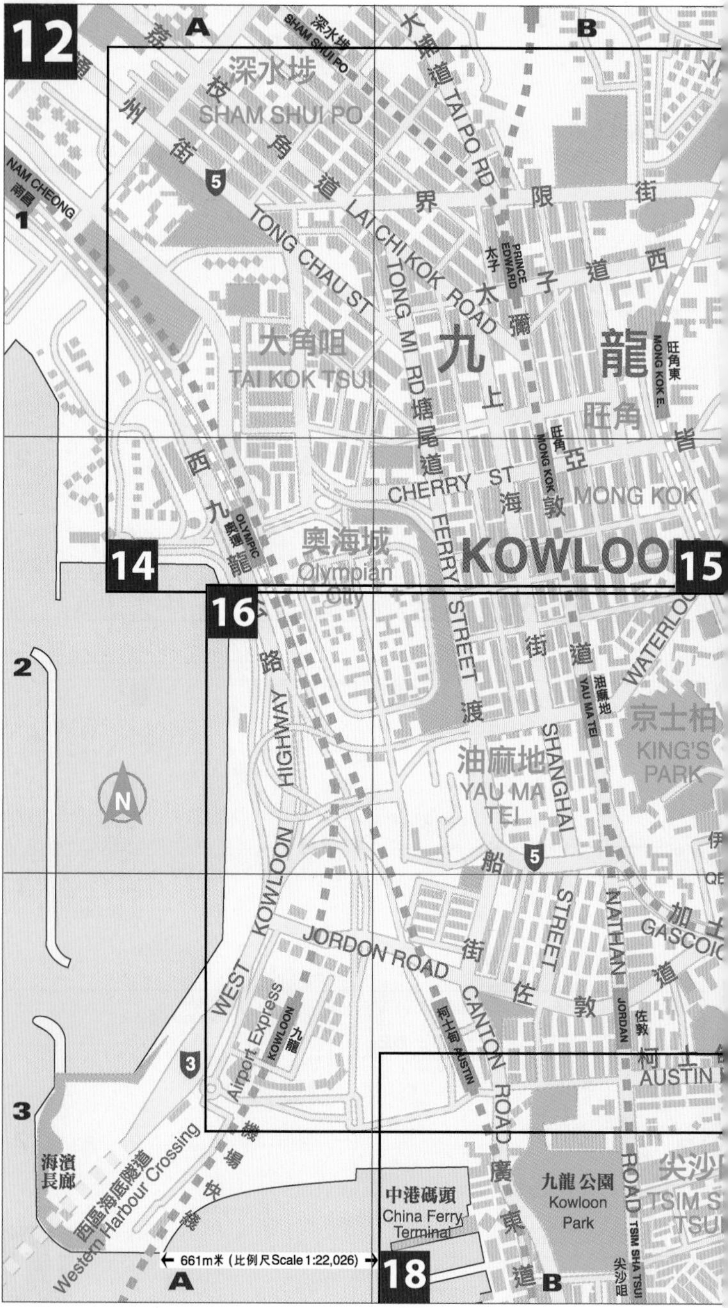
12
14
15
16
18
A
B
深水埗
SHAM SHUI PO
大角咀
TAI KOK TSUI
九龍
KOWLOON
旺角
MONG KOK
油麻地
YAU MA TEI
京士柏
KING'S PARK
奧海城
Olympian City
尖沙咀
TSIM SHA TSUI
九龍公園
Kowloon Park
中港碼頭
China Ferry Terminal
海濱長廊
TAI PO RD
LAI CHI KOK ROAD
TONG CHAU ST
TONG MI RD
CHERRY ST
FERRY STREET
WATERLOO
SHANGHAI STREET
NATHAN ROAD
GASCOIGNE
JORDON ROAD
CANTON ROAD
AUSTIN
WEST KOWLOON HIGHWAY
Airport Express
Western Harbour Crossing
西區海底隧道
NAM CHEONG
南昌
PRINCE EDWARD
太子
MONG KOK E.
旺角東
OLYMPIC
奧運
KOWLOON
九龍
AUSTIN
柯士甸
JORDAN
佐敦
YAU MA TEI
油麻地
TSIM SHA TSUI
尖沙咀
661m米 (比例尺Scale 1:22,026)

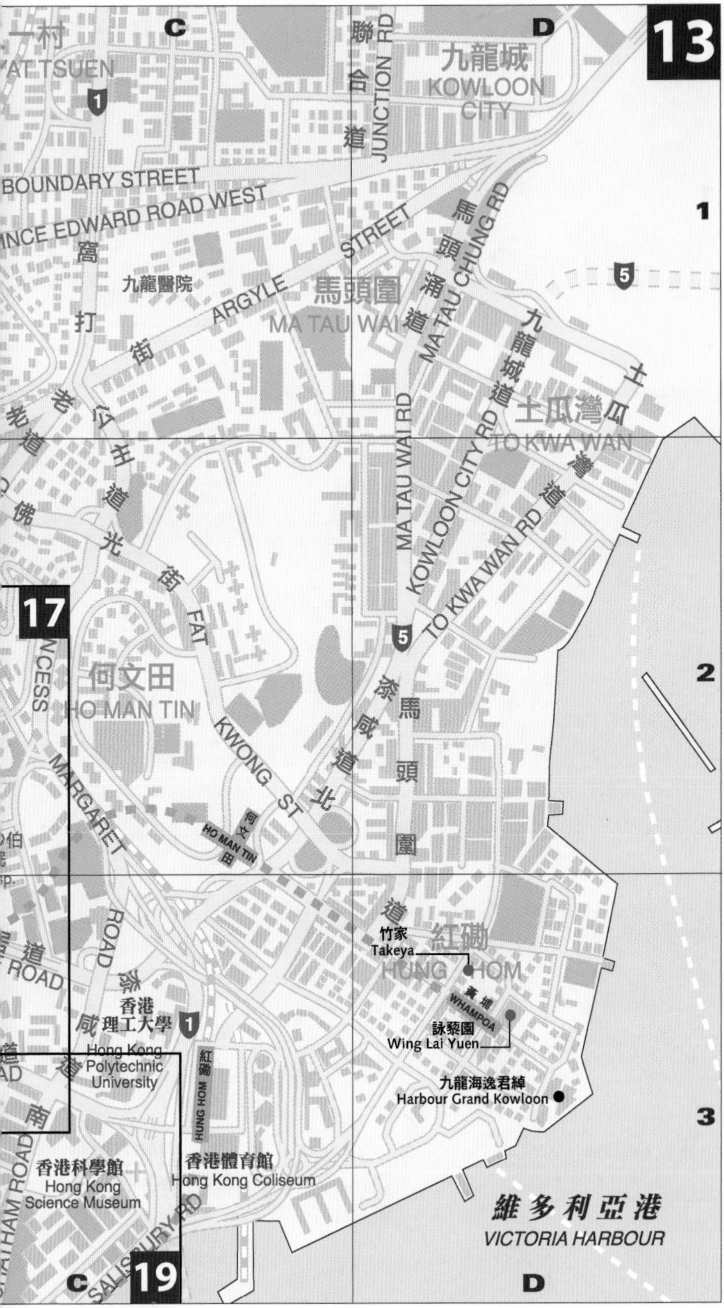
13
C
D
聯合道
JUNCTION RD
九龍城
KOWLOON CITY
BOUNDARY STREET
INCE EDWARD ROAD WEST
ARGYLE STREET
窩打老道
九龍醫院
馬頭圍
MA TAU WAI
馬頭涌道
MA TAU CHUNG RD
九龍城道
土瓜灣
TO KWA WAN
土瓜灣道
公主道
佛光街
MA TAU WAI RD
KOWLOON CITY RD
TO KWA WAN RD
17
何文田
HO MAN TIN
FAT KWONG ST
CESS
MARGARET ROAD
何文田
HO MAN TIN
漆咸道北
馬頭圍道
竹家
Takeya
紅磡
HUNG HOM
黃埔
WHAMPOA
詠藜園
Wing Lai Yuen
九龍海逸君綽
Harbour Grand Kowloon
香港理工大學
Hong Kong Polytechnic University
漆咸道南
紅磡
HUNG HOM
香港科學館
Hong Kong Science Museum
香港體育館
Hong Kong Coliseum
SALISBURY RD
19
維多利亞港
VICTORIA HARBOUR
1
2
3

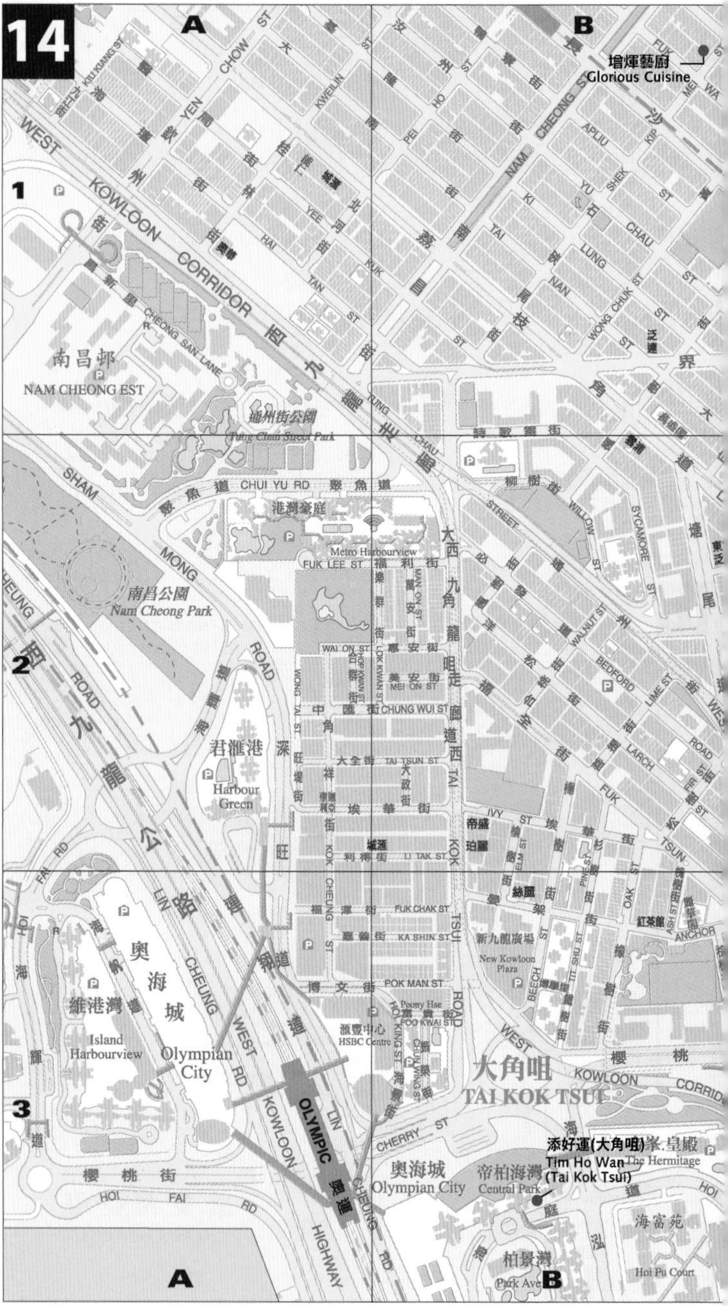
14
A
B
1
2
3
增輝藝廚
Glorious Cuisine
WEST KOWLOON CORRIDOR
南昌邨
NAM CHEONG EST
CHEONG SAN LANE
通州街公園
Tung Chau Street Park
CHUI YU RD
港灣豪庭
Metro Harbourview
FUK LEE ST
SHAM MONG ROAD
南昌公園
Nam Cheong Park
WAI ON ST
MEI ON ST
CHUNG WUI ST
TAI TSUN ST
LI TAK ST
FUK CHAK ST
KA SHIN ST
POK MAN ST
君滙港
Harbour Green
奧海城
Olympian City
維港灣
Island Harbourview
LIN CHEUNG RD
WEST KOWLOON HIGHWAY
OLYMPIC
奧運
匯豐中心
HSBC Centre
Peony Hse
FOO KWAI ST
TAI KOK TSUI ROAD
新九龍廣場
New Kowloon Plaza
大角咀
TAI KOK TSUI
CHERRY ST
HOI FAI RD
櫻桃街
帝柏海灣
Central Park
柏景灣
Park Ave
海富苑
Hoi Fu Court
添好運(大角咀)
Tim Ho Wan (Tai Kok Tsui)
The Hermitage
NAM CHEONG ST
APLIU ST
YU CHAU ST
TAI NAN ST
WONG CHUK ST
KWEILIN ST
YEN CHOW ST
PEI HO ST
KI LUNG ST
SHEK KIP MEI ST
FUK WA ST
TUNG CHAU ST
WILLOW ST
SYCAMORE ST
WALNUT ST
BEDFORD RD
LIME ST
LARCH ST
FIR ST
IVY ST
ELM ST
PINE ST
OAK ST
ASH ST
ANCHOR ST
BEECH ST
TIT SHU ST
HOI KING ST
CHUN WING ST
FUK TSUN ST
KOK CHEUNG ST
WONG TAI ST
HOP KWAN ST
LOK KWAN ST
NAN ON ST
KOWLOON CORRIDOR

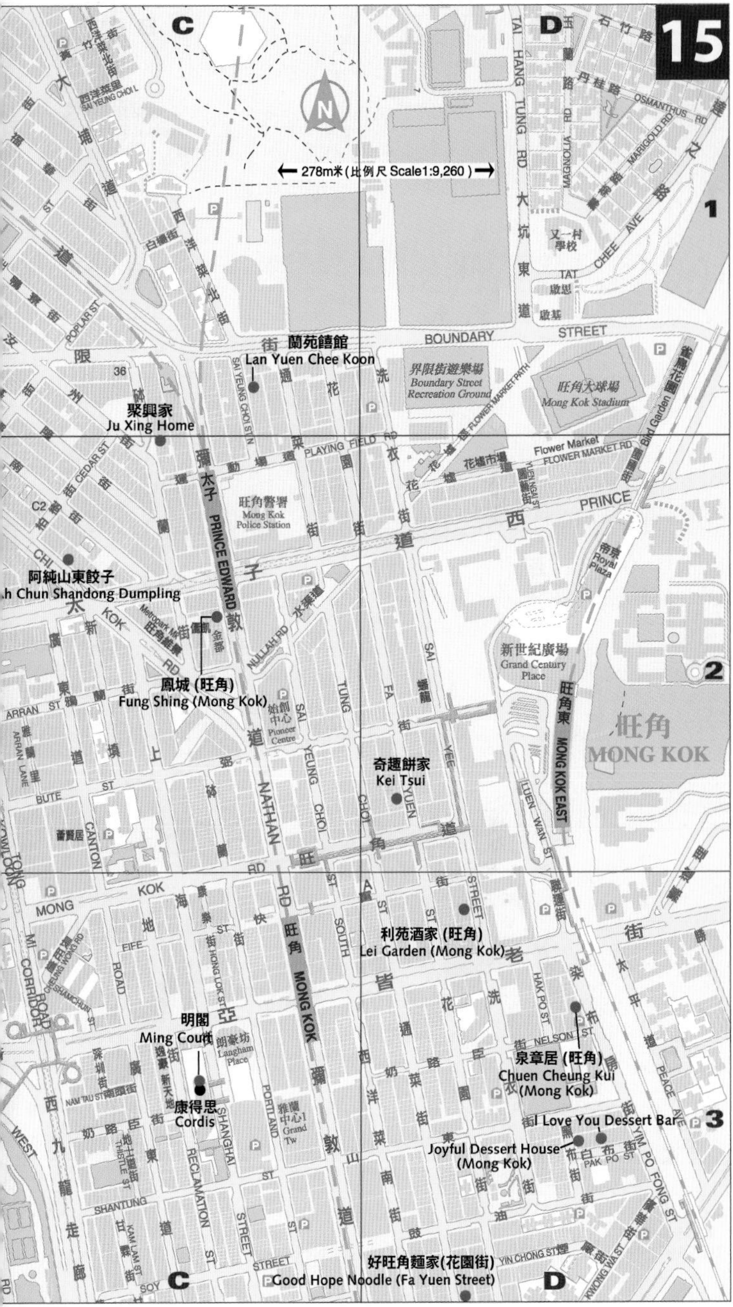
15
C
D
1
2
3
278m米 (比例尺 Scale1:9,260)
蘭苑饎館
Lan Yuen Chee Koon
聚興家
Ju Xing Home
阿純山東餃子
h Chun Shandong Dumpling
鳳城 (旺角)
Fung Shing (Mong Kok)
奇趣餅家
Kei Tsui
利苑酒家 (旺角)
Lei Garden (Mong Kok)
明閣
Ming Court
康得思
Cordis
泉章居 (旺角)
Chuen Cheung Kui
(Mong Kok)
I Love You Dessert Bar
Joyful Dessert House
(Mong Kok)
好旺角麵家(花園街)
Good Hope Noodle (Fa Yuen Street)
界限街遊樂場
Boundary Street
Recreation Ground
旺角大球場
Mong Kok Stadium
旺角警署
Mong Kok
Police Station
新世紀廣場
Grand Century
Place
帝京
Royal
Plaza
始創
中心
Pioneer
Centre
朗豪坊
Langham
Place
雅蘭
中心1
Grand
Tw
旺角
MONG KOK
BOUNDARY
STREET
PRINCE EDWARD
太子
PRINCE
NATHAN
RD
MONG KOK
旺角
MONG KOK EAST
旺角東
TAI HANG TUNG RD
大坑東道
CHEE AVE
OSMANTHUS RD
MARIGOLD RD
MAGNOLIA RD
PLAYING FIELD RD
FLOWER MARKET PATH
Flower Market
FLOWER MARKET RD
花墟市場
Bird Garden
YUEN NGAI ST
SAI YEUNG CHOI ST N
SAI YEUNG CHOI ST
TUNG CHOI ST
FA YUEN ST
SAI YEE ST
LUEN WAN ST
POPLAR ST
CEDAR ST
CHI KOK
NULLAH RD
ARRAN ST
ARRAN LANE
BUTE ST
CANTON RD
TONG MI RD
MONG KOK RD
FIFE ROAD
HONG LOK ST
SOUTH
ST
STREET
HAK PO ST
NELSON ST
PAK PO ST
PEACE AVE
YIM PO FONG ST
PORTLAND
RECLAMATION ST
SHANGHAI
SHANTUNG
KAM LAM ST
THISTLE ST
NAM TAU ST
CHEUNG WONG RD
SHAMCHUN ST
WEST KOWLOON CORRIDOR
KOWLOON
SOY
YIN CHONG ST
KWONG WA ST
36
C2
TAT
又一村
學校
西九龍走廊

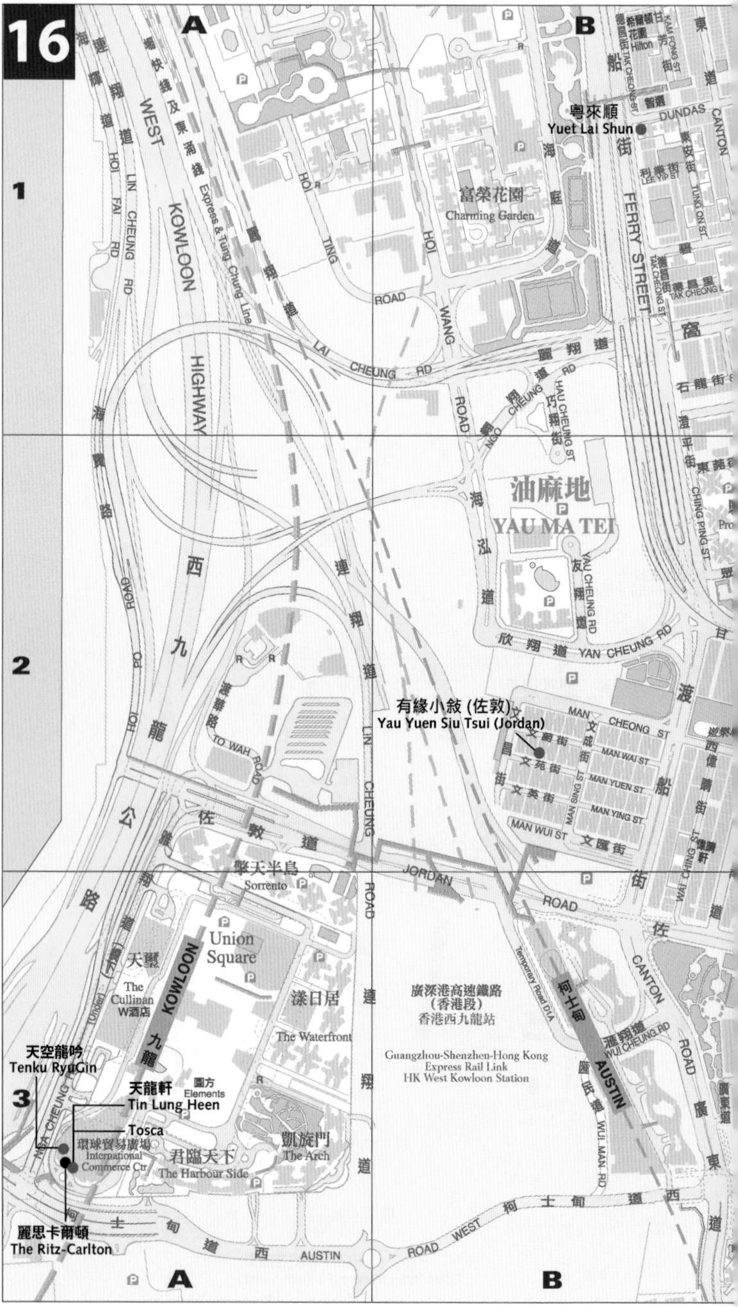
16
A
B
1
2
3
粵來順
Yuet Lai Shun
富榮花園
Charming Garden
油麻地
YAU MA TEI
有緣小敍 (佐敦)
Yau Yuen Siu Tsui (Jordan)
擎天半島
Sorrento
Union Square
天璽
The Cullinan
W酒店
漾日居
The Waterfront
廣深港高速鐵路
(香港段)
香港西九龍站
Guangzhou-Shenzhen-Hong Kong
Express Rail Link
HK West Kowloon Station
天空龍吟
Tenku RyuGin
天龍軒
Tin Lung Heen
圓方
Elements
Tosca
環球貿易廣場
International Commerce Ctr
君臨天下
The Harbour Side
凱旋門
The Arch
麗思卡爾頓
The Ritz-Carlton
WEST KOWLOON HIGHWAY
西九龍公路
機場快綫及東涌綫
Express & Tung Chung Line
LIN CHEUNG RD
HOI FAI RD
LAI CHEUNG RD
HOI TING ROAD
HOI WANG ROAD
FERRY STREET
NGO CHEUNG RD
HAU CHEUNG ST
YAU CHEUNG RD
YAN CHEUNG RD
TO WAH ROAD
LIN CHEUNG ROAD
JORDAN ROAD
佐敦道
MAN CHEONG ST
MAN WAI ST
MAN YUEN ST
MAN YING ST
MAN WUI ST
MAN SING ST
CANTON ROAD
AUSTIN ROAD WEST
柯士甸道西
AUSTIN
柯士甸
WUI CHEUNG RD
WUI MAN RD
Temporary Road D1A
DUNDAS
KAM FONG ST
TAK CHEONG ST
TAK CHEONG L
LEE YIP ST
TUNG ON ST
CHING PING ST
WAI CHING ST
Hilton
KOWLOON
九龍

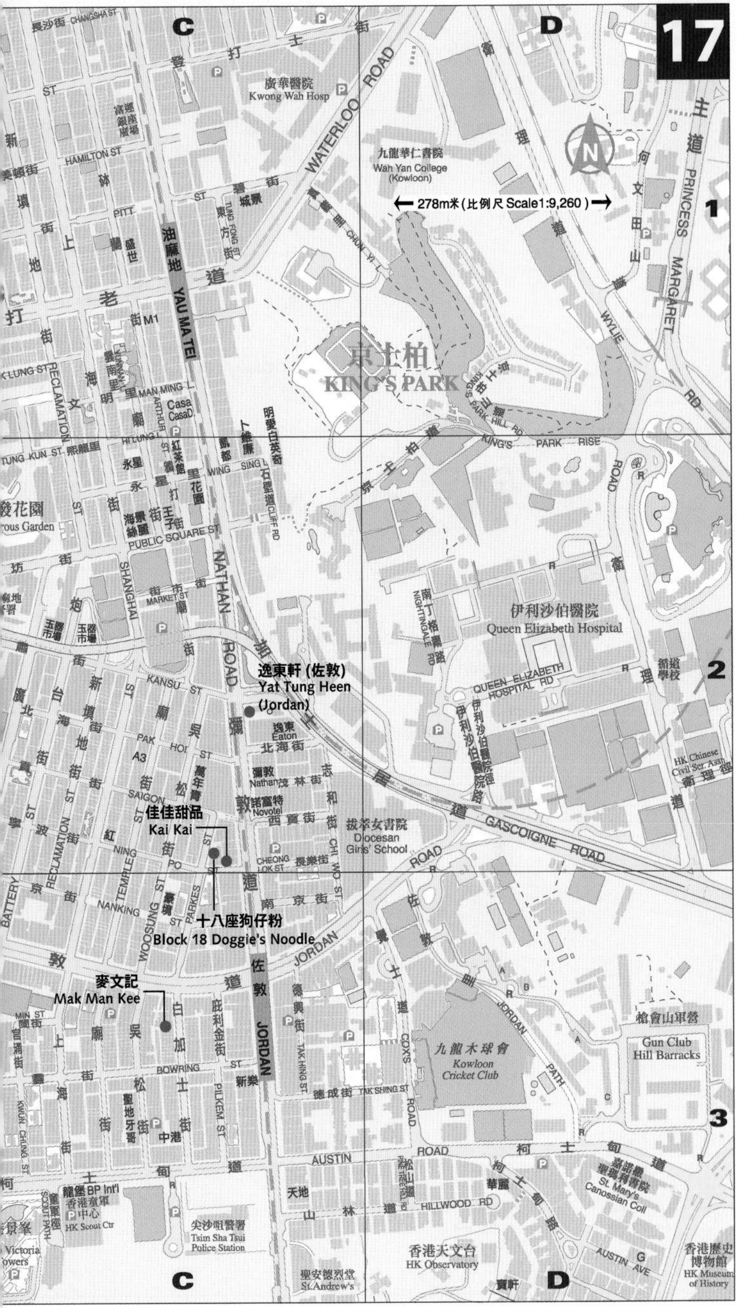
17
C
D
1
2
3
278m米 (比例尺 Scale1:9,260)
廣華醫院
Kwong Wah Hosp
九龍華仁書院
Wah Yan College (Kowloon)
京士柏
KING'S PARK
伊利沙伯醫院
Queen Elizabeth Hospital
逸東軒 (佐敦)
Yat Tung Heen (Jordan)
佳佳甜品
Kai Kai
十八座狗仔粉
Block 18 Doggie's Noodle
麥文記
Mak Man Kee
拔萃女書院
Diocesan Girls' School
九龍木球會
Kowloon Cricket Club
槍會山軍營
Gun Club Hill Barracks
尖沙咀警署
Tsim Sha Tsui Police Station
香港天文台
HK Observatory
香港歷史博物館
HK Museum of History
聖安德烈堂
St Andrew's
嘉諾撒聖瑪利書院
St. Mary's Canossian Coll
YAU MA TEI
油麻地
JORDAN
佐敦
NATHAN ROAD
GASCOIGNE ROAD
WATERLOO ROAD
PRINCESS MARGARET RD
AUSTIN ROAD
JORDAN ROAD
KING'S PARK RISE

18
A
B
1
2
3
柯士甸 AUSTIN
AUSTIN RD W 柯士甸道西
WUI MAN RD 匯民道
CANTON ROAD 廣東道
KWUN CHUNG ST 官涌街
SHANGHAI ST 上海街
TEMPLE ST 廟街
WOOSUNG ST 吳松街
PARKES ST 白加士街
PILKEM ST 庇利金街
San Diego 聖地牙哥
新樂 shamrock
恆豐 Prudential
柯士甸道
避風塘興記
Hing Kee
天地
港景峯 The Victoria Towers
龍堡 BP Int'l
香港童軍中心 HK Scout Ctr
童軍徑 SCOUT PATH
尖沙咀警署 Tsim Sha Tsui Police Station
富豪 (尖沙咀)
Fu Ho (Tsim Sha Tsui)
九龍公園游泳池 Swimming Pool
新同樂
Sun Tung Lok
翠亨邨 (尖沙咀)
Tsui Hang Village (Tsim Sha Tsui)
室內體育館 Sports Centre
地標 Landmark Centre - Piece
中港城 China HK City
國金軒(尖沙咀)
Cuisine Cuisine at The Mira
Whisk
The Mira
九龍公園
Park Lane Shopper's Boulevard 柏麗購物大道
彌敦道
皇家太平洋 Royal Pacific
港威大廈 Gateway
China Ferry Terminal 中港客運碼頭
香港文物探知館 HK Heritage Discovery Ctr
KOWLOON PARK
香港太子 Prince HK
海港城
唐人館 (尖沙咀)
China Tang (Tsim Sha Tsui)
九龍太平洋會
Sushi Tokami
(北座) 環球金融中心 World Finance Centre (南座)
清真寺 Jamia Masjid Islamic Centre
HAIPHONG RD 海防道
九龍公園徑
鼎泰豐 (新港中心)
Din Tai Fung (Silvercord)
新港中心 Silvercord
阿一海景飯店 (尖沙咀)
Ah Yat Harbour View (Tsim Sha Tsui)
TSIM SHA TSUI 尖沙咀
世界商業中心 World Comm Centre
新電訊中心 New T&T Centre
力寶太陽廣場 Lippo Sun Plaza
ASHLEY RD
HANKOW RD
LOCK RD
國際廣場 iSquare
GATEWAY BOULEVARD
HARBOUR CITY
朗廷
The Langham
唐閣
T'ang Court
Bostonian Seafood & Grill
Épure
海洋中心 Ocean Centre
PEKING RD 北京道
漢口中心 Hankow Ctr
京士(尖沙咀)
Qi (Tsim Sha Tsui)
九龍酒店 Kowloon
御寶軒
Imperial Treasure Fine Chinese Cuisine
KOWLOON PARK DRIVE
NATHAN ROAD
中間道
海運大廈 Ocean Terminal
馬哥孛羅香港 Marco Polo HK
夜上海 (尖沙咀)
Ye Shanghai (Tsim Sha Tsui)
基督教青年會 YMCA of HK
半島
The Peninsula
星光行 Star House
梳士巴利道
瑞樵閣
Chesa
香港太空館 HK Space Museum
吉地士
Gaddi's
嘉麟樓
Spring Moon
香港文化中心 HK Cultural Centre
鐘樓 Clock Tower
香港藝術館 HK Museum of Art
旅客諮詢中心 Visitor Info Centre
往中環 To Central
天星碼頭 Star Ferry Pier
往灣仔 To Wan Chai
九龍公眾碼頭 Kowloon Public Pier
尖沙咀
TSIM SHA TSUI
N
250m米(比例尺 Scale 1:8,333)

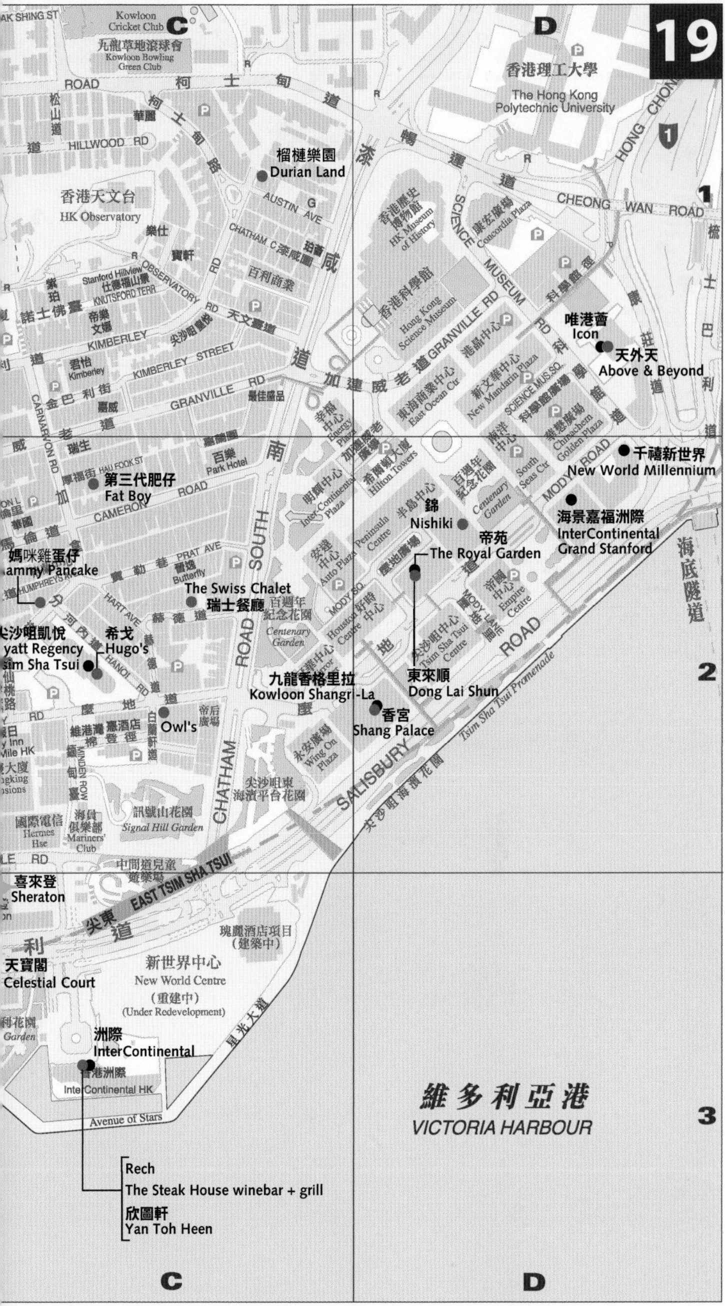
19
C
D
1
2
3
Kowloon Cricket Club
九龍草地滾球會
Kowloon Bowling Green Club
香港理工大學
The Hong Kong Polytechnic University
榴槤樂園
Durian Land
香港天文台
HK Observatory
AUSTIN AVE
CHATHAM RD
OBSERVATORY RD
KIMBERLEY RD
KIMBERLEY STREET
GRANVILLE RD
HILLWOOD RD
CARNARVON RD
CHEONG WAN ROAD
HONG CHONG
SCIENCE MUSEUM RD
GRANVILLE RD
香港歷史博物館
HK Museum of History
康宏廣場
Concordia Plaza
香港科學館
Hong Kong Science Museum
唯港薈
Icon
天外天
Above & Beyond
千禧新世界
New World Millennium
海景嘉福洲際
InterContinental Grand Stanford
MODY ROAD
第三代肥仔
Fat Boy
CAMERON ROAD
Park Hotel
媽咪雞蛋仔
ammy Pancake
PRAT AVE
HUMPHREYS AVE
HART AVE
HANOI RD
The Swiss Chalet
瑞士餐廳
尖沙咀凱悅
yatt Regency
sim Sha Tsui
希戈
Hugo's
CHATHAM ROAD SOUTH
錦
Nishiki
帝苑
The Royal Garden
Centenary Garden
Inter-Continental Plaza
Peninsula Centre
Auto Plaza
Houston Centre
MODY SQ.
Empire Centre
Tsim Sha Tsui Centre
South Seas Ctr
New Mandarin Plaza
East Ocean Ctr
Hilton Towers
Energy Plaza
Chinachem Golden Plaza
SCIENCE MUS.SQ.
東來順
Dong Lai Shun
九龍香格里拉
Kowloon Shangri-La
香宮
Shang Palace
Owl's
Wing On Plaza
SALISBURY ROAD
Tsim Sha Tsui Promenade
尖沙咀東海濱平台花園
訊號山花園
Signal Hill Garden
MINDEN ROW
Hermes Hse
Mariners' Club
海底隧道
喜來登
Sheraton
EAST TSIM SHA TSUI
瑰麗酒店項目（建築中）
天寶閣
Celestial Court
新世界中心
New World Centre
（重建中）
(Under Redevelopment)
洲際
InterContinental
香港洲際
InterContinental HK
Avenue of Stars
星光大道
Rech
The Steak House winebar + grill
欣圖軒
Yan Toh Heen
維多利亞港
VICTORIA HARBOUR

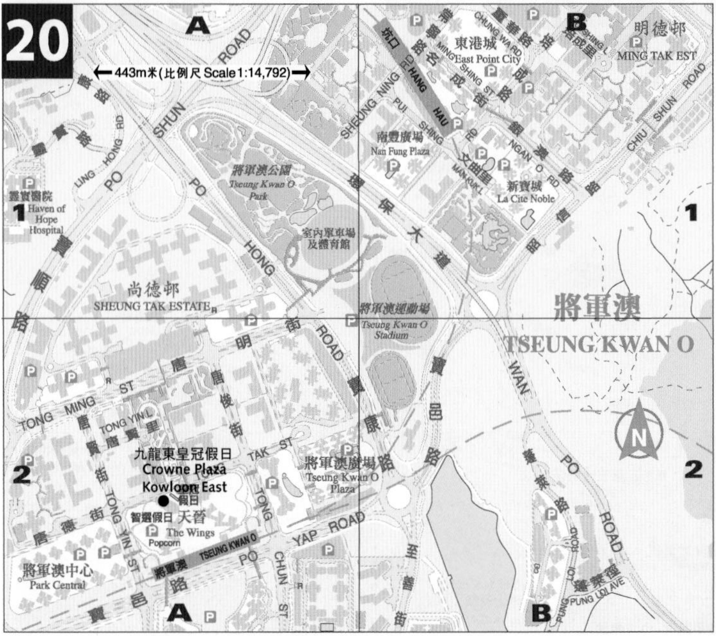

20
A
B
1
2
443m米(比例尺 Scale 1:14,792)
尚德邨
SHEUNG TAK ESTATE
將軍澳公園
Tseung Kwan O Park
室內單車場及體育館
將軍澳運動場
Tseung Kwan O Stadium
將軍澳
TSEUNG KWAN O
東港城
East Point City
南豐廣場
Nan Fung Plaza
新寶城
La Cite Noble
明德邨
MING TAK EST
靈實醫院
Haven of Hope Hospital
九龍東皇冠假日
Crowne Plaza Kowloon East
智選假日
天晉
The Wings
Popcorn
將軍澳廣場
Tseung Kwan O Plaza
將軍澳中心
Park Central
將軍澳
TSEUNG KWAN O
PO SHUN ROAD
PO HONG ROAD
LING HONG RD
TONG MING ST
TONG YIN ST
TONG YIN L
TAK ST
TONG CHUN ST
PO YAP ROAD
WAN PO ROAD
CHIU SHUN ROAD
SHEUNG NING RD
HANG HAU
PUI SHING RD
MING SHING ST
CHUNG WA RD
NGAN O RD
PUNG LOI RD
PUNG LOI AVE

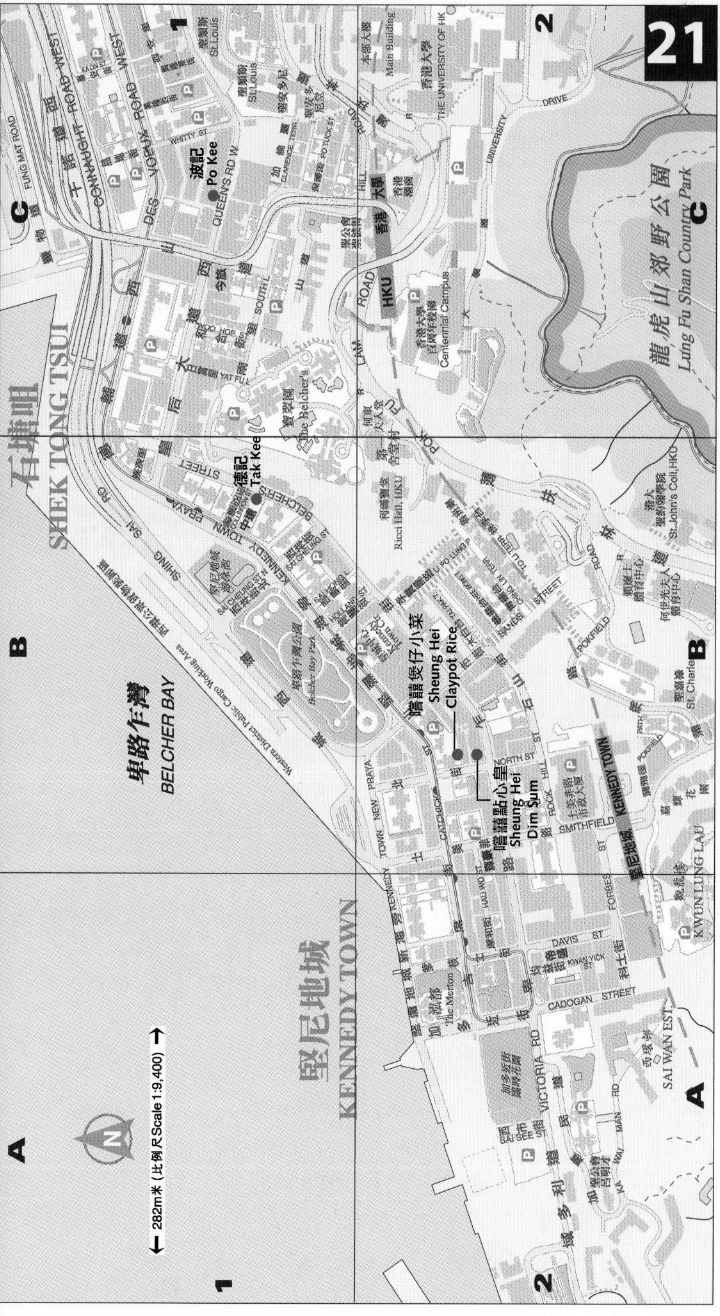
21
石塘咀
SHEK TONG TSUI
卑路乍灣
BELCHER BAY
堅尼地城
KENNEDY TOWN
龍虎山郊野公園
Lung Fu Shan Country Park
波記
Po Kee
德記
Tak Kee
嚐囍煲仔小菜
Sheung Hei Claypot Rice
嚐囍點心皇
Sheung Hei Dim Sum
HKU
香港大學
The Belcher's
Centennial Campus
Main Building
THE UNIVERSITY OF HK
Belcher Bay Park
The Merton
Western District Public Cargo Working Area
282m米 (比例尺Scale 1:9,400)
QUEEN'S RD W
DES VOEUX ROAD WEST
CONNAUGHT ROAD WEST
POKFIELD ROAD
VICTORIA RD
CATCHICK ST
KENNEDY TOWN PRAYA
NEW PRAYA KENNEDY TOWN
CADOGAN STREET
DAVIS ST
FORBES ST
SMITHFIELD
NORTH ST
SANDS STREET
UNIVERSITY DRIVE
KWUN LUNG LAU
SAI WAN EST.
Ricci Hall, HKU
St.John's Coll, HKU

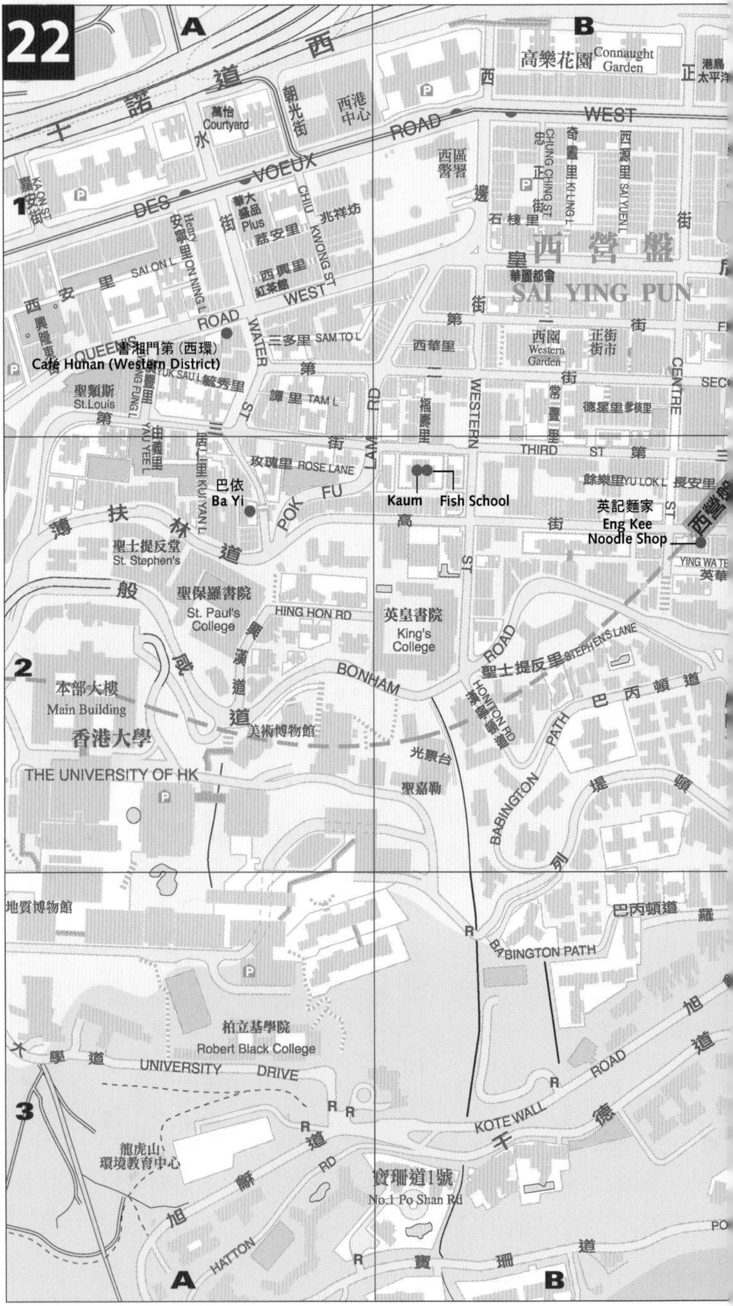
22
A
B
1
2
3
高樂花園 Connaught Garden
萬怡 Courtyard
西港中心
朝光街
DES VOEUX ROAD WEST
干諾道西
西區警署
CHUNG CHING ST
KI LING L
SAI YUEN L
石橋里
西營盤
SAI YING PUN
華大盛品 Plus
CHIU KWONG ST
兆祥坊
嘉安里
西興里
紅茶館
KA ON ST
Henry
安寧里 ON NING L
SAI ON L
QUEENS ROAD WEST
WATER ST
三多里 SAM TO L
書湘門第 (西環)
Cafe Hunan (Western District)
YUK SAU L 毓秀里
聖類斯 St.Louis
譚里 TAM L
西華里
西園 Western Garden
正街街市
德星里
多核里
CENTRE ST
WESTERN ST
福壽里
THIRD ST
玫瑰里 ROSE LANE
POK FU LAM RD
巴依 Ba Yi
Kaum
Fish School
餘樂里 YU LOK L
長安里
英記麵家
Eng Kee Noodle Shop
YING WA TE
英華
KU YAN L
YAU YEE L
由義里
居賢里
薄扶林道
聖士提反堂 St. Stephen's
般咸道
聖保羅書院 St. Paul's College
HING HON RD
興漢道
英皇書院 King's College
BONHAM RD
聖士提反里 ST. STEPHEN'S LANE
HONITON RD
巴丙頓道
本部大樓 Main Building
香港大學
THE UNIVERSITY OF HK
美術博物館
光景台
聖嘉勒
BABINGTON PATH
地質博物館
巴丙頓道
柏立基學院 Robert Black College
大學道 UNIVERSITY DRIVE
KOTEWALL ROAD
旭龢道
干德道
龍虎山環境教育中心
寶珊道1號 No.1 Po Shan Rd
HATTON RD
寶珊道

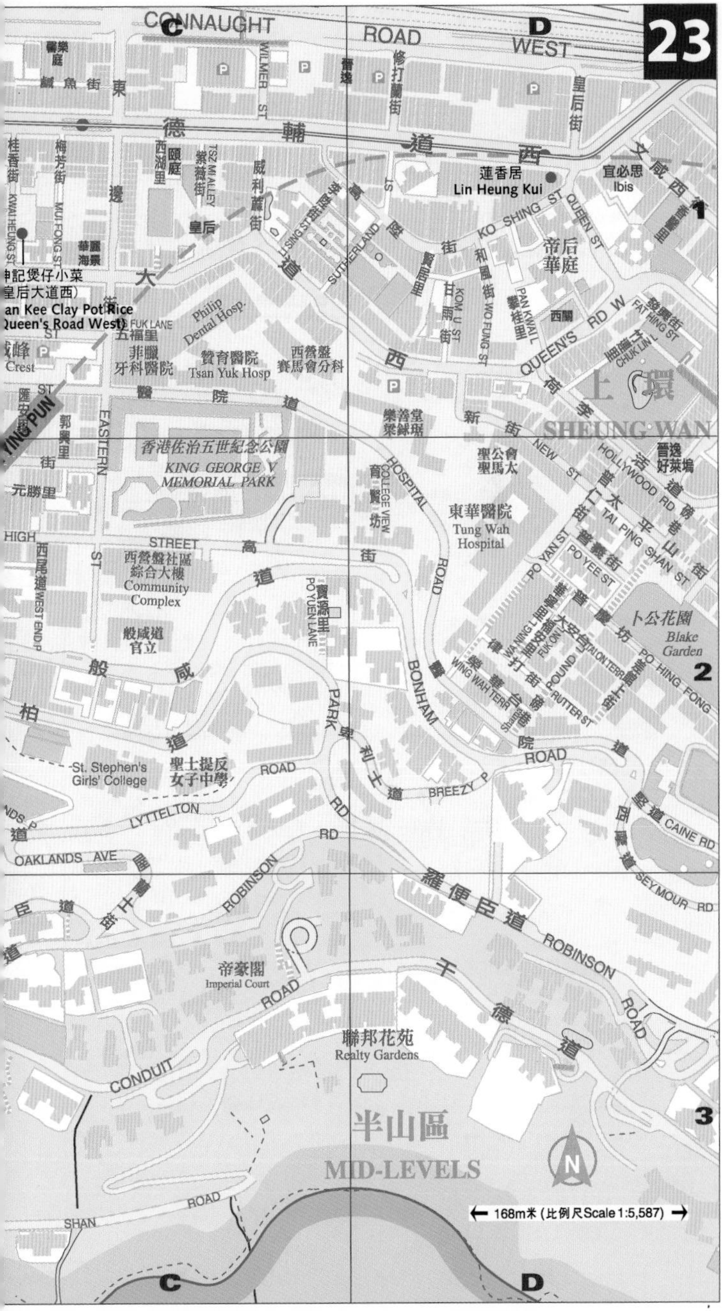

23
CONNAUGHT ROAD WEST
C
D
1
2
3
德輔道西
皇后街
修打蘭街
WILMER ST
威利麻街
TSZ MI ALLEY
紫薇街
西湖里
頤庭
桂香街
KWAI HEUNG ST
梅芳街
MUI FONG ST
華園
海景
皇后
蓮香居
Lin Heung Kui
宜必思
Ibis
文咸西街
KO SHING ST
QUEEN ST
高陞街
帝后
華庭
LI SING ST
SUTHERLAND ST
寶慶里
和風街
WO FUNG ST
甘雨街
KOM U ST
PAN KWAI L
攀桂里
西關
QUEEN'S RD W
發興街
FAT HING ST
竹連里
CHUK LIN L
上環
SHEUNG WAN
坤記煲仔小菜
(皇后大道西)
Kwan Kee Clay Pot Rice
(Queen's Road West)
FUK LANE
五福里
菲臘
牙科醫院
Philip
Dental Hosp.
贊育醫院
Tsan Yuk Hosp
西營盤
賽馬會分科
威峰
Crest
匯安里
郭興里
EASTERN ST
醫院道
西
新街
NEW ST
荷李活道
HOLLYWOOD RD
香港佐治五世紀念公園
KING GEORGE V
MEMORIAL PARK
樂善堂
樂銖瑶
聖公會
聖馬太
晉逸
好萊塢
育賢坊
COLLEGE VIEW
HOSPITAL ROAD
東華醫院
Tung Wah
Hospital
普仁街
太平山街
TAI PING SHAN ST
元勝里
HIGH STREET
高街
西尾道
WEST END P
西營盤社區
綜合大樓
Community
Complex
PO YAN ST
普義街
PO YEE ST
寶源里
PO YUEN LANE
卜公花園
Blake
Garden
般咸道
官立
WING WAH TERR
WA NING L
FUK ON L
大安台
TAI ON TERR
POUND L
RUTTER ST
PO HING FONG
普慶坊
BONHAM ROAD
柏道
St. Stephen's
Girls' College
聖士提反
女子中學
ROAD
PARK RD
東利士道
BREEZY P
堅道
CAINE RD
LYTTELTON
OAKLANDS AVE
RD
西摩道
SEYMOUR RD
羅便臣道
ROBINSON ROAD
ROBINSON
帝豪閣
Imperial Court
干德道
ROAD
聯邦花苑
Realty Gardens
CONDUIT
半山區
MID-LEVELS
N
SHAN ROAD
168m米 (比例尺Scale 1:5,587)

24
A
B
HK-MACAU FERRY TERMINAL
港澳碼頭
信德中心
Shun Tak Ctr
招商局大廈
China Merchants Tower
林士街多層停車場
干諾道西
干諾道中
上環 SHEUNG WAN
NEW MARKET ST
西港城
Western Market
Queen's Terrace
QUEEN'S RD W
BONHAM
WING LOK ST
TUNG LOI L
陳勤記鹵鵝飯店(上環)
Chan Kan Kee Chiu Chow
(Sheung Wan)
永安中心
Wing On Centre
無限極廣場
Infinitus Plaza
桃花源小廚 (上環)
Tim's Kitchen (Sheung Wan)
新園興記
Sun Yuen Hing Kee
荷李活道公園
Hollywood Road Park
SHEUNG WAN
Tate
Upper Modern Bistro
STRAND
中遠大廈
Cosco Tower
新紀元廣場
Grand Millennium Plaza
志魂
Sushi Shikon
Sushi
Wadatsumi
馨樂庭尚圜
Citadines Mercer
JERVOIS
Frantzén's Kitchen
卜公花園
Blake Garden
PO HING FONG
Bibo
麵鮮醬油房周月(中環)
Shugetsu Ramen
(Central)
Beet
VEA
One96
大班樓
The Chairman
九記
Kau Kee
GOUGH ST
名人坊
Celebrity Cuisine
蘭桂坊
Lan Kwai Fong
文武廟
Man Mo Temple
荷李活華庭
Hollywood Terrace
聚賢居
Centre Stage
BRIDGES ST
香港醫學博物館
HK Museum of Medical Sciences
CAINE LANE
WING LEE ST
合一堂
2
英華女學校
Ying Wah Girls' Sch
香港花園
HK Garden
SEYMOUR
一宝
Ippoh
HOLLYWOOD
木的地
蜜斗
The Noodle Hive
美麗台
Merry Terr
美麗閣
Merry Court
CASTLE RD
富景花園
Scenic Heights
猶太廟
Ohel Leah Synagogue
雍景台
Robinson Place
高雲台
Goldwin Heights
Belon
Le Souk
SOHO
ELGIN ST
STAUNTON
Escalator
Steak on Elgin
Blessings Garden
Excelsior Ct
Buxey Lodge
永德山莊
Scenecliff
雅賓利
Arts Mansion
康威園
Conway Mansion
康苑
Cliffview Mansions
慧明苑
Elegant Terr
清真禮拜堂
Jamia Mosque
嘉諾撒聖心商學書院
Sacred Heart Canossian College of Commerce
嘉兆臺
The Grand Panorama
CONDUIT ROAD
ROBINSON ROAD
MOSQUE JUNCTION
3
216m米(比例尺 Scale 1:7,194)
全景大廈
Panorama
中環（中區）
CENTRAL DISTRICT
N
A
B
ROBINSON

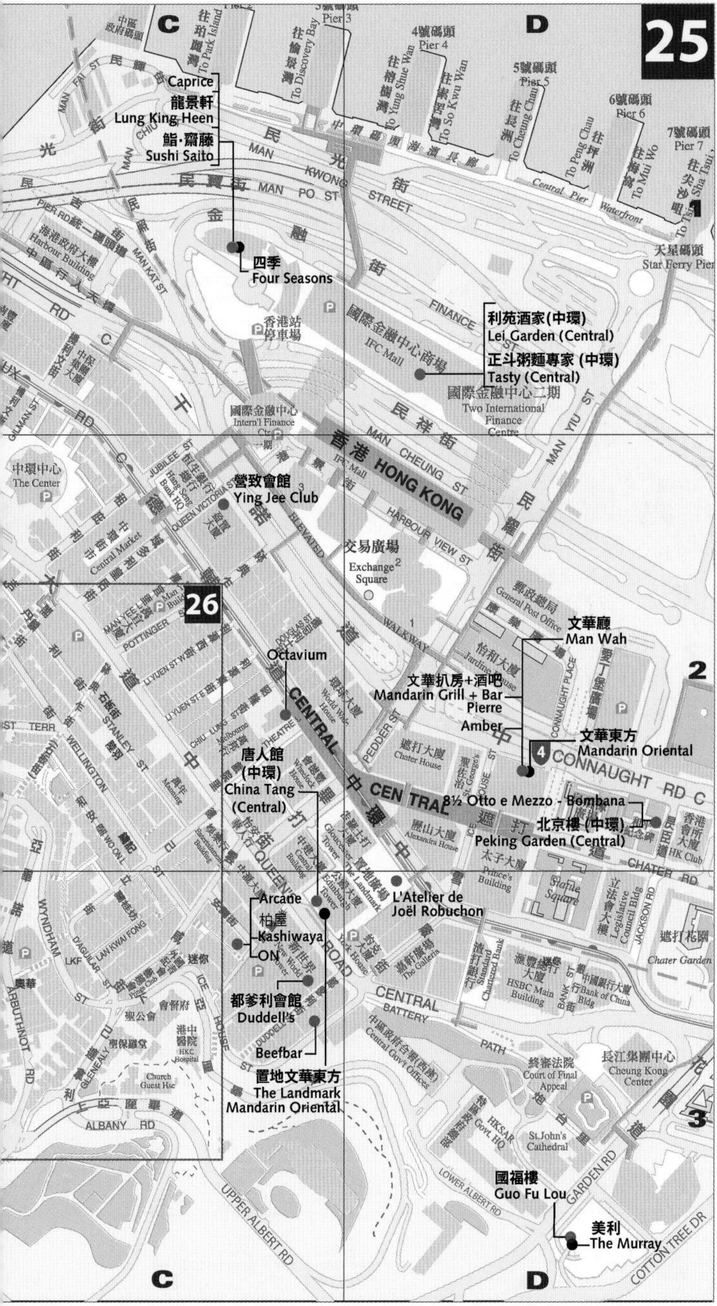
25
26
C
D
1
2
3
Caprice
龍景軒
Lung King Heen
鮨·齋藤
Sushi Saito
四季
Four Seasons
利苑酒家(中環)
Lei Garden (Central)
正斗粥麵專家 (中環)
Tasty (Central)
營致會館
Ying Jee Club
Octavium
文華廳
Man Wah
文華扒房+酒吧
Mandarin Grill + Bar
Pierre
Amber
文華東方
Mandarin Oriental
唐人館
(中環)
China Tang
(Central)
8½ Otto e Mezzo - Bombana
北京樓 (中環)
Peking Garden (Central)
Arcane
柏屋
Kashiwaya
ON
L'Atelier de
Joël Robuchon
都爹利會館
Duddell's
Beefbar
置地文華東方
The Landmark
Mandarin Oriental
國福樓
Guo Fu Lou
美利
The Murray
天星碼頭
Star Ferry Pier
國際金融中心商場
IFC Mall
國際金融中心二期
Two International Finance Centre
交易廣場
Exchange Square
中環中心
The Center
香港站停車場
HONG KONG
CENTRAL
CONNAUGHT RD C
CHATER RD
QUEEN'S ROAD
Central Market
Chater House
Alexandra House
Prince's Building
Statue Square
Legislative Council Bldg
HSBC Main Building
Bank of China Bldg
Chater Garden
Court of Final Appeal
Cheung Kong Center
St.John's Cathedral
Central Govt Offices
HKSAR Govt. HQ
General Post Office
Jardine House
World Wide House
The Landmark
The Galleria
HKC Hospital
Church Guest Hse
LKF
WYNDHAM
ARBUTHNOT RD
ALBANY RD
UPPER ALBERT RD
LOWER ALBERT RD
GARDEN RD
COTTON TREE DR
MAN YIU ST
FINANCE ST
HARBOUR VIEW ST
MAN CHEUNG ST
MAN KWONG STREET
MAN PO ST
PEDDER ST
CONNAUGHT PLACE
CENTRAL BATTERY PATH
Central Pier Waterfront

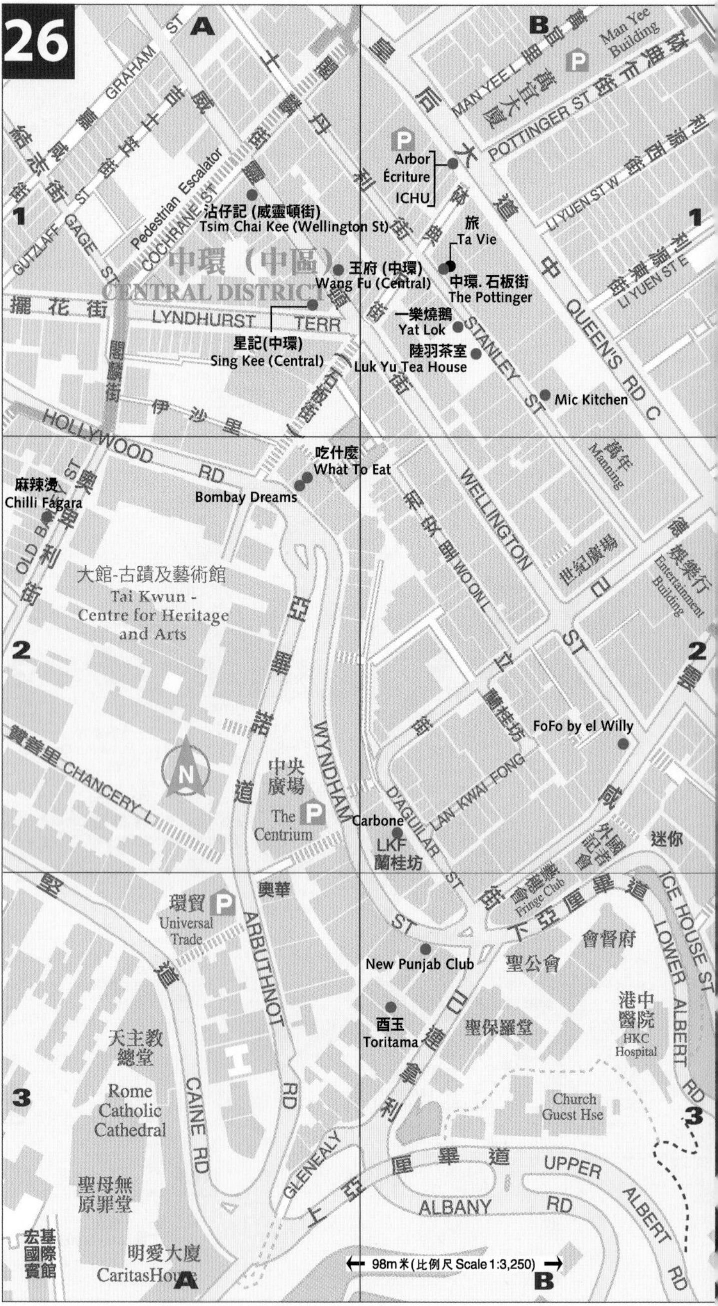
26
A
B
1
2
3
中環（中區）
CENTRAL DISTRICT
沾仔記 (威靈頓街)
Tsim Chai Kee (Wellington St)
王府 (中環)
Wang Fu (Central)
星記(中環)
Sing Kee (Central)
Arbor
Écriture
ICHU
旅
Ta Vie
中環. 石板街
The Pottinger
一樂燒鵝
Yat Lok
陸羽茶室
Luk Yu Tea House
Mic Kitchen
吃什麼
What To Eat
Bombay Dreams
麻辣燙
Chilli Fagara
大館-古蹟及藝術館
Tai Kwun -
Centre for Heritage
and Arts
FoFo by el Willy
Carbone
LKF
蘭桂坊
中央廣場
The Centrium
環貿
Universal Trade
奧華
New Punjab Club
西玉
Toritama
天主教總堂
Rome Catholic Cathedral
聖母無原罪堂
明愛大廈
CaritasHouse
宏基國際賓館
聖公會
會督府
聖保羅堂
港中醫院
HKC Hospital
Church Guest Hse
Fringe Club
Man Yee Building
Entertainment Building
Manning
世紀廣場
迷你
GRAHAM ST
GAGE ST
GUTZLAFF ST
COCHRANE ST
Pedestrian Escalator
LYNDHURST TERR
HOLLYWOOD RD
OLD BAILEY ST
CHANCERY L
WYNDHAM ST
ARBUTHNOT RD
CAINE RD
GLENEALY
D'AGUILAR ST
LAN KWAI FONG
WO ON L
WELLINGTON ST
STANLEY ST
QUEEN'S RD C
POTTINGER ST
MAN YEE L
LI YUEN ST W
LI YUEN ST E
ICE HOUSE ST
LOWER ALBERT RD
UPPER ALBERT RD
ALBANY RD
98m 米(比例尺 Scale 1:3,250)

27
A
B
250m米 (比例尺 Scale 1:8,333)
金鐘
ADMIRALTY
解放軍碼頭 PLA Berth
中西區海濱長廊
Central & Western District Promenade
EDINBURGH PLACE
大會堂
CITY HALL
龍和道
LUNG WO ROAD
中環軍營
Central Barracks
中國人民解放軍駐香港部隊大廈
添華道
TIM WA AVE
行政長官辦公室
立法會綜合大樓
Legislative Council Complex
LEGISLATIVE COUNCIL RD
分域碼頭
Fenwick Pier
干諾道中
夏愨道
CHATER RD
和記大廈
Hutchison House
美國銀行中心
Bank of America Tower
遮打花園
Chater Garden
MURRAY RD
LAMBETH WALK
美利道多層停車場
香港特別行政區政府總部
Hong Kong SAR Central Government Offices
添美道
TIM MEI AVE
中信大廈
Citic Tower
紅十字會總部
HK Red Cross Headquarters
FENWICK PIER ST
HARCOURT ROAD
遠東金融中心
Far East Fin Ctr
海富中心
Admiralty Centre
力寶大廈 II
Lippo Tw II
力寶中心
Lippo Ctr
力寶大廈 I
Lippo Tw I
中銀大廈
Bank of China Tower
COTTON TREE DRIVE
金鐘
ADMIRALTY
金鐘廊
Queensway Plaza
DRAKE ST
統一中心
United Ctr
MTR Construction Site
港鐵工地
夏愨花園
Harcourt Garden
(臨時封閉)
堅偉樓
Caine House
警政大樓
Arsenal House
警察總部
Police Headquarters
警政大樓東翼
Arsenal House East Wing
ARSENAL ST
花旗銀行廣場
Citibank Plaza
茶具文物館
Museum of Tea Ware
羅桂祥茶藝館
KC Lo Gallery
高等法院
High Court
金鐘道政府合署
Queensway Gov't Offices
QUEENSWAY
一座
One
香港公園
HONG KONG PARK
港島香格里拉
Island Shangri-La
太古廣場
PACIFIC PLACE
港麗
Conrad
Conrad Hotel
JW Marriott
Upper House
PARK AVENUE
Café Gray Deluxe
QUEEN'S ROAD EAST
皇后大道東
Three Pacific Place
KENNEDY ROAD
夏宮
Summer Palace
珀翠
Petrus
SUPREME COURT RD
JUSTICE DRIVE
JW萬豪
JW Marriott
奕居
The Upper House
英國文化協會
British Council
美國總領事館
British Consulate
MONMOUTH TERR
STAR ST
MOON ST
SUN ST
ELECTRIC ST
堅尼地道
中國外交部駐港特派員公署
BORRETT ROAD
BOWEN ROAD
港燈中心
HK Electric Ctr
BOWEN DRIVE
寶雲道
港島學校
Island School
Island Club
寶雲道花園
馬己仙峽道
Magazine Gap Towers
馬己仙
Magazine Heights
MAGAZINE GAP ROAD
PEAK ROAD
1
2
3

28
A
B
N
236m米 (比例尺 Scale 1:7,851)
1
2
3
博覽海濱花園
Expo Promenade
金紫荊廣場
Golden Bauhi
博覽道
香港會議展覽中心新翼
HKCEC New Wing
貿易發展局商貿資訊中心
TDC Business InfoCen
EXPO DRIVE
博覽道中 EXPO DRIVE CENTR
新滬坊
New Shangha
LUNG WO ROAD 龍和道
Grand Hyatt Steakhouse
港灣壹號
One Harbour Road
君悅
Grand Hyatt
分域碼頭
Fenwick Pier
LUNG KING ST
CONVENTION
會議道
香港會議展覽中心
HK Convention & Exhibition Centre
(往會場入口)
LEGISLATIVE COUNCIL
龍匯道
LUNG WUI RD
PIER ST
分域碼頭街
中信大廈
Citic Tower
紅十字會總部
HK Red Cross Headquarters
PERFORMING ARTS AV
FENWICK
香港演藝學院
HK Academy for Performing Arts
FENWICK ST
香港藝術中心
Art Centre
YMCA
瑞安中心
Shui On Centre
灣仔政府大樓
Wanchai Tower
港灣消防局
入境事務大樓
Immigration Tower
中環廣場
Central Pla
電訊大廈
Telecom House
稅務大樓
Revenue Tower
TIM MEI AVE
夏慤道
告士打道
GLOUC
4
堅偉樓
Caine House
美國萬通大廈
Mass Mutual Tower
夏慤大廈
Harcourt House
東亞銀行港灣中心
Bank of East Asia
六國
Luk Kwok
大新金融
Dah S Financia
港鐵工地
夏慤花園
Harcourt Garden
(暫時封閉)
警政大樓
Arsenal House
警察總部
Police Headquarters
警政大樓東翼
Arsenal House East Wing
ARSENAL ST
家全七福
Seventh Son
莎巴 (灣仔)
Sabah (Wan Chai)
車氏粵菜軒
Che's
留園雅敘
Liu Yuan Pavilion
新榮記
Xin Rong Ji
生記
Sang Kee
中國海外
QUEENSWAY
軒尼詩道
益新
Yixin
灣仔 WAN CHAI
JW Marriott
萬豪
遨舍衛蘭軒
Ozo Wesley
Wesley
ANTON ST
LANDALE ST
Butchers club
福臨門 (灣仔)
Fook Lam Moon (Wan Chai)
修頓中心
Southorn Centre
修頓遊樂場
Southorn Playground
修頓體育館
Southorn Stadium
Three Pacific Place
Le Garçon Saigon
Giando
Brass Spoon (Wan Chai)
LUARD RD
GRESSON ST
LUN FAT ST
Kelly's Cape Bop
O'BRIEN RD
星域軒
Star Crest
STAR ST
MOON ST
SUN ST
Akrame
SHIP ST
TAI WO ST
Bo Innovation
峇 (灣仔)
Qi (Wan Chai)
SWATOW ST
AMOY ST
LEE TUNG ST
SPRING GARDEN L
CROSS ST
STONE NULLAH
MONMOUTH TERR
洪聖廟
KENNEDY ROAD
St. Francis' Canossian
嘉諾撒聖方濟各書院
TAI YUEN ST
英迪格
Indigo
寶雲道網球場
BOWEN DRIVE
合和中心
Hopewell Ctr
QUEEN'S RO
胡忠大廈
Wu Chung Hse
FUNG WONG TERR
香港鄧鏡波書院
堅尼地道
BOWEN ROAD
寶雲道
A
B

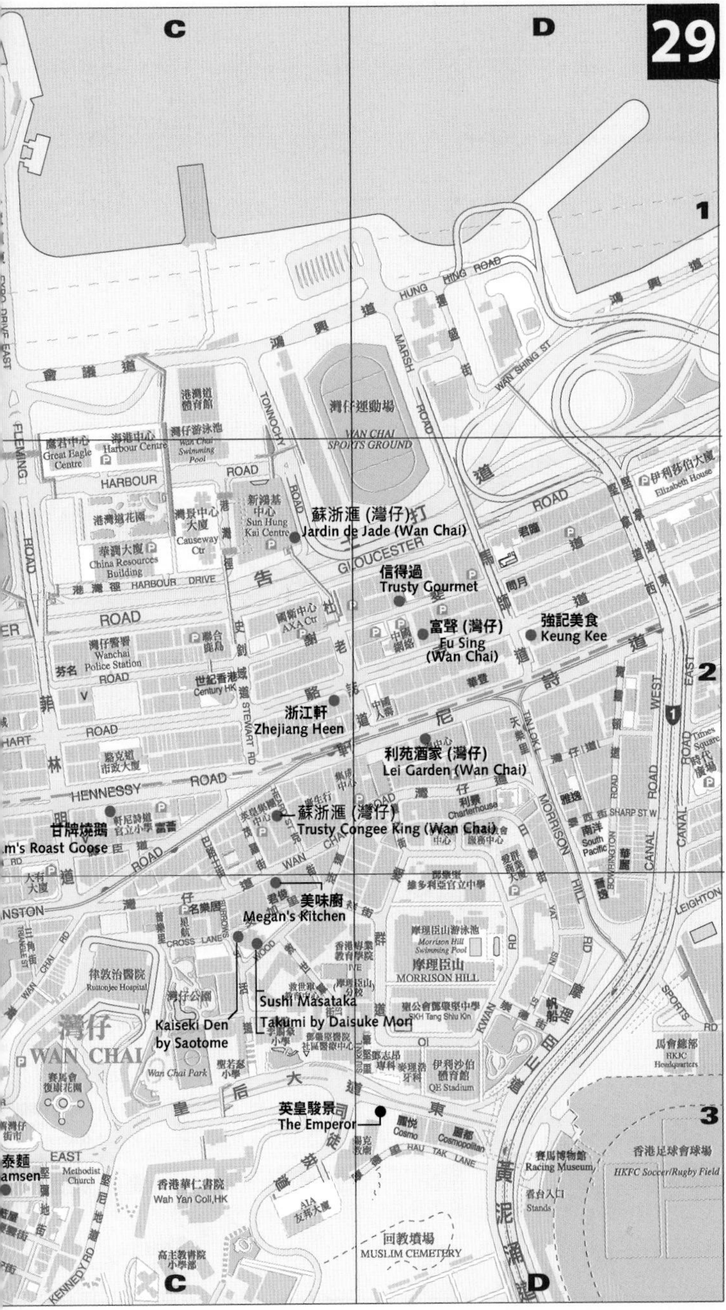
29
C
D
1
2
3
蘇浙滙 (灣仔)
Jardin de Jade (Wan Chai)
信得過
Trusty Gourmet
富聲 (灣仔)
Fu Sing
(Wan Chai)
強記美食
Keung Kee
浙江軒
Zhejiang Heen
利苑酒家 (灣仔)
Lei Garden (Wan Chai)
蘇浙滙 (灣仔)
Trusty Congee King (Wan Chai)
甘牌燒鵝
m's Roast Goose
美味廚
Megan's Kitchen
Sushi Masataka
Takumi by Daisuke Mori
Kaiseki Den
by Saotome
英皇駿景
The Emperor
泰麵
amsen
灣仔運動場
WAN CHAI
SPORTS GROUND
Great Eagle
Centre
Harbour Centre
Sun Hung
Kai Centre
Causeway
Ctr
China Resources
Building
Wanchai
Police Station
Century HK
AXA Ctr
Elizabeth House
Times
Square
Ruttonjee Hospital
灣仔
WAN CHAI
Wan Chai Park
Morrison Hill
Swimming Pool
MORRISON HILL
SKH Tang Shiu Kin
QE Stadium
HKJC
Headquarters
Racing Museum
HKFC Soccer/Rugby Field
Stands
Wah Yan Coll,HK
Methodist
Church
回教墳場
MUSLIM CEMETERY
Cosmo
Cosmopolitan
South
Pacific
Charterhouse
HARBOUR
ROAD
GLOUCESTER
HARBOUR DRIVE
HENNESSY
ROAD
STEWART RD
TONNOCHY
ROAD
MARSH
ROAD
HUNG HING ROAD
WAN SHING ST
FLEMING
ROAD
MORRISON
HILL
RD
CANAL
ROAD
WEST
EAST
SHARP ST W
BOWRINGTON
LEIGHTON
SPORTS
RD
HAU TAK LANE
CROSS LANE
WOOD
KWAN
KENNEDY RD
EXPO DRIVE EAST

30
A
B
N
161m米(比例尺 Scale 1:5,376)
1
2
3
奇力島
KELLETT ISLAND
香港遊艇會
Royal
HK Yacht Club
海底隧道
CROSS HARBOUR TUNNEL
警官俱樂部
Police
Officers Club
臨時直升機坪
HUNG HING RD
鴻興道
WAN SHING ST
運盛街
告士
CANNON ST
景隆街
信和廣場
Sino
鵬利中心
太湖海鮮城(銅鑼灣)
Tai Woo (Causeway Bay)
富臨飯店
Forum
ROAD
MARSH RD
GLOUCESTER ROAD
伊利莎伯大廈
Elizabeth House
PERCIVAL STREET
蛇王二
She Wong Yee
ROAD
JAFFE
堅拿道
銅鑼灣廣場二期
Involtini
LOCKHART
馬師道
斐道
謝斐道
駱克道
東
西
銅鑼灣
利園山道
何洪記
Ho Hung Kee
啟
KAI CH
軒尼詩道
TANG LUNG ST
登龍街
豫園
Shanghai Yu Yuan
La Bombance
RUSSELL ST
羅素街
時代廣場
Times Square
勿地臣街
波斯富街
LEE GARDEN
利舞臺廣場
Lee Theatre Plaza
SHARP ST EAST
霎東街
莆田(銅鑼灣
Putien
(Causeway Ba
禮頓中心
Leighton Ctr
YIU WA ST
耀華街
MATHESON ST
滬江(銅鑼灣
Wu Kong
(Causeway Ba
禮頓道
EAST ROAD
WEST
天樂里
TIN LOK L
寶靈頓道
灣仔道
SHARP ST W
霎西街
BOWRINGTON ROAD
CANAL ROAD
伊斯蘭中心
愛群商業大廈
Guardian House
日善街
MORRISON HILL
LEIGHTON ROAD
皇冠假日
Crowne Plaza
禮頓山
LEIGHTON H

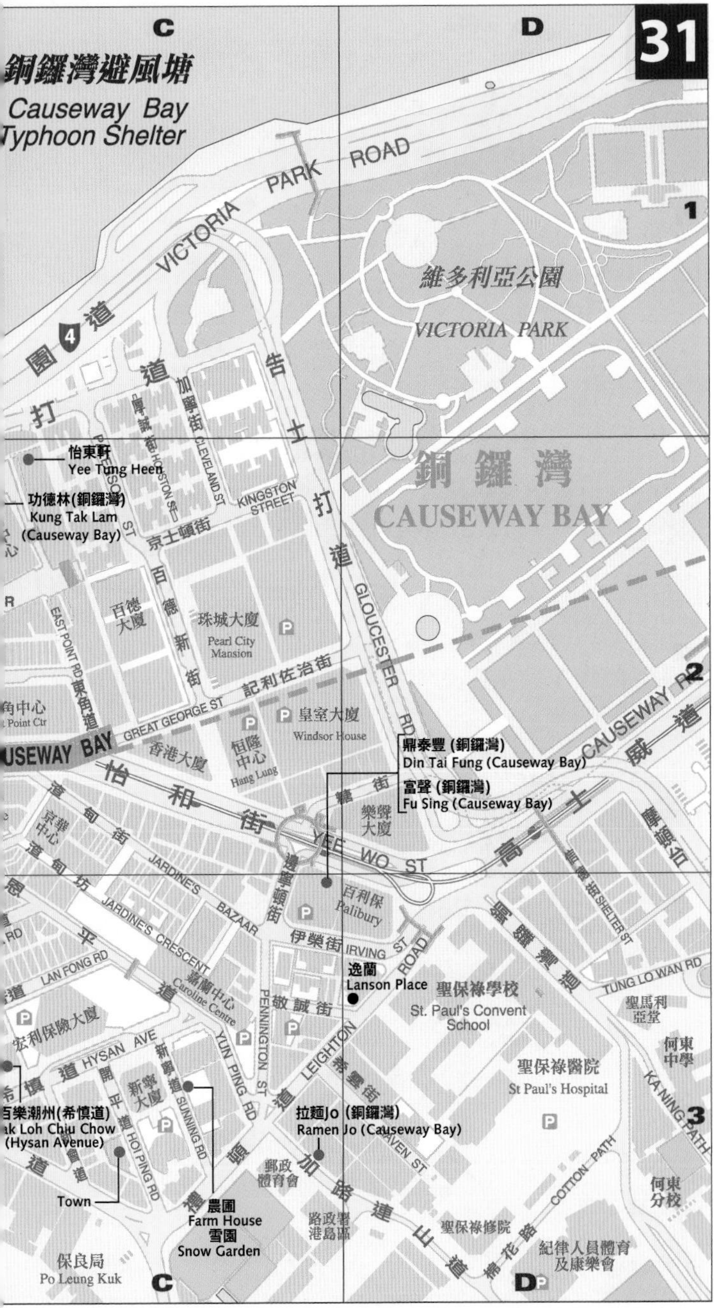
31
C
D
銅鑼灣避風塘
Causeway Bay Typhoon Shelter
VICTORIA PARK ROAD
維多利亞公園
VICTORIA PARK
銅鑼灣
CAUSEWAY BAY
怡東軒
Yee Tung Heen
功德林(銅鑼灣)
Kung Tak Lam (Causeway Bay)
CLEVELAND ST
KINGSTON STREET
京士頓街
GLOUCESTER RD
EAST POINT RD
東角道
百德大廈
珠城大廈
Pearl City Mansion
記利佐治街
GREAT GEORGE ST
皇室大廈
Windsor House
香港大廈
恒隆中心
Hang Lung
鼎泰豐 (銅鑼灣)
Din Tai Fung (Causeway Bay)
富聲 (銅鑼灣)
Fu Sing (Causeway Bay)
樂聲大廈
CAUSEWAY RD
YEE WO ST
怡和街
JARDINE'S BAZAAR
JARDINE'S CRESCENT
百利保
Palibury
伊榮街
IRVING ST
SHELTER ST
TUNG LO WAN RD
逸蘭
Lanson Place
聖保祿學校
St. Paul's Convent School
聖瑪利亞堂
何東中學
LAN FONG RD
嘉蘭中心
Caroline Centre
PENNINGTON ST
YUN PING RD
LEIGHTON ROAD
HYSAN AVE
新寧大廈
SUNNING RD
HOI PING RD
宏利保險大廈
百樂潮州(希慎道)
ak Loh Chiu Chow (Hysan Avenue)
Town
農圃
Farm House
雪園
Snow Garden
拉麵Jo (銅鑼灣)
Ramen Jo (Causeway Bay)
聖保祿醫院
St Paul's Hospital
KA NING PATH
COTTON PATH
郵政體育會
路政署港島區
聖保祿修院
紀律人員體育及康樂會
何東分校
保良局
Po Leung Kuk
1
2
3

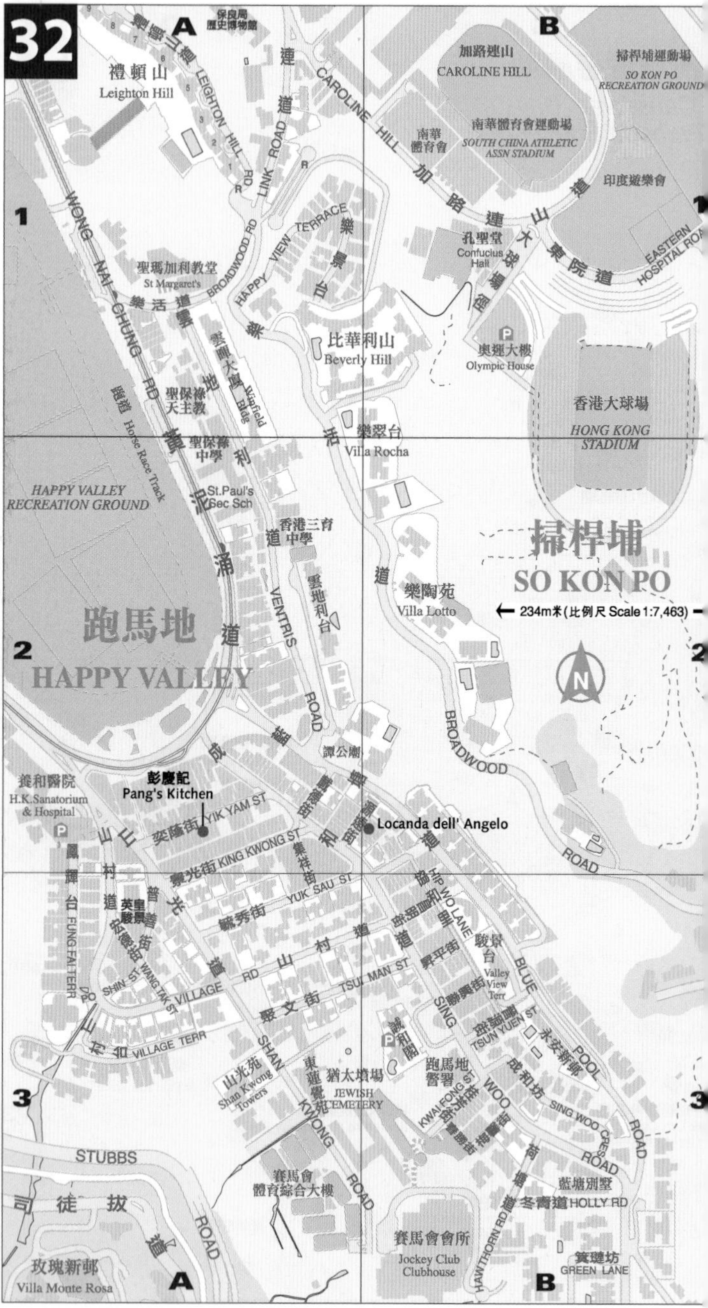
32
A
B
保良局歷史博物館
禮頓山
Leighton Hill
LEIGHTON HILL RD
LINK ROAD
CAROLINE HILL
加路連山
CAROLINE HILL
掃桿埔運動場
SO KON PO RECREATION GROUND
南華體育會
南華體育會運動場
SOUTH CHINA ATHLETIC ASSN STADIUM
加路連山道
印度遊樂會
孔聖堂
Confucius Hall
大球場徑
東院道
EASTERN HOSPITAL ROAD
WONG NAI CHUNG RD
BROADWOOD RD
HAPPY VIEW TERRACE
樂景台
聖瑪加利教堂
St Margaret's
樂活道
比華利山
Beverly Hill
奧運大樓
Olympic House
香港大球場
HONG KONG STADIUM
雲地利道
雲暉大廈
Winfield Bldg
聖保祿天主教
馬道 Horse Race Track
聖保祿中學
St.Paul's Sec Sch
樂翠台
Villa Rocha
HAPPY VALLEY RECREATION GROUND
黃泥涌道
香港三育中學
VENTRIS ROAD
雲地利台
樂陶苑
Villa Lotto
掃桿埔
SO KON PO
234m米(比例尺 Scale 1:7,463)
N
跑馬地
HAPPY VALLEY
BROADWOOD ROAD
譚公廟
養和醫院
H.K.Sanatorium & Hospital
彭慶記
Pang's Kitchen
奕蔭街 YIK YAM ST
Locanda dell' Angelo
景光街 KING KWONG ST
山村道
鳳輝台 FUNG FAI TERR
毓秀街 YUK SAU ST
HIP WO LANE
英皇駿景
普善街
宏德街 WANG TAK ST
SHIN ST
PO
VILLAGE RD
聚文街 TSUI MAN ST
駿景台
Valley View Terr
昇平街
SING WOO ROAD
BLUE POOL ROAD
TSUN YUEN ST
永安新邨
VILLAGE TERR
山村台
SHAN KWONG ROAD
山光苑
Shan Kwong Towers
猶太墳場
JEWISH CEMETERY
跑馬地警署
KWAI FONG ST
成和坊
SING WOO CRES
STUBBS ROAD
司徒拔道
賽馬會體育綜合大樓
藍塘別墅
冬青道 HOLLY RD
HAWTHORN RD
賽馬會會所
Jockey Club Clubhouse
玫瑰新邨
Villa Monte Rosa
GREEN LANE
1
2
3

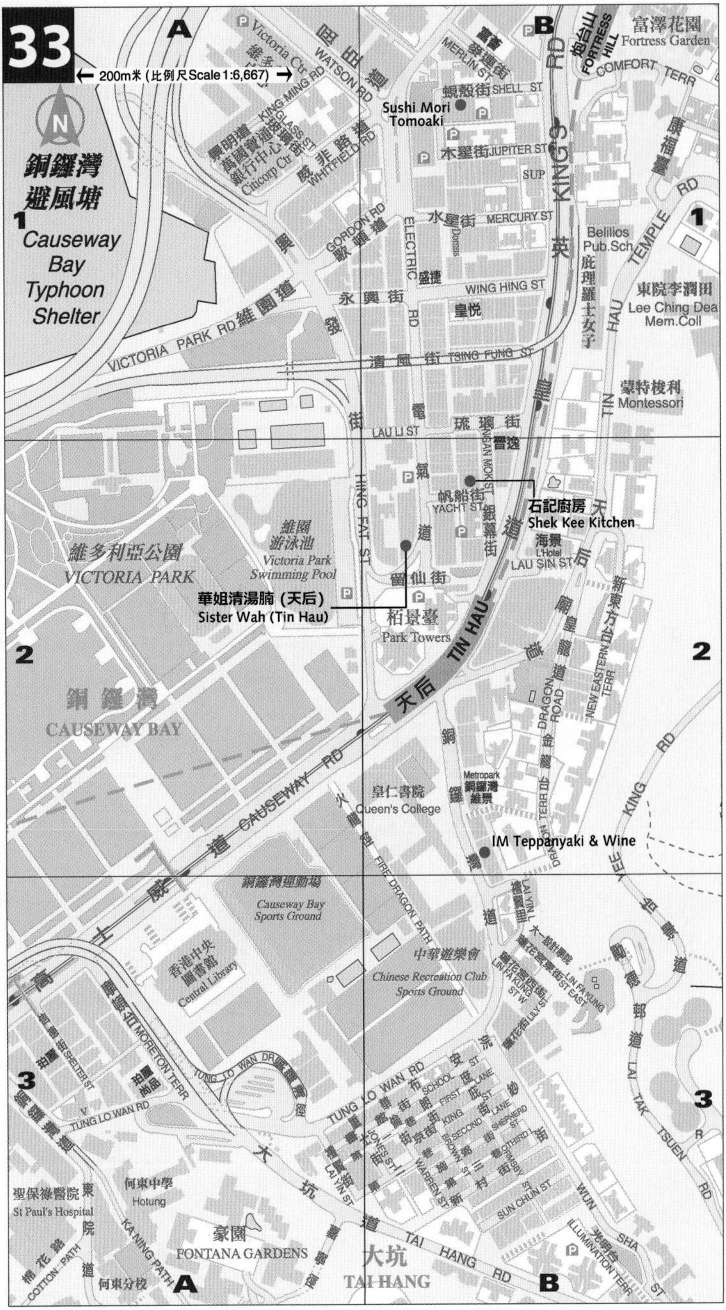
33
200m米 (比例尺Scale 1:6,667)
A
B
1
2
3
銅鑼灣避風塘
Causeway Bay Typhoon Shelter
富澤花園
Fortress Garden
炮台山 FORTRESS HILL
COMFORT TERR
VICTORIA PARK RD 維園道
WATSON RD
KING MING RD
GLASS ST
WHITFIELD RD
Citicorp Ctr
Victoria Ctr
MERLIN ST
SHELL ST
JUPITER ST
MERCURY ST
WING HING ST
TSING FUNG ST
LAU LI ST
GORDON RD
ELECTRIC RD
KING'S RD
TEMPLE RD
TIN HAU TEMPLE RD
Sushi Mori Tomoaki
Belilios Pub.Sch
東院李潤田
Lee Ching Dea Mem.Coll
蒙特梭利
Montessori
石記廚房
Shek Kee Kitchen
YACHT ST
LAU SIN ST
HING FAT ST
維多利亞公園
VICTORIA PARK
維園游泳池
Victoria Park Swimming Pool
華姐清湯腩 (天后)
Sister Wah (Tin Hau)
栢景臺
Park Towers
TIN HAU 天后
銅鑼灣
CAUSEWAY BAY
CAUSEWAY RD
皇仁書院
Queen's College
DRAGON ROAD
NEW EASTERN TERR
Metropark 銅鑼灣維景
IM Teppanyaki & Wine
KING RD
FIRE DRAGON PATH
銅鑼灣運動場
Causeway Bay Sports Ground
香港中央圖書館
Central Library
中華遊樂會
Chinese Recreation Club Sports Ground
LAI YIN LN
LIN FA KUNG ST W
LIN FA KUNG ST EAST
LILY ST
MORETON TERR
TUNG LO WAN DR
TUNG LO WAN RD
SHELTER ST
SCHOOL ST
FIRST LANE
KING ST
SECOND LANE
SHEPHERD ST
THIRD LN
BROWN ST
JONES ST
WARREN ST
ORMSBY ST
SUN CHUN ST
LAI YIN ST
LAI TAK TSUEN RD
WUN SHA ST
ILLUMINATION TERR
聖保祿醫院
St Paul's Hospital
何東中學
Hotung
KA NING PATH
COTTON PATH
何東分校
豪園
FONTANA GARDENS
大坑
TAI HANG
TAI HANG RD

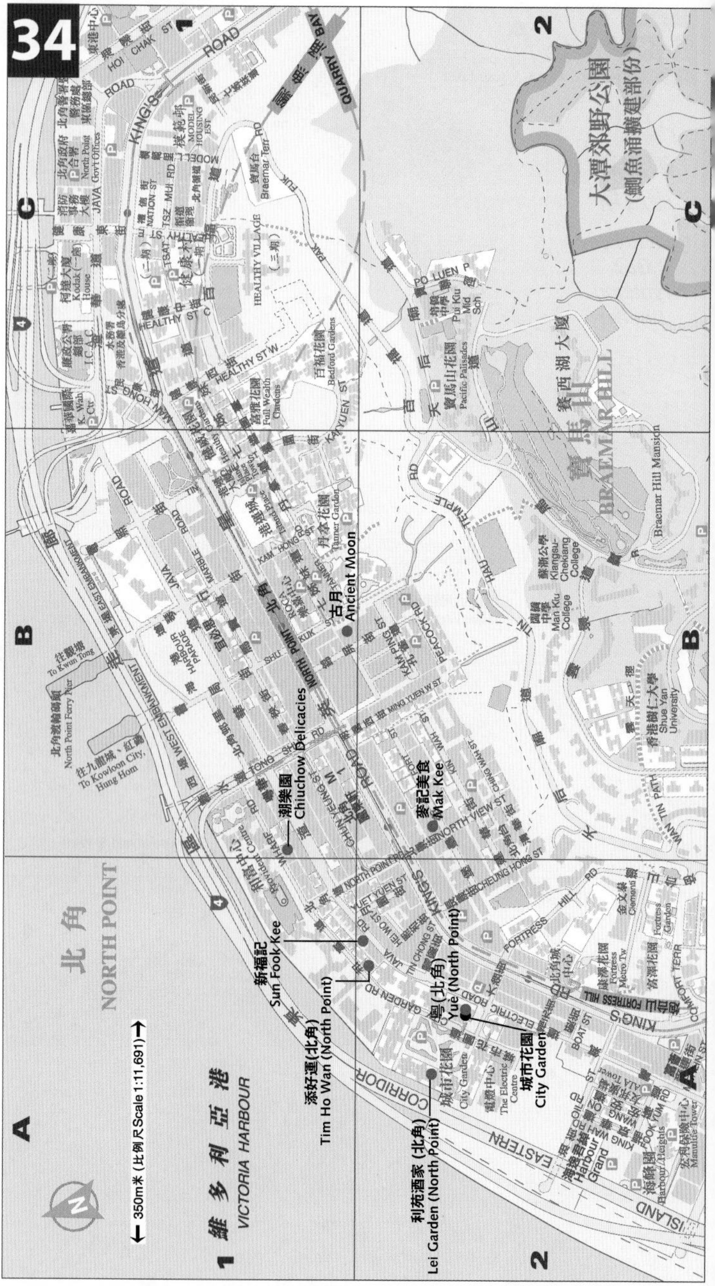
34
北角
NORTH POINT
維多利亞港
VICTORIA HARBOUR
350m米 (比例尺Scale 1:11,691)
新福記
Sun Fook Kee
添好運(北角)
Tim Ho Wan (North Point)
利苑酒家 (北角)
Lei Garden (North Point)
粵(北角)
Yue (North Point)
城市花園
City Garden
潮樂園
Chiuchow Delicacies
麥記美食
Mak Kee
古月
Ancient Moon
North Point Ferry Pier
To Kwun Tong
To Kowloon City, Hung Hom
KING'S ROAD
JAVA ROAD
EASTERN CORRIDOR
ISLAND
FORTRESS HILL
BRAEMAR HILL
寶馬山
Braemar Hill Mansion
Shue Yan University
Kiangsu-Chekiang College
Man Kiu College
Pacific Palisades
Bedford Gardens
Full Wealth Gardens
Tanner Garden
HEALTHY VILLAGE
Braemar Terr
QUARRY BAY
大潭郊野公園
(鰂魚涌擴建部份)
The Electric Centre
Harbour Grand
Harbour Heights
Manulife Tower
Fortress Metro Tw
Fortress Garden
Clementi
North Point Govt Offices
Kodak House
K. Wah Ctr
I.C.A.C.
Pui Kiu Mid Sch

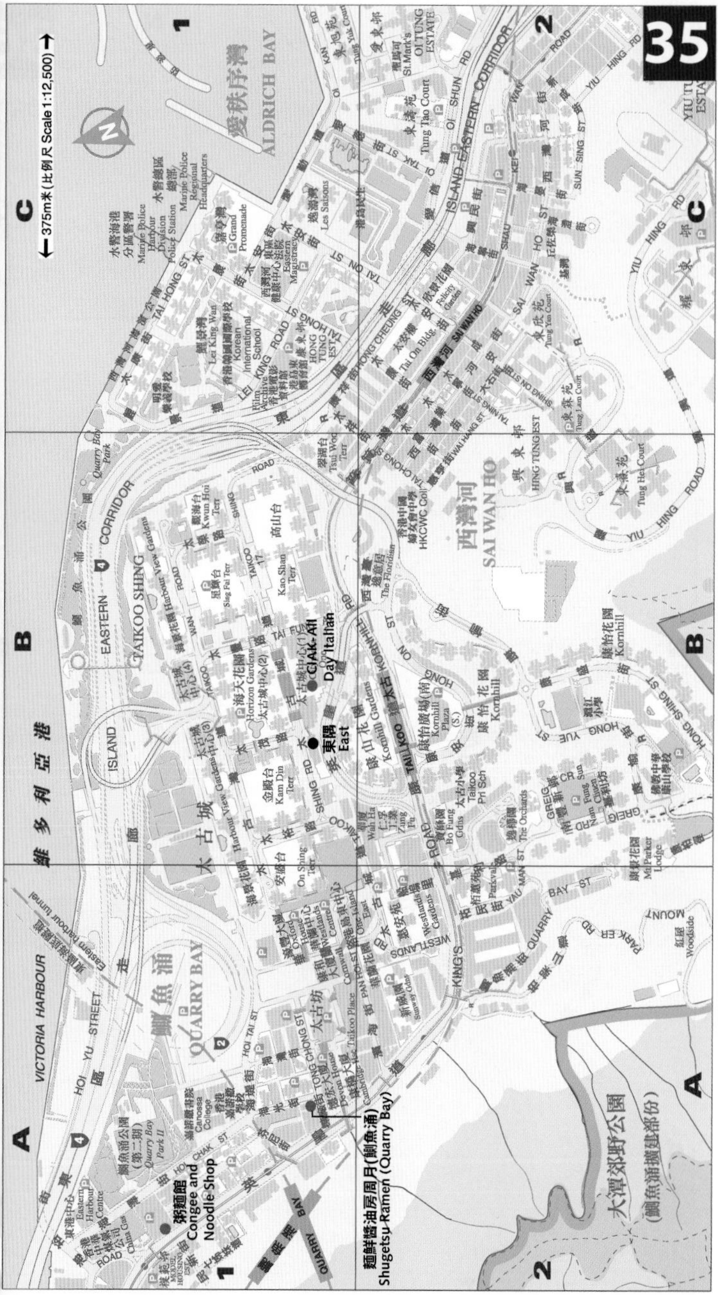
35
375m米(比例尺 Scale 1:12,500)
VICTORIA HARBOUR
維多利亞港
ALDRICH BAY
愛秩序灣
QUARRY BAY
鰂魚涌
TAIKOO SHING
太古城
SAI WAN HO
西灣河
ISLAND EASTERN CORRIDOR
KING'S ROAD
Eastern Harbour tunnel
粥麵館 Congee and Noodle Shop
麵鮮醬油房周月(鰂魚涌) Shugetsu Ramen (Quarry Bay)
東隅 East
GIAK-All Day Italian
大潭郊野公園 (鰂魚涌擴建部份)
Quarry Bay Park
Marine Police Regional Headquarters
Korean International School
Film Archive
Kornhill Gardens
Kornhill Plaza
Tung Hei Court
Tung Lam Court
Tung Yan Court
Tung Tao Court
OI TUNG ESTATE
HING TUNG EST
Taikoo Place
Canossa College
Grand Promenade
Les Saisons
Eastern Magistracy

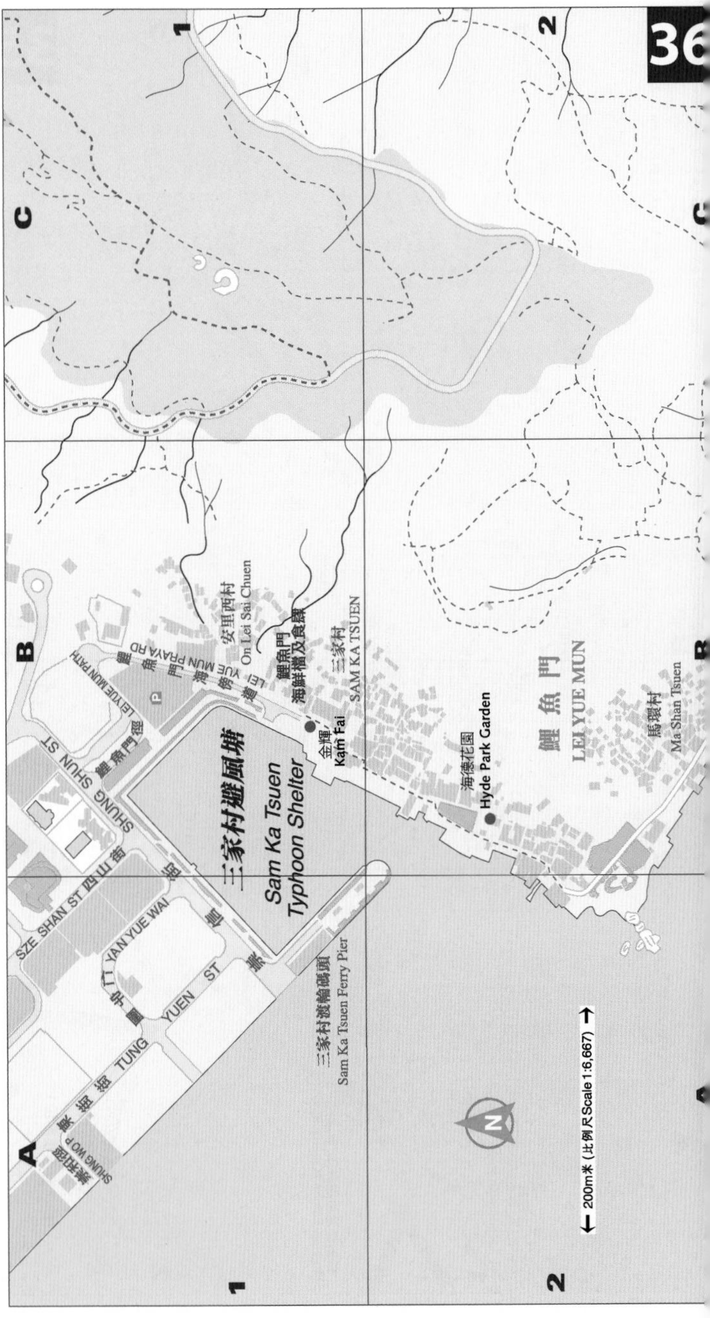
36
A
B
C
1
2
三家村避風塘
Sam Ka Tsuen Typhoon Shelter
鯉魚門
LEI YUE MUN
馬環村
Ma Shan Tsuen
海德花園
Hyde Park Garden
金輝
Kam Fai
三家村
SAM KA TSUEN
鯉魚門海鮮檔及食肆
安里西村
On Lei Sai Chuen
三家村渡輪碼頭
Sam Ka Tsuen Ferry Pier
SZE SHAN ST 四山街
SHUNG SHUN ST
崇信街
YAN YUE WAI
TUNG YUEN ST
東源街
SHUNG WO P
LEI YUE MUN PATH
鯉魚門徑
LEI YUE MUN PRAYA RD
鯉魚門海傍道
200m米 (比例尺Scale 1:6,667)

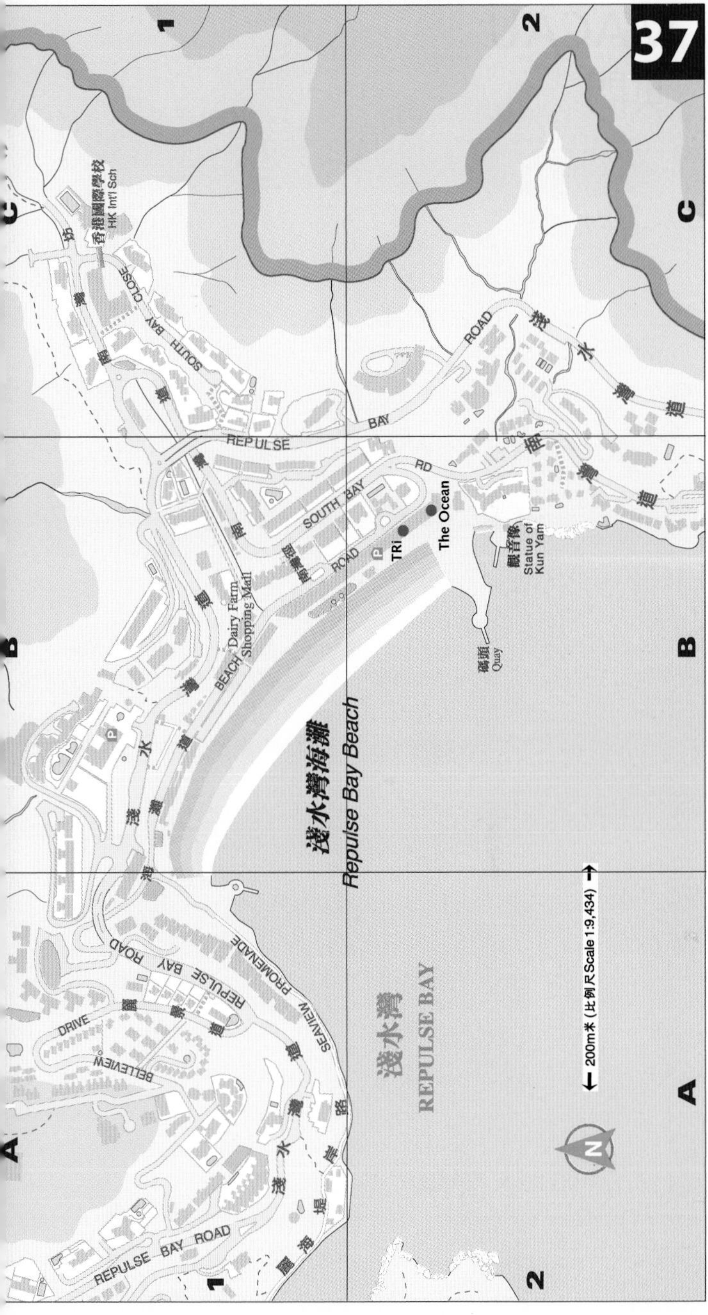
37
淺水灣海灘
Repulse Bay Beach
淺水灣
REPULSE BAY
200m米 (比例尺Scale 1:9,434)
觀音像
Statue of Kun Yam
碼頭
Quay
TRi
The Ocean
Dairy Farm Shopping Mall
香港國際學校
HK Int'l Sch
REPULSE BAY ROAD
淺水灣道
SOUTH BAY ROAD
南灣道
SOUTH BAY CLOSE
南灣坊
BEACH ROAD
BELLEVIEW DRIVE
麗景道
SEAVIEW PROMENADE
淺水灣海堤岸路
南灣徑
A
B
C
1
2

MACAU
澳門

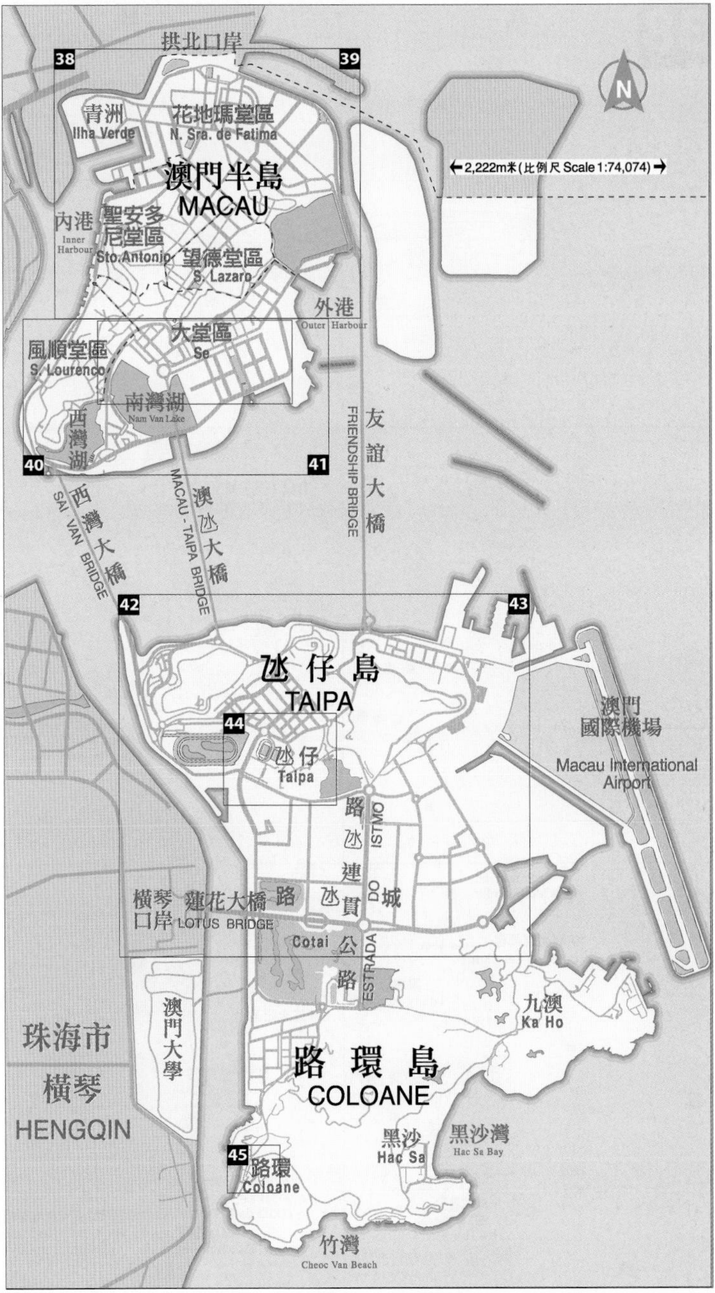

拱北口岸
38
39
青洲
Ilha Verde
花地瑪堂區
N. Sra. de Fatima
澳門半島
MACAU
←2,222m米(比例尺 Scale 1:74,074)→
內港
Inner Harbour
聖安多尼堂區
Sto.Antonio
望德堂區
S. Lazaro
外港
Outer Harbour
大堂區
Se
風順堂區
S. Lourenco
南灣湖
Nam Van Lake
西灣湖
40
41
友誼大橋
FRIENDSHIP BRIDGE
澳氹大橋
MACAU - TAIPA BRIDGE
西灣大橋
SAI VAN BRIDGE
42
43
氹仔島
TAIPA
澳門國際機場
Macau International Airport
44
氹仔
Taipa
路氹連貫公路
ESTRADA DO ISTMO
路氹城
橫琴口岸
蓮花大橋
LOTUS BRIDGE
Cotai
澳門大學
珠海市橫琴
HENGQIN
九澳
Ka Ho
路環島
COLOANE
黑沙
Hac Sa
黑沙灣
Hac Sa Bay
45
路環
Coloane
竹灣
Cheoc Van Beach

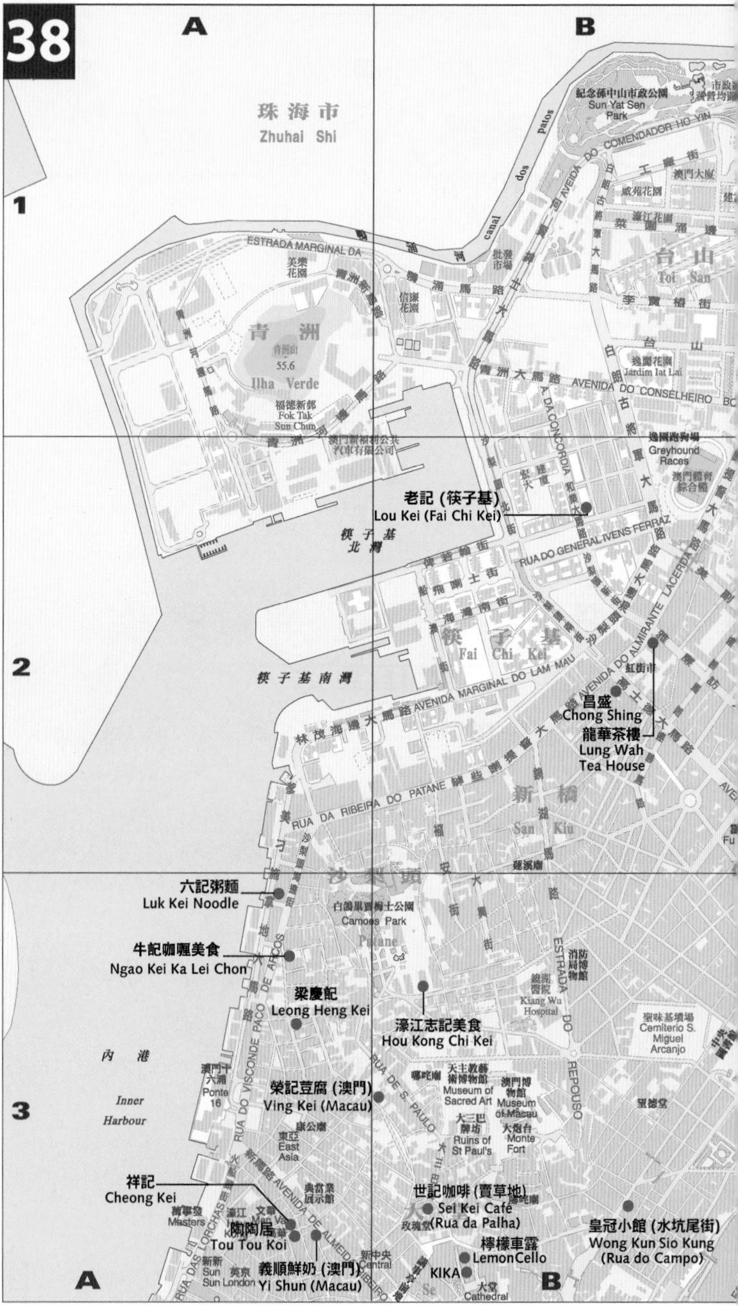
38
A
B
1
2
3
珠海市
Zhuhai Shi
紀念孫中山市政公園
Sun Yat Sen Park
canal dos patos
AVENIDA DO COMENDADOR HO YIN
ESTRADA MARGINAL DA
美樂花園
青洲
55.6
Ilha Verde
福德新邨
Fok Tak Sun Chun
澳門新福利公共汽車有限公司
台山
Toi San
逸麗花園
Jardim Iat Lai
AVENIDA DO CONSELHEIRO
A. DA CONCORDIA
逸園跑狗場
Greyhound Races
澳門體育綜合館
老記 (筷子基)
Lou Kei (Fai Chi Kei)
筷子基北灣
RUA DO GENERAL IVENS FERRAZ
筷子基
Fai Chi Kei
筷子基南灣
AVENIDA MARGINAL DO LAM MAU
AVENIDA DO ALMIRANTE LACERDA
紅街市
昌盛
Chong Shing
龍華茶樓
Lung Wah Tea House
RUA DA RIBEIRA DO PATANE
新橋
San Kiu
沙梨頭
六記粥麵
Luk Kei Noodle
白鴿巢賈梅士公園
Camoes Park
Patane
牛記咖喱美食
Ngao Kei Ka Lei Chon
RUA DE ARCOS
梁慶記
Leong Heng Kei
濠江志記美食
Hou Kong Chi Kei
鏡湖醫院
Kiang Wu Hospital
ESTRADA DO REPOUSO
聖味基墳場
Cemiterio S. Miguel Arcanjo
內港
Inner Harbour
澳門十六浦
Ponte 16
RUA DO VISCONDE PACO DE ARCOS
榮記荳腐 (澳門)
Ving Kei (Macau)
RUA DE S. PAULO
天主教藝術博物館
Museum of Sacred Art
澳門博物館
Museum of Macau
大三巴牌坊
Ruins of St Paul's
大炮台
Monte Fort
東亞
East Asia
RUA DAS LORCHAS
AVENIDA DE ALMEIDA RIBEIRO
祥記
Cheong Kei
萬事發
Masters
陶陶居
Tou Tou Koi
義順鮮奶 (澳門)
Yi Shun (Macau)
新中央
Central
新新
Sun Sun
英京
Sun London
世記咖啡 (賣草地)
Sei Kei Cafe
(Rua da Palha)
檸檬車露
LemonCello
KIKA
大堂
Cathedral
皇冠小館 (水坑尾街)
Wong Kun Sio Kung
(Rua do Campo)

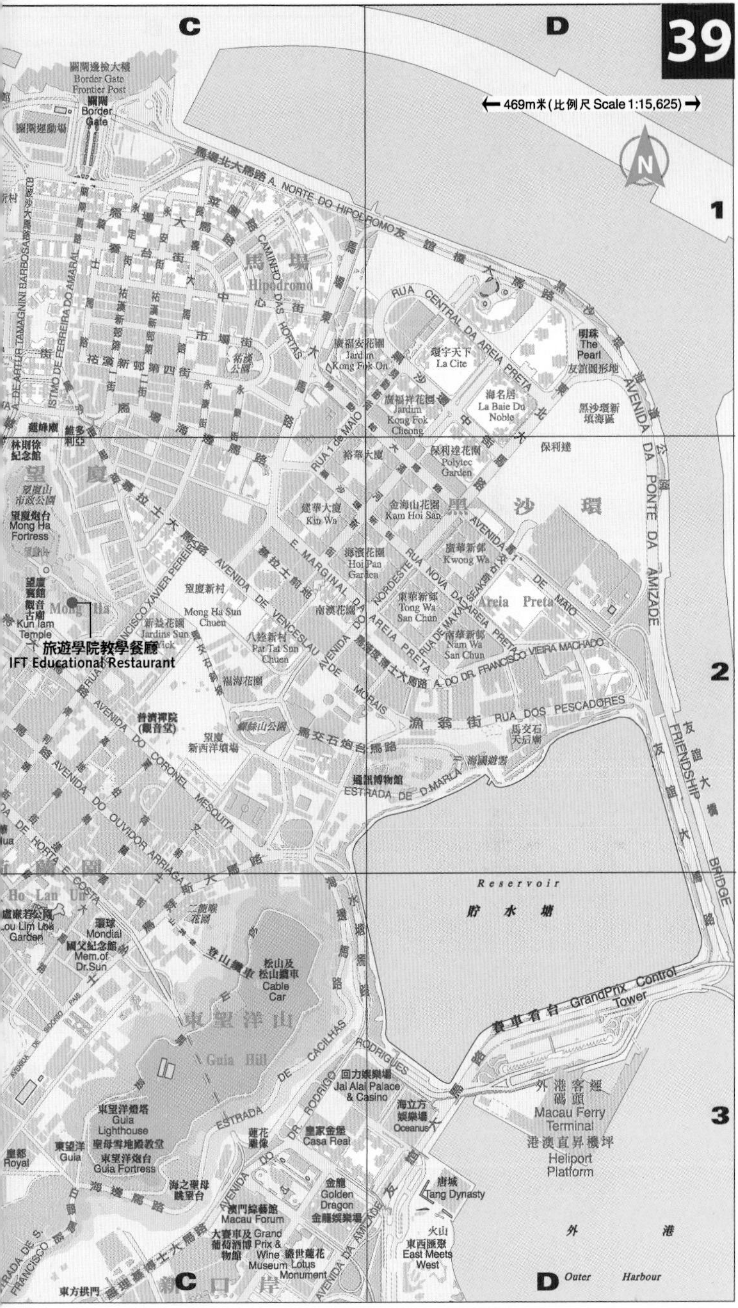
39
C
D
← 469m米(比例尺 Scale 1:15,625) →
N
1
2
3
關閘邊檢大樓
Border Gate
Frontier Post
關閘
Border
Gate
馬場北大馬路 A. NORTE DO HIPODROMO
友誼橋大馬路
馬場
Hipodromo
CAMINHO DAS HORTAS
RUA CENTRAL DA AREIA PRETA
廣福安花園
Jardim
Kong Fok On
環宇天下
La Cite
明珠
The
Pearl
友誼圓形地
廣福祥花園
Jardim
Kong Fok
Cheong
海名居
La Baie Du
Noble
黑沙環新
填海區
AVENIDA DA PONTE DA AMIZADE
保利達
保利達花園
Polytec
Garden
RUA 1 de MAIO
裕華大廈
黑
沙
環
建華大廈
Kin Wa
金海山花園
Kam Hoi San
海濱花園
Hoi Pan
Garden
廣華新邨
Kwong Wa
AVENIDA 1° DE MAIO
E. MARGINAL DA AREIA PRETA
RUA NOVA DA AREIA PRETA
東華新邨
Tong Wa
San Chun
Areia Preta
南澳花園
南華新邨
Nam Wa
San Chun
A. DO DR. FRANCISCO VIEIRA MACHADO
RUA DOS PESCADORES
漁翁街
馬交石
天后廟
祐漢新邨第四街
祐漢公園
趙偉廟
維多
利亞
林則徐
紀念館
望廈
望廈山
市政公園
望廈炮台
Mong Ha
Fortress
AVENIDA DE VENCESLAU DE MORAIS
AVENIDA DE ARTUR TAMAGNINI BARBOSA
ISTMO DE FERREIRA DO AMARAL
望廈新村
Mong Ha Sun
Chuen
新益花園
Jardins Sun
Yick
八達新村
Pat Tat Sun
Chuen
福海花園
望廈
賓館
觀音
古廟
Kun Iam
Temple
Mong Ha
旅遊學院教學餐廳
IFT Educational Restaurant
AVENIDA DO CORONEL MESQUITA
普濟禪院
(觀音堂)
望廈
新西洋墳場
螺絲山公園
馬交石炮台馬路
通訊博物館
ESTRADA DE D. MARIA II
AVENIDA DO OUVIDOR ARRIAGA
AVENIDA DE HORTA E COSTA
友誼大橋
FRIENDSHIP BRIDGE
Reservoir
貯水塘
Ho Lan Un
二龍喉
花園
盧廉若公園
Lou Lim Ieok
Garden
環球
Mondial
國父紀念館
Mem. of
Dr. Sun
松山及
松山纜車
Cable
Car
登山纜車
GrandPrix Control Tower
賽車看台
東望洋山
Guia Hill
ESTRADA DE CACILHAS
RODRIGUES
回力娛樂場
Jai Alai Palace
& Casino
海立方
娛樂場
Oceanus
外港客運
碼頭
Macau Ferry
Terminal
港澳直昇機坪
Heliport
Platform
東望洋燈塔
Guia
Lighthouse
聖母雪地殿教堂
東望洋
Guia
東望洋炮台
Guia Fortress
皇都
Royal
蓮花
雕像
皇家金堡
Casa Real
金龍
Golden
Dragon
金龍娛樂場
唐城
Tang Dynasty
海之聖母
眺望台
澳門綜藝館
Macau Forum
大賽車及
葡萄酒博物館
Grand
Prix &
Wine
Museum
盛世蓮花
Lotus
Monument
火山
東西匯聚
East Meets
West
外港
Outer Harbour
AVENIDA DA AMIZADE
東方拱門
新口岸

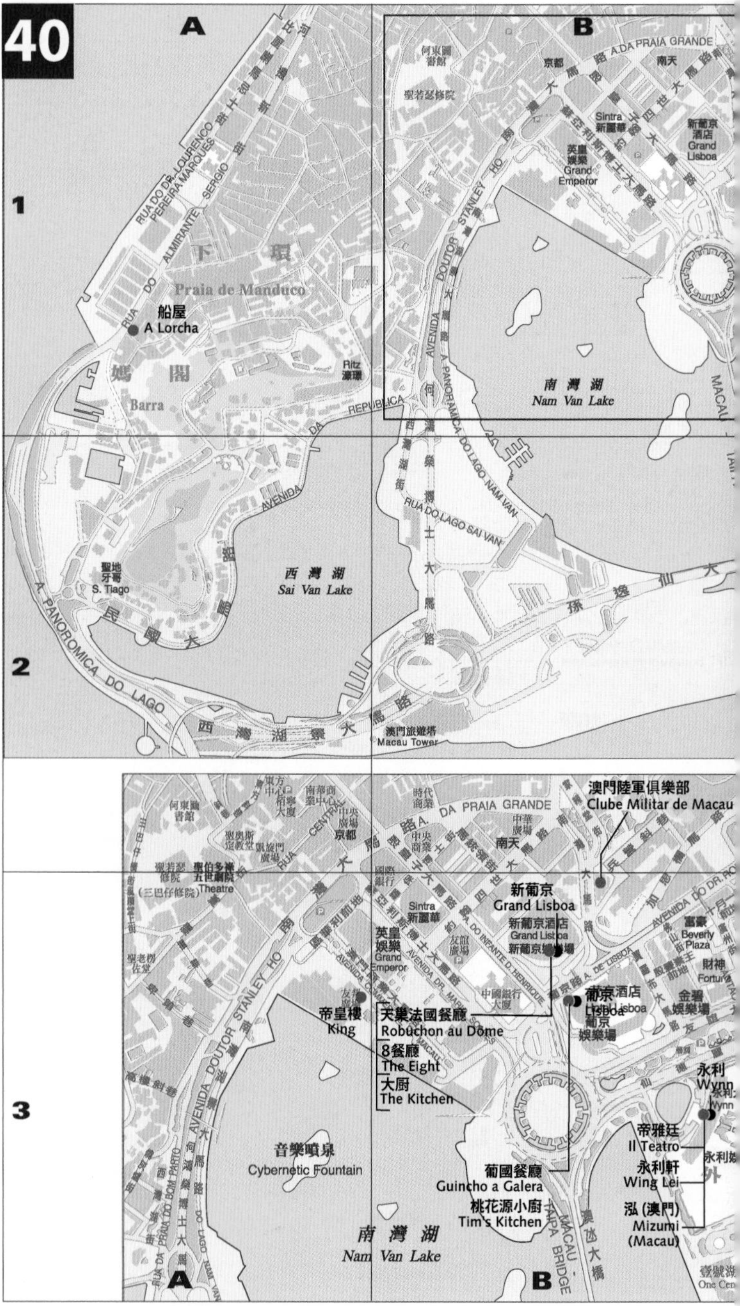
40
A
B
1
2
3
A.DA PRAIA GRANDE
京都
南天
何東圖書館
聖若瑟修院
Sintra
新麗華
新葡京酒店
Grand Lisboa
英皇娛樂
Grand Emperor
RUA DO DR. LOURENCO PEREIRA MARQUES
RUA DO ALMIRANTE SERGIO
下環
Praia de Manduco
船屋
A Lorcha
媽閣
Barra
Ritz
濠璟
AVENIDA DOUTOR STANLEY HO
AVENIDA DA REPUBLICA
A. PANORAMICA DO LAGO NAM VAN
RUA DO LAGO SAI VAN
南灣湖
Nam Van Lake
西灣湖
Sai Van Lake
聖地牙哥
S. Tiago
民國大馬路
A. PANOROMICA DO LAGO
西灣湖景大馬路
澳門旅遊塔
Macau Tower
孫逸仙大馬路
DA PRAIA GRANDE
澳門陸軍俱樂部
Clube Militar de Macau
新葡京
Grand Lisboa
新葡京酒店
Grand Lisboa
新葡京娛樂場
AVENIDA DO INFANTE D. HENRIQUE
AVENIDA DR. MARIO SOARES
A. DE LISBOA
富豪
Beverly Plaza
財神
金碧娛樂場
中國銀行大廈
葡京酒店
Hotel Lisboa
葡京娛樂場
帝皇樓
King
天巢法國餐廳
Robuchon au Dôme
8餐廳
The Eight
大厨
The Kitchen
音樂噴泉
Cybernetic Fountain
葡國餐廳
Guincho a Galera
桃花源小廚
Tim's Kitchen
MACAU - TAIPA BRIDGE
澳氹大橋
永利
Wynn
帝雅廷
Il Teatro
永利軒
Wing Lei
泓(澳門)
Mizumi (Macau)
聖伯多祿五世劇院
Theatre
(三巴仔修院)
RUA DA PRAIA DO BOM PARTO
壹號湖畔
One Central

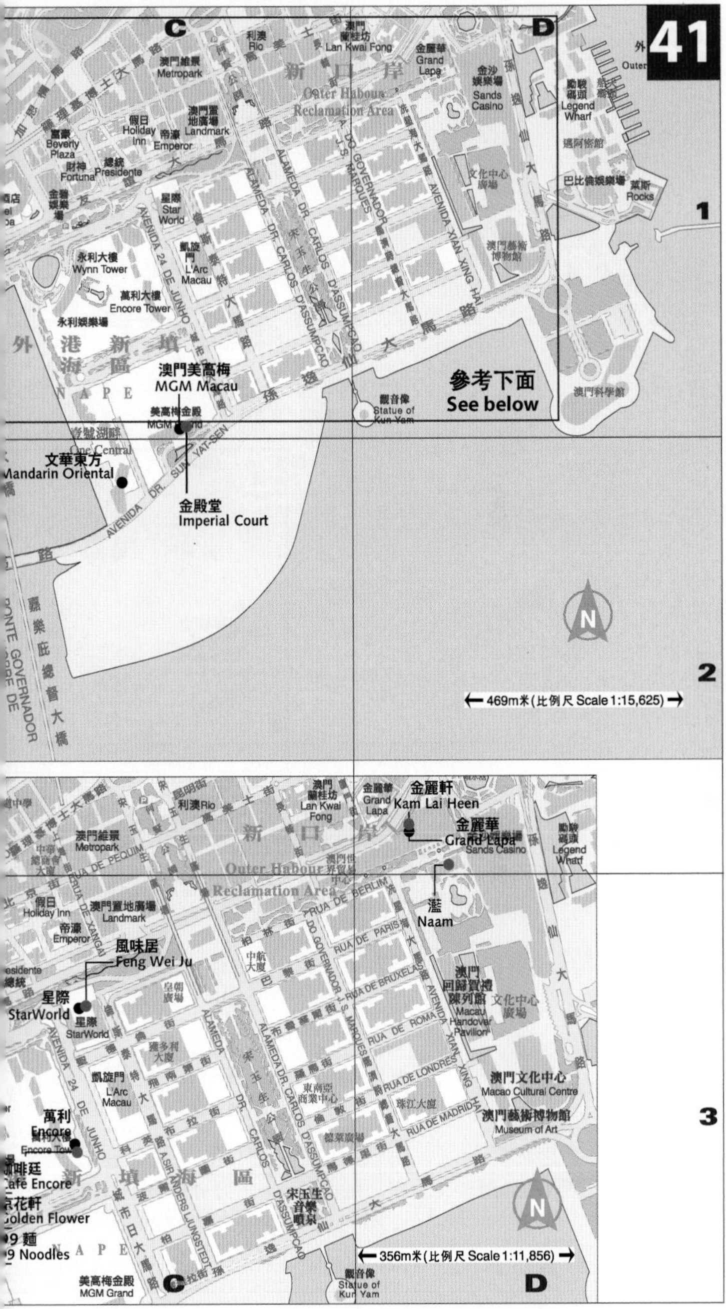
41
C
D
1
2
3
澳門蘭桂坊
Lan Kwai Fong
利澳
Rio
金麗華
Grand Lapa
澳門維景
Metropark
金沙娛樂場
Sands Casino
勵駿碼頭
Legend Wharf
澳門置地廣場
Landmark
假日
Holiday Inn
帝濠
Emperor
富豪
Beverly Plaza
財神
Fortuna
總統
Presidente
星際
Star World
巴比倫娛樂場
萊斯
Rocks
凱旋門
L'Arc Macau
永利大樓
Wynn Tower
萬利大樓
Encore Tower
永利娛樂場
外港新填海區
NAPE
新口岸
Outer Habour Reclamation Area
ALAMEDA DR. CARLOS D'ASSUMPCAO
AVENIDA XIAN XING HAI
AVENIDA 24 DE JUNHO
AVENIDA DR. SUN YAT-SEN
PONTE GOVERNADOR
澳門美高梅
MGM Macau
美高梅金殿
MGM Grand
壹號湖畔
One Central
文華東方
Mandarin Oriental
金殿堂
Imperial Court
參考下面
See below
觀音像
Statue of Kun Yam
澳門科學館
嘉樂庇總督大橋
469m米(比例尺 Scale 1:15,625)
N
金麗軒
Kam Lai Heen
金麗華
Grand Lapa
Sands Casino
Legend Wharf
澳門世界貿易中心
RUA DE PEQUIM
RUA DE XANGAI
RUA DE BERLIM
RUA DE PARIS
RUA DE BRUXELAS
RUA DE ROMA
RUA DE LONDRES
RUA DE MADRID
DO GOVERNADOR J. S. MARQUES
灆
Naam
風味居
Feng Wei Ju
星際
StarWorld
澳門回歸賀禮陳列館
Macau Handover Pavilion
文化中心廣場
澳門文化中心
Macao Cultural Centre
澳門藝術博物館
Museum of Art
凱旋門
L'Arc Macau
萬利
Encore
咖啡廷
Café Encore
京花軒
Golden Flower
99 麵
99 Noodles
ASIR ANDERS LJUNGSTEDT
宋玉生音樂噴泉
356m米(比例尺 Scale 1:11,856)
美高梅金殿
MGM Grand
觀音像
Statue of Kun Yam

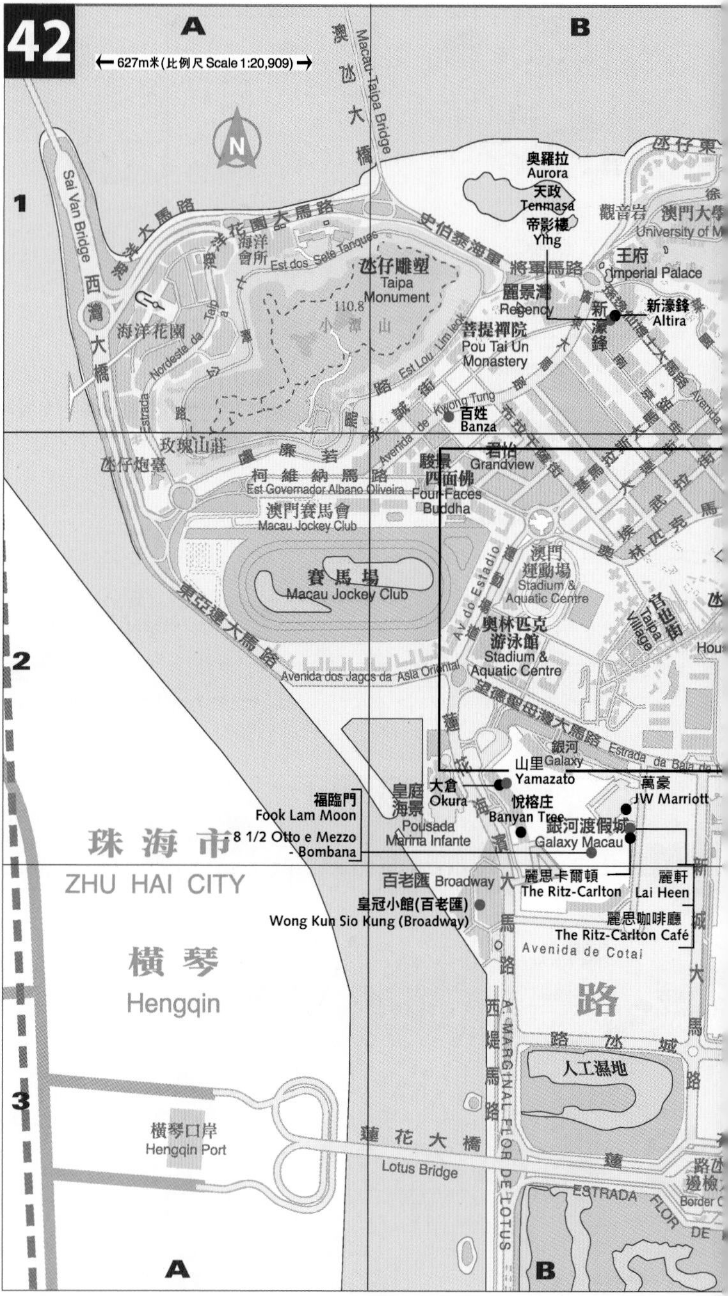

42
A
B
627m米(比例尺 Scale 1:20,909)
N
1
2
3
澳氹大橋
Macau-Taipa Bridge
Sai Van Bridge
西灣大橋
海洋大馬路
海洋花園大馬路
海洋花園
海洋會所
Est dos Sete Tanques
氹仔雕塑
Taipa Monument
110.8
小潭山
Estrada Nordeste da Taipa
史伯泰海軍將軍馬路
奧羅拉
Aurora
天政
Tenmasa
帝影樓
Ying
觀音岩
澳門大學
University of M
王府
Imperial Palace
麗景灣
Regency
新濠鋒
Altira
菩提禪院
Pou Tai Un Monastery
Est Lou Lim Ieok
Avenida de Kwong Tung
百姓
Banza
玫瑰山莊
氹仔炮臺
柯維納馬路
Est Governador Albano Oliveira
君怡
Grandview
駿景
四面佛
Four-Faces Buddha
澳門賽馬會
Macau Jockey Club
賽馬場
Macau Jockey Club
澳門運動場
Stadium & Aquatic Centre
奧林匹克游泳館
Stadium & Aquatic Centre
Av do Estadio
Taipa Village
官也街
東亞運大馬路
Avenida dos Jogos da Asia Oriental
望德聖母灣大馬路
Estrada da Baia de N
銀河
Galaxy
山里
Yamazato
大倉
Okura
萬豪
JW Marriott
悅榕庄
Banyan Tree
銀河渡假城
Galaxy Macau
福臨門
Fook Lam Moon
8 1/2 Otto e Mezzo - Bombana
皇庭海景
Pousada Marina Infante
珠海市
ZHU HAI CITY
百老匯 Broadway
皇冠小館(百老匯)
Wong Kun Sio Kung (Broadway)
麗思卡爾頓
The Ritz-Carlton
麗軒
Lai Heen
麗思咖啡廳
The Ritz-Carlton Café
Avenida de Cotai
橫琴
Hengqin
路氹城
人工濕地
西堤馬路
AV MARGINAL FLOR DE LOTUS
蓮花大橋
Lotus Bridge
橫琴口岸
Hengqin Port
ESTRADA FLOR DE
Border C

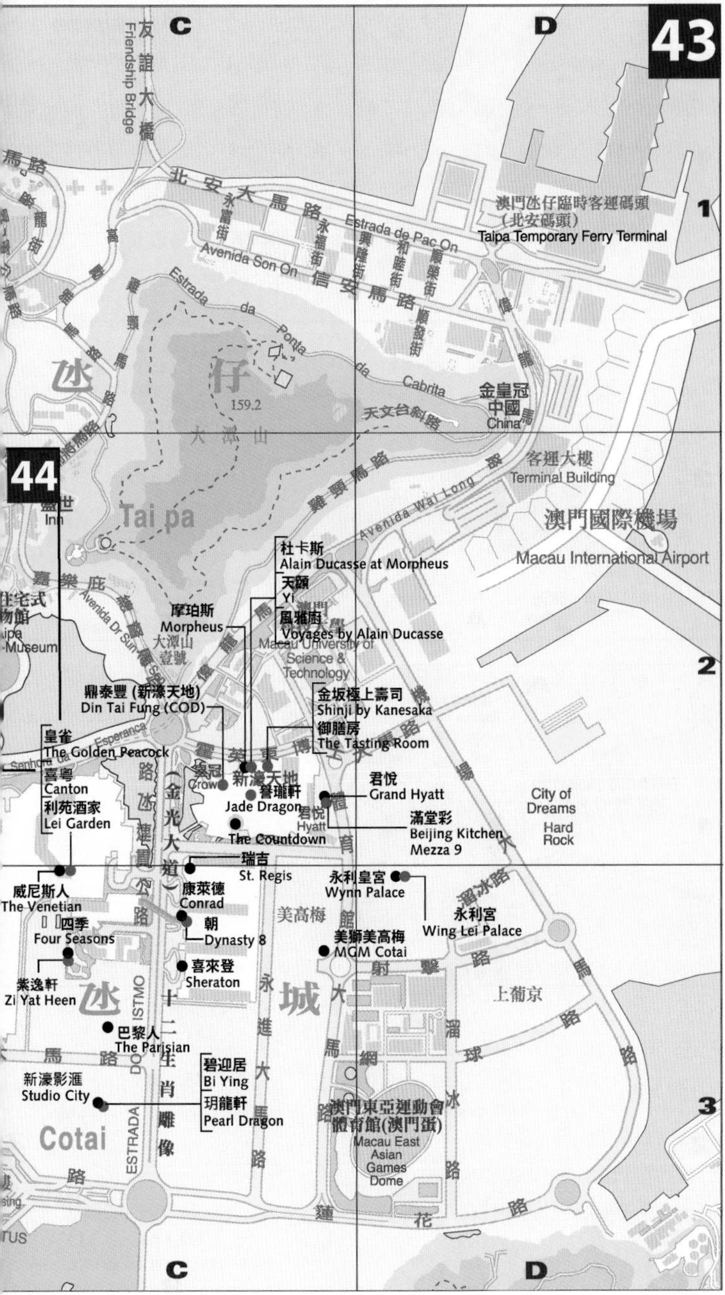

43
44
C
D
1
2
3
友誼大橋
Friendship Bridge
北安大馬路
Estrada de Pac On
澳門氹仔臨時客運碼頭
(北安碼頭)
Taipa Temporary Ferry Terminal
Avenida Son On
信安馬路
Estrada da Ponta da Cabrita
159.2
大潭山
天文台斜路
金皇冠中國
China
客運大樓
Terminal Building
雞頸馬路
Avenida Wai Long
澳門國際機場
Macau International Airport
Taipa
盛世
Inn
杜卡斯
Alain Ducasse at Morpheus
天頤
Yi
風雅廚
Voyages by Alain Ducasse
摩珀斯
Morpheus
大潭山壹號
Macau University of Science & Technology
Avenida Dr Sun Yat-Sen
鼎泰豐 (新濠天地)
Din Tai Fung (COD)
金坂極上壽司
Shinji by Kanesaka
御膳房
The Tasting Room
皇雀
The Golden Peacock
喜粵
Canton
利苑酒家
Lei Garden
Estrada da Baía de Nossa Senhora da Esperança
新濠天地
Crown
譽瓏軒
Jade Dragon
The Countdown
君悅
Grand Hyatt
滿堂彩
Beijing Kitchen
Mezza 9
City of Dreams
Hard Rock
金光大道
瑞吉
St. Regis
永利皇宮
Wynn Palace
永利宮
Wing Lei Palace
威尼斯人
The Venetian
康萊德
Conrad
朝
Dynasty 8
四季
Four Seasons
美高梅
美獅美高梅
MGM Cotai
喜來登
Sheraton
紫逸軒
Zi Yat Heen
氹城
上葡京
巴黎人
The Parisian
ESTRADA DO ISTMO
十二生肖雕像
碧迎居
Bi Ying
新濠影滙
Studio City
玥龍軒
Pearl Dragon
澳門東亞運動會體育館(澳門蛋)
Macau East Asian Games Dome
Cotai
蓮花路

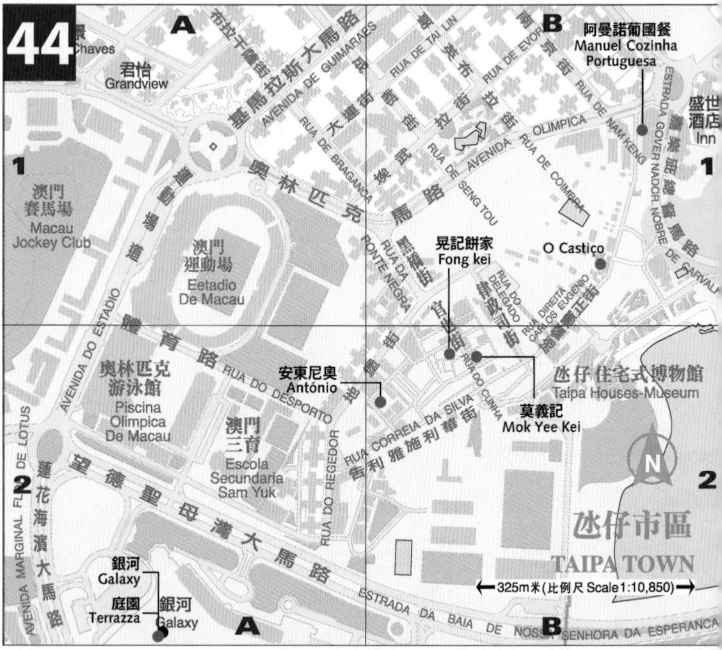
44
A
B
1
2
Chaves
君怡
Grandview
AVENIDA DE GUIMARAES
RUA DE BRAGANCA
RUA DE TAI LIN
RUA DE EVORA
RUA DE NAM KENG
阿曼諾葡國餐
Manuel Cozinha
Portuguesa
盛世
酒店
Inn
AVENIDA OLIMPICA
奧林匹克馬路
RUA DE SENG TOU
RUA DE COIMBRA
澳門
賽馬場
Macau
Jockey Club
澳門
運動場
Eetadio
De Macau
RUA DA PONTE NEGRA
黑橋街
晃記餅家
Fong kei
O Castiço
RUA DO DELEGADO
律政司街
RUA DIREITA CARLOS EUGENIO
官也街
RUA DO CUNHA
氹仔住宅式博物館
Taipa Houses-Museum
AVENIDA DO ESTADIO
體育路
RUA DO DESPORTO
奧林匹克
游泳館
Piscina
Olimpica
De Macau
安東尼奧
António
莫義記
Mok Yee Kei
澳門
三育
Escola
Secundaria
Sam Yuk
RUA DO REGEDOR
RUA CORREIA DA SILVA
告利雅施利華街
望德聖母灣大馬路
蓮花海濱大馬路
AVENIDA MARGINAL FLOR DE LOTUS
銀河
Galaxy
庭園
Terrazza
銀河
Galaxy
N
氹仔市區
TAIPA TOWN
325m米(比例尺 Scale1:10,850)
ESTRADA DA BAIA DE NOSSA SENHORA DA ESPERANCA

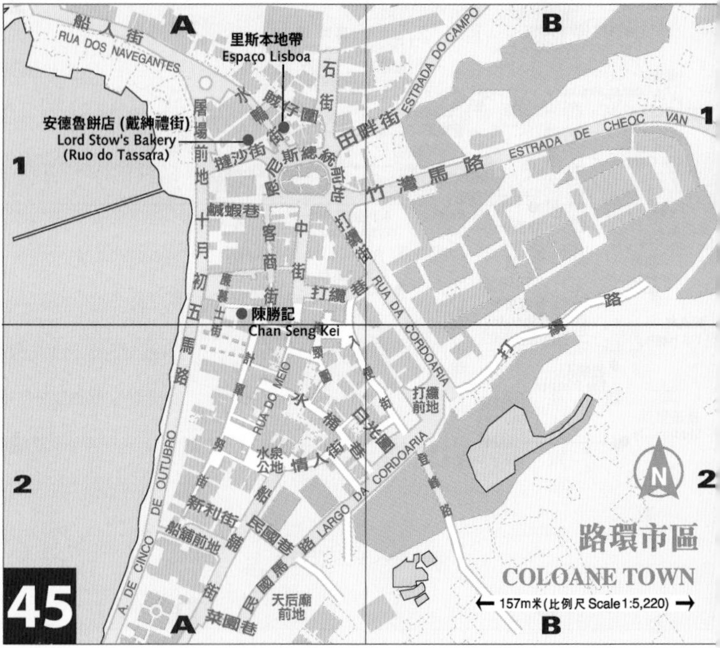
A
B
1
2
船人街
RUA DOS NAVEGANTES
里斯本地帶
Espaço Lisboa
石街
ESTRADA DO CAMPO
田畔街
ESTRADA DE CHEOC VAN
竹灣馬路
安德魯餅店 (戴紳禮街)
Lord Stow's Bakery
(Ruo do Tassara)
撻沙街
屠場前地
鹹蝦巷
客商街
中街
打纜街
十月初五馬路
打纜巷
RUA DA CORDOARIA
陳勝記
Chan Seng Kei
打纜前地
RUA DO MEIO
水泉公地
情人街
日光圍
N
路環市區
COLOANE TOWN
新利街
船鋪前地
民國巷
LARGO DA CORDOARIA
AVENIDA DE CINCO DE OUTUBRO
民國馬路
天后廟前地
菜園巷
157m米(比例尺 Scale1:5,220)
45

PICTURE COPYRIGHT
圖片版權

17 - SensorSpot/iStock , 18 - snvv/iStock , 19 - luchezar/iStock , 20-21-from left to right and top to bottom: ansonmiao/iStock - AzmanL/iStock - pushenok/iStock - Lisovskaya/iStock - ojoel/iStock - KontrastDesign/iStock - MielPhotos2008/iStock - 9200b0_32/iStock, 58 - Above & Beyond, 59 - Ancient Moon, 60 - Ah Yat Harbour View, 61 - Akrame, 62 - Amber, 63 - Ancient Moon, 64 - Arbor, 65 - Arcane, 66 - Michelin, 67 - Beefbar, 68 - Beet, 69 - Belon, 70 - Bibo, 71 - Bo Innovation, 72 - Bombay Dreams/Michelin, 73 - Bostonian Seafood & Grill, 74 - Brass Spoon/Michelin, 75 - Café Gray Deluxe, 76 - Café Hunan, 77 - Caprice, 78 - Michelin, 79 - Celebrity Cuisine, 80 - Celestial Court, 81 - Chan Kan Kee Chiu Chow, 82 - Michelin, 83 - Chesa/Michelin, 84 - Michelin, 85 - China Tang, 86 - China Tang/Michelin, 87 - Chinese Legend, 88 - Chiuchow Delicacies, 89 - Michelin, 90 - Chuen Kee Seafood, 91 - CIAK - All Day Italian, 92 - Michelin, 93 - Cuisine Cuisine at The Mira, 94 - 95, Din Tai Fung, 96 - Dong Lai Shun, 97 - Dragon Inn, 98 - Duddell's, 99 - Écriture, 100 - Michelin, 101 - Épure, 102 - Michelin, 103 - Fish School, 104 - Fofo by el Willy/Michelin, 105 - Fook Lam Moon, 106 - Forum, 107 - Frantzén's Kitchen, 108 - Fu Ho/Michelin, 109 - 111, Michelin, 112 - Gaddi's, 113 - Giando, 114 - Glorious Cuisine, 115- Michelin, 116 - Grand Hyatt Steakhouse, 117 - Guo Fu Lou, 118 - Michelin, 119 - Ho Hung Kee, 120 - 121, Michelin, 122 - Hugo's, 123 - Hyde Park Garden, 124 - ICHU, 125 - IM Teppanyaki & Wine/Michelin, 126 - Imperial Treasure Fine Chinese Cuisine, 127 - Involtini, 128 - Ippoh/Michelin, 129 - Jardin de Jade, 130 - Ju Xing Home, 131 - Kaiseki Den by Saotome, 132 - Kam Fai, 133 - Kam's Roast Goose, 134 - Kashiwaya, 135 - Michelin, 136 - Kaum, 137 - Michelin, 138 - Kwan Kee Bamboo Noodle/Michelin, 139 - Michelin, 140 - La Bombance, 141 - Michelin, 142 - L'Atelier de Joël Robuchon, 143 - Michelin, 144 - Le Garçon Saigon, 145 - Michelin, 146 - 152, Lei Garden, 153 - 154, Michelin, 155 - Loaf On/Michelin, 156 - Locanda dell' Angelo, 157 - 158, Michelin, 159 - Lung King Heen , 160 - Michelin, 161 - Man Wah, 162 - Mandarin Grill + Bar, 163 - Megan's Kitchen, 164 - Mic Kitchen, 165 - Ming Court, 166 - New Punjab Club, 167 - New Shanghai, 169 - Michelin, 170 - Octavium, 171 - ON, 172 - One Harbour Road, 173 - 8 1/2 Otto e Mezzo - Bombana, 174 - Pak Loh Chiu Chow, 175 - Michelin, 176 - Peking Garden , 177 - Petrus, 178 - Pierre, 179 - Michelin, 180 - Putien, 181 - 182, Qi, 183 - Michelin, 184 - Rech, 185 - Michelin, 186 - Sai Kung Sing Kee, 187 - Samsen, 188 - Michelin, 189 - Seventh Son, 190 - Shang Palace, 191 - Shanghai Yu Yuan, 192 - Michelin, 193 - Shek Kee Kitchen/Michelin, 194 - 195, Michelin, 196 - 197, Shugetsu Ramen, 198 - Michelin, 199 - Sister Wah, 200 - Michelin, 201 - Snow Garden, 202 - Spring Moon, 203 - Steak on Elgin, 204 - Summer Palace, 205 - Michelin, 206 - Sun Tung Lok, 207 - Michelin, 208 - Sushi Masataka, 209 - Michelin, 210 - Sushi Saito, 211 - Sushi Shikon, 212 - Sushi Tokami, 213 - Sushi Wadatsumi, 214 - Ta Vie, 215 - Michelin, 216 - Michelin, 217 - Tak Kee/Michelin, 218 - 219, Michelin, 220 - T'ang Court, 221 - Michelin, 222 - Tate, 223 - Tenku RyuGin, 224-225, Michelin, 226 - The Ocean, 227 - The Steak House winebar + grill, 228 - Mchelin, 229 - Tim Ho Wan, 230 -

Michelin, 231 - Tim Ho Wan, 232 - Tim's Kitchen, 233 - Michelin, 234 - Tin Lung Heen, 235 - Toritama, 236 - Tosca, 237 - Town, 238 - TRi, 239 - Trusty Congee King , 240 - Trusty Gourmet, 241 - Michelin, 242 - Tsui Hang Village, 243 - Upper Modern Bistro, 245 - VEA, 246 - Michelin, 247 - What To Eat/Michelin, 248 - Whisk, 249 - Wing Lai Yuen, 250 - Wu Kong, 251 - Xin Rong Ji, 252 - Yan Toh Heen, 253 - Michelin, 254 - Yat Tung Heen, 255 - Michelin, 256 - Yè Shanghai, 257 - Yee Tung Heen, 258 - Ying Jee Club, 259 - Yixin, 260 - 261, Yuè, 262 - Yue Kee/Michelin, 263 - Michelin, 265 - Zhejiang Heen, 266 - 270, Michelin, 271 - The Noodle Hive/Michelin, 276 - Citadines Mercer, 277 - City Garden, 278 - Conrad, 279 - Cordis, 280 - Crowne Plaza, 281 - Crowne Plaza Kowloon East, 282 - East, 283 - Four Seasons, 284 - Gold Coast, 285 - Grand Hyatt, 286 - Harbour Grand Kowloon, 287 - Hyatt Regency Sha Tin, 288 - Hyatt Regency Tsim Sha Tsui, 289 - Icon, 290 - Indigo, 291 - InterContinental, 292 - InterContinental Grand Stanford, 293 - Island Shangri-La, 294 - JW Marriott, 295 - Kowloon Shangri-La, 296 - Lan Kwai Fong, 297 - Lanson Place, 298 - Mandarin Oriental, 299 - New World Millennium, 300 - Ozo Wesley, 301 - Sheraton, 302 - The Emperor, 303 - The Landmark Mandarin Oriental, 304 - The Langham, 305 - The Mira, 306 - The Murray, 307 - The Peninsula, 308 - The Pottinger, 309 - The Ritz-Carlton, 310 - The Royal Garden, 311 - The Upper House, 328 - A Lorcha/Michelin, 329 - Alain Ducasse at Morpheus, 330 - Antonio, 331 - Aurora, 332 - Michelin, 333 - Beijing Kitchen, 334 - Bi Ying, 335 - Café Encore, 336 - Canton, 337 - 338, Michelin, 339 - Clube Militar de Macau, 340 - Din Tai Fung (COD), 341 - Dynasty 8, 342 - Michelin, 343 - Feng Wei Ju, 344 - Fook Lam Moon/Michelin, 345 - Golden Flower, 346 - Guincho a Galera, 347 - Michelin, 348 - IFT Educational Restaurant, 349 - Il Teatro, 350 - Imperial Court, 351 - Jade Dragon, 352 - Kam Lai Heen, 353 - King, 354 - Lai Heen, 355 - Lei Garden, 356 - 359, Michelin 360 - Mezza9, 361 - Mizumi (Macau), 362 - Naam, 363 - Michelin, 364 - 99 Noodles, 365 - Michelin, 366 - 8 1/2 Otto e Mezzo, 367 - Pearl Dragon, 368 - Robuchon au Dôme, 369 - Shinji by Kanesaka, 370 - Tenmasa, 371 - Terrazza, 372 - The Eight, 373 - The Golden Peacock, 374 - The Kitchen, 375 - The Ritz Carlton Café, 376 - The Tasting Room, 377 - Tim's Kitchen, 378 - Tou Tou Koi, 379 - Voyages by Alain Ducasse, 380 - Wing Lei, 381 - Wing Lei Palace, 382 - Wong Kun Sio Kung (Broadway)/ Michelin, 383 - Wong Kun Sio Kung (Rua do Campo), 384 - Yamazato, 385 - Yi, 386 - Ying, 387 - Zi Yat Heen, 388 - 389, Michelin, 391 - Michelin, 396 - Altira, 397 - Banyan Tree, 398 - Conrad , 399 - Encore, 400 - Four Seasons, 401 - Galaxy, 402 - Grand Hyatt, 403 - Grand Lapa, 404 - Grand Lisboa, 405 - JW Marriott, 406 - Lisboa, 407 - Mandarin Oriental, 408 - MGM Cotai, 409 - MGM Macau, 410 - Morpheus, 411 - Okura, 413 - Sheraton, 414 - St. Regis, 415 - StarWorld, 416 - Studio City, 417 - The Parisian, 418 - The Ritz-Carlton, 419 - The Venetian, 420 - Wynn, 421 - Wynn Palace

Michelin Travel Partner
Société par actions simplifiées au capital de 15 044 940 €
27 Cours de L'Ile Seguin - 92100 Boulogne Billancourt (France)
R.C.S. Nanterre 433 677 721

Dépot légal Novembre 2018

Printed in China: November 2018

E-mail : michelinguide.hongkong-macau@michelin.com

Maps : (C) 2018 Cartographic data Universal Publications, Ltd / Michelin
Printing and Binding: Book Partners China Ltd.

Robert Parker
WINE ADVOCATE

Welcome to RobertParker.com!

For more than 40 years, Robert Parker Wine Advocate has established itself as the independent fine wine guide on the international scene and is seen today as the most influential wine review globally.

Receive The Wine Advocate bi-monthly digital review and access a fully searchable database of more than 300,000 tasting notes, scores, articles and reviews.

Enjoy member's benefits brought to you by RP Benefits, rewarding you with special gourmet and wine experiences and privileges from our retail and F&B partners. Members also enjoy a privileged access to Matter of Taste, our worldwide series of events featuring wines rated RP90 and above in a Walkabout Tasting, Masterclasses and Dinners.

To activate your complimentary one-year Personal Subscription (valued at USD99) to The Wine Advocate, simply use the code below and register on RobertParker.com. Download the RP Benefits app on the App Store or Google Play to enjoy your member's benefits.

MHKMUyGJSs7